The Strange Death of Liberal England

GEORGE DANGERFIELD was born in Berkshire, educated at Oxford University and went to live in the United States in 1930. A former literary editor of *Vanity Fair*, Fellow of Princeton University and winner of the Pulitzer Prize for American History, his books include *The Awakening of American Nationalism* and *The Damnable Question: A Study in Anglo-Irish Relations.* He died in 1986.

The Strange Death
of Liberal England

George Dangerfield

Serif

London

This edition first published 1997 by
Serif
47 Strahan Road
London E3 5DA

Published in association with Stanford University Press 1997
Reprinted 1998, 2001

First published in New York by Harrison Smith and
Robert Haas, 1935

British Library Cataloguing-in-Publication Data.
A catalogue record for this book
is available from the British Library.

ISBN 1 897959 30 3

For Frances G. Wickes

Contents

Foreword

In 1935 the New York publishing house of Harrison Smith and Robert Haas published George Dangerfield's *The Strange Death of Liberal England*. Now, more than sixty years later, the book is as vital, if not more so, as when it was first published. It has had, eventually, a strong impact upon the historical profession, as well as something of an odd history. The original publishers quite soon went out of business and the book was not kept in print in America. It was published a year later in England for the first time by Constable, but in a slightly truncated form without the important epilogue on Rubert Brooke. Over the next 26 years it was a book known only, I believe, by a few, recommended by word of mouth and not, on the whole, given much attention by the historical profession or the reading public.

The author himself did not remain at all obscure. When the book was published Dangerfield was the literary editor of *Vanity Fair* in New York. After reading English at Hertford College, Oxford, where he was a contemporary of Evelyn Waugh's, he had, several years later in 1930, come to America and by the middle of the decade was an active figure in American literary life, reviewing extensively in various publications. He had already published a study of the Indian mutiny in 1933 and 1941 saw the publication of *Victoria's Heir* on the education of Edward VII. After the Second World War, he established a considerable reputation as an American historian, particularly of the early nineteenth century. *The Era of Good Feelings* won the Bancroft and Pulitzer prizes in 1953. *Chancellor Robert R. Livingstone* followed in 1960 and *The Awakening of American Nationalism: 1815–1828* in 1965. Then in 1976 he returned to his earlier interest in the brilliant *The Damnable Question: A Study of Anglo-Irish Relations*.

But for historians of Britain, the 'canonical' Dangerfield work is *The Strange Death of Liberal England.* As I have suggested, the book was more or less ignored by the historical profession when it was first published, being taken rather snobbishly as a volume of popular history. True, it was reviewed favourably by the young historian Stanley Pargellis, but in the middle-brow *Saturday Review.* 'J.E.T.' gave a favourable but dull review of the English edition in the September 1937 issue of *History*, with no acknowledgement, pro or con, of the brilliance of the writing, though he did tell his readers the central theme of the book: ' "It was not death which gave Imperial England such a disturbing appearance in the spring and summer of 1914." It was, on the contrary, a new and an exuberant life.'

But as far as I can discover, there was no review in the *American Historical Review*, the *English Historical Review* or other scholarly journals of the time. There was, however, an interesting review in the *New Republic* by H. N. Brailsford, who pointed out something of the central paradox of the book that the study both affirms and denies.

> To Mr Dangerfield's principal argument one might reply that English liberalism has not perished. As an attitude to life, based on an ethical and rationalist view of society, it survives in the main body of the Labour Party, in the Nonconformist churches, in a still influential press, and even in a wing of the Tory Party. It is still, with its mingled shrewdness and self-deception, the typical English way of thinking. What did die in its hour of seeming triumph was the Liberal Party.

With some minor modifications, a similar statement could be made today. At the same time, and this to my mind demonstrates the power of the book, the collapse of consensus and the rise of violence that Dangerfield wrote about during the period between 1910 and 1914 has also been a continual theme in the British past, frequently underrated. One might say this has never been more true than at this very moment.

In the 1950s I read a tattered copy of the original edition, to be found in the stacks of Harvard's Widener Library. My own paperback edition, the first, in 1961, is now in a similar state. Thomas Wallace, then a young editor at Capricorn, and I had the idea of bringing the book into print again after so many years of neglect.

I think that it is fair to say that there can be very few students of twentieth-century England in either country who do not read the book. While hundreds of academic monographs have been forgotten, *The Strange Death* continues as a major influence on how the period is viewed, and scholars and teachers spend considerable energy in coming to terms with the picture of England, in all its richness and complexity, presented in the book. Historians of the greatest distinction, acknowledging its qualities, have taken great pains to point out the errors of the work – nothing, of course, could more vividly attest to its vitality. And the interpretation will not die; no matter how often it may be knocked on the head, it has shaped the way the period is viewed. With its extraordinary literate and witty prose, its power of description and analysis, even if not presented in a traditional scholarly way, it is a study that will always have to be taken into account. There can be few works that are so alive after so many years, as likely to survive or as enjoyable to read.

What is the argument made in the book? It deals, with wonderful insight and imagination, considering that it was based just on published sources, as well as 'private information', as cited in the bibliography, on the four great rebellions in England of the period before the First World War, two more or less on the right, two more or less on the left. They were the attempts of the Conservatives in the House of Lords to preserve their powers against the Liberal Party and the determination of the Tories to preserve Northern Ireland as part of the United Kingdom; the vast increase in the number of industrial strikes and the militant efforts of the suffragettes to obtain the vote. It would appear that in these various campaigns, the Liberal Party had, on the whole, prevailed, but 'the dog it was that died.'

On the one hand Dangerfield has a certain nostalgia for this world, into which he had been born. He writes, in the very last lines of the book, when looking back from the vista of Rupert Brooke's grave:

> All the violence of the pre-war world has vanished, and in its place there glow, year into backward year, the diminishing vistas of that other England where the Grantchester church clock stood at ten to three, where there was Beauty and Certainty and Quiet, and where nothing was real. Today we know it for what it was; but there are moments, very human moments, when we could almost find it in our hearts to envy those who saw it, and who never lived to see the new world.

At the same time Dangerfield deeply admires – while treating them with witty irony – the vitality of the new movements. Their very espousal of violence was a sign of strength over the pieties of Liberal England. The escalation of violence in all the campaigns had its attractions until it was overwhelmed by the greatest violence of them all, the First World War, and Dangerfield, towards the conclusion of his book, gives that splendid quotation from Churchill about the afternoon of 24 July 1914: 'The parishes of Tyrone and Fermanagh faded back into the mists and squalls of Ireland, and a strange light began immediately, but by perceptible gradations, to fall and grow upon the map of Europe.'

Dangerfield raises, but does not solve, as the war prevented the issue being joined, the question of whether there would have been civil war. One suspects not, but one should not underestimate the possibilities of violence of the English: 'the grave matters' were not 'put to the test'.

As one of the most important books about the English past, as an example that history can be abiding literature, *The Strange Death of Liberal England* is available again. I envy those who will be reading it for the first time. It will also give perhaps even greater pleasure to those who will now have the opportunity to read it again.

Peter Stansky

Author's Foreword

Dear John,

You will remember how I first talked to you about this book. It seemed to me then that between the death of Edward VII and the War there was a considerable hiatus in English history. We knew something about the economic causes of war, and realized that the plutocracy of 1910–1914 was a terrible thing: and we knew a great deal about the jealousies of monarchs and the bewilderment of diplomats. Indeed, pre-war diplomacy had produced at least one great book, which was Mr Nicholson's portrait of his father. But what was the domestic life of England like in those years?

When I first thought of writing this book I had in mind a mixture of *Cynara* and Sophocles – the madder music, the stronger wine, the approaching catastrophe of which the actors themselves were unaware. My own recollections were not very helpful. My first memory is one of being held up to a window and shown Halley's Comet – which appears in the first chapter; and as for Rupert Brooke, who ends this book, I had not heard of him until 1918 when I was twelve years old and used to spend my money – I trust not as priggishly as it sounds – in the Poetry Bookshop in Theobald's Road.

It would have been a satisfactory drama, though, from a writer's point of view – that drama which I had imagined of a nation more or less dancing its way into war, to a sound of lawnmowers and ragtime, to the hum of bees and the popping of champagne corks. But it wouldn't have been true. For as soon as one begins to look into the subject one is confronted with a far more curious drama.

The year 1910 is not just a convenient starting point. It is actually a landmark in English history, which stands out against a peculiar background of flame. For it was in 1910 that fires long smouldering in the English spirit suddenly flared up, so that by the end of 1913 Liberal England was reduced to ashes. From these ashes, a new England seems to have emerged.

I realize, of course, that the word 'Liberal' will always have a meaning so long as there is one democracy left in the world, or any remnant of a middle class; but the true pre-war Liberal – supported, as it still was in 1910, by Free Trade, a majority in Parliament, the ten commandments and the illusion of Progress – can never return. It was killed, or it killed itself, in 1913. And a very good thing too.

I wish I could have given a chapter to the purely social scene – to fashions, furniture, manners, and taste in that plutocratic world. But such a scene cannot be contrived as yet. Many of its chief actors are still alive, which makes them difficult to handle; and most of the really significant memories, papers, diaries, letters, and so forth have still to be published. But one thing I am sure will eventually be established. That extravagant behaviour of the post-war decade, which most of us thought to be the effect of war, had really begun before the War. The War hastened everything – in politics, in economics, in behaviour – but it started nothing.

You know how much I hope that you will enjoy reading this book.

Affectionately,

G.D.

PART I

Their Lordships
Die in the Dark

May 1910 – August 1911

'The question is, shall we perish in the dark, slain by our own hand, or in the light, killed by our enemies.' Lord Selborne, in the House of Lords, 10th August, 1911.

Chapter One

The Comet

I

THE Right Honourable Herbert Henry Asquith was enjoying a brief holiday on the Admiralty yacht *Enchantress*, bound for the Mediterranean on some pleasant excuse of business. He had put in at Lisbon to dine with King Manoel of Portugal, and his reception in this precarious capital had been very gratifying. The *Enchantress* then headed for Gibraltar, and was rolling its valuable political freight about half-way between that rock and Cadiz when news was received that Edward VII was seriously ill. The yacht turned hurriedly and made for home, and was well past the Bay of Biscay when, at three in the morning of 7th May, 1910, a second message arrived. 'I am deeply grieved to inform you that my beloved father the King passed away peacefully at a quarter to twelve tonight (the 6th). GEORGE.'

The Prime Minister, sad and shaken, went up on deck and stood there, gazing into the sky. Upon the chill and vacant twilight blazed Halley's Comet – which, visiting the European heavens but once in a century, had arrived with appalling promptness to blaze forth the death of a king.

In London, darkness was gradually relinquishing the bleak façade of the dead king's palace and the crowds which still surrounded it, like the rising of a curtain upon some expensive melodrama, where the electric dawn gradually reveals a scene thronged with mourners. But here Mr Asquith held the stage alone, the only visible human being within the ghostly margins of sea and sky, staring up at that punctual omen. A character from one of Voltaire's tragedies would have done justice to this magian situation with an *où suis-je?* or a *Juste Ciel!*; but neither Mr Asquith's temperament nor his rather stolid figure had any business to monopolize so pregnant a scene.

He has recorded it in one lightless sentence in his *Fifty Years of British Parliament* and one can imagine his face, faintly illuminated in the twilight, a bland and weary face, in which frankness and reserve had long fought themselves to a standstill. A touch of flamboyance in the long white hair, a hint of fantasy at the corners of the mouth gave this face a certain incongruity, as though a passage of correct and scholarly prose had been set up in too fanciful a type. Mr Asquith was essentially a prosaic character.

The historian of pre-war England is at one grave disadvantage. Upon the face of every character he deals with there has stiffened a mask of facts, which only the acid of time can dissolve. Two centuries from now, Mr Asquith will be a fiction, a contrivance of taste, sensibility, and scholarship; perhaps they will see him then as a man extravagantly moderate, who was facing at this precise moment four of the most immoderate years in English history.

Such is the brief opening scene of a political tragi-comedy. And since dramatic irony consists of the audience's knowing what the actor does not know, it is at least an ironical scene. History unfortunately has decreed that the rest of the play should be somewhat wanting in nobility and balance; that it should be hysterical, violent, and inconclusive: a mere fragment of a play, with the last act unwritten. Yet, before the curtain was hastily called down in August 1914, Mr Asquith and the Liberal Party of which he was such a placid leader had already been dealt a mortal wound; and this he had no means of telling, as he stood on the damp deck, thinking kindly of the late king. Edward VII was an irritable man, but in his relations with his Prime Minister he had been frank and gracious, even when they disagreed. How would the new king behave, in the political crisis which lay just ahead? These thoughts occupied Mr Asquith all the way to Plymouth.

II

It was a full fortnight before the late king was permitted to rest with his fathers in St George's Chapel, Windsor. But there is hardly a recorded event in his last journey from London to Windsor – from the Highland lament in the late spring sunshine to the unseemly disarray of canons and choir in St George's Chapel – which does not recall some grief and disorder in the heart of things. Yet the melancholy pageant had been attended by a brave collection of foreign royalties, foreign diplomats, and Mr Theodore Roosevelt; it had been marked with every appearance of public sorrow; and had, taken all in all, done much credit to the Duke of Norfolk who staged it, and even more to the corpse himself. Edward had been loved.

But in that ponderous flesh which had gone, thus gloriously mourned, to its long home, one part at least was silenced by nothing more than worry. Whatever sickness – whether a common cold, or pneumonia, or over-indulgence – it was that killed the King, it was political controversy which occupied and alarmed his brain, and reduced his mental resistance to illness almost to a cipher.

When the funeral was over, there was a dinner at Buckingham Palace, where the visiting notabilities were served with the customary baked meats. After that nightmare dinner – so well described by Mr Roosevelt and M. Maurois – where the assisting royalties forgot the solemn purpose that had brought them there; where the King of Greece melted into tearful self-pity, and harsh things were whispered about the Tsar of Bulgaria – after that dreadfully comic banquet, the Emperor of Germany composed a letter to his Chancellor, von Bethmann-Hollweg. 'The outlook all round is black,' wrote this vigorous and partial observer. 'The Government is thoroughly hated. It is reported with satisfaction that in the days of the King's death and during his lying-in-state, the Prime Minister and others of his colleagues were publicly hissed in the streets and that expressions like "You have killed the King" were heard.' . . .

Some part of this hysterical missive was true. Though the Ministers had not been publicly hissed, nor were they hated, yet a certain controversy for which they were responsible had hastened King Edward into the shades. It is a controversy which has gone down into history attended with a great deal of frankly comic circumstance, and assisted into an unjust oblivion by such a chorus of English peers as might have sprung, fully coroneted, from the brain of Sir William Gilbert: yet during its petty career the English constitution was gravely threatened, and the Liberals emerged from it, flushed with one of the greatest victories of all time.

From that victory they never recovered.

Chapter Two

The Liberals
1906–10

I

THE England upon which Mr Asquith landed in May 1910, was in a very peculiar condition. It was about to shrug from its shoulders – at first irritably, then with violence – a venerable burden, a kind of sack. It was about to get rid of its Liberalism.

Liberalism in its Victorian plenitude had been an easy burden to bear, for it contained – and who could doubt it? – a various and valuable collection of gold, stocks, Bibles, progressive thoughts, and decent inhibitions. It was solid and sensible and just a little mysterious; and though one could not exactly *gambol* with such a weight on one's shoulders, it permitted one to walk in a dignified manner and even to execute from time to time those eccentric little steps which are so necessary to the health of Englishmen.

Whatever his political convictions may have been, the Englishman of the '70s and '80s was something of a Liberal at heart. He believed in freedom, free trade, progress, and the Seventh Commandment. He also believed in reform. He was strongly in favour of peace – that is to say, he liked his wars to be fought at a distance and, if possible, in the name of God. In fact, he bore his Liberalism with that air of respectable and passionate idiosyncrasy which is said to be typical of his nation, and was certainly typical of Mr Gladstone and the novels of Charles Dickens.

But somehow or other, as the century turned, the burden of Liberalism grew more and more irksome; it began to give out a dismal, rattling sound; it was just as if some unfortunate miracle had been performed upon its contents, turning them into nothing more than bits of old iron, fragments of intimate crockery, and other relics of a domestic past. What *could* the matter be? Liberalism was still embodied in a large political party; it enjoyed the support of philosophy and religion; it was intelligible, it was intelligent, and it was English. But it was also slow; and it so far transcended politics and economics as to impose itself upon behaviour as well. For a nation which wanted to revive a sluggish blood by running very fast and in any direction, Liberalism was clearly an inconvenient burden.

As for the Liberal Party, it was in the unfortunate position of having to run, too. It was the child of Progress, which is not only an illusion, but an athletic illusion, and which insists that it is better to hurl oneself backwards than to stand still. By 1910, the Liberals had reached a point where they could no longer advance; before them stood a barrier of Capital which they dared not attack. Behind them stood the House of Lords.

In its political aspect, the House of Lords was extremely conservative, quite stupid, immensely powerful, and a determined enemy of the Liberal Party. It was also an essential enemy. If anything went wrong, if one's radical supporters became too insistent, if one's inability to advance became too noticeable, one could always blame the Lords. It was therefore a melancholy fate which decreed that the Liberals should turn upon their hereditary foe; that they should spend their last energies on beating it to its knees; and should thereupon themselves – expire.

It was this impending and paradoxical crisis – this battle between the Liberals and the Lords – which had assisted Edward VII into his grave, and which now confronted a new and not very popular king called George V. . . .

II

In 1903, when Joseph Chamberlain – who had proved how insubstantial were party differences by being a Unitarian, a radical, and a Conservative at one and the same time – returned from South Africa with a plea for protective tariffs, it was unfortunate that his voice should have sounded like the voice of Cassandra, that unwelcome prophetess. But so it was. The Conservatives were drifting out of popularity like a swimmer caught in the undertow. Their prestige had suffered as the Boer War dragged on and England discovered how much blood it cost to run an Empire, particularly when that blood was spent in the prolonged and frequently ludicrous pursuit of a number of undaunted Dutch farmers. The Imperialist cause was useful enough so long as it kept the country in a state of sentimental rage; it had even divided the Liberals into two warring factions, slow to forgive each other: but now something realistic had to be done if the Empire were not to dwindle back into what a Liberal statesman had once described as 'one of the most idle and ill-contrived systems that ever disgraced a nation.'

So Chamberlain decided to prove, with characteristic force, that the Empire was a paying proposition. Markets had begun it, by markets it should live. The scheme he had in mind was this: to build a tariff wall around England for the single purpose of knocking holes in it, through which Imperial goods might pass; for you could not ask favours of the colonies without having something to give in return, and the colonies, alas, were all protectionist. The proposal was an ingenious one; yet the mere description of this singular Empire, free trader at heart and protectionist in all its limbs, was enough to damn the describer. For it carried with it one implication which nobody cared to face in 1903: it meant that England was no longer commercial dictator of the world; that the Empire of Free Trade must soon become one with Nineveh and Tyre.

Chamberlain had to show how true this was, but his words were heresy and defeatism to all but the very few. Free Trade had been an article of British faith – whether Liberal or Conservative – since the repeal of the Corn Laws: it had been a faith to which America and Europe had subscribed because they were in no position to do anything else; it had been rooted in the backwardness of other countries. To Englishmen of the nineteenth century it had represented that combination of the ideal and the profitable which is peculiarly English – while it stilled their consciences, it stuffed their pockets. From time to time the cry of Protection had been raised, but always in lean years and wavering accents.

Chamberlain wrecked his party. The 1906 elections, fought around this prophetic, precarious, and unpopular issue, resulted in a Liberal landslide.

But the Liberal Party which came back to Westminster with an overwhelming majority was already doomed. It was like an army protected at all points except for one vital position on its flank. With the election of fifty-three Labour representatives, the death of Liberalism was pronounced; it was no longer the Left. The Conservatives might have consoled themselves with the fact that they represented a logical Right; they might have waited to see what would come. But theirs was the gift of tongues, not of divination. To them, as to their opponents and the country at large, this Labour contingent rapidly lost its terror.

Even its twenty-nine professed socialists, those scandalous and impertinent revolutionaries, seemed prepared to vote with the Liberal majority, to wear frock coats, to attend royal garden parties, to become as time passed just a minor and far from militant act in the pantomime of Westminster.

The Conservatives were as sad and quarrelsome a pack as ever bayed a Liberal moon. And it was now, in this desolate political midnight to which Chamberlain had condemned them, that they turned to an old and faithful ally, an ally with whose aid – they openly but not wisely declared – they could run the country in or out of power. They turned to the House of Lords.

The House of Lords had been forgotten for nearly twelve years.

III

The soil of the eighteenth century was very rich. Far beneath its surface the struggles of history, long dead, worked their powerful chemistry: here were the corpses of feudalism and absolutism, in various stages of decay; here were the ashes of heretics, the blood of rebels, the nourishing mineral relics of ignorance and patriotism. There was scarcely an institution, political or social, which did not flourish in this earth and grow fat; and particularly was this true of the House of Lords. In 1700 it was a little assembly of great nobles, jealous, stubborn, and perverse; in 1801, through a lavish creation of peerages, it had come to represent the opulent and landed classes. In this way the bribery of George III and the vision of William Pitt had worked to a common end. The Crown was well rid of an obstinate and capricious enemy; the Constitution had gained its first distinctly conservative element. For the Lords never again demonstrated any desire for change. They fought the Whig Reform Bill in 1832; they killed the Liberal Home Rule Bill in 1884: over sixty years of startling progress had left them unmoved. The occasional voice of a Rosebery or a Dunraven, raised in this upper wilderness and crying for reform, died away unheard, and by 1906, when the Liberals returned to power after eleven years of opposition, their lordships were little better than a powerful Conservative caucus.

It was with these hereditary allies that Mr Balfour and his colleagues proposed to harry the vast majority opposed to them. Their lordships, after all, had almost unlimited powers. Looking at these noble statesmen in the early years of the twentieth century, it was impossible not to think that the English Constitution contained certain elements of almost reckless optimism. Ideally, their lordships were supposed to act in the interests of the electorate. When any piece of hasty or foolish legislation was sent up to them from the House of Commons, their business was to veto it, a course which, if it led to the government's resignation and a new election, would give the people another chance to express their opinion at the polls. And very nice too, always supposing their lordships to be gifted with the legendary wisdom of a witenagemot. Their boast was that they embodied the people's constitutional right to have the last word; that, since no party kept within the bounds of its election platform, they stood – a noble, uncomplaining buffer – between the country and all kinds of bruising legislation. Yet it was a curious thing that only about Liberal laws was the country offered its right to second thoughts: Conservative bills went through the Upper House unquestioned and unharmed.

In '84 and '94 the Liberals had threatened this hereditary obstacle with a large curbing of its powers, though nobody seemed to take these threats with quite the seriousness they deserved. A Commons sufficiently goaded could turn the House of Lords into a harmless jest by persuading the Crown to create such a horde of new noblemen as would overwhelm, with an obedient Liberal vote, any Conservative opposition their lordships could bring against them. And it was precisely this remote and laughable contingency which, in 1906, Mr Balfour and his Conservative minority refused to consider. And, refusing, ran themselves into one of the strangest constitutional comedies in English history.

It was clearly unwise to vex an opponent who had just been returned to Parliament with one of those majorities which mean that the people have spoken – to vex him, that is, otherwise than with words. The wise course would have been to wait. No government, however strongly supported in the Commons, can resist the melancholy climate of popular opinion, the gradual erosions of disillusion and boredom. The Liberal majority, as afterwards appeared, was built of showy but not very durable stuff; its splendid and somewhat arrogant 1906 façade would very soon have flaked and stained.

IV

But to the Conservative leader and ex-Prime Minister, Mr Arthur James Balfour, politics was little more than a serious game. He played it with the faintly supercilious finesse which belongs to a bachelor of breeding, and with a bitterly polite sarcasm which was quite his own. He had entered Parliament originally from that mixture of duty and idleness which made an English politician of the old school: in other words, because he could neither fight, preach, nor plead. In Westminster, being a member of the Cecil family, he was at least assured of a hearing.

He had become one of the more eminent of English philosophers at a time when English philosophy was at its lowest ebb: he pursued his speculations with the same earnestness and skill which he gave to golf, tennis, and the arrangement of dinner parties. He loved music, never got up till late in the morning, nor had ever been known to read a newspaper. He doubted everything on principle, but had never thought enough of life to distrust it. He was attractive, easy, and, as the years grew on him, fearless.

In his youth he had been known as 'pretty Fanny'; and indeed in those far days he looked rather like an attentuated gazelle. But with advancing age his face came more and more to resemble an engaging, even a handsome, skull: it carried into drawing-rooms and debates a skull's special property of hollow mockery, its eternal *memento mori* – which, since Mr Balfour was always affable and lively, gave him an air of mystery and even of enchantment.

Nobody had expected much of him when he first entered Parliament; but he had developed such a sinewy and subtle dialectic, such a know-ledge of Parliamentary tricks, such a display of every quality except passion and leadership, as delighted his friends and not infrequently confounded his enemies. This was the gentlemanly and intelligent being who brought his scattered Conservative following into their ill-judged assault upon the Liberal majority.

V

The Conservatives' tactics were simple, child-like, and brutal. In the Commons, they could only irritate their opponents with words: they looked to the obedient House of Lords to do the heavy work. And the Lords began by mutilating Mr Augustine Birrell's Education Bill be-yond hope of repair. Education in those days was a mysterious labyrinth, down whose crooked paths the Church of England and its sectarian opponents endlessly chased one another, fighting over what kind of religious teaching should be handed out to the children of

England's poor. This being a Liberal bill, the Church of England naturally got the worst of it; for the Church was traditionally Conservative.
But when the Lords killed it, nobody except the more rigid Non-con-
formists wept a tear over its perplexed and barren corpse, although Mr
Lloyd George – who pillaged the Scriptures without pity to adorn his
speeches–immediately pronounced against the evil of hereditary rule.

In the same session their lordships rejected a Plural Voting Bill,
designed to correct that old-fashioned injustice whereby certain property
holders could vote in more than one place. This was a frankly party
measure, and the Liberals contented themselves with threatening,
through the mouth of their Prime Minister, Sir Henry Campbell-
Bannerman, that 'the resources of the Commons are not exhausted.'
Meanwhile and with merely the politest whisper of a grumble the Lords
passed a Trade Disputes Bill which, backed by Labour and intended to
soothe the justly enraged Trade Unions,* was altogether too dangerous
to tamper with.

(It was when legislation of this sort appeared that the two political
parties at Westminster underwent a sorry transfiguration, becoming
one body with two vexatious heads. Each party, with a delicately un-
convincing air of being elsewhere, was treading a crude path of socialism: under twentieth century conditions, with a partly enfranchised and
largely dissatisfied working class, they could not do otherwise. The
Conservatives, who looked back to the subtle radicalism of Disraeli and
the more distant paternal schemes of Peel and St John, followed this
path with less concern than their opponents. The Liberals still cherished
at heart the teachings of Cobden and Bright, believed that state intervention was unforgiveable, and watched with a growing apprehension
the abyss which was opening between their theory and their practice.
That abyss was eventually to swallow them up. Meanwhile, as a kind of
capitalist left wing, they advanced upon social reform with noisy
mouths and mouselike feet.)

Their lordships next slaughtered a Licensing Bill, the object of which
was to curtail the number of public houses. In any Protestant country
liquor, religion, and politics are likely to go hand in hand. In England,
the Conservatives and the Established Church (whose priesthood was
and is a gentleman's profession) traditionally believed in a man's right
to drink strong waters: the Liberals and the Chapel (that is to say, the
Wesleyans, Congregationalists, Unitarians, and other severe, inde-

*See Part II, page 185.

pendent and socially vulgar sects) were inclined to protest, and sometimes even to believe, that drink was the Devil. In the public houses,
therefore, the Conservatives had a nice little chain of political fortresses,
where their cause was loyally upheld by poor men in their cups; and
these were not to be surrendered at any cost.

The country as a whole would have supported the House of Lords
in this latest move, if their lordships had not set about it in a highly
unprincipled manner. Instead of waiting to slay the bill with the courteous slow poison of a day's debate, two hundred and fifty noblemen
(apparently encouraged by a Conservative victory in a Peckham by-
election) met in open conclave at Lansdowne House, and there, in Lord
Lansdowne's drawing-room, voted its death. This was to insult not
merely the Liberal party, not merely the Temperance enthusiast, but
every right-thinking man in the country. When the Bill appeared in the
House of Lords, it was already dead, 'slain by the stiletto in Berkeley
Square', and not worth debating. And Mr Balfour still smiled upon
these tactics, affable and unconcerned: through the Upper Chamber he
was running the country, for all his pitiful minority in the House of
Commons.

VI

When Sir Henry Campbell-Bannerman died in 1908, it was like the
passing of true Liberalism. Sir Henry had believed in Peace, Retrenchment, and Reform, those amiable deities who presided so complacently
over large portions of the Victorian era, inspiring their worshippers
with so many generous sentiments and protecting them from so many
of the coarser realities. Sir Henry's political faith had been a noble one in
its day; but that day was over. It had condemned the Boer War, too
faintly; it had reformed the Army and the Navy, so that they became at
once more democratic and more deadly; it had proposed a new England,
where the worker should be free from the burden of ignorance, isolation,
and poverty, but for all its reform, the poor man remained poor. And
now almost the last true worshipper at those large, equivocal altars lay
dead – an elderly and rich Presbyterian whose three passions in life
were his wife, the French nation, and his collection of walking sticks.
He might well have murmured on his deathbed, like Sir Henry Savile,
'I am ready to depart, the rather that having lived in good times I foresee
worse': for indeed, in this new and hurrying century there was no place

for him. As for his successor – 'You are different from the others, Asquith,' said the old man, as he lay dying, 'and I am glad to have known you. God bless you!' And Mr Asquith became Prime Minister.

To many it seemed that the party's whole future now lay in this lawyer's disinterested hands; there were few men in England more gifted. Yet a certain lack of ardour, which often comes upon men who have given their youth to the Bar, was altogether against him in a time when only inspired leadership could keep his party on the heights – the slippery heights – it then occupied. If there could be such a thing as a Humour of Moderation, then Mr Asquith was the perfect example of it. He was ingenious but not subtle, he could improvise quite brilliantly on somebody else's theme. He was moderately imperialist, moderately progressive, moderately humorous, and, being the most fastidious of Liberal politicians, only moderately evasive. If he can be accused of excess it was in the matter of his personal standards, which were extremely high.

He had the sort of character which is so often found in the Senior Common Rooms of Oxford and Cambridge – that is to say, he was almost completely lacking in imagination or enthusiasm. The absence of these qualities does not prevent either dons or Ministers from getting through life in a very easy manner; the pleasures of the library, of the palate, of conversation or intrigue can generally make up for mere ardour. And there were plenty of good people in England who were only too grateful to Mr Asquith for being the kind of man he was and who – in consideration of his many decent virtues – were willing to forgive him for having married a lady of some wit and more exalted birth than his own who had taught him how to be moderately frivolous.

Above everything else, Mr Asquith was 'safe'. Like the party he led, he had been swinging gently towards the Right. People could assure themselves that no deep-laid radical schemes would ever be set stirring behind the modest portals of Number Ten, Downing Street. And that was as it should be. *Proximus Ucaligon ardebat.* . . .

VII

To Number Eleven, Downing Street, traditionally the Home of the Chancellor of the Exchequer, Mr David Lloyd George had now moved his goods and chattels. He had left his former office of President of the Board of Trade to Mr Winston Churchill, that volatile young convert from Conservatism, who complained bitterly that Mr Lloyd George had taken all the plums, and who originated unemployment insurance.

Mr George was a man set apart from his other colleagues on the Asquith cabinet. For one thing he had an irresponsible sense of humour; for another, he represented – or seemed to represent – all those dangerous and possibly subversive opinions which Liberalism, in its grave game of progress, was forced to tolerate. He was a great vote-catcher. His whole career had been set in terms of drama – to be correct, of sentimental drama; he had played his part with inspired and frequently sincere abandon; and his audience had spattered him generously with roses and eggs, both of which he seemed to enjoy.

If his convictions had been otherwise than emotional, he would have been a Socialist by this time. When he first exploded into English politics, an angry little solicitor from an uncouth, starved district in Wales, he brought with him something alien and dangerous. He was less a Liberal than a Welshman on the loose. He wanted the poor to inherit the earth, particularly if it was the earth of rich English landlords; and he wanted this with a sly, semi-educated passion which struck his parliamentary colleagues as being in very bad form.

The Boer War first brought him into prominence. He fought against it tooth and nail, and became generally hated as a leading pro-Boer – until the sad and sanguinary farce was over, when he was suddenly recognized as a man of vision.

But it may have been this successful termination to what had been, after all, a genuine campaign – a campaign inspired by deep personal distrust of empires and all imperial butchery – which turned his thoughts from the problems of maintaining a one-man Welsh revolution to the remote and dazzling chances of becoming an English prime minister. From then onwards he identified himself more closely with political Liberalism, putting himself before his party and his party before his principles. He became the idol of the radicals. Gentlemen of conservative tendencies and little humour (among whom, one cannot help feeling, were numbered in spirit most of his political colleagues) used to grumble that he would make a poor companion on a tiger hunt. And he would. He would have been on the tiger's side.

Fate, rather than Mr Asquith, seemed to have promoted him to the Exchequer. In composing his 1909 Budget he was faced with an enormous deficit, and forced to create new revenue for the Army, the Navy and Old Age Pensions. This was exactly the sort of position he was happiest in; he decided that now, when the financial outlook was particularly dark, was the time to attack.

The Budget he then contrived came to be known as the 'People's Budget', because it aimed a rude blow at the rich, and more especially at the Lords. It attacked the one interest which the Lords were known to cherish – the Land, the close and fruitful Goshen of society. Mr Lloyd George proposed an increase in death duties, a duty on undeveloped land – the present value of which, he declared, was a brazen fiction – a duty on coal and mineral royalties and a reversion duty on the termination of leases: to these he added, by way of revenge for the Lansdowne House 'stiletto party', tremendous duties on the liquor trade; and, as an appeal to socialist opinion, a super-tax on all incomes over £5,000 a year.

According to Mr John Burns, ex-Labour leader and Liberal careerist, the Cabinet deliberated upon this alarming document 'like nineteen rag-pickers round a 'eap of muck'. Most of them could probably see that in practice it was largely unworkable. Some of them were allied by birth, and all by friendship, with the rich whom it assaulted. And yet it had three advantages which could not be overlooked. It invested the whole party with an aura of progress which was badly needed after three none too progressive years in office; it was a loud champion of Free Trade; and it was a wonderful trap to catch the House of Lords in. To humble the House of Lords was the devout, vindictive wish of all good Liberals.

The question now was – how silly would their lordships be? By constitutional tradition, they could veto everything but a Budget: yet here was a Budget crying to be vetoed. It was like a kid, which sportsmen tie up to a tree in order to persuade a tiger to its death; and at its loud, rude bleating the House of Lords began to growl.

Their lordships prowled around it in their minds, meditating the last fatal leap. Should they kill it or not? If they vetoed it, the Government would have to resign, and Mr Asquith would go to the country not merely on the question of whether this Free Trade Budget was a good thing or not but also on the question of whether their lordships' power of veto was a good thing or not. And if the Liberals were re-elected, with however slender a majority, then the House of Lords would be in for trouble – a very fantastic kind of trouble, involving the not altogether credible creation of several hundred brand new Liberal peers.

Mr Balfour in the Commons, and the Marquess of Lansdowne in the

Lords, were all for letting the Budget pass. But the House of Lords had grown reckless, and its large Conservative majority of obscure and far from intelligent peers was in no mood to take advice.

VIII

To the constitutional comedy which now begins, Mr Lloyd George's Budget reads like one of those complicated prefaces which Messrs Ben Jonson, Bernard Shaw and others have been known to tack on to their printed works. If a motto were further needed, there could be none more apt than Sir William Gilbert's verse:

> *And if the House of Peers withholds*
> *Its legislative hand*
> *And noble statesmen do not itch*
> *To interfere with matters which*
> *They do not understand –*
> *Then bright will shine Great Britain's rays*
> *As in King George's glorious days.*

These lines, like a more and more melancholy refrain, seem to accompany all their lordships' subsequent follies. . . .

And while the House of Lords tried to make up its collective mind on this little matter of murdering the Budget, Mr Lloyd George decided to make a last assault. One July evening in 1909, therefore, he went down to Limehouse where, before a packed and partisan audience of East End cockneys, he delivered himself of one of the most inflammatory speeches of his whole career. Next morning, his printed words horrified many and many a respectable London breakfast table, and to many a country squire in his study must have sounded like the voice of vulgar doom. This, said England's comfortable classes, is revolution!

England has scarcely known a greater demagogue than this pre-war Lloyd George. His face, in its rare moments of repose, was elfin and commonplace, like a Barrie play: animated, it was something between an incomparable drama and a high-class vaudeville act. It was tragic, and sorrowful, and charming and comic by turns; it was lofty and it was low: emotions chased themselves across it like wind across a rain puddle, breaking it up into a hundred images. Without the magic of face and voice to support them, his speeches are not likely to survive; and one can only imagine the effect of this, the most famous passage in that famous Limehouse speech:

'*I was telling you I went down a coal-mine the other day. We sank into a pit half a mile deep. We then walked underneath the mountain, and we did about three-quarters of a mile with rock and shale above us. The earth seemed to be straining – around us and above us – to crush us in. You could see the pit props bent and twisted and sundered until you saw their fibres split in resisting the pressure. Sometimes they give way and then there is mutilation and death. Often a spark ignites, the whole pit is deluged in fire, and the breath of life is scorched out of hundreds of breasts by the consuming flame. In the very next colliery to the one I descended, just a few years ago three hundred people lost their lives that way. And yet when the Prime Minister and I knock at the door of these great landlords and say to them – "Here, you know these poor fellows who have been digging up royalties at the risk of their lives, some of them are old, they have survived the perils of their trade, they are broken, they can earn no more. Won't you give them something towards keeping them out of the workhouse?" – they scowl at us and we say – "Only a ha'penny, just a copper." They say, "You thieves!" And they turn their dogs on to us, and you can hear their bark every morning.*'

Exactly how much Mr Asquith enjoyed this caricature of himself, begging for coppers in such distasteful company and in all next morning's newspapers, is not known; but Mr Lloyd George was having the time of his life. He kept his audience howling with alternate rage and laughter; moment by moment, sentence by sentence, he assaulted the landlords, and outraged the gentry, and invited the dispossessed, and cozened the dissatisfied; he shouted and implored and wheedled and mimicked. It was a great performance.

And yet this spirited voice was not quite the voice of revolution – though thus it sounded in the anxious imagination of the Conservative press. It was a voice which nobleman and worker might have equal cause to distrust; it was a voice which would have been utterly lost in a world where there were no dukes to hate and no poor to pity: it was the inspired and concentrated clamour of the middle classes.

It was also Liberalism's extravagant last will and testament. All it really said was this – that the rich, who are beginning to get too much in their own hands, have got to pay. For all its large Welsh images and little Welsh impertinences, it looked back to that great nineteenth century delusion of an England where neither Wealth nor Work would ever combine; where a comfortable and independent bourgeoisie would make profits not too large to be indecent; where social ills would be medicined but never cured; and where the ideal man would come more and more to resemble an honest, tolerant, intolerable grocer. That delusion, not ignoble, of an eternal individualism was pretty faded, but still powerful enough to haunt Mr Lloyd George's speech, and to make his revolutionary language nothing more than the language of super-taxes and old age pensions.

But in the meantime, the speech had done its work. If their lordships had been violent about the Budget before, they were twice as violent now. Mr Lloyd George redoubled his efforts, uttering his underbred witticisms from a score of platforms in a voice as soft as snowfall; and up and down the country certain noblemen emerged from the rustic obscurity to which history had consigned them and began to trade public insults with their persecutor, which, though quite as unmannered as his, were unfortunately far less effective.

And as the day of debate in the House of Lords drew nearer, Mr Lloyd George had only one fear – that their lordships would suddenly recover their sanity and let his taxes through. But everything went according to plan. In normal circumstances the upper chamber was an empty place; it was only in crises such as this that it was filled with a horde of hereditary nobodies, possessed with a gentlemanly anxiety to do the wrong thing. It was these good folk who, after listening speechless to a debate of almost academic purity, withheld not the legislative hand. By a vote of 300 to 75, the Budget was rejected, constitutional precedent defied, the die cast.

Next morning, Mr Asquith announced that the rights of the Commons had been rudely challenged, and that he had no choice but to advise an immediate dissolution. Vainly Mr Balfour argued that the Budget was less a Money Bill than a new and brigandly fiscal policy: it was too late to save the day. In triumph, the Liberal cabinet resigned.

After a month of very dull electioneering, the country went to the polls in small numbers and recorded a lethargic opinion. As a result, the Liberals were so reduced, and the Conservatives so swollen, as to be almost equal in numbers: the Irish and Labour Parties held the balance of power.

Small wonder if, looking over these dispiriting figures, Liberals began to wonder whether they had not fallen into their own pit. If their party was to stay in power, it could only do so with Irish help. Betrayed Parnell's dream had come true at last. The Act of Union between

England and Ireland, so disreputable in its origins, so lamentable in its history, had at last revealed its great constitutional weakness. It had bestowed the control of Parliament upon a handful of men to whom England was an enemy, and whose support could only be won at the stiff price of Irish Home Rule. By these elections of January 1910, the Act of Union killed itself.

Killing itself, it killed the Liberal party: thereafter Mr Asquith and his colleagues were never to be separated from their Irish allies, for whom in their hearts they had no use at all. Irish Home Rule had been buried with Gladstone; in 1910, it was an academic question, no Englishman cared for it. And yet, if this 'People's Budget', having survived an election, were to pass through the Commons once again, Mr Asquith needed Irish votes. And the Irish were seriously opposed to Mr Lloyd George's land and liquor taxes; and would only join in passing them, and in the subsequent assault upon the House of Lords, on the strict understanding that Home Rule would follow.

Moreover they, and certain more radical members of the Liberal party, demanded that, before the Budget was passed and England saved from a threatening financial chaos, definite steps should be taken towards limiting the Lords' powers of veto. The mild majority of Mr Asquith's following and all the Opposition called for the Budget to be taken first. On 21st February, speaking with unusual nervousness, Mr Asquith declared that the Budget should go up to the Lords at once; faced a radical mutiny for the next week; meditated resignation; and eight days later announced in the House that his programme was 'somewhat modified'. He now proposed merely such financial measures as would tide the Government over the next few weeks; these passed, he would offer certain resolutions concerning their lordships' veto. The meaning of this was clear to everybody. Faced with an Irish and Radical desertion, he had thrown away all but the simplest pretence of independent action: in order to keep himself in power, he had made a bargain with the Irish. Under the gentle mockery of Mr Balfour, English constitutional history took on a new and forbidding shape – how forbidding, indeed how disastrous, time was yet to show.

IX

But neither the Liberals nor their tyrannical Irish allies could have their way with the House of Lords, without the help of one life, now very near its finish. The Government's next step was to pass a Bill through the Commons, limiting the Lords' veto; it would then be sent up to the Lords, who would scarcely pass it and vote their own death, unless they were bullied into doing so. And the only man who could bully them was Edward VII.

Edward VII faced this contingency with a justifiable uneasiness. Should the Lords refuse to destroy themselves, he would be advised to exercise his royal prerogative and create a multitude of new Liberal peers, who would obediently vote whichever way the Government told them. It was in his choice to exercise or not to exercise this prerogative. But it was generally supposed that his promise to exercise it would be enough; under such a threat, their lordships would have to yield. Better to vote their death themselves, than to have it voted for them; better to die as they were, a decent corpse, than to die ludicrously swollen with Liberal peerages. So everybody thought, and so King Edward thought, when he promised not to stand in Mr Asquith's way. But he would not, he said, absolutely guarantee to use his prerogative unless there were another election: if the country did not change its mind, if the Liberals were again returned, even to such power as they now held, he would do whatever he was advised to do.

Disgusted at the prospect of being used against the Lords, with whom he rather naturally sympathized, he did suggest a compromise. Of the six hundred peers, he proposed, let one hundred only have the right to vote, and let this one hundred be divided equally between Liberals and Conservatives. He made this suggestion hopefully to the Marquesses of Crewe and Lansdowne, respectively leaders of the Liberal and Conservative parties in the Lords; but neither nobleman could agree. What sort of selection would be made, they asked, but of the most obdurate and irreconcilable within either party? At that, the King determined that the choice no longer rested with him; he must do whatever the Government wanted. 'Thank God,' he said to Mr Reginald McKenna, the First Lord of the Admiralty, 'it's not my business.'

X

So, in a House of Commons where the atmosphere was irritable and bitter; where Mr Lloyd George had made unpleasant comparisons between the Opposition and officious penguins; where Lord Hugh Cecil had delicately likened Mr Lloyd George to a small boy deliberately dirtying his trousers in a puddle, and Mr Bonar Law had called the Government a worn and beaten fox – in such a House, Mr Asquith produced his veto Resolutions. There were three of them. To abolish by statute the Lords' veto on Money Bills; to restrict by statute the Lords' veto on legislation, so that if a Bill were passed by the Commons in three consecutive sessions, it should become law, no matter how the Lords voted; to limit the duration of Parliament to five years.

The first of these was safely passed on 5th April; and by Thursday, 15th April, the other two were through with majorities of round about a hundred. And on that same Thursday, the Prime Minister introduced his Parliament Bill. 'Whereas,' ran its preamble, 'it is intended to substitute for the House of Lords as it now exists a Second Chamber constituted on a popular instead of a hereditary basis, but such a substitution cannot immediately be brought about. . . .' (It was a clear victory for the Irish, the radicals, and all Single Chamber fanatics: the Government had postponed House of Lords reform indefinitely, for anyone who should be so foolish as to take it up, and to this day nobody has very seriously done so.) And on that Thursday night, as the clock's hands pointed to eleven and adjournment, Mr Asquith solemnly warned the Lords not to reject his Resolutions, unless they wanted the Crown to intervene; and the House adjourned in a storm of cheering on the Speaker's right and of wild, defiant yells on his left.

A few days later, the Budget was passed through both Houses, the Lords greeting it contemptuously with just a bare quorum. On 29th April, it received the Royal Assent – '*Le Roi remercie ses bon sujets, accepte leur bénévolence, et ainsi le veult.*' So, with a brief flourish of Norman French, the first stage of the battle ended. That revolutionary, that unbridled, that weary, that largely unworkable Budget of 1909 had come to rest at last; and no one but the Irish had any cause to smile.

XI

Parliament adjourned for Easter. Not without gaiety, Ministers and members departed. But the King had just returned from Biarritz with a bad cold, a dangerous cold which despondency over the crisis just ahead of him did nothing to mitigate. In the starlit early morning of 7th May, newsboys awoke all the crooked streets of London. 'Death of the King', they shouted. 'Death of the King'. By noonday, England was in black.

Chapter Three

Their Lordships Die
in the Dark

I

WITH the passing of the Budget and the death of King Edward, the battle with the House of Lords moved out into the open. And if the controversy that now began seems faded and freakish as we look back on it, yet it serves to prove that politics, like a tarnished mirror, must always return some reflection of the national destiny. For a moment, as they pass to and fro in this dim, reflected area, the figures in the quarrel assume a larger importance than is theirs by right as individuals. Their shapes waver and dissolve, until you could almost swear that personages more ancient had taken their place; for the fight between Lords and Commons, which came to such an ignoble ending one year later, was the last ragged skirmish of a long and sometimes heroic struggle.

The whole importance of this quarrel, which the Lloyd George Budget finally precipitated, lies in its reference to two very simple propositions: aristocracy must be powerful; aristocracy must be responsible. English aristocracy, more ancient in principle than in birth, had fought for, and won, and was now losing its economic power: it was the mournful duty of politics to shadow forth its loss of responsibility by taking away its parliamentary leadership.

It would be easy to relegate this dispute to a mere phase in party warfare, and to forget its large implications. But this was no parochial affair. It was a struggle between two doomed powers: between the middle-class philosophy which was Liberalism and the landed wealth which passed for aristocracy and found its living symbol in the House of Lords. With the Lords' power of veto went all those claims to economic leadership which had formerly belonged to the owners of great estates.

And if Mr Asquith's Resolutions and his Parliament Bill meant anything, they meant that the land's political power was on the wane as well. Away with it, and away with English aristocracy, too: it had become too old-fashioned to do its work.

There is a barbarism in politics, not unhealthy, which decrees the death of any institution which has lost its economic meaning; just as savage kings and chieftains were once slaughtered when they were no longer able to lead in battle or beget children. (But those who made themselves the instruments of this archaic doom had to be young and healthy and brave. Otherwise the same doom would come upon them.

Could the Liberal party succeed where the House of Lords had failed? Could it govern the country? Or was it perhaps too feeble and too faint-hearted to avoid, in its turn, a swift and correct destruction?)

II

When the funeral ceremonies for King Edward were over, Mr Asquith went northward to Skye and in the scented calm of that remote island sat down to write a memorandum to his new sovereign. It is a pity that this document has not survived; it must have been a lucid treatise on the functions of monarchy. It must have conveyed, beyond any doubt, a polite warning of the dangers which lay ahead, and a slightly alarming air of unconcern, and even of condescension. For the Prime Minister's opinion of George V was much the same as everybody else's. The new king had no political experience whatsoever. He had once been a sailor; he had acquired some knowledge of a good many foreign coaling stations, but very little of the world at large. Politicians supposed him a man with Tory principles and a short temper: beyond that, they knew and supposed nothing.

To the mass of his subjects he meant nothing. His father was a hard king to follow. Edward VII represented, in a concentrated shape, those bourgeois kings whose florid forms and rather dubious escapades were all the industrialized world had left of an ancient divinity: his people saw in him the personification of something nameless, genial and phallic, the living excuse for their own little sins. And he had been a good king, after his fashion. The blood of his ancestors, agitated by so many crises and so many loves, had taught him to combine duty with indulgence; every beat of it was a warning to constitutional behaviour. He was never tyrannical, he was never loud, or ill-mannered; he was just comfortably disreputable. How right it seemed, under his kindly dispensation, that humanity's fondest sins should be drummed from church and chapel only to find refuge in the Throne! Englishmen had never cared for a respectable monarch: witness the fate of King Charles, whom the

Commons executed, and of King Arthur who, in idyll after idyll, received a mortal wound from Lord Tennyson.

And George V was respectable. As was not unusual in the history of the Hanoverian dynasty, he had been in opposition to his father, only the opposition was silent and moral, not political. People who were very much at home with King Edward in Buckingham Palace could never have found their way into Marlborough House, where the Prince and Princess of Wales held a small and severe court. Here all was order and tranquillity; here the virtues of family life were cultivated: and it was these things which, to the dismay of smart London, were now to be transplanted to Buckingham Palace.

A month after King George's accession, one ray of hope lit up the general disillusion. A gentleman by the name of Mylius had been circulating from time to time in England a republican sheet called *The Liberator*. There was nothing in *The Liberator* which posterity is likely to cherish except its quaint belief that monarchs and not millionaires were the symbols of twentieth century tyranny, and the fact that it was published in Paris by an enterprising but not very honest Hindu. With King George on the throne, however, Mr Mylius and his Hindu friend, animated by republican ardour and a natural tendency towards mud-slinging, saw fit to revive a somewhat tepid scandal – namely that the King had been married to an admiral's daughter in his youth, and that his present marriage was bigamous. The circulators of this malodorous little *histoire* were simple enough to hope that an ugly mob would soon be battering at the palace gates as the result of it. But the consequences were not quite so violent. Mr Mylius, being the only partner available, was summoned to appear in court to answer a charge of libel; and England sat back in the pleasant hope that its new king would prove a gay dog after all.

But Mylius had chosen for the King's first wife a lady whom George V had seen only twice and never so much as spoken to, and his evidence was very soon torn to pieces by Sir Rufus Isaacs, the Attorney-General. Mylius refused to plead in his own defence. The King had accused him, not as a king but as a private citizen, and unless his accuser appeared in court and took the witness stand, he would not and could not make a proper defence. King George, somewhat hysterical by now, pleaded for a chance to vindicate himself in this rather unseemly fashion; but in the end Mr Mylius was condemned, unheard, to a few months of prison.

The country as a whole was very disappointed. From the disingenuous flattery of the polite magazines, there had already emerged the message that the new King was not going to be fashionable. It now appeared that he was going to be dull. Dullness was almost unforgivable in 1910: and the disinterested and loyal character of the new King was blandly overlooked.

III

For royal virtue or vice the politicians cared nothing. What they feared was royal inexperience. The Liberals wondered whether George V would not prove too susceptible to Tory blandishment, as so many of his intimate friends were Tories. The Tories felt that he should be allowed some breathing space before being subjected to the dubious subtleties of ministerial advice. After all, it was up to him now. He alone could create new peers.

Prompted by Mr Asquith, therefore, King George now proposed an armistice, in which the leaders of both parties should get together and compose their differences in quiet discussion. A Constitutional Conference was arranged. It was to be held in Lansdowne House, scene of the 1908 'stiletto' meeting. Mr Asquith, Mr Lloyd George, Mr Augustine Birrell, and Lord Crewe represented the Government; Messrs. Balfour and Austen Chamberlain, and Lords Lansdowne and Cawdor spoke for the Conservatives. Neither side was in the least hopeful.

But while the King found his political bearings, and the country recovered from its grief, both sides were perfectly willing to talk. Their deliberations were shrouded in secrecy, to the discomfort of back benchers in either party, and of amateur politicians all over the country; though if we examine the suggestions which were made across Lord Lansdowne's table (as distinct from the suggestions which were made, as it were, under it) there seems to be no reason why the country should not have been allowed to know of them.

The discussions ranged over a wide but insubstantial and haunted field. What should the relations of the two Houses be in the matter of finance? What machinery could be found to prevent persistent disagreement between Lords and Commons? How could the composition and numbers of the House of Lords be so regulated as to make it act fairly between the two parties? Mr Balfour and his colleagues were prepared to yield over finance. No more lordly tampering with budgets.

The Commons could have entire control over Money Bills. The Lords would accept the Speaker's certificate as a guarantee that no other legislative material had been tacked on to them. This large and inevitable concession, yielded with a sigh of relief, was the only lucid agreement.

Not that the Conservatives were backward with what an earlier vocabulary would have called 'cheapening'. They dangled all kinds of fantastic bargains before the indifferent noses of Asquith, Lloyd George, Birrell, and Crewe. They offered to discard the hereditary principle; they were willing to accept joint sittings of the two Houses on all matters of 'constitutional', as opposed to 'ordinary' legislation. (But what was 'constitutional' legislation? Nobody knew. It is an axiom of English constitutional theory that no precise difference exists between 'constitutional' and 'ordinary' legislation.) The one thing they were not ready to sacrifice was the essentially Conservative character of the Upper House. And that was the one thing which mattered.

Pericles said of unwritten laws that they bring 'undeniable shame to the transgressors'. The Lords had transgressed in 1909 when, armed with their legal rights, they rejected the Budget: but who could say that these eight good gentlemen, closeted like conspirators in Lansdowne House, were not committing a far more serious trespass? To reform the House of Lords meant to set down in writing a Constitution which for centuries had remained happily unwritten, to conjure a great ghost into the narrow and corruptible flesh of a code.

IV

For this Constitution, which haunted the Lansdowne House Conference, was nowhere set forth in an Instrument. It had no visible body. A Magna Carta, an Apology, an Act of Settlement, an Act of Union, had printed themselves across the ribbed sands of English history like the footsteps of an unseen traveller, a mighty ghost. Materialized, this spectral Constitution would have been a very monster, bearing a horrid mixture of features, from Norman French to early Edwardian; a monster flagrantly improvised, illogically permanent; a monster which existed on the principle that every grievance had a remedy, but that no grievance was eternal and no remedy a panacea.

It was this variegated spirit, the genius of English history, which mocked the rather idle labours of those eight gentlemen in Lansdowne House.

In July 1910, the Conference was still vaguely optimistic, or so the Prime Minister announced. Resisting an invitation to Lord Crewe's country house – for fear that the country would accuse it of being influenced by 'Crewe's champagne' – Lord Crewe kept a good table – it worked on until 10th November, when it finally agreed to disagree. What it had stumbled over, not once nor twice, was the now threatening problem of Irish Home Rule. And it had attempted to settle this, not over the conference table, but by the more devious and subterranean ways of politics.

Who cared for Home Rule in 1910? To the Liberals it was an abstraction, a cause with the glamour gone from it, a dead thing. The Conservatives had always opposed it from a traditional belief that some medicinal mixture of 'evolution' and artifice would dose away Ireland's desires.

But Home Rule was on the way; it was the unavoidable result of a restriction of the Lords' veto. The Irish party as good as held Mr Asquith's I O U – Home Rule was to be paid to them in return for those eight score votes of theirs which had put the Budget through. A Home Rule Bill was to be one of the first pieces of legislation which, passing through the Commons on three consecutive sessions, would become law, however the Lords voted.

Both Liberals and Conservatives felt that Irish interference in their present constitutional quarrel was highly objectionable. Politics was still for the most part a gentlemanly profession, a fencing match with buttoned foils, a serious game; and now it was probably to be broken up by an invasion of brawling Celts, armed with lethal weapons and in deadly earnest. Parliament had little use for deadly earnestness. Its members kept their wrath for debate, or brought it out with a flourish on the public platform; they rarely carried it into private life with them. In private life they were all gentlemen together, Liberal and Conservative alike.

How often, in those still untroubled days, had political hostesses been gratified with the sight of Messrs Balfour and Asquith sauntering into their drawing-rooms arm in arm! That afternoon in the House Mr Balfour had possibly visited some of his choicest sarcasms on Mr Asquith, and after dinner Mr Asquith would have to hurry back and answer them; meanwhile they were very good friends. If there was to be music, Mr Balfour would certainly stay; his skull's face wreathed in smiles, he would wave a charming good-bye to the Prime Minister, who was going to be very destructive about him in Parliament that evening. It was all very gentle and gay; and now it was to be spoiled by a number of Irishmen who had the singular bad taste to be in earnest about the freedom of their country.

Yet the only way for Mr Asquith to escape from his Irish obligations was by coalition with the Conservatives; in which case he would be allowed to restrict the Lords' veto in return for Imperial Preference and compulsory military service. This was a most improbable exchange, and in any case coalition was scarcely possible except in a time of acute business depression, when capitalists of the right and left wing would naturally cling together. And business in 1910 was still capable of managing its own affairs. None the less, some such scheme was discussed during the Lansdowne House armistice, and was ultimately quashed – as Mr Lloyd George maintains in his *Memoirs* – by a certain Mr Akers-Douglas, a retired and soon to be ennobled mediocrity whom the Conservatives regarded as the fount of wisdom.

And yet, however remote coalition must have seemed to such veterans as Asquith and Balfour, there were younger men in either party who took it more seriously. On the Conservative side, a young and rising politician, Mr F. E. Smith, was openly in favour of a 'real and honest truce'. There was little which Mr Smith concealed from his dear friend, the young and risen Liberal politician, Mr Winston Churchill. He even looked further afield. In October he wrote to Austen Chamberlain: 'It seems to me that Lloyd George is done for unless he gradually inclines to our side in all the things that permanently count.' This may seem curious language to use about the predatory author of the People's Budget; but it was shrewd enough. Mr Lloyd George, much softened by the courtesies of Lansdowne House, had come to have something of a fondness for the younger Conservative mind: it was elastic, it was businesslike, and above all it was in a hurry. Perhaps, for a little while, that old ghost of a Fourth Party peered wickedly into Lord Lansdowne's innocent windows; it would have been very exciting for young and ambitious politicians to throw over their venerable leaders and try to run the country for themselves.

But once again the terms of such a bargain would have been too heavily in the Conservatives' favour. Besides which, the would-be young coalitionists very much distrusted one another, and rightly.

None of them was disinterested; each was for himself. So 'the great arrangement' of Mr Smith's dreams faded away, like the mirage it really was. And shortly afterwards the Conference itself broke up, with nothing accomplished.

On 8th November Mr Asquith admitted to 'an apparently irreconcilable divergence of opinion'. Two days later, the eight gentlemen met for the last time in Lansdowne House. Just before their final conference began, Mr Balfour took Mr Asquith aside and murmured, in pessimistic tones, that he saw nothing ahead of him but chagrin and retirement. He was quite right.

11th November found Mr Asquith at Sandringham, where King George had been whiling away these ominous last days. The Prime Minister explained as gently as he could what the future might be expected to bring forth. The previous afternoon, the Cabinet had agreed to ask for an immediate dissolution. There would have to be another election, in which the country must decide for itself whether the Commons or the Lords should prevail. If the Liberals were returned once more, then His Majesty would be advised to use his royal prerogative, and create at one swoop a swarm of something like five hundred peers.

The Prime Minister merely stated his case and left. King George was face to face at last with the crisis which had so darkened his father's last days. In great trouble, he returned to London.

At about three o'clock in the afternoon of 16th November, Mr Asquith appeared in Buckingham Palace. With him was Lord Crewe – 'as if he needed a witness' as critics remarked, not sure what the Prime Minister was up to, but sure that it was nothing good. The two Liberal leaders, of course, had come to ask for His Majesty's decision in the matter of using his prerogative, should that unpleasantly comic course become necessary.

There could scarcely have been two men whom George V would less rather have met. But 'I have never seen the King to better advantage,' Asquith noted that same evening; 'he argued well and showed no obstinacy.' These condescending phrases do not conceal the fact that there was something for the King to argue about. What a humiliating thing they had come to ask of him! Peerages were often bestowed upon the wrong men for the wrong reasons; but they were none the less rewards, they were honours. You had to work your way through Parliament for them, or pay money for them, or write poetry for them;

they were not to be had for nothing. Suddenly to ennoble some five hundred obscure and undeserving men, simply as a political measure, was to turn the House of Lords into a vulgar joke. It was to make a joke of the royal prerogative. It was a melancholy and maddening step for any sovereign to contemplate who was at all serious about his dignity. So George V naturally 'argued well'. And Mr Asquith, benign and gentle, softened his demands as much as possible. After all, the prerogative might never actually be used; the mere threat of such a farcical punishment would likely bring their lordships to heel. And in any case, he said, he was not asking for absolute guarantees; all he wanted was a 'hypothetical understanding': *if* he took the responsibility of advising another election, and *if* he then retained his majority, would the King agree to create peers?

The King, not used as yet to Mr Asquith's language – so lucid and so evasive – asked if that was the advice which would have been tendered to his father. 'Yes, sir,' said Mr Asquith, 'and your father would have consented.' So George V agreed that there seemed to be no alternative. Begging him to keep this conversation a secret, Asquith and Crewe took their leave, very well contented.

And while the King, unhappy but a man of his word, pretended to his friends that there had been no understanding (at Windsor, a month later, Lord Lansdowne suggested to his uncomfortable sovereign that a creation of peers was 'inconceivable') the new elections took place. The country was indifferent, and politicians were hard put to it to stir up its lethargy. Just before Dissolution, the House of Lords had been presented with the Parliament Bill, the Bill which had arisen from Mr Asquith's Resolutions. It had then offered to accept the most sweeping reforms, if only it could retain its veto. 'Ah, gentlemen,' sighed Mr Asquith at Hull, 'what a change! This ancient and picturesque structure has been condemned by its inmates as unsafe.'

V

Up to the last moment of those December elections of 1910, the Tories laboured to produce alternatives. But the more they laboured, the more they resembled Dr Johnson's criminal, who started to write a book two weeks before his execution. 'Depend upon it, sir,' said Dr Johnson, 'when a man is going to be executed in a fortnight, it concentrates his mind wonderfully.'

Perhaps they had some little hope of reprieve. But the industrial North was still firm against Tariff Reform, even Tariff Reform wrapped in loyal bunting and called Imperial Preference. In sodden weather, the country returned its weary and sarcastic opinion. Liberals – 272; Conservatives – 272: it was, once again, an Irish-Labour majority which gave Mr Asquith his mandate to overwhelm the Lords. But here, as Mr Birrell remarked, here was 'the sudden emergence of a certainty'. Nothing could save the Lords now. The country had given Mr Asquith its lazy permission to proceed; it had also invited him to take the consequences.

When the new Parliament assembled on 22nd February, 1911, Mr Asquith still said nothing about his 'hypothetical understanding'. Balfour and Lansdowne, though they believed that Irish and Labour pressure would force the Cabinet 'to play the bullies in the Royal closet', still put some faith in George V's powers of persuasion. He might yet stir the ministerial conscience, they hoped, if that organ were not wholly atrophied.

In the House of Lords, meanwhile, Lord Morley – the Liberal Lord President of the Council – coldly remarked that reformed or unreformed (and proposals of reform were still being desperately advanced), regenerate or unregenerate, their lordships would lose their veto. It was then that the Old Order suddenly lifted its head. . . .

A large number of England's peers had been christened by Mr Lloyd George, in his happy Budget days, 'the backwoodsmen'. The only public source of knowledge about these hereditary statesmen was Debrett's *Peerage*, in whose detailed pages they – with their wives and families, their cousins and their aunts – afforded the curious snob a spare and stilted gratification. Otherwise, they lived an obscure and doubtless a useful existence on their country estates, scattered through the length and breadth of England, and were locally familiar as landlords, magistrates, and Lords-Lieutenant. During the Season, they would come to London, usually for the Eton and Harrow match; and you could see them in the illustrated papers, glaring with a mixture of contempt and alarm at their modern enemy the photographer, who snapped them hopefully at Lord's cricket ground or in the park.

For many years they had gone about their rural business, not troubling the country and by the country untroubled. During the long, long days of Conservative rule, they never entered the House of Lords; in its red-leather wastes they would have been lost and miserable, and Tory

Bills were peaceably voted through without them. But when the Liberals came back in 1906, with their huge majority and their formidable Labour tail, there was a faint shudder in the country homes of England, and one or two strange and speechless Tory faces were observed, lurking in the dark, far corners of the House of Lords. The backwoodsmen were on the move.

Divisions were so infrequent in the Upper Chamber before 1906, that 'when one occurs', a Bishop was heard to remark in the Athenaeum Club, 'the peers cackle as if they had laid an egg'. But as the Liberal Government presented its Education Bill, its Licensing Bill, its Plural Voting Bill, the peers began to have something to divide about. And whom else should the Conservatives call upon to murder Liberal legislation but their vast reserves of rural, unremembered Tory lords? It was these men, these landed noblemen, whom Lloyd George assaulted in his Limehouse speech and afterwards; and his audiences, townsfolk for the most part, began to think of them as virtual barbarians who crawled from their country fastnesses simply and solely to vote against good Liberal Bills; who made vast fortunes from the toil of miners, lived on the spoils of the church, robbed the railway companies; and who, when the Chancellor asked them for a halfpenny, just a copper, incontinently turned their dogs upon him.

It was with such worthies that the fate of the Parliament Bill now rested. They were scarcely the villainous barons of Mr Lloyd George's imagination, but they did want to retain their right of ruining legislation. The idea that they were old-fashioned and useless, though unfortunately a true one, troubled them not a little, and it was in May 1911 that they showed definite signs of revolting.

This revolt first showed its head at a luncheon given by Lord Willoughby de Broke, a genial and sporting young peer, whose face bore a pleasing resemblance to the horse, an animal which his ancestors had bred and bestridden since the days before Bosworth Field. Willoughby de Broke was not a 'backwoodsman' in the purest – or Lloyd George – sense of the word. He had attended quite a few sittings of the House of Lords, and had even delivered a speech there, much to Lord Lansdowne's gratification, on the subject of canteens in Territorial summer camps. He had voted faithfully against the People's Budget, and honestly believed that England's assorted masses should be treated as he treated his gamekeepers, grooms and indoor staff – that is, kindly and firmly. He had quite a gift for writing, thought clearly, and was not more than two hundred years behind his time.

Over this amiable peer's luncheon table, in May of 1911, revolt first reared its coroneted head. Oddly enough, its leader was none other than Lord Curzon, the embittered ex-Viceroy of India whom Lloyd George's Budget had pushed back into political life. Curzon, surely one of the most brilliantly pompous men in England, rather enjoyed the aristocratic gesture, particularly when it emphasized nothing more than his own importance. In this instance he did not believe that the King would ever be advised to create peers; that was unthinkable, 'a fantastic dream'. So – 'Let them make their peers,' he said with an idle and easy conscience: 'We will die in the last ditch before we give in.' His words were soon to be used against him.

The Conservative party was dividing into two. On the one were the 'Ditchers', who believed in fighting the Parliament Bill all the way, on the assumption that Mr Asquith was bluffing and would never dare advise a creation of new peers. On the other hand were the 'Hedgers', composed of the more venerable and statesmanlike Conservatives, who rather thought the time had come to climb down and passively vote away their own powers. The Ditchers first advertised themselves on 23rd May. On that day the Parliament Bill came up to the House of Lords, to be greeted with an excellent debate and a Ditcher threat of grave amendments in committee.

In Buckingham Palace and Downing Street it was realized, with a shudder of genuine surprise, that the Lords were going to fight.

VI

On Empire Day, Mr F. E. Smith and Lord Winterton gave a fancy dress ball at Claridge's. In the middle of the ball-room floor, among the Junos and the Ceres and the Cleopatras and the Louis Quinze duchesses and the pink tulle ballet girls and the young politicians in velvet with jewelled snuff-boxes, stood Mr Asquith and Mr Balfour, dressed in ordinary evening clothes. At midnight a way was cleared through the rout for the figure of a peer, wearing robes of state, and bearing on his coronet the legend '499: just one more vacancy': it was Mr Waldorf Astor. This delicate allusion to the Royal Prerogative was greeted with rounds of applause, from Mr F. E. Smith in his eighteenth century white satin, and Mr Winston Churchill in his scarlet domino, and Lord Charles

Beresford in his black false nose and black veil, and all the rest of that expensive gathering; and not the least from Mr Balfour and Mr Asquith, who seemed to think it an excellent joke.

Perhaps it was. Perhaps the realities of the situation were to be gauged, as one nettled correspondent suggested to *The Times* of 26th May, 'by the vagaries of a mock peer in tinsel, in the presence of the Prime Minister and the Leader of the Opposition'.

VII

With the beginning of June, the newspapers paid less and less attention to this unpredictable question. Everything was now consecrated to the approaching Coronation, at which (perhaps for the last time) the peers would assist in an unreformed condition.

One English Coronation is very like another; each has the same backward look. Each is a celebration of the past. Each rehearses, for a long hour or two, the glory that has departed; and, with a ritual plundered from Rome and only half-domesticated, calls to the dead in solemn mummery. King George's Coronation of 22nd June, 1911, has inspired little except a piece of excellent prose from Miss Sackville-West. Its weighted majesty was lightened by only a few human moments. The pleasant Comte d'Haussonville, seated in his blue-draped *tribune* and waiting for the show to begin, admires the opposite spectacle of Mr Balfour, *'qui, trouvant sans doute l'attente longue, dort'*. The Speaker regards with suppressed annoyance the unmannerly behaviour of the German Crown Prince. Lord Morley, exhausted at an early stage of the ceremony, suddenly thinks, 'This would be a splendid moment to die.' A Baroness is discovered sitting among the Countesses, and ejected with polite horror. Beyond the Abbey walls there waits another sort of life; the big hats, the 'reasonably' corseted figures, the high collars, the twentieth century. But here only the past is alive.

And the King and Queen have gone back at last to the Palace; the Peers, festive and comic anachronisms in robes and coronets, are wining and lunching in Westminster Hall. In the blue-hung Abbey the Thrones are empty, the altar has retired into its Protestant obscurity, the chapels are filling with shadows. The whole pageant of an hour ago, purple and trumpets and chorus, was, after all, insubstantial: it has faded back where it belongs, where no beauty is found and no songs echo, into the illustrious tombs and vaults of Westminster Abbey, and the trifles of dust which inhabit them.

The next day was the day of the Royal Progress, when a procession representing the Empire, with the King-Emperor in its midst, was to pass round London, to gratify as many of England's citizens as could crowd within sight of it, heirs one and all of the palm and the pine and the far-flung battle line. It was also a Bank Holiday. Londoners arose to uncertain weather, a fitful and watery sunshine and a rainy wind.

They decided, however, that this would be a good day for going into the country, and left their city to a fairly moderate assembly of provincials and foreigners.

At eleven o'clock, when the King and Queen left Buckingham Palace, their carriage and escort were momentarily lighted with a shaft of sunshine, and again at Hyde Park Corner the sun crept over helmet and cuirass and pennoned lance. A Royal Pavilion had been built at Wellington Arch, where the visiting royalties sat: 'a blaze of glorious colouring', said *The Times*, glad of this polyglot and largely doomed concourse. As the King and Queen drew near the whole royal Babel came smartly to its feet, and George V, clutching his carriage door, stood up to bow towards the day's most spontaneous greeting.

Now that her monarchs had ceased to govern, England rather expected some enthusiasm to be shown about them. Royal processions were supposed to be regarded as something between a circus, a Lord Mayor's Show, and a minor apocalypse. But as this procession rounded Hyde Park and entered Piccadilly, it appeared to have started out almost for nothing.

Perhaps the threat of rain had kept spectators away. '*Pleuvoir sur le Roi et la Reine*,' thought the affronted d'Haussonville, watching events from a window, '*songez donc!*' Or it may not have been the rain. Possibly '*il y ait un peu moins de monde à Londres qu'on ne le prevoyait*': in other words, nobody cared. For Piccadilly was so thinly lined that not a loyal soul there had even to stand on tiptoe. Already, along this sparse and whispering route had gone the Colonial and Indian processions. The Indian princes were well received, because of their plumes and jewels and cloth of gold. But the troops from Canada, Australia, New Zealand and South Africa, the Ministers of Crown Colonies, the Dominion Premiers went by unacclaimed, drab symbols of an empire whose frontiers marched with the sun, and whose capital was taking it altogether too much for granted. It was like a march of rather dull toys.

And the King and Queen, riding politely welcomed through miles of London, carried back few warming memories except of a burst of applause here and there and the huzzas of their foreign cousins and the friendly handkerchiefs of Lords Lansdowne and Selborne waving from the steps of Devonshire House....

The visiting royalties were feted and sped on their way – which led through the Balkan Wars to 1914: England was to see few of them again. At Stafford House, banked with crimson carnations, and Grosvenor House, filled with blue hydrangeas, the royal sons and daughters of Europe, Asia and India danced and bowed and, towards midnight, supped. It is difficult to say which those luxurious, ironic suppers better resembled – the feast of Trimalchio or the feast of Damocles.

VIII

But now, with the chivalrous rites of the Coronation fresh in memory, the Ditcher faction girded itself for combat. It is perhaps a just comment on England of 1911 that this last battle to preserve aristocracy should have taken on a strident and comic disguise. Many of the Ditchers were earnest men and men of good-will, who, gazing back in spirit to the mellow vistas of a pastoral England, truly believed that the country was better off under the guidance of men of birth. Even the industrial era, they reasoned, had found noblemen at the helm; who had better served their country through the machine-ridden latter half of Victoria's reign than those honest survivals of a landed and predatory aristocracy – the Duke of Devonshire and the Marquess of Salisbury?

But the unhappy comic spirit which took possession of this last desperate sally of the Ditchers, was due to the fact that – apart from their hatred of Home Rule and their fears for political Conservatism – they were instinctively horrified by reality. In their minds, to attack the House of Lords was to attack an ancient and virtuous talisman. There was a certain magic in the hereditary principle. That most peerages sprang from the curious powers of survival in some obscure medieval family, or from a dishonest bargain struck in the eighteenth century, or from a talent for guessing right on the stock exchange, or from a genius for keeping business projects on the windy side of the law – this they could not or would not recognize. To them, the House of Lords was the mysterious symbol of Breeding. They rallied to its protection, as savages rally to protect a house of an idol.

The most primitive idols, even those which have long been abandoned to the jungle and the sand-drift, are land-marks in the journey of the human soul: they represent a search for coherence in the confusions and fears of living. So this venerable House of Lords was not simply a constitutional relic of the great landed fortunes; it was also a fetish, it meant the ideally paternal responsibility of the noble few. And though this meaning was quite irrelevant to the twentieth century, yet those who tried to preserve it were not merely idle men or arrogant men. They saw the passing of certain values which at their best were very high and at their worst were very human; they did not realize that life consists in change, that nothing can stand still, that today's shrines are only fit for to-morrow's cattle. Clinging to the realities of the past, they prepared to defend their dead cause to the finish.

For a while they were satisfied with their official leader. On 4th July, in committee, Lord Lansdowne offered an amendment to the Parliament Bill which proposed that all Bills affecting the Crown, the Succession, the Establishment, or the Union should be subject to a referendum, an amendment which implied a determination to keep all such questions as Home Rule beyond the mere decision of a majority in the Commons. Moreover, the Parliament Bill, when it emerged from committee on 5th July, was not at all the Bill which the Commons had submitted; it was quite unrecognizable. Mr Asquith affected astonishment. Why bother to have an election? he asked the House of Commons: the Lords had so amended his Bill that it embodied, in a less conciliatory manner, all those suggestions which had been made, and rejected, at last year's conference.

The Government could not resign, for the country would not stand a third election. The only course left him was to lay all his cards on the table.

On 17th July, he had an audience of King George. On 18th July, Mr Lloyd George arrived, like Hermes, on Mr Balfour's doorstep. With a sly, sweet gravity, highly irritating to his hearers, he told Mr Balfour and Lord Lansdowne that only yesterday the King had pledged his word to create peers, and that this was simply the confirmation of a promise given as far back as December 1910. The Government, he said, was determined to pass its Parliament Bill through the Lords, and unamended, but it had no desire to proceed with a creation of peers. On the contrary, the Lords had still a few more days in which to come to reason. Until 24th July, when Mr Asquith purposed to announce the

King's decision, the Commons would not deal with the Lords' amendments. But when they did deal with them – and here at last he revealed the whole situation – they would not return them with the usual statement of objections; they would return them rudely *en bloc*, with a downright warning that unless the Bill went through in its original shape the certain consequence would be a deluge of brand new coronets.

'An unheard-of thing', Lord Lansdowne told Lord Knollys, the King's secretary: never before had the House of Lords been so grossly, so studiously insulted. But as far as he and Mr Balfour were concerned, the game was now up; the King had given his guarantee; it was useless to go on fighting. He said as much when the Parliament Bill went through its Third Reading in the Lords on 20th July: the amendments, he said unhappily, could only be insisted upon 'so long as we remain free agents'.

This was the white flag. And up jumped the septuagenarian Earl of Halsbury; and Lansdowne knew, as one bitter sentence followed another, that he could no longer answer for the sanity of his followers.

IX

On that same evening, Mr Asquith sat in his room in the House of Commons, composing a letter.

Dear Mr Balfour } [he wrote]
 Lord Lansdowne

I think it courteous and right, before any public decisions are announced, to let you know how we regard the political situation.

When the Parliament Bill in the form which it has now assumed returns to the House of Commons, we shall be compelled to ask the House to disagree with the Lords' amendments.

In the circumstances, should the necessity arise, the Government will advise the King to exercise his Prerogative to secure the passing unto law of the Bill in substantially the same form in which it left the House of Commons; and His Majesty has been pleased to signify that he will consider it his duty to accept, and act on, that advice.

Yours Sincerely,

H. H. ASQUITH.

Under these chilly sentences the dust of rumour, which had been rising like a cloud around the King and his Ministers, settled into bleak and final fact. Next morning, the Conservative peers met at Grosvenor

House at half-past ten, in great consternation and about two hundred strong, moved to Mr Balfour's house at half-past eleven; and finally split apart at Lansdowne House that afternoon. In the mounting summer heat, the nerves of both sides – Hedger and Ditcher, realist and romantic – were stretched and ragged. Lord Lansdowne's strategy was clear and sensible: when the Commons returned the Parliament Bill in its original shape, he would advise unconditional surrender. But he made the mistake of announcing this decision in the most lukewarm fashion, and then of asking for opinions. Whereupon – 'I shall divide', Lord Halsbury shouted, 'even if I am alone'; and the Duke of Somerset and Lord Willoughby de Broke declared themselves willing to follow this ancient into the ditch; and other less articulate peers were understood to mutter agreement.

Nothing definite could be done until Mr Asquith made his announcement the following Monday; with this small respite Lord Lansdowne consoled himself. In angry little groups of three and four, their perspiring lordships came out into the stagnant heat of Berkeley Square. A reporter asked Lord Halsbury what was going to happen. The antique rebel glared at his questioner: 'Government by a Cabinet controlled by rank socialists,' he snapped, and could not be persuaded to say more. . . .

Halsbury was generally considered a fine example of English breeding; belonging to the impoverished cadet branch of a noble family, he had fought his way up to the Woolsack and an earldom. His little body, large head and enormous mouth gave him a curious resemblance to Tenniel's picture of Lewis Carroll's Duchess, which in its turn curiously resembles a great English gentleman. And Halsbury was a great English gentleman, a species of creature which often behaves in a dutiful and disinterested fashion, but is also capable of more eccentricity than all the gentlemen in Europe combined.

Well seconded by Lord Willoughby de Broke, he now prepared to humble Lord Lansdowne, Mr Balfour, the Liberals and the Crown. Willoughby de Broke's job was to rally the 'backwoodsmen'. In the escutcheoned pages of Debrett's *Peerage*, he discovered names so long buried in rustic quiet that few men could have known what their owners looked like. To these he wrote a letter, asking for their valuable votes against the unamended Parliament Bill with such success that, on 23rd July he declared that he could count on more than a hundred peers. Another labourer in this heraldic vineyard was Mr F. E. Smith, who –

his schemes for a coalition overthrown – acted as assistant secretary with a grave, careless, and extravagant humour.

Mr F. E. Smith was the product of Lancashire and Oxford. The son of middle-class parents (his father was a Birkenhead lawyer), he had learned at Oxford the infinite pleasures of spending the money one does not possess. For four brilliant years at that University, he had lived very well on scholarships and credit; had overcome by his wit, his good looks, his games, a sense of intellectual superiority and a certain Lancastrian stubbornness – the prejudices of all but a few of his contemporaries; and had decided quite correctly that fame and wealth were his whenever he was ready to seize them. He was called to the Bar. He got into Parliament. An almost unknown young barrister from the Northern Circuit, he astonished the Commons of 1906 by one of the most brilliant maiden speeches ever heard in their House, a speech which – if it had not been marred by the verbal trickery of an Oxford Union debater – would be sure of a high place in the history of English eloquence. He was not a great parliamentarian, so his friend Winston Churchill said; but that was because he never took Parliament quite seriously. His emotions, which were far less mature than his devastating and brilliant mind, made him cruel and pert.

He was tall, dark, slender and a little over-dressed. His eyes and hair were lustrous; the first from nature, the second from too much oil. His mouth had always a slightly contemptuous droop, his voice was a beautiful drawl. He had acquired, not diligently but with too much ease, the airs of a fox-hunting man who could swear elegantly in Greek. Many people loved him, most distrusted him, some despised him, and he despised almost everybody. In his later career as Earl of Birkenhead he served himself more faithfully than his God or his country, and has been left naked to his biographers; who, when they come to dealing with him, will discover among other less creditable attributes that he was without question the most fascinating creature of his times.

His motives for entering the lists with Halsbury and Willoughby de Broke were sufficiently mixed. He rather fancied himself in extravagant rôles; he had an ambition to finish up in the House of Lords, and longed for it to stay powerful until he could get his peerage; his friend Austen Chamberlain (with his father, the dying Joseph Chamberlain) was an ardent Ditcher; and he longed to have his revenge on Mr Balfour. Mr Balfour had severely snubbed him. Offered a Privy Councillorship in the non-partisan Coronation Honours List, he had received a note from his leader, suggesting that he should not sit on the front Opposition Bench, although this was the right of all Privy Councillors.

By administering this deadly snub to one of the most brilliant of his followers, Mr Balfour showed how little he was in touch with all the younger Conservatives. For Smith he had a particular dislike, because Smith was an upstart on the make; but there was elsewhere an alien spirit abroad. In these new earthquake times, his whole pragmatic world was splitting and crumbling under his feet; now, in his own party, gaped the inevitable, unsightly fissure. It was not that he disliked arrogance or intransigeance; he himself, beneath his casual manner, was capable of both: but he could never take either quality very seriously. His party had played a losing game since 1910, and possibly he had been to blame for not playing hard enough: the only thing left now was to lose gracefully, with an air. But though he was pessimist enough to suppose that most men were incapable of wisdom or foresight, yet, like some pessimists and most Tory veterans, he lacked imagination. He could not put himself into another man's shoes; particularly into the narrow shoes of such young political macaronis as F. E. Smith, Austen Chamberlain, Lord Hugh Cecil, and others of his rebellious following. Among the clubs, and the drawing-rooms, and the week-end parties there drifted the little phrase 'BMG' – Balfour Must Go. He heard it with chagrin and resignation; he knew that the Ditcher revolt was partly aimed against his leadership: on 23rd July, he learned that control was no longer in his hands.

On the afternoon of that day, Mr Asquith and his wife drove to Parliament through quite a cheering crowd. The Prime Minister was rightly contented with the world. Before him lay the delectable prospect of a triumphant reception; of a silent and attentive audience; of those luminous and tireless sentences with which he was going to proclaim that the Crown had yielded to the Liberal cause.

Mrs Asquith went up into the Ladies' Gallery, and found them standing on their chairs with excitement. Below them, a crowded House waited for her husband's arrival; and her heart beat high as a roar of welcome greeted him, walking up the floor.

Questions were disposed of. The Clerk read out the First Order of the Day: 'Parliament Bill: consideration of the Lords' Amendments.' There was another Homeric shout from his party as Mr Asquith rose. His speech was lying on the brass-bound box on the Table; waiting for the cheers to finish, he smoothed it out. At last, in a dead silence, he opened his mouth to speak.

But he had scarcely reached midway in his first sentence, when, from the seats behind Mr Balfour, came a shout of 'Traitor! Traitor!' From a corner seat below the gangway Lord Hugh Cecil, white with rage, took up the monotonous burden. 'Traitor! Traitor!' chanted the Opposition.

Mr Balfour lounged on the front Opposition bench, the faintest shadow of concern on his dreamy face betraying his disgust and amazement: this scene was not of his making, it had clearly been concerted among a small Ditcher minority. The Opposition cry was now rising to a hoarse and angry yell. The Speaker was helpless. There had been nothing like this since 1893, when members fought with disreputable fists along the floor of the House.

For three-quarters of an hour, Asquith faced his tormentors. Sometimes the noise died down long enough for him to read one sentence from his manuscript. Then he would be overwhelmed again with hoots and jeers. Every now and then Lord Hugh Cecil, his gaunt Elizabethan frame shaken with ludicrous passion, would stand up and scream, 'You've disgraced your office!'

To the very end Mr Asquith preserved his reputation as a consummate parliamentarian. At first he did not seem to notice the din; but as the brutal minutes passed, his mouth grew hard and his impassive face went slightly pink with fury. It was a piece of gallantry which did him credit but won him no mercy. In the Ladies' Gallery above, Mrs Asquith scribbled a note and sent it down to Sir Edward Grey, where that baronet sat remotely on the Treasury Bench. 'For God's sake,' she wrote, 'defend him from the cats and the cads.' Sir Edward read it, and sadly tore it up. Indeed, it was Will Crooks, of the Labour party, who struck the first blow for decency. He sat near enough to Lord Hugh to be heard. 'Many a man,' he shouted, 'has been certified for less than half of what the noble lord has done this afternoon.'

Thus rebuked by one of his social inferiors, Cecil almost collapsed; and in the half silence which followed, Sir Edward Carson rose to move adjournment. The Speaker remarked, with icy politeness, that the debate had not yet opened, and F. E. Smith immediately leaped to his feet. His careful mask of contempt thrown off, 'F.E.' was not without vulgarity; and the din began all over again. The Irish party started to shout. John Redmond, their leader, had been certainly audible to those around him when he said, 'If these damned Englishmen choose to make bloody fools of themselves, that's no reason for us not to behave.' Nor was it: but among the Irish ranks there was a small and capricious minority, led by William O'Brien, who looked and behaved like a slightly demented minor prophet, and who now enlivened the proceedings with an eldritch scream of, 'What ruffian said "McNally"?' 'McNally', it appeared, was a name you could not mention among Irishmen, belonging as it did to an informer of the early nineteenth century; and the Irish, forgetting the larger quarrel around them, started to exchange strange insults among themselves at the tops of their far from inconsiderable voices.

This was more than even Mr Asquith could stand. 'I am not going to degrade myself,' he said; and dropped his papers on to the box before him, and sat down.

Never before, in the history of Parliament, had a Prime Minister been refused a hearing: this was the beginning of what Asquith afterwards described as 'the new style'. Meanwhile Mr Balfour rose to answer a speech he had not heard, and to imply some criticism of the rebels behind him. Balfour was listened to in silence, but was followed by the revengeful F. E. Smith, whose very appearance inspired the Liberals with such justifiable fury that they completely lost their heads. Both sides began to yell at once; eyes gleamed in fury; fists were brandished aloft: for a moment it seemed as if the benches would empty themselves into battle on the floor. 'F.E.' could get no further than 'Mr Speaker', and having said these words some half a dozen times, he gave up and joined in the general hullabaloo. Whereat the Speaker, acting under the new Standing Order No. 21, adjourned the House without question being put, 'a state of grave disorder having arisen'.

One thing was certain. The Tory rebels had done no good either to themselves or the cause they were promoting. If the champions of hereditary government were a learned upstart and a noble hooligan. . . .

But F. E. Smith and Lord Hugh Cecil, leaders of what was afterwards known as 'The Cecil Scene', were unrepentant: others might and did apologize to the Prime Minister (who found the rewards of martyrdom well worth an hour's torture); these two became more vigorous in opposition than ever. As a protest against Mr Balfour's leadership, 'F.E.' left his customary seat behind the front bench and joined his noble colleague below the gangway.

X

The Ditchers could number – besides Lords Halsbury and Willoughby de Broke – Lord Milner, Lord Selborne, the Salisbury family (the Marquess in the Lords, and Lord Robert and Lord Hugh in the Commons), the dying Joseph Chamberlain and his son Austen, Sir Edward Carson, and F. E. Smith; behind this assorted leadership was a shadowy gathering of peers whom Willoughby de Broke claimed for his own, and whose exact numbers no man could guess. Lansdowne and Curzon (the latter a hurried convert to the Hedger persuasion, and much hated by the Ditchers therefore) knew that they could count on two hundred noblemen to support their policy of not challenging a division on the unamended Parliament Bill – in other words, of refusing to vote. Lord Crewe, the Liberal leader, controlled seventy-five lords, who would vote obediently for the Bill. So that Willoughby de Broke's backwoodsmen, if they amounted to no more than eighty, could defeat the Bill, force the King into an ordeal of wholesale creation, and subject the House of Lords to a grotesque and intolerable enlargement.

In an atmosphere thus charged with Tory humours, the Government could only wait and hope; but Lansdowne was now trying to persuade the more selfless of his patricians into an act of what the Romans would certainly have called *religio* – into voting, that is, with the Liberal peers and against their own convictions. Alarmed, the Ditchers rallied at a great No Surrender Dinner in the Hotel Cecil banqueting room on 26th July, where the central piece of decoration was the bald head and mutton chop whiskers of Lord Halsbury, who had consented to act as chairman. Eighteen hundred people, wilting in the summer heat, listened to a series of polite attacks upon Mr Balfour, and tried to remember that theirs was a truly baronial cause.

A sudden awareness of vanishing nobility visited each of the actors. 'I trust your splendid Earl is none the worse for last night's banquet,' Carson wrote to Lady Halsbury the next morning – as though, the Ditchers having now set their backs to a crumbling feudal wall, no other language were suitable to their predicament than such as might have been thought up by that eager medievalist, Mr Maurice Hewlitt.

The Conservative rebels needed something more than fine words and full dinners. On 27th July, Lord Robert Cecil wrote to F. E. Smith from Edinburgh, declaring that the party as a whole could not be made to fight. Nor could it. It contented itself with moving a vote of censure on 7th August – 'that the advice given to His Majesty by His Majesty's Ministers, whereby they obtained from His Majesty a pledge that a sufficient number of peers would be created to pass the Parliament Bill in the shape in which it left the House of Commons, is a gross violation of constitutional liberty, whereby the people will be precluded from again pronouncing upon the policy of Home Rule'.

Even Mr Balfour's dialectical subtlety was not able to preserve this fragile argument from disintegration: the more delicately he phrased his sentences, the more he entangled himself in that veil which hangs between monarch and Parliament, until at last there was scarcely a shred of it left. The King, he said in brief, had only just come to the throne and lacked experience, and a sad advantage had been taken of him; and with that, it appeared, he disassociated himself from any further part in the controversy. In vain Mr Asquith laboured to mend what his opponent had marred: Mr Balfour's retreat had left the Crown open to every miserable breeze of rumour, and King George, already alarmed by the Cecil scene, now insisted that something better than this should be done for him. Next day Lord Crewe did his best in the Lords, when he said that 'His Majesty had faced the contingency . . . with natural, and, if I may be permitted to use the phrase, with legitimate reluctance'; and with that the unsatisfied King had to content himself. Mr Asquith insisted that nothing more could be said; for he could not appear to have coerced his sovereign.

But the Crown at least would not take refuge in the ditch along with Halsbury, Smith and the rest of those mixed companions. Lord Knollys, the royal secretary, openly lobbied for the Hedger cause, much to the fury of the extremists, who did not hesitate to call their sovereign a traitor – though a traitor to what it would have been hard to tell.

On 8th August, the Commons rejected Lord Lansdowne's amendments. On 9th August, the Lords began their great debate, and adjourned with everything still uncertain. Lord Lansdowne's following had increased to three hundred and twenty peers; Lord Morley said that the Government's supporters now numbered eighty, with a strong probability that most of the bishops would vote for the Bill; as for the Ditchers, gossip had it that their ranks were thinning.

There were some who still declared that Mr Asquith would never advise a wholesale ennoblement, for all his threats. But the curious reader may discover, in Messrs J. A. Spender and Cyril Asquith's biography of the Prime Minister, a long list of possible peers which Mr Asquith drew up at that time, and which contained among many others the names of Anthony Hope Hawkins, Gilbert Murray, and Thomas Hardy. None of these gentlemen had been approached, of course, and it is doubtful if any would have accepted; but since the Prime Minister's imagination did not blench at the image of Mr Hardy in a coronet, it may be assumed that his intentions were serious. The Office of Works, moreover, was known to be thinking of the possibilities of Westminster Hall as a temporary House of Lords, since the present chamber would not have room enough for the invasion of five hundred brand new barons.

On the night of 9th August, at a Ditcher gathering in Lord Salisbury's house, Willoughby de Broke declared that he could count on one hundred and twenty votes. But six were ill, and several might 'run out' at the last moment. He was not in the best of spirits.

XI

On 10th August, the debate entered its final stage at half-past four of a sweltering afternoon: the mercury had climbed to 97° in the shade, the highest temperature recorded in seventy years. Some miles away, from out of the tropically moist East End, the paralysis of a transport strike was slowly creeping towards London's heart.

Nobody knew how the Lords would vote. Not Mr Asquith who had retired to Wallingford, his voice reduced to a hoarse whisper from nervous fatigue: not King George, waiting anxiously in Buckingham Palace. The King had come up from Cowes only three days before, with pleasant memories of a great sun and a fresh breeze and the roads filled with yachts; of how the King of Spain's yacht fouled the Warner Lightship and of how everyone waited anxiously for the Kaiser's *Meteor* to lose the King's Cup; and now, in the heat of London, he faced the dull reality of a Ditcher victory.

Could the Ditchers win? For once, the House of Lords was actually *debating*, and its final decision lay in the dark lap of chance, at the mercy of anger and caprice and rhetoric. That afternoon, packed breathless into box and gallery, London's smartest audience waited for the final clash which might yet precipitate a summer swarm of peers.

Lord Lansdowne began the debate in the lame, explanatory fashion of one who knows that trusted friends and colleagues have turned against him. He believed, he said, that the country would support him in an action whereby 'five hundred English gentlemen will not have taken their seats in this House upon conditions which I can only describe as humiliating and disgraceful'. And surely the exiguous safeguard of a two years' veto was better than a vast Liberal majority which would, when the Conservatives were again returned to power, prove obstinate and obstructive.

Lord Halsbury was up, his tiny figure shaken with wrath. Why were the Diehards responsible for a creation of Liberal peers? It was just as if a highwayman came and said, 'Give me your watch or I'll cut your throat,' and when you did not give him your watch, remarked, 'You are the author of your throat's being cut.' The whole Bill, he shouted through the cheers of his supporters, was wrong and immoral.

The Upper Chamber was behaving in a most unusual manner. The dignity, the courtesy, the somnolent inaudible voices, all were fled; even the old, familiar faces were distorted with rage or shadowed with suspicion. For a long while it seemed that the Ditchers were going to win: they made more noise, they aroused more enthusiasm. In vain the Archbishop of Canterbury announced that he would no longer abstain from voting *for* the Bill, being incensed at 'the callousness – I had almost said "levity" – with which certain noble Lords contemplate a course of action which would make them the laughing stock of the Dominions.' In vain Lord Camperdown – aghast at this new thought of the crude laughter of Canada, the hoarse, subterranean mirth of Australia – declared himself for the Government. He was answered by the Duke of Norfolk, premier peer of England, who threw the weight of his prestige into the Ditcher balance.

But when Lord Willoughby de Broke unwisely declared that the whole threat of a creation was 'pure bluff', Lord Morley rose and pronounced what every sensible man knew to be the last word. Morley was nervous and unhappy. 'I have to say,' he answered, 'that every vote given tonight against my motion is a vote in favour of *a large and prompt creation of peers.*'

These last words had a humorous, explosive sound not inappropriate to the punishment they threatened. As William IV had once said of the great Reform Bill, the Bill would pass either with or without a creation of peers. Nor could its consequences be avoided, so Morley thought as he sat down; it was not hereditary rule alone which was to endure a change tonight; something had happened to Ireland, too. She was no longer a hopeless suppliant: suddenly she brooded above their lordships' heads, a sinister and powerful Sphinx.

But the Ditchers considered neither the immediate present nor the resolving future. Their rage increased. They observed, with a violent contempt, the shadows of premonition which had crept over Morley's empty and chiselled face. They were left with the single determination to die on their feet, as though the feudal cause they upheld demanded no less of them. And so the speeches went on, while the long summer twilight withdrew from the stained glass windows, and the lights were lit, and the heat grew thick.

Lord Curzon, the Ditcher renegade, made his last appeal to reason. Lord Halsbury's party, he said, would find perhaps that they had wrought 'irreparable damage to the Constitution, their own party, and the State'. A pulpit speech, a pulpit speech, Lord Halsbury screamed, scarcely waiting for Curzon to sit down. His voice sank. He left the final decision of right or wrong to God and his conscience. Lord Rosebery followed him, pursuing to the end his self-appointed rôle of political anchorite. Rather than subject the House of Lords to degradation, he would vote for the Government, and thereafter never enter its precincts again.

And Lord Selborne finished the debate. 'The question is, shall we perish in the dark, slain by our own hand, or in the light, killed by our enemies. . . . It is because we do believe in our consciences that the course we are taking is the course of duty and the course of wisdom that we will follow Lord Halsbury into the Lobby.'

XII

With these grave and touching sentences, the House prepared to divide. Those in the galleries peered downwards, stirred beyond themselves, half conscious that history would be made within the next few minutes. The Chamber emptied quietly, until at last there was nothing left to fix the eyes upon but an expanse of red leather benches and a deep green carpet. Some who were there swore afterwards that the lights burned lower, and that they could hear in the lobbies a ghostly, insistent whisper, like the whisper of a disaffected crowd.

The silence held for a good ten minutes. Then, quite suddenly, the House began to fill again. From the right and the left of the Throne trod two thin lines, keeping level with each other until amost the end.

From a gallery above the Throne, Lords Lansdowne and Curzon watched breathless. But at last they knew the Hedgers had won; for it was the line on the right which held out longest. The Clerk handed a slip to the Government teller. 'On Question that this House do not insist upon the said Amendments, their Lordships divided: Contents, 131; Not-Contents, 114.' Their Lordships had decided to die in the dark.

From the crowded galleries there came a long, an almost inaudible, groan. Then members of the House of Commons went clattering and crowing through the Lobbies to their own chamber, where Irishmen and Labourites rose to cheer. For a while, the peers lingered in small groups on the floor; then they, too, dispersed. . . .

'It wasn't our fault,' Lady Halsbury cried to the people who pressed against her carriage windows in Parliament Square. She was 'boiling with rage'. She had already refused to shake Lord Lansdowne's hand when she met him at the door of the Princes' Chamber. Others were no more forgiving. In the 1900 Club, a queer little Tory stronghold in St James' Street, the leading Ditchers gathered in wrath and amazement, and from there, but little cooled, made their way to the Carlton Club, where a great crowd awaited them. There was some wild talk of revenge, and if any Tory peer who had voted with the Government dared show his face that night, he was greeted with shouts of 'Traitor!' and 'Judas!' 'We have been beaten by the Bishops and the Rats,' George Wyndham cried, and so it was. A scrutiny of the lists revealed the fact that some dozen Conservative peers had sacrificed themselves, and that all the Bishops, except their lordships of Worcester and Bangor, had voted with the Government. On the other side appeared names so perfectly obscure that few men in public life had so much as shaken their owners' hands before that night. Another word for 'Rat', it seemed, was 'Realist'.

The result had been in doubt up to the very end. The Duke of Norfolk had come in with eight followers, and nine Ditchers – after a harrying final talk with their consciences – had decided to abstain. One, at least, had done so from sheer panic at having to record a verdict of any kind: a certain duke, whose name has never been divulged, offered his support to Willoughby de Broke, and actually appeared on the fatal night. Since this nobleman was of a particularly restless and indecisive character, Willoughby de Broke took the precaution of hiding the ducal hat. But to no avail. Seized with alarming doubts at the very last minute, the noble duke left the House literally on the run, and disappeared hatless into the night.

Altogether it had been the closest shave. If all the Ditchers had stood their ground, and there had been no Rats, the vote would have gone against the Bill: as it was, the Bishops and the Rats were to be thanked for saving everyone from an extremely ludicrous if not indecent situation. The *Globe* hoped that no honest man would take these gentlemen by the hand again, that their friends would disown them, their clubs expel them: the *Observer*, with no less gratitude, remarked, 'There can be no closing of the ranks while there are traitors in the ranks, unexpelled and unrebuked.'

And the Parliament Bill was now a Parliament Act; the Constitution, still unmaterialized in its mighty progress, had planted one more large footstep in the sands of history. Its appearance was an ominous one. It meant the death of aristocracy and it meant the resignation of Mr Balfour: above all, it meant the triumph of everything that Parnell had suffered for. When Lord Rosebery, four bishops and ten unimportant peers signed their names to a protest in the little-used House of Lords Protest Book, the casual reader must have seen little more there than the lamentations of fifteen gentlemen concerning the curtailment of an obviously unfair veto. But those were more prophetic subscriptions and, like hieroglyphics, they were beyond the common reading. They set forth three years of undignified bickering, a gun-running, a mutiny, a threat of civil war; and, beyond these, more indistinct and more awful, the barricades of Easter Week and the long, blood-stained wastes of the Troubles.

For the moment, however, there was peace. The King 'has gone off happy' – said his secretary, Lord Knollys – 'and please God we shall have no more crises.' But Providence, as most men feared, was not to be so merciful: it may temper the wind to the shorn lamb, but not to the dying sheep.

(*Dying!* In the streets of London, the last horse-bus clattered towards extinction. The aeroplane, that incongruous object, earthbound and wavering, still called forth exclamations of rapture and alarm. Country roads, with blind corners and precipitous inclines, took a last revenge upon the loud invading automobile. There was talk of wild young people in London, more wild and less witty than you would ever guess from the novels of Saki; of night clubs; of negroid dances. People gazed in horror at the paintings of Gauguin, and listened with delighted alarm to the barbaric measures of Stravinsky. The old order, the old bland world, was dying fast: and the Parliament Act was its not too premature obituary. . . .)

If rumours of earthly actions ever reach the dead, one wonders what Mr Gladstone's subtle and pompous soul made of this great Liberal victory: or how the Duke of Devonshire received the news in that place where his slow-moving conscience was now doubtless reconciling itself to eternal bliss. In their day, would the House of Lords ever have dared to reject a Budget? And if it had, would Mr Gladstone have advanced to revenge himself with the dubious but necessary support of eight score Irish patriots? Was not this triumph, after all, only the last uphill charge of a weak and almost leaderless army?

PART II

Hubris

1911 – 13

Chapter One

'Animula Vagula . . .'

I

THE consequences of the Parliament Act were not heroic. Biographers of those gentlemen who were fated to play a leading rôle in the domestic events of the next three years have treated this period in the lives of their heroes with a certain nonchalance: they have, in fact, hurried past it, and have taken up the thread of their story at the point where England's statesmen were to be seen in a more advantageous light – directing, muddling, or dying in the most hideous war in human history. English biography adroitly stops in 1910 and starts again in 1914. But the story of these years deserves to be told, if only for the spectacle it affords us of a democracy passing from introspection to what looks very like nervous breakdown. Unfortunately it cannot be told with the biographer's privilege of selecting only what pleases him; the procession of minor incidents must be allowed to shuffle its way through these pages unhindered by any nice considerations of art or form.

I set it in motion with something of an apology. One day in the life of a contemporary dictator will provide more instances of fruitless insanity, of misplaced tyranny and sudden caprice than will appear in all these pages put together. This is not a record of personalities but of events; and not of great events but of little ones, which, working with the pointless industry of termites, slowly undermined England's parliamentary structure until, but for the providential intervention of a world war, it would certainly have collapsed. The structure remains, a not unsightly patchwork: it is still agreeably haunted by one of its former inhabitants, who slowly died there during the years 1910–14. It was in these years that that highly moral, that generous, that dyspeptic, that utterly indefinable organism known as the Liberal Party died the death. It died from poison administered by its Conservative foes, and from disillusion over the inefficacy of the word 'Reform'. And the last breath which fluttered in this historical flesh was extinguished by War.

II

To reduce the Liberal Party to a definition would be like attempting to reduce the glandular contours of a circus Fat Lady by simply talking her thin. It was an irrational mixture of whig aristocrats, industrialists, dissenters, reformers, trade unionists, quacks and Mr Lloyd George: it preserved itself from the destructive contradictions of daily reality by an almost mystical communion with the doctrine of *laissez-faire* and a profound belief in the English virtue of compromise. Its leadership was as mixed as were its principles. The Asquith Cabinet was very far from being the democratic group which its radical supporters might have wished for. Lloyd George, Lord Morley, John Burns, the ex-strike leader, Lord Loreburn, Mr Asquith himself – these men were enough in the spirit of the times to have worked themselves up from nowhere or almost nowhere; and perhaps Lloyd George and Burns had still some remnants of selfless affection for the class they sprang from. But the rest – they were of the ruling classes. The forms of democracy were a means of keeping in their possession a power which, they believed, was theirs by right. Some of them were peers who owed their place there to the fact that they had inherited their titles – thus preserving within the Cabinet some relic of that aristocratic whiggery which had been the bane and the support of Mr Gladstone. Of these Lord Loreburn afterwards remarked, when asked by a friend for an opinion of them – 'Liars, sir, and thieves.' It was not a friendly Cabinet.

And those of them who sat on the Treasury Bench in the House of Commons, what was it about *them* which so peculiarly irritated their opponents in those last pre-war years? Was it their almost cynical alliance with the Irish? Or was it their easy tolerance of that milk-and water socialism which, mingled with a few drops of personal vitriol, Lloyd George was prescribing for the electorate? These things, perhaps, but something more than these.

Along that row of distinguished and original faces there would pass from time to time, as lightly as a shadow upon the waters, an alarming, an alien, spirit. It invaded and effaced the dignified construction of Mr Asquith's features, it crept about the corners of Mr Lloyd George's eyes, with imponderable fingers it ruined that noble forehead which was Mr Winston Churchill's, it reduced the hatchet lines of Mr McKenna's face to the lesser proportions of a ladylike paper-knife – a spirit dangerous and indefinite, *animula vagula blandula*, the Spirit of Whimsy, which only afflicts Englishmen in their weakness.

It greets you with an engaging smile out of the imperfect photographs of those days. But to choleric gentlemen of the Opposition who watched it hovering over the troubled waters of debate, it was not so engaging. In the hush of crisis, in the tumult of abuse, or when the stuffy air of the Commons seemed almost to glitter with the shining, salt ripples of sarcasm – there it played, airy, remote and irresponsible.

Chapter Two

The Tory Rebellion

I

WITH the House of Lords no longer able to prevent it, Home Rule was now a certainty. Mr Asquith had promised it, when he bargained for Irish support for his Budget and his Parliament Bill. Nobody knows exactly what bargain he had struck then, whether it was a written pledge or just a gentleman's agreement; he and John Redmond, the Irish leader, carried that secret with them to their graves.

It may have been merely a gentleman's agreement, for Redmond was always to preserve a rather touching faith in the Liberal Party. He succeeded Parnell, when memories of that tragic O'Shea divorce case still offended the delicate nostrils of English Protestantism; and, just as he himself was never hurt by scandal, so was he never touched by that cold flame which burned in his former leader. He was fond of Parliament; its dignified ritual, its devices, and subterfuges, and intrigues all meant more to him than perhaps they should mean to an Irish leader, and it was often said of him that he had been so long in Westminster that he had forgotten what Ireland was like. In appearance he resembled a hawk: not, indeed, the hawk whose poised shadow casts a silence on the hedgerows beneath him, not the 'blue beak ember'; but a tamed and weary hawk. And it was not Parliament alone which had tamed him: beneath his outside of remote and almost Roman gravity there beat the heart of a squire. And whenever in the next few years occasion arose for his outside to prove itself, to present a stern and implacable opposition to Liberal compromise, to insist on full payment for his earlier support – then that betraying heart, the heart of a gentleman with a nice little estate in County Wicklow, would suddenly get the better of him. He would think, he would retreat, he would half yield: and then the occasion had passed. He was a living contradiction; and it was the fate of the Liberal Party to give itself into the hands of a contradiction and not of a Parnell. A Parnell would probably have been driven to put it out of office; a contradiction could only lead it deeper and deeper into the mires, and the mists, and the squalls of Irish politics – and eventually lose it there.

What Asquith and Redmond had agreed upon would have been simplicity itself under one condition – a united Nationalist Ireland. To separate Ireland from its Union with England, *that* would not have been the major operation which Gladstone had attempted, not in 1911. In 1911 Ireland was surprisingly respectable, and the old picture of its lean, outrageous peasantry, its filthy cabins which bred starvation and treachery, its unsuitable religion, its illogical refusal to see the beauties of lowliness and reverence as ordained by the Anglican Catechism, its permanent lust for stabbing England in the back – this old picture, so lamentably ill-conceived because conceived by an oppressor, was already fading from the English mind.

In 1901 the Wyndham Land Act – the most constructive piece of legislation in the history of England's relations with Ireland – began slowly putting the land back where it belonged, in the hands of the Irish farmers. The old abuse of foreign landlords who took the best soil for themselves and the best pasture and drove their tenants into huddling wretchedly together on barren land which hardly yielded the rent, that old abuse of an English Ascendancy backed up by rapacious squireens, had now been corrected and in the course of time would disappear. If only Ireland had been united, how easily Liberals and Conservatives would have persuaded themselves to grant the extremely modified freedom of Home Rule! But Ireland was not united.

In the northern province of Ulster there lived a community of Protestants, descended sometimes from dour Presbyterian Lowland Scots, sometimes from English settlers. Ireland which, with the coloured breath of its climate and the odour of its haunted soil, had tamed the Norman and the Dane, and absorbed the Belgians in Wexford, and seen even the remains of Cromwell's soldiers yield before the gentle charm of Tipperary – Ireland had laid its hand upon even the most forbidding foreign elements in Ulster. A surprisingly large number of original Celts survived the infamous 'clearances' and remained, in unregenerate Catholicism, to fill the southern counties of Ulster and sometimes to mingle the unhappy charm of their blood with the cold blood to the north of them: the mists and the rains and the long twilights worked their spell. And the result had been not to soften the Ulster Protestant but to set him apart. The Ulster Protestant liked nobody but himself.

He was the Orangeman. Every year, on the anniversary of the Battle of the Boyne when William of Orange slaughtered the bewildered and abandoned forces of James II – ('Change kings,' they shouted, 'and we'll fight you again') – he beat his knuckles raw on the drum. Those monotonous Orange drums were the voice of Ulster. They beat out a contempt for all Catholics; they were the savage undertone of that Protestant Ascendancy which had once driven the best Catholic families to live in underground cellars, which had persecuted and impoverished and fattened on Southern Ireland, and which still remained – in the shape of a disestablished but unfortunately not dispossessed Church – to fill the ancient cathedrals and churches with the mingled smell of rotting hassocks and inefficient scrubbing. The Protestant Ascendancy, though essentially it had been a profitable union of landlords and clergymen, had always smiled upon the northern Orangeman; he was part of it in the sense that he had been spared by it, and he was part of it in the sense that he had learned from it. He utterly despised his Catholic neighbours, they were no countrymen of his: they were a lower order of human being. 'The crown of the causeway,' ran one of his typical rhymes, 'on road or street, and the Papishes under my feet.' Another name for the Catholics was 'Croppies'. Mr Wingfield-Stratford quotes a passage from one characteristic Orange toast to the memory of William III, the victor of the Boyne: 'And may all Croppies be rammed, slammed, jammed and damned into the great gun that is in Athlone, and may I be standing by with a lighted torch to blow them in innumerable fragments over the Hill of Blastation. . . .' The Orange population of Ulster was thrifty and industrious but not lovable.

And it had no love for England. It was quite alone; it owed no allegiance to anyone but itself and the grim God it had fashioned in its own likeness. England was a convenience, England existed to see that no Catholic Irish Parliament ever controlled affairs in Ulster; and at all times when such control seemed unlikely, the Ulsterman was a convinced and stubborn radical who, at the least sign of interference from England, turned angry and rebellious.

By some trick of history which only Southern Irishmen could understand, who still thought of Ulster as the fighting province, the 'right arm of Ireland' – from Ulster came some of the greatest of Irish patriots. And yet it was this inexplicable province, whose sons could rise to the heights of selfless patriotism and sink to the sourest depths of bigotry, which alone stood between Ireland and Home Rule.

Ulster's support of the Union with England was partly religious and partly economic. To its fears of Catholic intolerance, of priestly despotism, was added the premonition that, under an Irish parliament, Catholics would take all the best positions, and once in possession of them, would have no ability to perform what they had undertaken. Belfast merchants and manufacturers were convinced that an Irish parliament would ruin them, through taxation, through mismanagement, through legislation which would favour agriculture at the expense of industry. After all, they argued, the Catholics of Ireland had for generations been deprived of administrative experience. What did Southern Ireland know about industry? When one tried to answer that question it became all too clear that England had first of all reduced the Catholic Irish, through starvation and exile, to a point where they were properly 'available' for industry, and had then seen to it that industry was never available for them. When Grattan's Parliament ended in that corrupt Union with England, all hopes of an industrial Ireland ended with it, and while other nations passed on into the nineteenth century Ireland lingered in the eighteenth. Spiritually and economically, southern Ireland was still in the eighteenth century when Asquith and Redmond struck their bargain.

It is not to be supposed that English Conservatives had any feelings of bosom friendship for Ulster. Ulster's 'loyalty' was loyalty to Ulster; and nobody could quite forget that when the Board of National Education was first set up, Ulster had blossomed overnight with revolutionary 'gun-clubs', and that when the Church Act was passed Ulster had threatened to 'kick the Queen's Crown into the Boyne'. That was not so very long back; and in 1911 all its talk of British citizenship, and Crown, and Empire, and Constitution was simply a way of finding synonyms for the Protestant Ascendancy. No, Ulster was not lovable, and the Conservative Party did not love it; but, looking round for a weapon with which to replace the Lords' veto, its eye lit upon...Ulster's bigotry. With Ulster's bigotry it could break the Liberal Party.

What a lovely argument lay in its mouth! The Liberals were professed lovers of freedom, yet here they were, all ready to offer Ireland Home Rule at the expense of the Ulster minority; they were offering something which might perhaps only be achieved by the forcible coercion of the northern Protestants; they had impaled themselves on the horns of a dilemma and, with the proper political pressure, they might easily perform there a really very humorous act of self-immolation. Deprived of the Lords' veto, the Conservatives turned from Westminster, and, with a cynical abandon, started to beat the Orange drum.

II

The Tory Party, in the course of absorbing the doubtful or angry
Liberal, had acquired another *alias* – it was also the Unionist Party.
Unionists were originally gentlemen who could not see eye to eye with
Mr Gladstone in the matter of Home Rule for Ireland – in other words,
the Conservatives plus Mr Joseph Chamberlain and his ex-Liberal following; then they became gentlemen who believed in solving the Boer
problem *vi et armis*; then they were the advocates of militant imperialism: and now, when the question of Home Rule was once more in the
air, their very name implied that they were ready to resist Home Rule by
any means that came to hand. From Joseph Chamberlain they had
inherited something rather less reasonable than Tariff Reform; they had
inherited a taste for fighting, simply for fighting's sake.

In the days of Mr Gladstone, Home Rule had been something to
fight against, because Imperialism had not then been tarnished with Boer
blood. Home Rule, to the imperialist of the '90s, was like gashing the
very heart of a glorious Empire. But the imperialist of 1911 was not quite
so romantically minded; he knew perfectly well that to give Ireland a
Parliament, which, at its best, could be little better than a glorified
County Council, would do the Empire no harm at all; and he had
more than a suspicion that an unsupported Ulster could probably be
made to consent without too much difficulty. The word 'Unionist' fitted
snugly round the Conservative mood, like an iron glove around a fist.
It had very little to do with Ireland: it had a great deal to do with beating
the Liberal Party into an irremediable mess of political blood and
brains.

And the Unionists had acquired a new leader. In November 1911,
Mr Balfour resigned from that position, explaining in a characteristic
speech to his constituents of the City of London that he was too tired. He
was succeeded by Andrew Bonar Law. Bonar Law was chosen by a
compromise, since the party could not decide between the equally
powerful claims of Messrs Walter Long and Austen Chamberlain; but,
like many men who are chosen through compromise, he was exactly
suited to the particularly brutal policy the Unionists were about to
adopt.

He was a man *without unction* – so Sir Walter Raleigh has described
him in one of his letters, adding unreasonably that he loved men without

unction. If so, Sir Walter was one of the few people in England who could have felt anything much more than a liking for Andrew Bonar Law, who contrived to hide a mild and retiring disposition behind an appearance of rasping, uncomfortable self-consciousness. He was a Scotch-Canadian, and a Presbyterian; his father had once occupied an Ulster manse. His face was sad, his forehead crumpled; he had an unfortunate habit of saying the wrong thing in debate. He was absolutely honest, and he was excessively Tory in the matter of having no political imagination whatsoever: when attacked by men more subtle in dialectics than himself, he generally took refuge in a remarkably unpleasing rudeness.

The really dangerous thing about Andrew Bonar Law was the fact that he was too close in spirit to Ulster's bigotry: his leadership provided an admirable screen for the cynical manoeuvres of his colleagues on the Opposition Bench.

III

As for Ulster, ever since the elections of January 1910, she had been brooding over the prospect of Home Rule. The first sign of activity was a renewed interest in the Loyal Orange Institution which, founded to 'keep alive the principles of the Whig Revolution of 1688', had fallen into a justified disrepute, and only appeared in force on 12th July of each year, when its members marched under banners, beat drums, and vilified the Pope. But its system of separate lodges, allied to a Grand Lodge in each county, made it an effective framework for organized Unionism, and to it flocked a varied and abusive assortment of country gentlemen, Protestant clergy, business men, professional men, farmers, and Protestant artisans. In January 1910, when it became clear that Mr Asquith had allied himself with the Irish Nationalists under Redmond, Protestant Ulster went Unionist almost to a man.

Under the guidance of Mr William Moore, M P for North Armagh, it gave birth to an Ulster Unionist Council, the purpose of which was to form a union of all local Unionist Associations, and keep them in constant touch with the parliamentary representatives in Westminster. And, its former leader – Mr Walter Long – having been elected to a London seat in January, on 21st February, 1910, it chose Sir Edward Carson to fill his place.

Sir Edward was fifty-six years old, a barrister, a great advocate, and a

Southern Irishman. People of a suspicious nature began to wonder aloud why he should impair a lucrative practice by plunging himself into the parochial furies of Orange politics: he was not fond of unnecessary exertion, he preferred law to politics. Was it perhaps vanity, they asked, which had driven the Member for Dublin University into the Ulster camp? The question showed how very little was yet understood of the peculiar nature of the troubles which lay ahead. Sir Edward was not vain. He was a fanatic, and he was particularly a fanatic on the question of the Union between England and Ireland. He believed in the Union between England and Ireland, not simply as a man who believes in an effective constitutional system, but as a religious man might believe in the marriage between his parents which, if annulled, would turn him into a bastard. And he hated Home Rule, not merely as an Irishman who, though Southern, was a Protestant and made a fat living at the English Bar, but rather as a religious man might hate a moral evil. Home Rule, indeed, was so hateful to Sir Edward that he had not bothered to inquire into its nature. And those who did not realize what Sir Edward could do with an evil into the nature of which he had not bothered to inquire, had only to cast their minds back to a certain famous and sordid trial, when Oscar Wilde was defendant and one Carson, QC, was prosecutor. For two days Carson had endured the painful barbs of Mr Wilde's platonic wit, but he had clung grimly to his task until, in what seemed the very moment of defeat, he had caught Mr Wilde off his guard. And he had then reduced Mr Wilde from a debonair philosopher to a rather fat and greasy gentleman with a peculiar taste for pot-boys. When Sir Edward's moral fervour was aroused, he would fight; he would fight against any odds, particularly against odds which might make him look ridiculous; and when it came to fighting against Home Rule, he would take on the English Parliament and the English Army and, if ever he caught one or other of those institutions in a careless or hesitant or even a sympathetic posture, there was every chance that he would win.

Many politicians did not believe that Sir Edward was quite up to the physical strain of leading Ulster. He suffered from a bad digestion, bad nerves, insomnia, and melancholy; his rather craggy face, with its dark eyes brooding above the heavy mouth and brutal chin, was already the face of an invalid. But they had forgotten what moral fervour could do for Sir Edward, and they had no idea at all of what Sir Edward could do when he was in the grip of moral fervour. Otherwise, they would not have been too happy at the thought of his leading any parliamentary party. For his was a nature which will often succeed in the court-room, which is welcome on platforms, and at home in dissenting pulpits; but a nature, also, which ought never to be allowed within the walls of a parliament, so long as parliaments remain the interesting playgrounds of democracy. Sir Edward was of granite all compact; Celtic granite. He could not play; above all things, he could not play with his principles. And yet it was one of the contradictions of his nature that he could turn his principles against themselves, and attempt to overthrow the Constitution in the name of the Constitution, and discredit the Crown in the Crown's honour. This arose from no subtlety in him, no curious and inner clash of qualities, but rather from a lack of subtlety. It is told of him that, on the final day of the House of Lords debate, he was met by a young peer at the Chamber door, who asked him, 'What's the betting?' ' "Betting!" ' was the cold answer. 'Is *that* all you think of when the Constitution is in the melting pot?' Had it ever even occurred to him that, if the Constitution really was in the melting pot, he and his Diehard friends were responsible for putting it there? Unfortunately, it had not. Such thoughts were for less limited characters; for the kind of characters, perhaps, which, in the days of Gladstone and Disraeli, had given the mighty battles of Parliament something of the air of a profound game. If Parliament utterly changed its character in the last years before the War, and threatened to destroy itself by putting off those decencies which had hitherto preserved it from complete reality (and in the face of complete reality no parliament can survive) – that was due to Tory violence and Liberal weakness. And Tory violence owed not a little of its strength to Sir Edward Carson, who was not merely an intelligent fanatic, with all the absence of humane qualities implied in that phrase, but also an Irishman. And he was never more Irish than when he was preaching disaffection in the name of a loyalist party and from the front bench of the Tory Opposition. Behind such a peculiar combination as Carson and Bonar Law, what could the Tories not achieve?

It was not until September 1911 that Sir Edward really came in touch with his Ulster followers, since his political activities up to that date had been devoted to assisting Lord Halsbury in his desperate attempt upon the Royal Prerogative. But now that the Lords had voted away their veto, now that a Home Rule Bill was bound to become law some time in 1914, Sir Edward felt that his place was in Ulster. On 23rd September, therefore, on the lawns of Captain James Craig's mansion of Craigavon above Belfast Lough, he confronted a vast audience of inquisitive Ulstermen. Most of them had never seen him before. To what sort of man, they wondered, had they committed themselves? The answer was beyond measure reassuring. Sir Edward used little rhetorical artifice, his metaphors were infrequent, his imagery spare, his gestures limited; but, speaking in a curiously vibrant voice and in accents seldom heard north of the Boyne, he told his audience exactly what it wanted to be told.

Gazing away towards the far, blue Antrim coast beyond the estuary, he declared that – contrary to Liberal opinion – Ulster was more uncompromising than ever in its opposition to Home Rule. 'We will yet defeat the most nefarious conspiracy that has ever been hatched against a free people. . . . Make no mistake; we are going to fight with men who are going to play with loaded dice. . . . Our demand is a very simple one. We ask for no privileges, but we are determined that no one shall have privileges over us. We ask for no special rights, but we claim the same rights from the same Government as every other part of the United Kingdom. We ask for nothing more; we will take nothing less. It is our inalienable right as citizens of the British Empire, and Heaven help the men who try to take it from us.'

Whether a small Protestant minority was not, in fact, claiming a somewhat special privilege in interposing itself between the rest of Ireland and a freedom which the rest of Ireland desired; and whether it did not ask a highly particular right, when it claimed to be free of the decisions of a majority in the Imperial Parliament – these were speculations into which neither Sir Edward nor his audience made any pretence of entering. 'We must be prepared,' Sir Edward pronounced in his peroration, '. . . and time is precious in these things – the morning Home Rule is passed, ourselves to become responsible for the government of the Protestant Province of Ulster.'

What did this mean? Was it a bluff? a means of arousing public sympathies in England? a way of forcing a weak Liberal government into resignation, by holding above its head the sad prospect of civil war? This is what the Liberals thought it to be, and this is what the Tories certainly intended it to be: for it would be easy to give the hated Parliament Act a farcical appearance by proving that, on its very first application, it would inevitably end in bloodshed. 'Believe me,' said Carson at Portrush, 'any Government will ponder long before it dares shoot a loyal Ulster Protestant, devoted to his country and loyal to his King.'

One thing, at least, had emerged into the realm of fact. A commission of five leading Orangemen – Captain James Craig, MP, Colonel Crawford, MP, the Right Honourable Thomas Sinclair, Colonel R. H. Wallace, CB, and Mr Edward Sclater – was already devoting its energies to the drawing up of 'a Constitution for the Provisional Government of Ulster.'

IV

And from the long procession which found its way to Craigavon on 23rd September, yet another fact emerged. One little group of men had caught and held everybody's eye. While the rest were content to shuffle along in a vague formation of fours, every man in this group held his head up, his shoulders back, and did his more or less successful utmost to keep in step. On inquiry, it was discovered that these worthies were from County Tyrone, and that they had been learning military drill all by themselves; and thereafter, inspired by their example, other small contingents of Orangemen could be seen drilling in parks, playgrounds and athletic fields, sometimes with rough pieces of wood to take the place of firearms, and always with that awkwardness which belongs to people who have no instinct for obedience. It was not an inspiring sight, but Colonel R. H. Wallace was quick to perceive what he called its 'importance'. The Colonel was a lawyer who had served in the Boer War, and still retained a thirst for military action; he consulted with Mr James Campbell (afterwards Lord Chancellor of Ireland) who assured him that any two Justices of the Peace could authorize drill and other military exercises in the districts under their jurisdiction, if certain conditions were observed. In January of 1912, the Colonel actually made application to the Belfast magistrates in the name of the Belfast Grand Lodge, of which he was Grand Master, and the lodges under its control, in which the lodges 'gave their assurance that they desire this authority as faithful subjects of His Majesty the King, and their undertaking that such authority will be used by them only to make them more efficient citizens for the purpose of maintaining the Constitution of the United Kingdom as now established and protecting their rights. . . .' These somewhat treasonable conditions, which blankly ignored Parliament's constitutional right to change the Constitution, appeared to be acceptable to the Belfast magistrates; and it was not long before an Ulster Volunteer Force was recruited from the Orange Lodges, the Unionist Clubs, and from such unaffiliated citizens as desired to be made 'more efficient'. Placed under the guidance of the Province's military men, and provided with quantities of dummy wooden rifles, it marched hither and yon along the damp Ulster roads, and skirmished about among the Ulster fields, to the huge delight of the English radical press, which found it excellent copy for humorous articles. The only trouble was, as men of a pessimistic turn of mind were beginning to point out, that the 'Coercion' Act, prohibiting the importation of arms into Ireland, was no longer in force; and there was really nothing to stop those wooden rifles from becoming something more deadly. Which, in the course of time and with the help of Tory subscriptions, is just what they became.

Meanwhile it was noised abroad in Ulster that Mr Winston Churchill, who had just left the Home Office for the more congenial Admiralty, was coming to Belfast to speak about the virtues of Home Rule; worse still, beside him on the platform would be Messrs Redmond and Dillon of the Nationalist Party. All this had been arranged by the Ulster Liberal Association, whose chairman, Lord Pirrie, was generally considered to be one of Belfast's more unloved citizens. Lord Pirrie, *The Times* correspondent wrote on 18th January, 1912, 'deserted Unionism about the time the Liberals acceded to power, and soon afterwards was made a peer; whether *propter hoc* or *post hoc* I am quite unable to say, though no Ulster Unionist has any doubts on the subject.' And if this were not enough, Mr Churchill intended to speak in Ulster Hall, and there was 'something impudent and impious in the proposal that this temple of Unionism should be profaned by the son of the man who assisted at its consecration.' (The *Saturday Review*, 27th January, 1912.)

That Mr Churchill was impudent, not even his best friends could deny; he had brought impudence to a fine art, so that his most spectacular effects in the world of politics were always achieved with an air of having thumbed a nose at all that was tardy and tedious in human affairs. But he was not impious; and, if he had been, he would not have been impious towards the memory of his brilliant and tragic father. It was true that Lord Randolph Churchill, in the days when Mr Gladstone was aiming at Home Rule, had gratified his audience at the opening of Ulster Hall with the famous slogan – 'Ulster will fight, and Ulster will be right.' But Mr Churchill, while writing a biography of Lord Randolph, discovered the following passage in a letter which his father wrote to Lord Fitzgibbon in February 1886: 'I decided some time ago that if the GOM went for Home Rule, the Orange card would be the one to play. Please

God it may turn out the ace of trumps and not the two.' In other words, Lord Randolph Churchill was playing in 1886 precisely the same cynical game which the Tories were playing in 1912; so that when the Unionist press accused Mr Churchill, as it did with abandon, of 'dancing on his father's grave' by trying to promote the cause of Home Rule in Ulster Hall, it made the rather childish mistake of supposing that there was a grave to dance on; Lord Randolph's political body was not buried in Orange soil. Indeed, if this wayward genius could have observed his son's activities in 1912, he would more likely have done so with approbation than with sorrow, blood being generally thicker than politics.

Mr Churchill's motives in offering to go to Belfast were not altogether unmixed: he pursued the limelight as wholeheartedly as any man in England. But the limelight, when Mr Churchill was in pursuit of it, behaved with the caprice of an *ignis fatuus*. It took all Mr Churchill's activity – of which he fortunately possessed his full share – first to get himself within range of the precious light, and then to hold it on himself for any appreciable length of time; and the English political scene was therefore from time to time bedazzled with sudden, unpredictable flashes, in which Mr Churchill would be discovered in an attitude at once humorous, arrogant, and comic. And this was not altogether his fault. Brilliant and capable as he undoubtedly was, he could have found his way into the headlines at least as consistently as Mr Lloyd George did, if he could have enjoyed Mr George's advantage of humble birth. But his most radical gestures were ruined by the fact that he was a Marlborough, that he was quite incapable of indentifying himself with the public, for whom he seemed to cherish a sort of genial disdain. By nature flamboyant, insolent in his bearing, impatient in his mind, and Tory in his deepest convictions, he was a curious person to be found holding a responsible position in the Liberal Party, and few men could have been more distrusted, or have taken a more curious pleasure in being distrusted. As a result, whenever he occupied the news it was always in a manner that was slightly *farouche* and highly infuriating.

To these characteristics, Mr. Churchill added a strong taste for battle. The blood of his ancestor, the first Duke of Marlborough, occasionally cantered through his veins, like a colt through a meadow, with the most alarming and peculiar results. In December 1910, for instance, when he was still Home Secretary, three sergeants of the City Police were killed by rifle fire while investigating a burglary in a

Houndsditch jewellery shop, and the whole of Whitechapel was thereupon combed by an extra police force, hunting for one 'Peter the Painter', whom the authorities believed to be responsible for this outrage. 'Peter the Painter' – otherwise Peter Straume of Riga – was said to be a famous anarchist, and the newspapers followed the search for him with the liveliest interest. The discovery, in a Mr Moroutzeff's house in Gold Street, of a pistol, six hundred cartridges, one hundred and fifty Mauser bullets, and numerous 'dangerous' chemicals, provoked a number of front page stories concerning the extremely mythical existence of anarchist arsenals in the East End of London. The police pursued their inquiry with greater diligence. At last, on the night of 3rd January, 1911, they closed in on Number 100, Sidney Street, Stepney. It was a bitter night, with a little snow falling. Number 100 stood barred and silent. Stones were thrown at its windows, and the answer was a burst of fire; whereupon the constabulary hurried into cover, carrying with them one casualty, a sergeant with a light chest-wound.

When morning broke, the whole district was alive with policemen, seven hundred and fifty strong, to whom had been added nineteen Scots Guardsmen who had come all the way from the Tower with a Maxim gun, and kept up a continual fire from the shelter of a neighbouring brewery. Stories of this besieged and murderous nest of anarchists, whose numbers no man could guess, spread through London and were carried to every newspaper in the kingdom. By midday, Mr Churchill had arrived upon the scene.

There was, of course, nothing to prevent a conscientious Home Secretary from personally investigating such a battle-ground as Sidney Street had now become. But most Home Secretaries would have done so with as little ostentation as possible. Not so Mr Churchill. He drove down from Whitehall in his car, and stepped out – an imposing figure in a silk hat and a fur-lined coat with an astrakhan collar. His silk hat and astrakhan collar crept from door to door; They peered round corners; They exposed Themselves to random bullets; They were to be seen in earnest consultation with soldiers and police officials.

As the number of anarchists in Number 100 grew momentarily in Mr Churchill's imagination, he agreed that a couple of field guns from the Royal Horse Artillery depot in St John's Wood should be summoned immediately, and himself suggested that Royal Engineers from Chatham ought to be on hand, in case the hordes of besieged could only be reduced by mining operations. But while the artillery still rattled through distant streets, and before the Engineers were so much as notified, wisps of smoke were seen to curl from the broken windows of Number 100. The fire brigade arrived, and was told to keep away from such a hornet's nest, which was soon briskly alight from top to bottom. The police prepared to advance, but Mr Churchill waved them back; accompanied only by an inspector and a guardsman armed with a double-barrelled sporting gun, he strode towards the front door. The inspector kicked it in. There was no resistance, no burst of gunfire. The anarchists were quite dead . . . all *two* of them. Of 'Peter the Painter' there was no sign at all.

It was fortunate for the Government that there was something more than a Sidney Street side to Mr Churchill's character. Fond as he was of warfare and drama, he was also one of the most capable administrators in Liberal history; and, given the right opportunity, he could merge both sides of himself with the most startling effect. He could even repress that unfortunate, that powerful impulse towards publicity which gave so many of his public adventures the appearance of a poorly staged *opéra bouffe*. In October 1911, he was offered the post of First Lord of the Admiralty; he was paying a visit to Mr Asquith in Scotland, and the two were walking in sight of the twilit Firth of Forth when the Prime Minister made his proposal. At that very moment two battleships, vast in the gathering darkness, glided into view. It was just as though Nature herself had opened some mysterious box and dropped into the Home Secretary's hand two magnificent toys. 'I accepted with alacrity,' he afterwards wrote in *The World Crisis*. Thereafter the Admiralty yacht *Enchantress* was his home and his office; he spent eight months of every year afloat in it. He visited every dockyard, every shipyard, every naval establishment in the British Isles and the Mediterranean; no point of strategic importance, no piece of Admiralty property but he became thoroughly acquainted with it. 'On the wall behind my chair, I had an open case fitted, within whose folding doors spread a large chart of the North Sea. On this chart every day, a Staff Officer marked with flags the position of the German Fleet. Never once was this ceremony omitted until the War broke out. . . .' (*The World Crisis*, Vol. I, p. 70.) Fleet, and squadron, and flotilla, the guns, the tubes, the 'murderous queens' of steel, all these were his to play with, to polish, to perfect; the administration of these precise and sanguinary toys touched some rich, secret place in his imagination so that, lost in a drama as solitary as that of a child which plays by itself, he yet contrived to bring the whole Navy into a state of efficiency which would have been altogether beyond the powers of an ordinary First Lord. That all this should have occurred under a Liberal Administration is not without its irony; but it is typical of Mr Churchill's character that he should have been the Minister responsible for its occurrence.

And it must have cost him some effort to bestir himself from his efficient dream and go to Belfast. But the scent of battle was in the air; the newspaper headlines beckoned; there were stupid minds all waiting to be outraged. It was impossible for him to resist such congregated opportunity. The Orangemen of Belfast were infuriated, and, since the consequences of their fury were apt to be deplorable (two thousand Catholic workers had already been driven from the shipyards in scenes of considerable brutality), it was openly feared that they might do Mr Churchill some physical damage. Mr Churchill, whom nobody ever accused of cowardice, appeared to regard this prospect with equanimity. Not so the Orange leaders, who realized the destructive effect that any rioting would have on English opinion at this early stage of the game. On 17th January, however, the Ulster Unionist Council announced that it observed 'with astonishment the deliberate challenge thrown down by Mr Winston Churchill,' and that it was resolved to prevent his Home Rule meeting from being held in Ulster Hall. In other words, if Mr Churchill insisted on speaking there, he would have to take the consequences. Mr Churchill did not insist; he had gained his point. The whole Liberal press was seething with fury over this unwarranted interference with freedom of speech. . . .

But he still had to find a building fitted for his purpose. The Opera House? Alas, the manager of the Opera House (who was said to have been tempted with an offer of knighthood) could not see his way to letting Mr Churchill use it. Building after building was considered and discarded, until at last the Government was reduced to hiring a marquee from Scotland and arranging for the meeting to be held on the Celtic Football Ground, which was situated at a safe distance from Ulster Hall. It also imported five extra battalions of infantry and two extra squadrons of cavalry; while the Unionist Council, fearing that some of its less cultivated followers would stone the soldiery, responded with an appeal 'in view of the Ulster Hall victory . . . to abstain from any interference with the meeting on the Celtic Football Ground,' and had this appeal pasted on all the Belfast hoardings.

At Larne, where he landed on the morning of 8th February, Mr Churchill was greeted by a large crowd of Unionists, who sang 'God Save the King' *at* him; though the First Lord, on his journey across, had been engaging on no more unpatriotic thoughts than how he could best deal with the Kaiser's recent threat of a *Luxus Flotte*. At Midland Station, there was another hostile reception. Outside the Grand Central Hotel, where he lunched, a numerous congregation of Orangemen was only restrained from violence by the brooding presences of Sir Edward Carson and Lord Londonderry on the opposite balcony of the Ulster Club. In Royal Avenue, down which he drove towards the football ground, he was gratified by the sight of enormous and revolting effigies of himself and Mr Redmond, stuck on poles; while the crowd, by what the Unionist Mr McNeill has delicately described as its 'involuntary swaying', threatened to overturn the car with himself and Mrs Churchill in it.

A little further on, in Falls Road, circumstances were abruptly changed. It was the images of Carson and Londonderry which now leered from the poles, and a purely Nationalist crowd which surged forward to shake Mr Churchill by the hand. . . .

The speeches were made; the marquee on the Celtic Football Ground emptied itself into the gathering damp darkness. In Royal Avenue and York Street, the Unionists lingered in great numbers to have another chance at Mr Churchill. But Mr Churchill's exit was less dignified than his entrance. Through a dirty labyrinth of by-streets he was driven, much against his own inclinations, in secret haste to the Midland terminus; and was off by special train for Larne, before his enemies around the Grand Central Hotel realized that he had escaped them.

After all the speeches and the threats and the precautions, the day seemed to have spent itself in a poor anti-climax. And yet this, almost the last sincere Liberal invasion of Ulster, was not without its implications. In the first place it showed that Orange Ulster was extremely unwilling to give any opponent a chance to speak freely. And in the second place it showed that all Ulster was not Orange. Some part of the Nationalist crowd which thronged into Belfast that day must have come in from across the border; but the great majority of it was from Ulster. If Ulster had such an active Catholic minority, then there was even more trouble ahead; but how particularly complicated that trouble could become nobody learned until 1914.

V

The really sinister intentions of the Tory Party first revealed themselves on 26th January, about a fortnight before Mr Churchill's serio-comic excursion to Belfast. The Tories have been kindly treated by history, which has overshadowed their Ulster conspiracy with the vast bulk of the subsequent War, so that today this conspiracy is almost forgotten; and they have been kindly treated by psychology, which contends, not without truth, that England was in such a dangerous state of hysteria in the last two years of 1912–14, that even the most outrageous acts then committed must find some excuse. But the Tory mind, none the less, did concoct nothing less than a rebellion in those years; and perhaps the most disagreeable thing about this rebellion was that it was set on foot in the name of Loyalty.

Since it ended with nothing more sanguinary than the hasty slaughter of some few Irish citizens in Bachelor's Walk in Dublin, it might be considered of very small importance, but in its peculiar way it is one of the most monstrous events in English constitutional history, and certainly the most deadly event in the history of English Liberalism; for in that obscene little spatter of blood on the Dublin quays the word *Finis* was written to the great Liberal battles of the nineteenth century....

The Tory philosophy, up to the beginning of the War, might be summed up in this way: Be Conservative about good things, and Radical about bad things. This philosophy, so far as can be seen, has only one flaw: it was always the Tories who decided what was good and what was bad. This kind of decision can be made time and time again with the best results; but it contains, in its very essence, some fatal and arbitrary elements, and the mere effort of having to make it has been known to produce any number of fanatics, tyrants, martyrs, minor prophets, and, indeed, most of the disagreeable creatures which have ever plagued this long-suffering planet. In 1912, the Tories decided that a Parliament controlled by a Liberal majority was a Bad thing.

Everything they did in the next two years was aimed, not against Home Rule, but against the very existence of Parliament. Because Liberalism was already almost moribund, in spite of its appearance of health, their conscious aim was to destroy Liberalism: because the whole mood of that pre-war England was sudden, sombre, and violent, their unconscious desire was to ruin an institution which they were pledged to protect. An utterly constitutional party, they set out to wreck the Constitution; and they very nearly succeeded.

On 26th January, 1912, the first steps were taken, when a meeting of ten thousand people in the Albert Hall was addressed by Mr Bonar Law. Referring to the Orange wrath at that time stalking through Belfast, he said: 'We who represent the Unionist Party in England and Scotland have supported, *and we mean to support to the end*, the loyal minority [in Ireland]. We support them not because we are intolerant, but because their claims are just.' Sir Edward Carson followed him with one of those enormous threats for which he was soon to be famous: 'I am here tonight under the most tragic circumstances, with the possibilities of grave and difficult operations in Belfast and in Ulster within almost a few days'. Here he referred to Mr Churchill's little visit. He then projected himself more freely into the future. 'I am here to tell you solemnly and honestly that we intend to see this matter through. The cost may be great, the sufferings may be terrible.' These speeches seemed at the time nothing more than the legitimate bombast of a disgruntled Opposition; but were they? Was there not, in the voices of both speakers, a new and sinister ring? It is true that the end envisaged by Mr Bonar Law was nothing more than a Liberal capitulation before his threats of civil war; words and words only, he thought, were to be his weapons: he did not then realize that those who preach disaffection are sometimes obliged to practise it. As for Sir Edward, who knows what schemes were stirring in his dark and uncompromising brain?

The Government, meanwhile, announced that its Home Rule Bill would not be presented until 11th April; and, with everyone still uncertain what the provisions of this Bill would be, the Ulster Unionists proposed to hold a monster demonstration at the Show Ground of the Royal Agricultural Society at Balmoral, a suburb of Belfast. And it was at this demonstration that Mr Bonar Law made his second plunge into rebellion. On the evening of the 7th, while the church bells were still ringing for Easter evensong, he set out from London with a retinue of seventy Unionist MP's. They arrived at Larne on the following morning; and while they were still tossing on the midnight waters of the Irish Channel, the presses of the London *Morning Post* were engaged with a poem of Rudyard Kipling's, which was to appear on the next day's front page.

'*What answer from the North?*' Mr Kipling blared in perhaps not his happiest tones:

One Law, one Land, one Throne.
If England drive us forth,
We shall not fall alone.

Nobody could say that, when Mr Bonar Law arrived on the Ulster shores, he had not been pursued thither with trumpets from London.

Nor was his welcome any less vociferous than the verses of Mr Kipling. At every wayside station he was greeted by enthusiastic and persistent mobs, which thrust addresses upon him, and wrung his hand, with all the dour, drab fervour of Irish Presbyterians. 'If this is how you treat your friends,' he said with characteristic maladroitness, 'I am glad that I am not an enemy.'

At Belfast, they could scarcely drive through the streets. At the Reform Club – once the headquarters of Belfast Liberalism – an address was presented to the Unionist leader, which stated that the Government's conduct would 'justify loyal Ulster in resorting to the most extreme measures in resisting Home Rule.' Mr Bonar Law was not backward. 'On behalf of the Unionist Party,' he said, 'I give you this message, that, though the brunt of the battle will be yours, there will not be wanting help from "across the Channel".' On his way to Mount Stewart that afternoon, a stop was made at Comber, where 'he asked himself how Radical Scotsmen would like to be treated as the Government was treating Protestant Ulster. "I know Scotland well," he replied to his own question, "and I believe that, rather than submit to such a fate, the Scottish people would face a second Flodden or a second Bannockburn".' (R. McNeill, *Ulster's Stand for Union*, p. 82.) The grim triumph which had been his all the way from Larne was going to his head with something of the effect of sour wine. To say that it intoxicated him would be too weak and pleasant a phrase. It poisoned him.

At Balmoral, the next day, there gathered what Sir Edward Carson claimed to be one of the largest assemblies in the history of the world; and that 'was hardly by hyperbole,' *The Times* correspondent declared in a moment of almost idiotic bliss. And at this historical gathering the sedition preached by Mr Bonar Law, who led off with a scholarly appeal to Ulster's worst fighting instincts, was nearly surpassed by Mr Walter Long. 'If they put Lord Londonderry and Sir Edward Carson in the dock,' roared Mr Long, 'they will have to find one large enough to hold the whole Unionist Party.' Whereat Mr Bonar Law and Sir Edward Carson turned towards each other, clasped hands, and maintained this affecting attitude long enough for the whole assembly to realize that they were doing their level best to look like generals on the eve of battle. And then, while everyone stood with bared heads, Sir Edward released Mr Law, and strode to the front of the speakers' stand. 'Raise your hands,' he shouted. 'Repeat after me – "Never under any circumstances will we submit to Home Rule".' In the centre of the show grounds was a signalling tower, with a flagstaff ninety feet tall: and while the audience, and the Marquess of Londonderry, and the Protestant Primate, and the Presbyterian Moderator, with obedient thunder intoned those words after Sir Edward, a Union Jack was broken from the flagstaff. It measured forty-eight feet by twenty-five. It was the largest ever woven. Patriotism could do no more.

VI

Two days later, Parliament re-assembled after its Easter recess. It was now dimly aware that it was being threatened with a civil war, engineered by its own Opposition – the 'loyal' oratory of Balmoral suggested nothing less; and its mood was nervous and belligerent. Mr Asquith, moving for leave to introduce the Home Rule Bill, quoted a passage from one of Mr Bonar Law's more recent speeches – 'The present Government turn the House of Commons into a market place where everything is bought and sold. In order to remain a few months longer in office, His Majesty's Government have sold the Constitution. . . .' At this, the following peculiar piece of dialogue travelled to and fro across the Table.

The Prime Minister: 'Am I to understand that the Right Honourable gentleman repeats here, or is prepared to repeat on the floor of the House of Commons...'

Mr Bonar Law: 'Yes.'

The Prime Minister: 'Let us see exactly what it is: It is that I and my colleagues are selling our convictions.'

Mr Bonar Law: 'You have not got any.'

The Prime Minister: 'We are getting on with the new style.'

'*The new style*'; how ridiculously, how perilously far it was from the masterly sarcasms of Mr Balfour!

Four days later, the Home Rule Bill was given its first reading. In these days, when the British Empire is of so spiritual a structure that any large piece of it could break away with scarcely a groan, that Bill seems a meagre thing to have aroused such consternation in the imperialist mind. It was built on the old Gladstonian formula of transferring purely Irish matters to the Irish Parliament, while it reserved for the Imperial Parliament at Westminster all questions touching the Crown, the making of peace or war, treaties and foreign relations, new Customs duties, and certain other services. The Royal Irish Constabulary was to be under the Imperial Parliament for the next six years. The Irish Parliament could not establish and endow any religion, nor impose any religious disability. The Common Treasury remained, so that, though the Irish Parliament could raise new taxes, it could add no more than 10 per cent to the income tax, death duties, or customs duties imposed by the Imperial Parliament. An elaborate financial arrangement put England under the necessity of providing some two million extra pounds a year; and it was arranged that forty-two Irish members should sit in the Imperial Parliament. 'The Bill was not an extreme one,' says J. A. Spender, Mr Asquith's biographer. It certainly was not. If ever a nation was huddled into perpetual swaddling clothes by a piece of legislation, Ireland was so huddled by Mr Asquith's Home Rule Bill. Presented with the merest travesty of a parliament, it was further to be gratified with the quite odious prospect of hunting hither and yon for new subjects for taxation. The only satisfactory feature in the Bill was the fact that it did not mention the possible exclusion of Ulster....

Gathered in force for the occasion, and blandly concealing the fact that it regarded the whole thing with mingled alarm and resignation, the Cabinet sat on the Treasury Bench to listen to this momentous document. What its private counsels had been during the previous month, we can only guess; once and once only, as though some curtain were momentarily lifted upon a half-lit stage, we catch a shadowed glimpse of its melancholy deliberations. The Prime Minister and his colleagues, George V was told in a report dated 6th February, had decided to warn Mr Redmond:

'that the Government held themselves free to make changes, if it became clear that special treatment must be provided for the Ulster counties, and that in this case the Government will be ready to recognize the necessity, either by amendment or by not pressing the Bill on under the provisions of the Parliament Act.'

Either compromise or surrender: with the Parliament Act scarcely six months old, these were to be the heroic alternatives, and of these only compromise was really tolerable. And yet the Irish problem was already beyond the reach of compromise. Protestant Ulster, at a pinch, might agree to be divided off from the rest of Ireland: but what would Catholic Ulster say? What would the Southern loyalists say? Above all, what would the Nationalists say, determined as they were to have a whole country or nothing? The more Mr Asquith and his colleagues thought about it, the more they realized that, under a warning like this, Mr Redmond would have no choice left him; he would be obliged to put them out. And so, shuddering at the very thought of such a clean death, they reversed their decision, and determined to say nothing.

The most politic silence breeds uncertainty. Was it perhaps from some inner suspicion that the Liberals were about to let him down, that Mr Redmond greeted this wretched Bill with an overwhelming eulogy? A general who believes that his allies are deserting him, has to rally them as best he can. 'What I want to say is this – that, viewing this Bill as a whole, I say here – and in what I say I speak for my colleagues on these benches – it is a great measure. . . . It is a great measure, and we welcome it. . . . If I may say so reverently, I personally thank God that I have lived to see this day.' His whole speech, delivered in more passionate tones than was his wont, was continually interrupted by Unionist jeers and catcalls, while, with polite applause, the Liberal leaders signified their stern intention to force Ulster into submission.

On 9th May, the Second Reading, moved by Mr Churchill, was passed through with a Government majority of 101, and an exclusive English majority of 39. On the morning of 11th July, when the Bill went into Committee, an anxious group of Ulster MP's and Peers gathered at Stafford House; in the afternoon one Agar-Robartes, a Liberal from Cornwall, was going to propose an amendment to the effect that the four counties of Antrim, Down, Derry and Armagh should be excluded from the jurisdiction of the Irish Parliament – and the question was, should the Ulster Unionists support this amendment or oppose it? The Government had prepared what seemed at first a very pretty trap. If the Ulstermen supported the amendment, they would seem like a very poor kind of Irishmen for agreeing to partition their country, and they would certainly be accused of betraying their Protestant friends in the South. If they opposed it, English opinion would condemn them for attempting to obtain by fighting what they could have had by legislation. To make the trap more complete, this amendment – which the Government itself would oppose – was to be moved by one of the Government's own following who, because he was known as a stern evangelical, would thus obscurely pacify the wide anti-Catholic feeling in Liberal circles: for one of the disquieting features of the Home Rule Bill was that it offered its limited freedom to men who loved the Pope.

Sir Edward Carson, however, perceived that this trap was in reality no trap at all, and he easily persuaded that worried group at Stafford House to give their support to Mr Agar-Robartes. The amendment, he explained, could be turned against the Bill; it could wreck the Bill. All they had to do, in the course of debate, was to explain that Home Rule without Ulster would be a farce, and that they supported the amendment for precisely that reason.

That afternoon, Mr Agar-Robartes – summarizing his argument in the phrase 'Orange bitters will not mix with Irish whiskey' – started a debate which was to continue, with increasing bitterness, for three days. In the course of it Mr Bonar Law made the perhaps unparalleled statement, bristling with treasonable hints and invitations, that if the Government used troops to coerce Ulster, 'Ministers who gave that order would run a greater risk of being lynched in London than the loyalists of Ulster would run of being shot in Belfast.'

On the third day, Sir Edward proved to the angry Liberals how easily he had avoided their little trap. It was true, he said, that he and his followers accepted the amendment – but 'we do not accept this amendment as a compromise of the question. There is no compromise possible.' On the contrary, they accepted it because it denied the very spirit of the Bill, which had been framed for the whole of Ireland. Mr Augustine Birrell, speaking with all the prestige of Chief Secretary for Ireland, had said that, without Ulster, Home Rule would be 'truncated'. Sir Edward agreed. But he drew a different conclusion. Mr Birrell's conclusion was that 'therefore you must force Home Rule upon Ulster. I draw the conclusion that you ought not to have Home Rule at all.' This dialectical feat did Sir Edward a great deal of credit, and made the Government look remarkably foolish; but it scarcely concealed the fact that the Ulster leader and his friends were not going to attempt any constructive suggestions.

Mr Lloyd George did what he could to save his party from utter shame. He suggested that Protestant Ulster was now deserting its loyalist friends in the South; and, having driven in this worm-eaten little wedge, went on to remark that Sir Edward's speech was altogether too

indefinite. 'Is there a demand from the Protestants of those four counties
... that they should not go in to help at all in an Irish Parliament to protect the rest of the Protestants of Ireland? What, therefore, is the demand
of Ulster? Not that she should be protected, not that she should have
autonomy herself, but the right to veto autonomy to the rest of Ireland.
That is an intolerable demand.'

The amendment was defeated, but, in defeating it, the Government's
majority sank to sixty-nine.

And now, by whatever secret virtue it is which relieves anything of
its terrors once it is put into words, the principle of exclusion for Ulster
became generally acceptable to all Unionists. With what smooth and
plausible airs Mr F. E. Smith proclaimed this to the Orangemen of
Belfast on 12th July! Ulster, he said, had publicly accepted the idea of
separate treatment as an alternative to maintenance of the Union as a
whole. If the Unionists could not keep all Ireland, he implied, at least
they could keep Ulster; and no Home Rule Bill would be acceptable,
unless it contained a provision that Ulster was to be excluded. What
could be more reasonable?

And what, we might ask ourselves today, could be more impossible,
if the Liberals were to keep faith with Mr Redmond?

But Mr Smith's words were perhaps not so important as the effect
they had upon him. This was the first time that he had been permitted to
represent his party on one of these occasions, and he was determined to
comport himself in a proper manner. That day, the 222nd anniversary
of the Battle of the Boyne, was ushered in with what *The Times* described
as 'the softest of soft Irish mornings'. It was raining heavily. By nine
o'clock, however, the city's streets were filled with shouting Protestants,
the city's air was terrible with banners – the most terrible of which, from
an æsthetic point of view, was one of King William III on horseback. The
higher Orange officials were borne to the rendezvous in cars and
carriages, 'for the mud was great'; but the rank and file splashed along in
garish detachments, each Lodge having its distinctive head-dress, sash,
and banner. Once at the meeting place, the various Lodges stuck their
banners into the mud and disappeared on their proper business of beating
drums and scaring Catholics; and when Mr Smith arrived, he discovered
that his audience consisted of Orange notables, banners, and some few
damp folk who were too listless to do anything more active than listen.
He laboured, moreover, under the double disadvantage of a marked
English accent and the fact that, as leading speaker, he felt obliged to

cloak his more rebellious sentences with some appearance of legality; so that his small audience understood very little of what he said, and liked even less of the little it understood. Everything – the weather, the peculiar disappearance of his audience, and poor reception given to his speech by what audience there was – combined to put Mr Smith into a very dispirited frame of mind. But it was one of his characteristics that, though he always tried to do things in a reasonable and legal fashion, if reason and legality proved ineffective, he would jump to the opposite extreme with the most acrobatic abandon. This was why he had supported Lord Halsbury. And this was why, having discovered that Ulster cared nothing for decency, he determined never to make that mistake again. And he never did.

VII

On 27th July, a monster Unionist meeting was held at Blenheim Palace, the home of the Duke of Marlborough, head of Mr Winston Churchill's family. Here the genius of Vanbrugh and the correct hand of Capability Brown had preserved – in the vast proportions of the palace, in the wide lawns, the rose gardens, the little temples – the very essence, serene and terrible, of the eighteenth century. Here, as though purely distilled from the confused and muddy waters of time, the spirit of majesty and reason and order, of cruelty and arrogance, stood in cold beauty among the little hills of Oxfordshire. And here, amidst this palpable and breathing memory, Mr Bonar Law made his third crude step into rebellion.

The Government's policy, he said, was part of a 'corrupt Parliamentary bargain,' and it had no right 'to carry such a revolution by such means.' Circumstances being what they were, he told his fifteen thousand hearers, he could imagine no lengths to which Ulster Unionists might go where the Unionist Party, and the public at large, would not follow them in sympathy. A clearer incitement to violence could not have been made. And Carson – 'King' Carson he was now called by the Liberal press – followed with a warlike speech. 'We shall shortly challenge the Government,' he concluded, 'to interfere with us if they dare, and shall with equanimity await the result.' At these words, Mr F. E. Smith rose in tremendous excitement and cried, 'Should it happen that Ulster is threatened with a violent attempt to incorporate her in an Irish Parliament, I say to Sir Edward Carson, "Appeal to the young men of England!" ' The echoes of these speeches, hurtling back from those impersonal presences, the walls and windows of Blenheim, had a kind of madness in them. Mr Law and Mr Smith and Sir Edward Carson seemed no longer responsible. Now, if ever, the Liberal Party needed the help of its dead giants: its present leaders were too weak and careless to withstand such an attack. Writing of Blenheim later, in *Fifty Years of British Parliament* (Vol. II, p. 154), Mr Asquith said, 'The speeches and the action taken upon them were no longer – to quote language I had used of Mr Balfour twenty years before – "the conditional incitements of an academic anarchist".' He was right. Speaking very soon after the meeting, he said that Mr Bonar Law's speech marked 'an absolute end to Parliamentary Government.' He was right. In the late autumn, again, he said, 'The reckless rhodomontade at Blenheim in the early summer, as developed and amplified in this Ulster campaign, furnishes for the future a complete grammar of Anarchy.' He was right. Sad for the Tory Party that it should have been so; and sadder still for the Liberals that Mr Asquith could never live up to the lucid vigour of his own words.

It was the beginning of the 'silly season'. Parliament had gone into summer recess, and its members, having nothing better to do, filled the correspondence columns of the newspapers with alternate abuse and support of the Blenheim speeches. Mr Churchill also took his pen in hand and, in two published letters to a Scots constituent, set forth an indictment of Ulster and her Unionist supporters. Mr Churchill has emerged today from all the vicissitudes of his political career with at least the reputation of being one of the finest writers of prose in contemporary England; and it was because they dealt a very telling blow beneath the Unionist fifth rib that *The Times* described these two letters as 'a turgid homily – a mixture of sophistry, insult, and menace.' But if Mr Churchill hoped that he would alienate Unionist support among the general public, he was wrong. Only the pen of a Jonathan Swift, at its very deadliest, could have done that. There was a method in the Unionist madness. Such was the state of English nerves in those days, that violence made a stronger appeal to the public than any other form of speech and action. The tide was already turning against the Liberals. In South Manchester, in Crewe, in North Manchester, even in Midlothian – Mr Gladstone's old seat – by-elections had gone or were to go against them. As the Tory rebellion proceeded from Craigavon on to Balmoral, and from Balmoral on to Blenheim, it seemed that they had nothing to oppose to it but the highly literate wrath of their printed words.

And now Sir Edward Carson prepared himself for another supreme effort. Certain Ulster Unionists were afraid that the spirit of enthusiasm and solidarity in Ulster might fade away if the people, animated by speech after speech in meeting after meeting, were allowed to disperse to their homes without any means being taken of securing their sense of 'mutual obligation'. Hounds need 'blooding': the Ulstermen needed a Covenant. Carson agreed with this notion, but declared that no empty pledge would serve their purpose. The people must be given something they could honour, something to keep them in shape until his precious Ulster Constitution was fit to spring upon them, something which – rightly worded and prepared – would fill their spirit as suddenly as a squall fills the sails in dead weather.

On 17th August it was announced in the press that 28th September would be set aside in Ulster as Ulster Day, when loyal Orangemen would pledge themselves to a Solemn Covenant, the terms of which were not yet settled. That powerful pledge, so essential to Ulster's health, was still to be cast into words. One day Captain Craig was sitting in the Constitutional Club in London, knitting his brows over a piece of paper. He was thinking. At this interesting moment, Mr B. W. D. Montgomery, secretary of the Belfast Unionist Club, appeared, and asked Craig what he was doing; and Craig replied that he was 'drafting an oath for the people at home.' Whereupon Mr Montgomery had a brain-wave. What could be more suitable, he suggested, than the old Scots Covenant, which not only was a fine document, but breathed a harsh, militant Protestancy very congenial to the modern Orangeman? They found what they were looking for in the Club Library; but when they submitted their find to the Commission of Five, it was seen that its language, though finely constructed, was altogether too involved, and the Scots Covenant was accordingly re-vamped by the editorial hand of the Right Honourable Thomas Sinclair. The draft was then submitted to all Protestant Churches, and the Presbyterian Moderator immediately objected that it bound its signatories for all time, and he thought it wrong for any Christian to bind himself to such an oath. The phrase 'throughout this our time of threatened calamity' was thereupon added, to the apparent satisfaction of the Moderator's conscience, if that is what it can be called.

News of this fresh Ulster move had a profound effect upon England.

It was useless for the Liberal press to keep up its cry that Carson was 'bluffing'; a bluff is only a bluff when someone has the courage to call it. The Government's courage, whimsical at all times, was now almost non-existent; and this could be seen from a letter which Mr Churchill wrote to Mr Redmond on 31st August. 'The opposition of three or four Ulster counties,' wrote the First Lord, 'is the only obstacle which now stands in the way of Home Rule. You and your friends ought to be thinking of some way round this. No doubt you are, with your usual political foresight. The Unionist Party,' he continued, 'have now staked their whole power to fight Home Rule on this foundation. Remove it, and the path in my judgement is absolutely clear.'

Remove it! This advice shows how very little Mr Churchill, wrapped up in his dream of battleships, and how very little the whole Liberal Cabinet understood of Ireland. Or was it perhaps that they understood Mr Redmond too well? Had they discovered, through some blind intuition, that Mr Redmond cared more for Home Rule than for Ireland, that he had played English politics too long, and was now able to persuade himself that an Act of Parliament carried with it some divine assurance of Irish freedom? However this may have been, Mr Redmond himself was uneasily aware of his own separation from reality. He knew that he could not 'remove' the obstacle of those Ulster counties. Behind his back, without his consent, beyond his disposal, a new Ireland had grown up – the Ireland of the literary renaissance, of the Abbey Theatre, of the Gaelic League, of the still insignificant Sinn Fein, even of Larkin's Trade Union. To the various but concentrated spirit – so careless of what happened at Westminster – of this new Ireland, those Ulster counties were essential: the nation must be a 'seamless garment', a whole country from north to south.

'I do not believe,' Mr Churchill went on, 'that there is any real feeling against Home Rule in the Tory Party apart from the Ulster question, but they hate the Government, are bitterly desirous of turning it out, *and see in the resistance of Ulster an extra-Parliamentary force which they will not hesitate to use to the full.*' The italicized passage does much credit to Mr Churchill's acute political sensibilities; but this was his blithe, insensible remedy – 'I have been pondering a great deal over this matter, and my general view is just what I told you earlier in the year – namely, that something should be done to afford the characteristically Protestant and Orange counties a moratorium of several years before acceding to the Irish Parliament. I think the time approaches when such an offer should be made; and it would come much better from the Irish leaders than from the Government. No one can doubt that the winter session will be critical. Much is to be apprehended from a combination of the rancour of a party in the ascendant and the fanaticism of these stubborn and determined Orangemen. These opinions are personal, so far as I am concerned; they have not been arrived at from consultation, and are for your private eye alone.'

Mr Redmond could only have read this letter with alarm and chagrin. What could it mean but that Mr Churchill was weakening? His Belfast experience, his respect for his father, his buried Toryism, his friendship for F. E. Smith – the cause might be in any one of these things, or it might have had its origin in caprices and eccentricities that Redmond could not even guess at. But Churchill and Lloyd George had been the two most strenuous upholders of Home Rule; and it was Redmond's fortune that, of the whole Cabinet, these two should be the most wayward and fantastic. A puff of wind, 'an anything, a nothing', might turn Churchill from his allegiance; an uneasiness among the Nonconformist ranks, a feeling that they walked too closely yoked with Rome in the Irish question, a growing preoccupation with his Insurance and Land campaigns – and Lloyd George would withdraw his support. As he perused the plausible meditations of Mr Churchill, Mr Redmond must have felt that his Liberal allies were, gradually but perceptibly, creeping from the scene of battle. . . .

It was fortunate that Sir Edward Carson had no opportunity to peep over Mr Redmond's shoulder as he read this letter. Things were already going too well for him. On 19th September, before an audience of hand-picked reporters and his own entourage of Ulster MP's, he read his Covenant aloud. The setting he chose for this revelation was the arcade leading to the Craigavon tennis court, and he stood aloft on a stone step, which now bears an inscription recording the event. 'Ulster's Solemn League and Covenant,' he intoned. 'Being convinced in our consciences that Home Rule would be disastrous to the material well-being of Ireland, subversive of our civil and religious freedom, destructive of our citizenship, and perilous to the unity of the Empire, we, whose names are underwritten, men of Ulster, loyal subjects of His Gracious Majesty King George V, humbly relying on the God whom our fathers in days of stress and trial confidently trusted, do hereby pledge ourselves in Solemn Covenant, throughout this our time of threatened calamity to stand by one another in defending for ourselves and our children our cherished position of equal citizenship in the United Kingdom, and in using all means which may be found necessary to defeat the present conspiracy to set up a Home Rule Parliament in Ireland. And in the event of such a Parliament being forced upon us we further solemnly and mutually pledge ourselves to refuse to recognize its authority. In sure confidence that God will defend the Right we hereto subscribe our names. And further, we individually declare that we have not already signed this Covenant. God save the King.'

A campaign to inspire the future signatories with a proper enthusiasm for this pretentious document was started at Enniskillen on 18th September, the day before Sir Edward's apocalyptic appearance in the Craigavon arcade. Two squadrons of mounted yeomanry, armed with lances, met Sir Edward at the Enniskillen station and escorted him to Portora Gate, where 40,000 Unionist Clubmen, drawn from the surrounding agricultural districts, straggled past him in military order. The Portora Gate Hotel 'began to fill "with clergymen, landlords, and ladies", while outside these aristocratic precincts, sauntered bearded Protestant peasants, of extraordinary age, if they had, as was stated, "always remained faithful to the memory of King William".' (George Peel. *The Reign of Sir Edward Carson*, p. 66. He was quoting from *The Times* of 19th September, 1912.) The meeting was first addressed by Lord Hugh Cecil, whose speech was somewhat above the heads of his audience, upon whom he urged, as a way of softening religious difficulties, the policy of 'merging their religious parties in the life of the wider community.' Nothing could have been further from an Orangeman's desire than to soften any religious differences; and though Lord Hugh, who was an ardent leader of the ritualist right wing in the Church of England, probably knew what he meant, his hearers made no attempt to follow him in his Romish speculations. Nor is there any record that he was invited to speak in Ulster again. Sir Edward put matters right by declaring roundly, when his turn came, that Enniskillen was 'one of the outposts, near to the zone of danger, and among our enemies.' This was the sort of language which the landlords, the clergymen, the ladies, and the bearded peasants had come to hear.

During the next nine days demonstrations were held at Lisburn, Derry, Coleraine, Ballymena, Dromore, Portadown, Crumlin, Newtownards, and Ballyroney. At Coleraine, Martin Ross – co-author of the charming *Experiences of an Irish RM* – was one of the spectators; filled with loyalist enthusiasm, she had travelled all the way from her South to be present. But the brutally comic spirit which haunted all Sir Edward's activities laid its hand also upon this pleasant lady's thoughts. She watched the crowd pouring out of Coleraine's streets on to a green hill by the River Bann. A pavilion had been built for the speakers, facing the hill, and a strong east wind strained at its many flags, and whipped the blue waters of the Bann behind it. To the enchanted Martin Ross, seated in the pavilion, a lovely miracle of silence seemed to be laid upon the vast audience, whose remoter faces were already being swallowed up in the advancing rim of twilight. She listened to the Orange oratory with increasing rapture. But when Mr F. E. Smith rose to speak, her enthusiasm knew no bounds. 'I have seen,' she wrote, 'a face so inscrutably youthful, so immutably serious, *in a deal at the Dublin Horse Show....*'

At Portadown, a town traditionally grim, Carson was received with something like military honours. His escort presented arms with dummy rifles, the Union Jack was dipped at his approach, and the pageant was further enlivened with two pieces of artillery, made of wood which had been painted a steel grey, and accompanied by an ambulance and a group of nurses. At the sight of this remarkable piece of mummery, F. E. Smith exclaimed, 'The battle is won already!' ('Yes!' Mrs Smith wrote to her sisters. 'We all thought the dummy cannons absurd. It was only at Portadown that they had them. We none of us knew anything about it. We all said: "How the Radicals will laugh!" ')

On 27th September, there was an overflow meeting at Ulster Hall designed to steel Orange hearts for what Sir Edward had called 'the most serious matter that has ever confronted them in the course of their lives.' Such was Sir Edward's description of the Covenant. Mr R. McNeill was even more impressive. His name for the Covenant was the '*Sacramentum*'.

The '*Sacramentum*' – the word has a peculiar aptness. On 28th September, through streets lined with silent, bareheaded and reverent Orangemen, Sir Edward Carson strode to the City Hall; he was preceded by a banner of faded yellow silk, with a black star in the centre, and a scarlet cross on a white ground in one corner – the selfsame banner which had been carried in front of William of Orange at the Battle of the Boyne, two hundred and twenty-two years before. At the City Hall, in the open space directly beneath its door, the altar awaited Sir Edward – a square table covered with the Union Jack; around it, grouped in a semi-circle, and dappled with the rich passage of the mid-day sun through a great stained-glass window behind them, stood this altar's assistant priests – the Lord Mayor and Corporation, the Harbour Commissioners, the Water Board, the Poor Law Guardians. The crowd beyond the door pressed closer as Sir Edward advanced to the table, and, kneeling, signed the Covenant. He was followed by the Marquess of Londonderry, Lord Charles Beresford, the Bishop of Down, the Presbyterian Moderator, and a prosperous series of Privy Councillors and Members of Parliament. It was an affecting moment. At H. W. Nevinson's side, as he watched it as representative of the *Manchester Guardian,* stood J. L. Garvin, editor of the *Observer*, 'and with characteristic worship of big personalities, he kept telling me that he loved Carson.' (H. W. Nevinson. *More Changes, More Chances*, p. 376.)

All day long, Carson and F. E. Smith harangued the multitude, as it moved in and out of City Hall. That evening they dined at the Ulster Club, and afterwards, their man-drawn carriage toiling for sixty-three minutes through a ten minutes' stretch of shouting street, arrived in triumph at the quay.

'Don't leave us,' the mob was heard to mourn (or so *The Times* correspondent positively declared), 'you mustn't leave us!' The two tall, dark figures hesitated for a gratified moment or two, and –

'It was only when someone pointed out that Sir Edward had work to do for Ulster in England that the crowd finally gave way and made an opening for their hero....'

Beyond the quay-shed doors lay *RMS Patriotic*, her main cabins banked with flowers. As she slowly drew off into the gathering dusk towards England, and as long as they were within earshot of land, her passengers listened to the harsh Belfast voices troubling the dark waters with 'Auld Lang Syne' and 'God Save the King'.

The Ulster *Sacramentum*, so melodramatic, so obvious, and yet, in its curious way, so macabre, at last convinced the most reluctant Liberals, and the even more reluctant Mr Redmond, that Home Rule could not be attained simply by passing a Bill three times through Parliament. No less than 471,444 men and women had signed the Covenant, and the effect of this news upon the House of Commons was to put that venerable chamber into a very bad temper. Temper the Commons had already displayed that autumn. There was a famous occasion when the Government whips were caught off their guard, and, on a vote concerning the

Financial Resolutions for the Home Rule Bill, Mr Asquith had gone down to defeat by 228 to 206. It was a sad story; while the Liberals innocently spent their afternoon elsewhere, not expecting a division until after dinner, the Unionists flooded the Lobby at four o'clock, and the Government was 'snapped'. The next day, Mr Asquith, quoting a formidable list of precedents from Sir Robert Peel to Mr Balfour, refused to resign; the House adjourned in a scene of considerable disorder; and the literary Mr R. McNeill suddenly picked up a book – which happened to be a manual containing rules and advice for observing good behaviour in Parliament – and threw it with some force at Mr Churchill, striking him shrewdly on the side of his face. Never one to refuse combat, Mr Churchill advanced upon Mr McNeill. Mr McNeill advanced upon Mr Churchill. As Members crowded about the Table, unwilling to miss a moment of this promising bout, Mr Will Crooks sang the first line of 'Auld Lang Syne', somebody started to laugh, and the light of battle died from the eyes of the First Lord and his opponent. The next day, apologies were offered and accepted very handsomely on the floor of the House; but from that incident onwards, it was noticed, Liberals and Conservatives gradually abandoned their pleasant habit of strolling down to the House together; gradually they dropped all pretence of being on speaking terms; until at last they held aloof from one another like the enemies they were.

If Liberal rage was nourished by the appearance of hateful reality in Ulster, the Unionists were moved to sedition by quite different reasons. For the first time since 1903 they were actually united. After much doubt and uncertainty, in the course of which Mr Bonar Law's leadership was seriously threatened, they had decided to wrench from their Tariff Reform platform, with all the circumstance of official action, that unpopular, that splintered plank of 'Food Taxes'. This almost surgical feat of carpentry accomplished, they were now ready to pour the pure vials of their wrath, no longer vitiated by dissension, full upon the heads of their Liberal opposites. . . .

VIII

It has sometimes been said of the Parliamentary Session of 1913, that it was one of the dullest in history. And this was true, in the sense that Parliament could hardly congratulate itself on its position in English affairs. It was simply a parade ground through which there marched, in close order, large blocks of Home Rule Bill; it was also a place where Sir Edward Carson, invested with all the majesty of a petty king, would suddenly appear and whence he would as suddenly disappear into the mists of Ulster or into mistier consultations with his Tory allies. On 1st January, he moved an amendment proposing the total exclusion of Ulster, which was defeated by a majority of 97; and thereafter, apparently unconcerned at such a trivial pantomime, he watched the Bill go through its third reading, disappear into the House of Lords, be rejected by the Lords with a majority of 257, and come back to wait in the Commons until the time was ripe for it to follow the same procedure once again. Nothing emerged from this planetary progress except one fragment of more or less unrelated dialogue. Towards the end of the debate on 1st January, Mr Bonar Law remarked:

'These people in the North-east of Ireland, from old prejudices perhaps more than from anything else, from the whole of their past history, would prefer, I believe, to accept the government of a foreign country rather than submit to be governed by honourable gentlemen below the gangway [i.e. the Nationalists].'

Mr Churchill seized upon this passage. 'I refer,' he said, 'to the statement that Ulster would rather be annexed to a foreign country.' . . . He could get no further. He waited for a lull in the Opposition wrath. 'If you do not listen to me,' he murmured sweetly, 'it is a matter of total indifference.' Nobody was more conversant with the whole art of irritating opponents: he smiled, he shrugged his shoulders, he kept his feet. In a little while, he could make himself heard again. 'Ulster,' he repeated in saccharine tones, 'would rather be annexed to a foreign country than continue her allegiance to the Crown.' While the Opposition benches yelled at him, Mr Churchill smiled upon them with the blandest and most calculated air of infuriating patience. At last he was given a third chance to speak; he threw his spear with exact and unscrupulous aim. 'This then is the latest Tory threat. Ulster will secede to Germany. . . .'

Let the Tory execrations which followed this timely thrust fade away into the silence, and with them all considerations as to whether or not a Cabinet Minister has any right to play with such barbed innuendoes in a time of peace – there remains the unhappy fact that Mr Churchill could not have spoken more directly at the country's fears. Or should one not say 'fears'? Should one, after all, say no more than 'fantasies'? What was the public's feeling towards its future enemy? When you read the jocund thrusts at Germany in the *Punch* of those days, or look at Heath Robinson's humorous cartoons of a possible Prussian invasion, or remember that 'Saki' could write a novel in 1913, in which the Kaiser, having subdued all England, was apparently abashed if not utterly vanquished by the gallant refusal of a troop of Boy Scouts to march past his imperial self – you cannot resist the conclusion that public fears of Germany were a kind of self-indulgence. In the War Office, and the Foreign Office, and the more enlightened sections of Fleet Street – here they knew how near to the precipice the world was. But the public? The public was only aware of an inner tension, a need for stimulants; and what could be more exciting than to gather all the political rages, all the class hatreds, all the fevers for spending and excitement and speed, which then seemed to hang like a haunted fog over England – to gather them and condense them into one huge shape and call it *Germany*? Thus agreeably hagridden, thus desperately and delightfully alarmed, the people of England could perhaps forget the domestic crises which advanced upon them hour by hour. Germany was about as real to them as Japan is real today to the Eastern seaboard of the United States: a threat – certainly; a menace – beyond a doubt. But so is plague still a menace, and the second coming, and communism, and death.

The irony in this was purely tragic. Out of the reality which was to burst upon it not two years later, the public made an island melodrama; it was pleased to prophesy, not knowing that it was a prophet. To men of real foresight, to professional alarmists, to gentlemen with armaments to sell in a hurry – it gave the same eager response: it cried as easily for eight dreadnoughts as it let its flesh creep over the thought of London improbably honeycombed with anarchists. The thought of a conscript army horrified it, yet it fed its growing hysteria on the thrilling notion that an army would have to be used – very soon and – who could tell? – perhaps to turn back a German invasion. Its almost primitive sense of theatre was a blessing to editors in need of copy; it was also a blessing to merchants with more sinister commodities for sale. . . .

The airship melodrama of 1913 was doubtless prompted at each stage by the manufacturers of aircraft; but its chief actors were the public, the press, and certain ghostly sounds and presences; and, in its utterly unreal presentation of realities to come, in its childish gravity, its enthusiasm, its unself-consciousness – it is so typical of the assorted hysterias of pre-war England, that it deserves to be repeated in some detail. It was in this sort of general atmosphere, it should be remembered, that the

Tories succeeded in reducing Parliament to a dull and quarrelsome farce.

It was in February 1913, after Mr Churchill had reached an agreement with Admiral von Tirpitz about preserving the ratio of eight English dreadnoughts to five German, and after the Navy had become in consequence too insipid for drama, that stories suddenly appeared – in the *Daily Mail* and other sensational papers – of airships hovering at midnight over the East Coast. That these airships were German was quite beyond question. What else could they be? But it was not until 24th February that rumour turned into fact. 'AIRSHIP OVER THE EAST COAST' shouted the *Daily Mail*'s headlines of that date – 'MANY WITNESSES.' There was to be no more uncertainty on the subject: the *Daily Mail* knew all.

The first act of this aerial melodrama opened at Selby, in the West Riding of Yorkshire. There were four witnesses. (1) A solicitor of Selby saw two hovering lights in the sky, at 9.15 of Friday evening, 21st February. (2) An insurance manager, standing in Church Fenton Station with a party of Selby business men, observed – not three-quarters of an hour later – 'an airship with strong searchlights playing on the railway lines.' It was high at first, he said, but soon descended almost to the roofs of Church Fenton. There it lingered for some twenty minutes, while he and the business men held their breaths; then it was off at a great speed, showing for the first time a wicked red and green light along each side. (3) A countryman of Riccall in the East Riding saw an airship at 8 p.m., and, being sharper of hearing than the rest, actually distinguished the whirr of its engines. (4) A commercial traveller was driving near Ellerton between ten and eleven that night, when he and his horse were startled by a very bright light 'from an airship or something' which passed across the road in front of him and proceeded rapidly towards Bridlington. This concluded the evidence. There was no doubt about it: the Germans were flying about over England.

With a fine editorial caution, however, the *Mail* remarked, on 25th February, 'Whether or not we accept the circumstantial evidence that a strange airship was seen hovering over British territory on Friday and Saturday, it must be taken as certain that this country has recently been visited by foreign aircraft.' And its conclusion was that the country very badly needed 'a large provision of dirigibles' – which, to be sure, the exhibitors at the Aero Exhibition at Olympia would have been very glad to supply.

Three days later, the *Whitby Gazette* took up the cry:

WANTED, AN AIR MINISTER

ENGLAND AT GERMANY'S MERCY

NORTH-EAST COAST SURVEYED NIGHTLY BY DIRIGIBLES

FURTHER APPEARANCES OF AIRSHIP AT WHITBY.

And further appearances there were, attested by the most trustworthy witnesses. A gentleman meditating upon the stars from his bedroom window in Skinner Street, Whitby, saw a light moving slowly northward: it was not a star; it was too dull for an ordinary star, too slow for a shooting star. 'I am presuming,' he concluded solemnly, 'that I saw *the* airship.' A Mr William Prentice, Jr, walking round by Larpool at a quarter to eight in the evening, saw the airship, too, travelling at a great rate towards Eskdaleside. It had a red light in the bows and a greenish light at the stern; as Mr Prentice watched it, it shut off its lights, 'lifted a little,' and began hovering round and round. 'I went towards Ruswarp and up Ruswarp Lane, and I could see the machine in the air all the time. At about twenty minutes past eight o'clock the airship proceeded towards Pickering, or York, travelling sixty or seventy miles an hour, I should think. . . .' There were others who had seen it with alarm, he added, and these would certainly bear him out that the airship appeared to be about a mile above the land, and – the night being 'dark but starlight' – was plainly visible as a cigar-shaped vessel with a platform beneath. The explanation came about a week later, though not from the press. The airship was a farmer, wheeling a creaking wheelbarrow loaded with manure along a hill-top; a light swinging from a broomstick, which had been tied to the wheelbarrow, guided his footsteps through the dark. How he and his load developed a red light in the bows and a green light in the stern; or how they suddenly disappeared at seventy miles an hour towards Pickering – these facts are beyond the flight of all but the rarest imaginations. But the airship was not permitted to remain just a load of manure. On the same night, in Bedale post office many miles away, a young clerk was told by his colleague, quite simply, 'There is an airship outside.' He went out at once. 'There was no doubt,' he informed the *Whitby Gazette*. 'It was an airship.' He could bring a dozen witnesses to support him. A Whitby sea-captain, at about the same time, was attracted by a very bright light, a little to the north of Venus which, when he reached for his telescope, became 'enshrouded in a haze.' It was all very mysterious, but the *Gazette* had no doubts whatsoever: Germans were at work, surveying the Yorkshire wolds. Had not the steamer *Orcadia* just put into Kirkwall, fresh from the North Orkneys, with tales of a dirigible seen in the eye of day off Sanday Island? What the Germans could be doing so far north and above those unstrategic seas, nobody knew; and, indeed, the airship was so distant that some few doubters in the crew thought it was a flock of birds.

Birds it turned out to be – a flight of geese, fleeing southwards from the dead Arctic February, as they often do if the climate becomes too cold for them. But by now airships were seen everywhere – in Lancashire, above the West coasts, over the South. As late as 8th March, the people of South Wales were terribly alarmed by the planet Venus, hung low in the sky and veiled with clouds. At last, the discovery of a fire-balloon on the Yorkshire moors put an end to the whole business, while Germany rocked from end to end with mirth over this 'Flying German' who had haunted the English heavens: but in May the *Daily Mail*, undeterred, promoted a monster meeting at the Mansion House to demand more airships. The meeting was thinly attended, the public being now absorbed in the deadly intentions of German waiters; and Mr Balfour and Lord Rosebery, who had taken the whole thing seriously enough to promise to speak, somehow discovered that they had other engagements.

IX

If these mythical airships served no other purpose, at least they projected their searchlights into the dim recesses of the public mind. Clouded with fearful dreams of anarchists and invasions, responsive only to romance, active only in riot, how could that mind be reached except through methods which earlier politicians would not even have considered? Its apathy towards such a constitutional problem as Home Rule exactly coincided with the Tory Rebellion; and Mr Bonar Law was able to pacify his conscience with the thought that public opinion was not to be aroused except by talk of guns and bloodshed, and hints of mutiny, and treasonable exhortations. 'If treason prosper, none dares call it treason.' But then, he began to ask himself, was treason prospering? It was easy for him to send a message to Belfast on the 12th July – 'Whatever steps you may feel compelled to take, whether they are constitutional, or whether in the long run they are unconstitutional, you have the whole Unionist Party, under my leadership, behind you.' But it was Sir Edward

Carson who delivered the message, Sir Edward Carson who received the applause, and Sir Edward Carson – there was no getting away from it – who controlled the party. If those unconstitutional steps which Ulster might feel compelled to take led towards bullying the Government into resignation, Mr Law would be content; but he had an uneasy feeling that they might actually lead to bloodshed, and that Carson and his volunteers would not be upset if they did. 'The Tory Party,' Sir Almeric Fitzroy wrote in his diary on 15th July, 'have committed themselves so deeply in Ulster . . . that there is no way of retreat open.'

The Tories could not retreat into Parliament. They had already made that refuge untenable. There was no choice but to go on. Looking round for some reputable way to get rid at once of Sir Edward and the Government, they lit upon the Crown. For some months now, George V had been subjected to all kinds of back-stairs advice; but lately more eminent and responsible voices were beginning to whisper in the royal ear. Lord Lansdowne, Mr Balfour, and Mr Bonar Law – each in his own way – thought that the King would be within his constitutional rights if he dissolved Parliament and forced another election on the question of Home Rule; Lord Rosebery and, of course, Mr Asquith, were convinced that such action would be a *coup d'état*, which, when undertaken by a comparatively untried king, would more likely wreck the Crown than mend the Irish problem.

For a while, London was filled with rumours that the King intended to abdicate. Nothing could be further from George V's character; or could show more clearly how little he was understood. He had one of the most active consciences in England; he was conscientiously determined to do his duty; his whole disposition was towards peace. He was certainly not the man to vanish from a scene which called for his presence; but, though he had no intention of yielding to the delicate and dubious importunities of Lord Lansdowne, Mr Balfour, and Mr Bonar Law (who, to be sure, did not consider wrecking the Crown until it became reasonably probable that Sir Edward might yet wreck them), yet he would much rather sign the Home Rule Bill in ink than in blood. So he did everything that he could to moderate Tory language on the one hand, and on the other to bring the leaders of both parties into friendly consultation. England has had more brilliant and more spectacular monarchs than George V, but surely no monarch more suited to assist its democracy through a period of what was beginning to look very like nervous breakdown.

The King's movements towards peace were much assisted by a letter sent to *The Times* by Lord Loreburn – the irascible ex-Lord Chancellor, who had hitherto been known as a stubborn supporter of the purest Home Rule. This missive, published on 11th September, sternly reproved the Government for not treating the Northern Province separately, for not suggesting a settlement by consent. It was useless for the Cabinet to recall, with legitimate animosity, that when some such proposal had been made in its secret deliberations at least two years before, Lord Loreburn had very firmly quashed it. The deed was done. Although a *Times* editorial pounced upon this letter as a confession that 'as a permanent solution, the Irish policy of the Government is indefensible,' the Government knew better than to hit back. Peace was in the air. True, peace has many names, and the least of these is 'policy'; but a peaceful policy is better than nothing at all. The King was inviting leading men of either party to Balmoral, and that was how Lord Crewe and Mr Bonar Law came to play golf together at Deeside one September afternoon, when Mr Law confessed – though he spoke with his usual rancour – that Federal Home Rule (by which presumably he meant one parliament for Southern Ireland, another for Ulster, another for Scotland, another for Wales, with the Imperial Parliament over them all) was not impossible. The Liberal Ministers, assembled in an Arran castle towards the end of September, apparently decided to accept Mr Law's olive-twig. While Mr Lloyd George – still somewhat subdued by the Marconi Scandal* – tried to divert the public mind with a new Land Campaign, Mr Asquith, Mr Churchill, and Sir Edward Grey punctuated the month of October with admissions that Ulster might – just *might*, they would go no further – not be altogether bluffing.

In vain Mr Redmond protested, at Limerick on 12th October, that the division of Ireland into two nations 'is to us an abomination and a blasphemy' – he had already put himself into the hands of his Liberal allies. And his Liberal allies perceived, as one sees a crack of light under a dark door, the beginnings of indecision within the Unionist ranks. Mr Bonar Law was losing his nerve. Now was the time to suggest that a partition of Ireland was not so abominable or so blasphemous; and when Mr Churchill hinted as much in the Commons on 29th October, Mr Law replied, in a voice that vibrated with – was it hesitancy? or was it perhaps fear? – that the nation was drifting towards the tragedy of civil war.

* See pages 250/251.

The next evening, speaking at Newcastle-on-Tyne, he made himself even clearer. 'The Ulster people and their leaders,' he said, 'have not consulted us. It is their responsibility, and it is a responsibility from which Sir Edward Carson does not shrink.' Was he preparing to desert Sir Edward, as the Liberals were preparing to desert Mr Redmond? For the moment, it seemed so. Mr F. E. Smith was rumoured to be talking, once again, of a coalition ministry. Could it be that English politicians were deciding, at this very last moment, to settle the problems of Ireland in their own way and in their own Parliament?

But if they were, they had reckoned without Sir Edward Carson. That dark mind, that cold and powerful temperament, were already at work. If the Liberals had scented a weakness in the Unionist Party, Sir Edward was aware of an even greater weakness in the Liberal leadership. He was not the man to let an opportunity slip, or to watch his friends desert him without lifting a hand to drag them back. The Loreburn letter convinced him that there was a deep division in the Government between those who believed that Ulster could still be coerced, and those who believed that she could not; he knew he could increase this division by increasing his own threats. As for Mr Bonar Law and Mr F. E. Smith, he had no fear – he knew how to play upon them.

If the Unionists withdrew their active support, if the Liberals healed their division, Ulster would have to be content with some scheme of local autonomy under an Irish Parliament; this was not to be borne, it was not even to be considered. On with the Civil War! He had already, on 24th September, produced his famous Ulster Constitution – which was, to be sure, the most impossible system of involved bureaucracy ever created by the ingenuity of man. Three days later, he held a review of 7,000 Belfast Volunteers, led by their new Commander-in-Chief, General Sir George Richardson (retired); and the general's galloper was none other than the Right Honourable F. E. Smith, KC (who was known as 'Galloper' Smith from then onwards). The next morning a religious service was held in Ulster Hall, and was attended by Carson and Smith. The sermon was delivered by a North Antrim clergyman, dressed for the occasion in a frock-coat, a light waistcoat with shining metal buttons, a low-cut collar, and a white bow tie, who thundered that if King George had been present at yesterday's review – 'He would have said, "I am not afraid of Germany" '; and went on to draw an elaborate comparison between Sir Edward and Joshua. . . . Ah, no! Sir Edward need have no fears about Mr Smith; the 'Galloper', his sense of drama and his sense of humour equally involved, might talk about coalition, but he would not desert. There remained Mr Bonar Law.

But Mr Bonar Law's mind was not long in making itself up. Even while he considered how he could bring his party back into some appearance of constitutional propriety, even while he hesitated, retreated, meditated desertion, the activities of Sir Edward in Ulster worked upon his spirit like some powerful magic. A meeting with Mr Asquith on 6th November settled the matter once and for all. Ostensibly the two leaders sympathized with each other upon the difficulties which beset them; but the very sight of Mr Asquith – so tired, so passive, and above all so gentlemanly – was too much for Mr Bonar Law. Here before him – in the quiet person of the Prime Minister – was the whole Liberal Party. It was weary, it was ailing, and it could be broken. All considerations of decency and restraint vanished from that moment; the danger point had been passed; on with the Tory Rebellion!

But Mr Asquith, too, seemed to have carried from that meeting a new resolve. To Mr Law's suggestions of either a General Election or permanent exclusion of Ulster from the Bill, he had, he told Mr Redmond, 'given no countenance.' At the next Cabinet, Mr Lloyd George proposed that a certain area of Ulster – as always 'to be agreed on' – should be excluded from the operations of the Bill for five years. Sir Edward Carson, of course, would not accept this; but it might prevent an uprising in Ulster, for men do not take up arms to fight against something which will not happen for five years. The Cabinet was impressed but it could not see its way to agreeing. This was on 17th November. On 24th November, Mr Redmond composed an almost desperate memorandum to the Prime Minister. The Tories, he said, had now discovered that 'they had to confront a Minister who would meet with firmness any overt movement on their part'; he begged Mr Asquith to make no offer of concessions which 'would be calculated to give new strength and new hope to the Orange movement.' This contradictory document was read to the Cabinet on the morning of 25th November, and the Cabinet was once again impressed.

But not Mr Lloyd George. The Irish problem was diverting attention, not merely from Parliament, but from his own Land Campaign; he began to discover in himself a convenient sympathy with the Ulster Protestants. That afternoon, he had a secret consultation with Mr Redmond. He urged his proposal upon the Irish leader. Things had gone so far, he said, that some offer would have to be made; the

Government had found a store of ninety-five thousand rounds of ammunition in Belfast, and it was believed that Sir Edward would shortly hold a review of *armed* men. The Cabinet, he hinted, was really very much in favour of excluding Ulster for five years.

Mr Redmond made no attempt to argue with this new, volatile, but too adequate adversary. He simply remarked that he stood firm by his memorandum – there must be no concessions to Ulster. But the misgivings which rushed upon him, those he might conceal in his words, but not in his voice; and Mr Lloyd George hastened to reply that, without concessions, he, Lord Haldane, Mr Churchill and Sir Edward Grey might resign, which would mean a general *débâcle* and a very serious setback for Home Rule. Mr Redmond refused to yield: Home Rule would have a second chance in future years; but if Mr Lloyd George resigned, would *he* have a second chance? Mr Redmond thought not. 'It would mean the end of L.G.'s career' (he noted, setting down his conversation afterwards) 'and would be a far more serious thing for the Liberal Party – it would mean the end of the Liberal Party for a generation, *perhaps for ever. He admitted this.*'

This sort of fencing, though swift and skilful, could serve no purpose: Mr Redmond would not give up Home Rule, Mr Lloyd George would not resign. Both the Irishman and the Welshman had gone too far on their separate paths to draw back, both were irrevocably committed to the Liberal Party. But was Mr Lloyd George simply bluffing? Mr Redmond had some suspicions that he was. And these were amply confirmed in the next two days, the 26th and the 27th, when Asquith and Birrell took occasion to inform the Irish leader that the Cabinet had by no means favoured Mr Lloyd George's suggestion; oh, dear no, they had been very much opposed to it; 'nothing definite had been decided about seizing the arms, etc. etc.'; and as for Carson, they would not dream of making him an offer.

There were rumours, indeed, that the Cabinet had already put out tentative feelers towards Carson. But if Mr Redmond heard these rumours, he never mentioned them, to do so would only make matters worse. He had other worries, other perplexities.

X

Behind Mr Redmond's back, a new kind of Irish patriotism was growing up. He might groan inwardly, but there it was; he might bury his head deep in the shifting sands of strictly constitutional procedure, but sooner or later he would have to stand upright and look this new opponent in the face. There was no getting away from it – Ireland was developing an independent mind; it was no longer inclined to believe that its whole future lay in the delicate and difficult manoeuvres of conflicting English parties, which appeared to think of it as something between a pawn and a confounded nuisance. And the truth was that Sir Edward Carson was by no means hated by the southern Nationalists; in fact, he was rather admired. Here was an Irishman who not only defied the English Parliament, but defied it successfully and forcibly and with threats of bloodshed. That he defied it in the name of loyalty to England scarcely mattered; the point was that what he could do, other Irishmen could do. It was a matter of ancient history that the 'sheen of arms' in Ulster was a signal to the rest of Ireland; and perhaps the rest of Ireland – demanding Home Rule and an undivided country – ought soon to fall upon Sir Edward and his followers with a kind of affectionate ferocity. On 15th December, Sir Roger Casement, an Ulster Nationalist, went down to address a Nationalist meeting in Cork, and when his speech was over, called for three cheers for Sir Edward Carson. Sir Roger's unusual, and perhaps extreme, desire for abstract justice had been much increased by two revolting investigations which he had conducted in tropical countries for the English Government; and the good citizens of Cork so misunderstood his meaning that they dismembered the chairs in wrath and hurled them at his head. But Casement, in his peculiarly unbalanced fashion, had expressed what everybody was beginning to feel. Carson was – perhaps the word is somewhat exaggerated, but none other seems to serve – rapidly turning into an Irish hero.

Elsewhere, this was becoming all too plain. On 26th November, a public meeting was held to organize the Nationalist Volunteers. The Committee behind this movement, which had been going on all summer, was headed by Professor Eoin MacNeill, a temperamental Celtic scholar, with some gift for demagoguery. As Vice-President of the Gaelic League, he had done a great deal for the revival of the Gaelic tongue – which was the League's optimistic object; and had already scored what was considered a triumph for Irish Nationalism by having the Gaelic tongue made an essential subject for matriculation in the National University. In October he published an article in the League's official paper, calling on Ireland to arm; and this article was read with enthusiasm by Padraic Pearse, who, with a number of other Ulster

Nationalists then engaged in recruiting for the Irish Republican Brotherhood, had been thinking along very much the same lines. Pearse and his republican friends, all of them admirers of Carson's rebellion, thereupon joined forces with MacNeill and his constitutional friends; Colonel Maurice Moore – George Moore's brother – offered the Volunteers his military knowledge; and, by the beginning of December, the movement was well on foot.

What was Mr Redmond to do? He comforted himself with the reflection that the United Irish League and the Ancient Order of Hibernians – his most influential backers – were altogether opposed to the Volunteers. But then the leaders of the Volunteers had had the temerity to suggest that the United Irish League and the Ancient Order of Hibernians no longer represented the spirit of Ireland; that they were, in fact, no more than the creaking components of an old-fashioned, hide-bound, and greedy political machine. Worse still, Professor MacNeill seemed to take it for granted that Mr Redmond would assume control of these Volunteers, become a sort of general in action against Sir Edward Carson, and abandon his beloved weapon of eight score votes in Parliament for the more dubious equipment of an indefinite number of Irish guns. You might as well present a practiced swordsman with a blunderbuss, and beg him to let fly: Mr Redmond was at a loss to think what had happened to Ireland.

And this was not all. The Dublin strikes that summer had produced in Messrs Larkin and Connolly a new menace to Mr Redmond's peace of mind. Mr Larkin, who had a semi-mystical enthusiasm for riot, Guild Socialism, and the freedom of Ireland, was not destined to prove much more than a thorn in the side of the English Trade Union Congress. But Mr Connolly had offered himself and his burning oratory to the cause of Irish Nationalism; and Mr Redmond could not quite see himself marching in step with syndicalist workmen. Moreover, from those Dublin strikes even stranger figures were emerging. There was, for instance, the Countess Markievicz, who, as Eva Gore-Booth, had successfully dislocated her father's industries with a series of local strikes, and who now, in the intervals of serving soup to strikers, was organizing a body of Irish Boy Scouts, with the object of sending these children into battle with the Volunteers. Tall, wild-haired, near-sighted, this generous and warm-hearted lady assiduously drilled her scouts in the vacant lots of Dublin, and frequently broke, as was her habit when excited, into fluent French couched in a strong English accent. Then there was Captain

James White, DSO, son of Field-Marshal Sir George White, the hero of Ladysmith. Captain White had lost his emotional balance in the Boer War, and had been pursuing it ever since; at the moment he had chased it into Larkin's camp, and was busy organizing the more rebellious of Larkin's strikers into a Citizens' Army, the precise object of which nobody could discover.

And lastly, there was Arthur Griffith's Sinn Fein. As late as 1915, Mr Redmond was calling Sinn Fein 'the temporary cohesion of isolated cranks'; and perhaps he was right, perhaps Sinn Fein was never more than a convenient name. But the emergence of a convenient name is not without its significance, and in 1913 Sinn Fein, though still a lonely journalistic movement, was none the less on the move; and there was something in Sinn Fein – was it the gift of prophecy, or was it just independence? – which troubled Mr Redmond, even while he affected unconcern. Ireland was changing, and it was changing without his consent; he knew that if he was to get Home Rule in a constitutional manner, he would have to hurry, for – with events hurling onwards at their present speed and towards what unthinkable destination! – the Parliament at Westminster would very soon be helpless.

Could he rely on Mr Asquith? He did not know; but he realized that his whole future, and that pacific future which he desired for Ireland, hung upon Mr Asquith and the Cabinet. If only they would face Sir Edward and the Tories with the serene and secure majesty of an affronted Parliament! If only (and this was the more bitter thought) he had put them out of power a year ago, at the first sign of weakness and before he himself had been drawn irrevocably into the whirlpool of their indecision. The waters turned around aimlessly and without rest: the Cabinet could not make up its mind whether it should yield or fight or whither it should move; and when at last it moved – such are the inevitable results of indecision – it moved in the wrong direction. On 7th December, two proclamations were issued, forbidding the importation of arms into Ireland.

The Ulster press openly gloried in this. These proclamations aimed themselves – whether intentionally or unintentionally – straight at the Nationalist Volunteers. The illegal importation of arms was a simple thing if you had money, and the Ulster Volunteers had money; Tory wealth was prepared to supply them indefinitely. But, at the time of the proclamations, the other Volunteers were almost penniless – they could not afford to charter ships, and bribe officials, and go through all the expensive processes of gun-running. When the proclamations were withdrawn six months later, Ulster had all the guns she needed. Small wonder that, by Christmas 1913, Mr Redmond had realized that the Cabinet was against him; and had half agreed that the Home Rule Bill should continue on its passage to and fro between the Commons and the Lords with an amendment tacked on to it, permitting the temporary exclusion of the Province of Ulster. By the end of November he had called Lloyd George's bluff; by the end of December he had discovered that there was no bluff to call.

Yet 'temporary exclusion' itself meant less than nothing. While Sir Edward held court at Craigavon, Mr Bonar Law rushed onwards into rebellion in his support. The Unionist leader had altogether recovered from his attack of conscience. Deserted by the Crown, enraged by the fragile fatalism of Mr Asquith, encouraged by the resounding successes of Sir Edward Carson, he threw all caution to the winds. And help came to him, not from on high, but from some quarter scarcely less providential. Early in the year, Field-Marshal Earl Roberts, a national idol, and the hero of Heaven knows how many campaigns, grew very interested in the fate of Ulster, and even went so far as to suggest that he himself should assist the Ulster Volunteers, if no other commander could be found for them. The gallant and endearing old gentleman was, however, not a little doubtful as to the propriety of his entering the scene in person: after all, as a Field-Marshal, he was still on the active list. In June, however, he discovered an effective substitute. 'His name,' he wrote to Colonel Hickman of the Ulster Provisional Government, 'is Lieutenant-General Sir George Richardson, KCB, c/o Messrs Henry S. King and Co., Pall Mall, S.W. He is a retired Indian Officer, active and in good health.' And thereafter, with all Lord Roberts' vast prestige behind him, Sir George took command of the Volunteers.

At Antrim, on 21st September, Sir Edward improved upon this position with a large pronouncement – 'We have pledges and promises from some of the greatest generals in the army that, when the time comes and if it is necessary, they will come over to help us keep the old flag flying and to defy those who dare invade our liberties.' These words were, of course, directed at the Liberal Cabinet; for even those Ministers who believed that Ulster could and should be coerced, knew that the will of Parliament could not be done without the Army. Should the impossible occur, and the Army refuse to obey its orders, the Parliament Act and Parliament and the whole theory of representative institutions would simultaneously collapse. No wonder then that, when this speech appeared in the next day's newspapers, general opinion maintained that 'King' Carson was bluffing again. Bluffing he was, in some measure, and in some measure he continued to bluff until August 1914: he would certainly rather kill the Parliament Bill and the Government with threats, than kill his fellow countrymen with bullets. To that extent he, and Mr Bonar Law, and all the Tory rebels saw eye to eye. But his Antrim speech, so full of vague phrases, so resonant with the conditional menaces of a political orator, was by no means altogether bluff. Through its labyrinth of words one clue led with singular directness to the War Office, and specifically to the office of the Director of Military Operations, where Major-General Sir Henry Wilson, an Ulsterman of sanguine temperament and considerable gifts, sat spinning a contradictory web in which the Army should be at once involved more closely with France and also rendered so mutinous in temper that it would refuse to obey the Government in any gesture against Ulster. Of all positions in the Cabinet, that of Secretary for War was least grateful; it had played strange tricks upon those who held it; and its present incumbent, Colonel Seely, was not to be spared its goblin machinations. Whether Colonel Seely suspected that the War Office, with Sir Henry Wilson's help, was slowly being honeycombed with Tory intrigue, will never be known: but he gave no sign. Other quarters, however, seemed to be better informed than the Secretary for War. In October, the *Daily Telegraph* was able to say that 'any attempts to break the loyalists of Ulster by the armed forces of the Crown will probably result in the disorganization of the Army for several years.' In November the *Pall Mall Gazette* and the *Observer*, both under the editorship of J. L. Garvin, the most influential of Tory journalists, suggested that all Unionists should leave the Territorial Army, and do their best to prevent others from joining it. As for Sir Henry Wilson, that gifted observer noted in his diary for 25th November:

'Wherever I look, to China, to India, to Egypt, to South Africa, to Morocco, to Europe, everything is restless and unsettled, and everyone except ourselves is getting ready for war. This frightens me. Our Territorials are falling down . . . our regulars are falling down . . . our Special Reserve is a thing *pour rire*. And we are doing nothing.'

Nothing, that is, except to see that His Majesty's forces were indisposed to obey His Majesty's Government.

The effect upon Mr Bonar Law of these pointed remarks and scarcely less pointed rumours, was extremely inspiriting; he could not contain himself any longer. In Dublin on 28th November, he made one of the most reckless speeches of his whole career:

'I remember this,' he said, 'that King James had behind him the letter of the law just as completely as Mr Asquith has now. He made sure of it. He got the judges on his side by methods not dissimilar from those by which Mr Asquith has a majority in the House of Commons on his side. There is another point to which I would specially refer. In order to carry out his despotic intention the King had the largest army which had ever been seen in England. What happened? There was no civil war. Why? Because his own army refused to fight for him.'

A more extraordinary appeal to the Army had never been made, it is safe to say, by any Opposition leader. And when it was made, something died: that attitude of critical and grumbling respect for government, which had been fostered through over two hundred years of revolution and reform, expired upon Mr Bonar Law's breath. It had to die: it was too old, and not healthy; but it was curious that a Tory leader should have pronounced its obsequies. The immediate effect of Mr Bonar Law's speech became apparent as the year passed. The position of Parliament had shrunk – beneath this singular attack of politicians and generals – to something almost purely topographical. Parliament had become so many square yards in the Borough of Westminster; so many cubic feet of talkative air and pseudo-Gothic masonry; so many echoes in an inconvenient chamber where several hundred gentlemen sullenly debated. Its position in the English scene had been usurped by two forces – Sir Edward Carson and, vague but menacing, the British Army.

Chapter Three

The Women's Rebellion

I

IF in the Tory Rebellion – which the last chapter halted in mid-career – there is something outrageous and desperate, something murderous even in its mildness, yet in the end the whole process seems to resolve itself into a political melodrama, moving with infinite slowness towards an unknown destination. The actors may rant as they please, the imitation thunders and lightnings roar and flicker, the backdrop with a parliament painted on it may be exchanged for a lurid suggestion of horror and despair – but still, when the echoes have faded and the lights are dimmed and the curtain goes down on that tedious and tawdry act, what have we left but the memory of some recognizable English politicians in the recognizable posture of having lost their heads?

But as the frock-coated cast goes through its ill-directed paces, we are uncomfortably aware that we have missed something. The death of an attitude? An attitude of respect for the processes of democratic government? An attitude which in itself was no more than two hundred years old, and which was afterwards reborn – not with the same secure, complacent, and satisfying appearance – but reborn none the less?

There is more to it than that. In the menaces of Sir Edward Carson, and the extravagances of Mr F. E. Smith, and the fulminations of Mr Bonar Law, and the hesitations of Mr Asquith, and even in the acquiescence of Mr Balfour – was there not evident, horrible but inevitable word, a neurosis? To pursue a neurosis through the endless involutions of a political system; to observe, in the movements of those fundamentally decent figures, the effects of weariness, insecurity, and fear; to ask from what origin sprang those impulses which could make the legislators of England talk in terms of toy soldiers, and incredibly drag a party quarrel into the arena of civil war – such a task, from the very outset, seems quite impossible. Yet some such inquiry has to be made. For surely when an ancient Constitution is impiously investigated in a fit of bad temper, the historian is faced with a crisis which, in one shape or another, constantly recurs through the history of our times. The explanations are not difficult. The Land had lost its power, therefore the Lords lost theirs; the Irish, for the first time in the history of the Union, and with no Lords to defeat them, could impose their will on a weak Liberal cabinet; and the Liberal cabinet was weak because, in that stage of capitalism, it no longer represented an effective Left: no wonder the Tories tried, by such crude means as lay immediately at hand, to medicine this incurable economic sickness, and no wonder their methods seemed to hasten rather than delay its course. But are these really the explanations? Or rather, do they explain all that there is to explain? It is the habit of contemporary philosophy to mesh every succeeding crisis in the ordered and apparently inescapable nets of economic theory; but, somehow or other, when the nets are dragged brimful into the light of day, one thing seems to have evaded them, and that the most important catch of all. They have been dropped into swarming waters at the likeliest times; they have been watched with skill and manoeuvred with infinite patience; but they have never quite snared that inconvenient and unpredictable entity – the human soul. Yet it is the human soul which – as in all crises, so in the Tory Rebellion – finally disposes the course of events. To mention the word 'soul' in connection with Sir Edward Carson, Mr F. E. Smith, Mr Bonar Law, Mr Asquith, and Mr Balfour might seem incongruous, not to say romantic, if by 'soul' one meant that spiritual essence which variously manifests itself in the ecstasies of saints, the fugues of Bach, and the iambics of Aeschylus.

But – fortunately or unfortunately – the word is susceptible of a lower definition, and may even mean that irrational side of human nature which, for all the enlightenments of civilization still persists in responding to images so long buried in history that no one can positively say where they began or where they will end. This sort of irrational and unconscious element may possibly be discovered in the vagaries of pre-war English politicians; indeed, there is no avoiding it. For the Tory Rebellion was not merely a brutal attack upon an enfeebled opponent – that is to say, political; it was not merely the impassioned defence of impossible privileges – that is to say, economic: it was also, and more profoundly, the unconscious rejection of an established security. For nearly a century men had discovered in the cautious phrase, in the respectable gesture, in the considered display of reasonable emotions, a haven against those irrational storms which threatened to sweep through them. And gradually the haven lost its charms; worse still, it lost its peace. Its waters, no longer unruffled by the wind, ceased to reflect, with complacent ease, the settled skies, the untangled stars of accepted behaviour and sensible conviction; and men, with a defiance they could not hope to understand, began to put forth upon little excursions into the vast, the dark, the driven seas beyond. When Mr Bonar Law incited the Army to mutiny, his boat was already out; when Sir Edward Carson played upon the fury of Orange Ulster, he had left the haven, too; and so with Mr F. E. Smith, and Lord Halsbury, and Lord Hugh Cecil, and the rest. Would they manage to keep afloat, by baling out with some little political bucket? Would they sink? Would they put back? These questions were never settled; for, alas, the waters in which they found themselves were soon to be adventured upon by the whole western world, to be widely strewn with the wreckage of Liberal faiths, and to encompass us all today.

But the death of Liberal England – the various death of security and respectability – may not be considered simply as a loud prelude, passing suddenly into war. It was a brief but complete phase in the spiritual life of the nation. And though the Tory Rebellion refuses to reveal, in any kind of a satisfactory fashion, the irrational nature of this phase, the historian cannot excuse himself from seeking it elsewhere.

II

The politicians refuse to be anything but politicians; there remain the women. What can hardly be seen in the activities of one sex, may possibly discover itself – however reluctantly – in those of the other. On first thoughts, the activities of Englishwomen during those unnaturally distant years between 1910 and 1914 are merely an agreeable, disturbing extension of what had been going on for more than twenty years. *Emancipation* is the word; it conjures up all sorts of new visions – from tennis and bicycling to the inner sanctums of offices, where, for the first time, in all her glory, and at starvation wages, woman was beginning to compete with man. The most convenient way of approaching this question is through the wardrobe. The female form, as the century progressed towards war, was being released from the distortions and distentions of the Victorian era; no longer did woman insist, with what seems to our more modest gaze an extreme salaciousness, upon the erotic attractions of her hips and her buttocks, thrusting these portions of herself, well padded and beribboned, into the eye of the yearning male. By 1910 the womanly body had begun to look very like a womanly body. Corsets were reasonable, skirts scarcely dragged in the mire and the dust, evening gowns were more *svelte* than swollen. Towards 1912, daring ladies slashed their evening skirts well up to the knee, and set off their attractive slimness with outrageous head-dresses of plumes; and by day the influence of Bakst appeared in effective combinations of barbaric colours; and somehow the conversation whispered over luncheon tables and behind palms suited itself to these desirable changes.

The female wardrobe, with its endless combinations of colours and varieties of material, with its infinite suggestions of new social relationships, offers itself as a convenient short cut into history: but is the history thus arrived at by any chance true history? Is it in the peccadilloes of a 'smart set', in the emancipated whisper in some fronded embrasure of a ducal drawing-room, in the activities of a county tennis court, that the shadowy depths reveal themselves? The du Deffands and de Carrières of an earlier day, the Mrs Asquiths of this Georgian world we are thinking of, are, it is true, an essential decoration, a guide-post even, a clue to mysteries long vanished: and yet, along with the wit, the wardrobe is faded. Where are they now, the silks and the feathers and the fans? How many men have tried to preserve, in the faint lisp of silk as it curtseys, in some exact description of an exotic perfume, in the nods and nuances of a salon, the very accents and distillations and subtleties of a buried past! And how few have succeeded! The light thus thrown shows up only what time itself has discarded as worthless.

> ... *and in one place lay*
> *Feathers and dust, today and yesterday.*

But as we turn over the Georgian wardrobe there, among that reasonable collection of charming stuffs and shapes, appear two preposterous contrivances – a stiff starched collar, very like a man's, and a hard straw hat, very like a man's. And, as we contemplate these unappetizing, these almost incredible phenomena, we realize that the pre-war female wardrobe has, after all, led us straight into life....

The early twentieth century woman would try at times, as accurately and uncomfortably as possible, to make herself look masculine. And when we ask, why did she try to make herself look masculine? – then, upon the heels of that apparently simple inquiry, there crowd such a host of warnings and suggestions, such a bevy of revolutionary causes from such unexplored depths, that we feel something like Odysseus, when he poured a little blood into a trench and discovered that he was faced with the whole assembly of hell. The stiff starched collar and the hard straw hat are, at best, inconsiderable clues, but they are positive; and it is a positive movement we are now to inquire into.

For the Women's Rebellion – the outrageous Suffragette Movement of 1910–14 – was above all things a movement from darkness into light, and from death into life; and, like the Tory Rebellion, its unconscious motive was the rejection of a moribund, a respectable, a smothering security. The reasons for this are too manifold and too obscure to be pressed into a few paragraphs, but there is one which might profitably be selected for examination. Woman, through her new awareness of the possibilities of an abstract goal in life, was, in effect, suddenly aware of her long-neglected masculinity. And the consequences of this were extreme. With a vital energy, the manifestations of which were abandoned and eccentric, she pursued her masculinity first into politics – which seemed the most likely thicket in which to bring it to bay – then into the secret recesses of her own being; and though her quarry was always agile enough to remain one jump ahead of her, her pursuit was to be of incalculable service to the women who came after. At the time, to be sure, it did not seem so. The Suffragettes were always in a minority, and their behaviour, to say the least of it, was neither sensible nor endearing. But if we follow them through all the steps of their peculiar career, we may get some notion of other forces then sweeping through England; until at last we may even catch a glimpse, fleeting but complete, of that new energy which rose like a phoenix from the strange death of the pre-war world and rushed headlong on to the battlefields of Flanders and the blood-stained beaches of Gallipoli.

Beneath the political and economic motives in the disintegration of Liberal England, there lies the psychological motive – the abandonment of security. In the case of the women it was the abandonment of what was, in the worst sense of the word, a *feminine* security. The legacy which their Victorian predecessors had bequeathed them was a purely negative one – the legacy of conscious adaptation to the rôle of Perfect Wife. The Victorian woman was the angel in the house, the Griselda of her pompous day, the helpmeet who conceived children in submission and without desire, the eternal inferior. Her whole career lay in marriage, her security was founded in her husband's ability to provide for her, her ambition satisfied itself in helping him along his path through the world. These were her conscious desires, but could she live up to them?

Unfortunately, she could not. The tyrant of the breakfast table, the bed, and the parlour hearthrug, the crude and insensitive creature who took everything to himself, fame, education, even the unholy pleasures of love – how easy it was to yield to him in the mind and betray him in the spirit! Beneath the idle and artificial wife, below the diligent helpmeet, behind that cunning ambush of blushes and fainting fits – there stood the primitive woman, the biological female. Let the male be deferred to by all means; there was another and more subtle way of reducing him. He could be mothered. What strange visions are conjured up by these innocuous words, what sudden glimpses of an almost savage reality! In the Victorian bed-room and dining-room and parlour there sits, not an amiable wife, but a submissive tyrant, who is more than ready to be browbeaten and put upon so long as her husband remains unconsciously dependent upon her, in his dual rôle of master and child.

In this lamentable separation between the outer and the inner life, the Victorian matron was at least able to satisfy one of her deepest instincts; indeed it is scarcely too much to say that, by subtly undermining his masculinity, she took her revenge upon her domestic oppressor. But the unmarried woman was in no such case. Everything was denied her. Education, business, love – all were impossible. Sometimes a Florence Nightingale would release her stores of masculine energy upon the unspeakable horrors of the hospitals at Scutari or the intolerable stupidities of an antiquated War Office; sometimes a Charlotte Brontë would dip her pen in passion instead of ink and scandalize the world with some scorching revelation of her complicated soul. But how few these women were, and how few their opportunities! When a husband is a woman's career, the woman without a husband is as good as dead. She must colour her drab existence with good works, gossip, hypochondria, and religion, until at last – unused and unwept – she dies. Such are the results of living in a world of men.

The Victorian woman's sense of an impersonal goal – her masculinity – had, on the face of it, been ruined by nearly a century of humility and dependence; yet, in a thousand repressions and resentments and dreams and desires lay the means to restore it again. But how was this to be done? It is one of the seeming paradoxes of life that woman's impersonal goal will ultimately be discovered in that principle of personal relationship, whihc is her highest and most individual contribution to life. And surely it was to personal relationship that the Victorian woman had sacrificed herself. But had she? Had she not rather sacrificed herself to her own security? Had she not assumed that personal relationship depended upon an individual human being outside herself and not upon the principle within herself? Had she not projected her sense of an impersonal goal upon a man, only to bring it back to herself? If this was so, then she had set a vicious circle in motion; and how was the circle to be broken? One thing was clear: by living only in relation to a single man, woman had become separated from her own womanhood, and, by fair means or foul, she must get it back again.

It is doubtful if these considerations occurred to the average pre-war woman, except in terms of an unconscious dissatisfaction. She may have assumed that the process known as emancipation would, by gentle and imperceptible degrees, restore the balance between the sexes: and perhaps, in an ideal world endowed with infinite patience, this is what would have happened. But the world of the soul is neither ideal nor patient, and its vital energies have never allowed themselves to be harnessed by reason. The neglected masculinity of woman refused to wait upon time, and that strange, unlovely, but valuable phenomenon known as the Militant Suffragette Movement was the result of its refusal.

The militant suffragettes did not actually become militant until November 1910; and from then until the war they were always in the minority. This was only to be expected. For all her mistakes – and they were many and fantastic – the militant suffragette lived in the present, and must be enrolled among the makers of history. The process of making history can, in her case, be divided into two distinct stages. At first, her instinct warned her that only by asserting their masculinity could women hope to become women again, and for a time she was willing to make use of a long established argument and demand for women a political equality with men; in other words, she wanted the Vote. But it would be ingenuous to suppose that the suffragette was ultimately concerned with anything so reasonable as the suffrage. What good would the Vote do her, when and if she had it? The arguments in its favour were numerous and convincing, and she had them all at her finger tips: but did they go deep enough? Her instinct assured her that they did not. Gradually she began to draw upon the masculine element within herself, not simply as something which confirms an argument, but rather as a food which sustains and energizes life. And the food, re-enforced by the repressions of a century, was not unnaturally too strong for her. Those high starched collars, those hard straw hats, what are they, after all, but the fugitive and casual symbols of acute psychological dyspepsia?

Beside the discomfort of her undigested masculinity (which made her increasingly arrogant towards men), the woman of the present – the pre-war suffragette – suffered from another and equally formidable affliction. She was haunted. Whether she sat or walked or talked or slept, in public and in private, there crept about her an enervating, a lax, a lamentable atmosphere – the cloudy desires of hundreds of thousands of unmarried women, condemned to do nothing. In this atmosphere of the unlived female life, which invaded – unasked and irresistible – the remotest rooms of her being, she was restless and irritable. Here too, it seemed, were to be discerned the scattered and wasting elements of a great female principle.

How were they to be fused once more? Her answer to this perplexing question was a revolutionary one – she must overthrow that personal security which had kept women lurking for so long behind the coat-tails of their men. To recover her womanhood woman must go out into the wilderness, there to be alone with herself and her sisters. It is the custom among certain primitive tribes for marriageable girls to spend some time in the woman house, to learn the wisdom of women; and it was from some secret yearning to recover the wisdom of women that the homosexual movement first manifested itself, in 1912, among the suffragettes.

This was the second stage in the making of pre-war feminine history. It was achieved in disorder, arrogance, and outrage. It was melodramatic, it was hysterical, it was in a hurry. It possibly deserves every bad epithet but one – it was not perverse. People very frequently damn the sins they have no mind to, whether in sex or literature or politics, by calling them perverse; but perversity, if it means anything at all, means the conscious and deliberate preference of something low before something high, of death before life. And this pre-war lesbianism – which, in any case, was more sensitive than sensual – was without any question a striving towards life.

Naturally enough, these Georgian suffragettes were odious to men, whom they regarded more and more as coarse and inferior creatures; but they were also odious to women. The majority of pre-war women lived in the past, clung to their respectable and moribund security, and dreaded even the limited independence which the Vote would assure them. And perhaps, in their heart of hearts, they knew that they were doomed – to live.

For the revolution was on its way, and the way it took was the way of all revolutions. Its end was a valuable one – the solidarity of women, the recovery of their proper place in the world; its means were violent and dubious. But no revolution has ever taken place without the sudden, the unbridled uprising of long suppressed classes and long ungratified desires; without cruelty and rage: nor is a revolution anything but the savage assault of right instincts upon wrong ideals. The Georgian suffragette was not personally attractive, or noble, or *clairvoyante*. People who make history very seldom are. Providence has bestowed upon them an instinctive response to the unrecognized needs of the human soul, and though this response is often wry and more often ridiculous, life could scarcely progress without it. By 1910 the ideal of personal security through respectability had become putrid: therefore it was necessary that it should die. And to accomplish its death there assembled, crowding up from the depths of the female soul, as uncouth a collection of neglected instincts, hopes, hatreds, and desires, as thorough going a psychological *jacquerie*, as ever came together at any time in human history....

III

Emmeline Pankhurst was a fragile little woman, not more distinguished in her appearance than other pretty little women who have worn well. She was the widow of a Lancashire barrister; and it is recorded of the late Mr Pankhurst that he busied himself with things like the municipal drains and rights for women, at a time when drains and women were supposed, the one to smell and the other to blush unseen. In short, the late Mr Pankhurst was something of a socialist; and Mrs Pankhurst assisted him in all his projects, and held all his theories, and when he died she was inconsolable.

She was not meant to spend the rest of her life as a Lancashire widow. However neat and charming she might look behind a tea-table, when the firelight and the lamplight met and mingled in the beautifully polished silver; however gently her hands would play among the teacups (and Victorian novelists have assured us that a woman's hands are never more lovely than when so engaged); however softly and carefully her voice would exchange, with some casual visitor, the banalities of the day; there was – and who could doubt it who had ever met her? – something restless in the appearance of Mrs Pankhurst. She was by no means resigned to her lot. It may have been her face which betrayed her: those delicate features, chiselled by an ingenious artificer in a momentary absence of inspiration, would suddenly grow tense; the thin nostrils would contract; and in the pleasant eyes there would flare, swift and inconsequential, a thin flame; and any little thing might bring about this transformation. People would leave her comfortable fireside with a distinct impression that they would not care to have Mrs Pankhurst for an enemy. And they were right.

One cause her husband had bequeathed her which seemed particularly suited to her type of mind. The niceties of municipal politics, the procrastinations of Fabian reform – these matters were not essentially of interest to Mrs Pankhurst. She felt that they could get along very well without her; that they required, above all, a measure of self-abnegation: a woman could do valuable work in these fields, but most of it would have to be done patiently, intelligently, and behind the scene. And it is not known of Mrs Pankhurst that she ever proposed to spend her widowhood behind any scene, if there was the slightest chance of getting in front of it.

But the cause of Woman's Suffrage – here at least she could pursue, with unflagging diligence, her late husband's work. Women had already obtained, or were clearly destined to obtain, all the minor recognitions that a political democracy can afford; only one reward, but that the most vital and the most obstinately contested, was still denied them – the Vote. To the Vote, therefore, Mrs Pankhurst offered her life. Those thin nostrils had scented battle from afar; those pleasant eyes would suddenly flame with prophetic vision; and the fragile hands, clenching themselves in meditative moments, would seem already to be clasping the proud banner, the oriflamme, which they and they alone should bear before the advancing hordes of dedicated women.

'One fight more,' as Florence Nightingale said to Sidney Herbert, 'the best and the last.' But could Mrs Pankhurst be its leader? At times, she doubted it. At times she was overwhelmed with the dismal fact, but none the less an important fact in the late 1890s and early 1900s, that she was only the widow of a Manchester lawyer, with little money and no connections. A small group of women, meeting in her house in 1903, to form the Women's Social and Political Union, did, in fact, so work on the feelings of one MP that a private member's Bill, proposing woman's suffrage, actually reached the floor of the House, where it was drowned with laughter: and Mrs Pankhurst and her friends, arrived from Manchester for the occasion, gathered in a protesting huddle around the statue of Richard I (who would hardly have been in sympathy with them), and were patiently 'moved on' by the police. And again, in 1906, Mrs Pankhurst was with difficulty restrained by her two daughters from making a scene in the House of Commons itself. 'You have baulked me,' she wept, 'both of you! I thought there would have been one little niche in the temple of fame for me!'

She underestimated herself; she was not to be baulked of her niche. But how could it be reached? There were other women's suffrage associations; the Conservative women had one; and Mrs Fawcett, the widow of a man high in Liberal circles, had another: and both were in possession of something very much to be desired, social prestige. Mrs Pankhurst had none; and the more she realized that, allied with these women, she would always be in the background, the more clearly it dawned upon her that they were wrong. They seemed to expect that the Vote would be given them out of a kind of political chivalry; and that, once in their possession, it would be used simply to help the men. They seemed to think of politics as if it were an enlargement of the Home, where the womanly hand might gently restrain man from making mistakes in things he did not understand – such as social service, remedies for prostitution, and the treatment of the unmarried mother – but would refrain from him in all matters of national importance. This was all very well; but Mrs Pankhurst did not think it was nearly good enough. If you approached the men in a ladylike and supplicatory manner (and in such a tactical scheme she knew that she herself could only take a very secondary place) they would never give you what you wanted, they would put you off for ever. And she was quite right. For it is one of the peculiarities of human living that it often takes ambition and self-interest to arrive at the truth.

For a while the W S P U did not dissociate itself from the movement as a whole; but another very obvious element in human living is the fact that a powerful personality, an indomitable will, must always make itself felt. Between 1903 and 1910, the women's suffrage cause made considerable progress; and in the agitated manner of its progress one can discern the influence, however obscure, of the mind of the Manchester widow. At first, the women's processions, with their wavering banners, their long skirts, and shy faces, were observed with indulgence and laughter. There was a famous story of how, one day, as one of these processions passed through the streets of a midland town, two young men, of somewhat effeminate appearance, offered to carry one of the banners;

and those in the procession could not help wondering why, thereafter, the laughter which greeted them was far louder than before. At last they realized what the joke was about. The banner which the two young men supported – with difficulty, for it was large and heavy – bore this legend – MEN HAVE VOTES, WHY CAN'T WE?

But the mood was not long to remain gentle. Slowly it began to dawn upon England that the women really meant business; slowly, and with great resentment, the word 'suffragist' changed to the word 'suffragette'. Cabinet Ministers appeared on political platforms with a wary look; at any moment, and in the very middle of their speech, they might be heckled by some young woman, who would have to be dragged out in scenes of great disorder, not to say impropriety – for portions of her clothing were frequently left behind in the struggle. Very soon, the ticket-holders for more important meetings were carefully examined; and all suspicious women were turned away: but, with perverse ingenuity, the creatures would disguise the slimmest among them as messenger boys, or the most imposing as dowagers; and, somehow or another, if they intended to heckle a Minister, heckle him they did. Rather melancholy little pickets would linger in Downing Street, with little banners, which they waved at the Prime Minister. Sittings of the House were disturbed by eldritch screams from the Ladies' Gallery. Mottoes were chalked on pavements. In Hyde Park, in 1908, a gathering of two hundred and fifty thousand women listened to the preaching of the cause from various platforms. It seemed as if – in that spiritual seraglio to which the Victorian woman, married and unmarried, had been condemned – eager hands were already picking at the locks: and if the gates were ever thrown open, the guards overwhelmed – what would come out? Decent men and women shuddered at the thought. But one thing was certain: as the years advanced, and the suffragettes grew more obstinate and temperamental, every threatening movement, every picket, every banner, every immodest assault upon tradition and propriety of these 'petticoated, long-stockinged, corseted females,' led back at last, through all the labyrinth of opinions, whimsies, and organizations, directly to Mrs Pankhurst and the WSPU.

IV

It is almost impossible to write the story of the Woman's Rebellion without admitting certain elements of brutal comedy. An Aristophanes alone could do it justice. From the spectacle of women attacking men there rises, even in this day, an outrageous, an unprincipled laughter. And when a scene as ordinary as English politics is suddenly disturbed with the swish of long skirts, the violent assault of feathered hats, the impenetrable, advancing phalanx of corseted bosoms – when, around the smoking ruins of some house or church, there is discovered the dread evidence of a few hairpins or a feminine galosh – then the amazing, the ludicrous appearance of the whole thing is almost irresistible.

And its chief actors – say what you please, they are not very lovable. You are forced to ascribe to Mrs Pankhurst and her daughter Christabel certain motives of self-interest, certain moments of exhibitionism, which do not especially commend themselves. They and their associates were courageous enough; some of them stood more physical torture than a woman should be able to bear: but then, as the scene unrolls itself and their sufferings increase, how can one avoid the thought that they sought these sufferings with an enraptured, a positively unhealthy pleasure? They chose to be martyrs; and the world has never loved a martyr. (A reasonable number of traitors, poisoners, thieves, and debauchees have been assisted from this life quite cleanly and quickly with a rope or an axe: for the martyr has been reserved, at least in memory, the shower of arrows, the lions, the flaying, and the boiling oil. And perhaps the reason is that the martyr positively demands that his end shall be made as bitter as possible; as though he thought that the last, protracted quiver of his tortured nerves were adding an extra polish to his crown in heaven, or a final flourish to his footnote in the history books.)

It is difficult to look behind the appearance for the intention; and even more difficult to admit that the intention, once found, is valuable and vital. But that is the truth. Mrs Pankhurst, her daughters, and her colleagues – for all their extravagances – are among the makers of history; they were fighting their way out of death into life; and what they did had to be done. They submitted to the outrageous handling of policemen and toughs as early Christians once submitted to the lions. It is true that, if we were to meet some of those early Christians today, we should not choose them for a quiet drink in the bar or a cosy talk over the fireside. They were doubtless an unlikely collection of human beings. But the state of Roman civilization made them essential, and by their deaths they saved the world from heaven alone knows what moral ruin. The suffragettes were, in their way, equally unlikely and un-companionable; yet they assisted woman no little way towards the re-discovery of the place which was really hers in the world. Their methods were bad and mistaken; but their ultimate motives shine, as a lamp shines through a fog. And, before they are subjected to the unkindly processes of narrative, one would like to pause here and do them honour.

V

The first characteristic scene in the Woman's Rebellion does not open until November 1910. Mrs Pankhurst, now the acknowledged leader of the militant suffrage movement, had agreed that, with a new king on the throne, it would be more seemly for the women to declare an armistice. But she was also determined that the WSPU should be more downright in its methods; for experience had taught her that nothing short of a profound and prolonged shock would ever persuade Mr Asquith's Government to give women the Vote.

The Government – uneasily aware that Mrs Pankhurst's was one of those causes which Liberalism ought to uphold – had tried to rid itself of responsibility by declaring that women's suffrage was not a party measure. But when a highly controversial question is removed from party politics, the chances are that it will never get anywhere; and Mrs Pankhurst, with her former knowledge of the vagaries and procrastinations of municipal politics, had a shrewd suspicion that Mr Asquith, that consummate parliamentarian, never *intended* woman's suffrage to get anywhere.

As early as February 1910, the Government had shown some disposition to yield, and, for at least a short while, Mrs Pankhurst thought that Mr Asquith might – just *might*, she had no reason to suppose more – have come over to her way of thinking. The WSPU, if it had any political affiliations, was a Labour movement, but a number of Liberal women were known to be in sympathy with it, and a wise Prime Minister would not want to offend them. As his part in the truce, Mr Asquith professed himself ready to smile upon what was known as the Conciliation Bill, which would enfranchise about a million women: to be specific, women owners of business premises paying £10 a year rental and upwards, and women householders; and when the Bill came up for its first reading on 12th July, it was passed by 299 to 189.

But that, in effect, was as far as the Bill ever got. Now Mrs Pankhurst was to have all her suspicions justified; now, moving with some finesse but not too delicately, the Ministerial hand played havoc with all her aspirations. The question at issue seemed to be a very simple one: should the Bill go to a Grand Committee of the House, or to a Committee of the whole House; in the first event, a special Committee would deal with it promptly and separately while the Commons transacted their usual business; in the second, special facilities from the Government would be needed to bring it safely through the Committee stage. The second reading was secured after an interesting debate, in which Mr F. E. Smith appeared as the women's most obdurate opponent; but when a second division was taken, as to which Committee should see the Bill on to its third reading, Mr Asquith let it be known that he wished all franchise bills to go to a Committee of the whole House; and a number of the Bill's sincerest supporters agreeing with him (whether from carelessness or loyalty), to a Committee of the whole House the Bill went, by a vote of 320 to 175.

The Bill had been exiled into a very wilderness; and Mr Asquith's was the hand which had sent it there. For a day or two, Mrs Pankhurst did not comprehend the enormity of what had been done to her; but at last she realized that the Bill would never reach its third reading unless the Cabinet agreed to give it facilities. And then she realized, too, that facilities would never be given. The treachery of the Government, the stupidity of her own supporters in the Commons – how could these things be borne? For a while she did nothing; the truce should be kept; she could be patient. But when Parliament re-assembled in November, and if nothing were done – then they should see what it was to thwart her!

But November found Mr Asquith in the midst of his battle with the Lords, with an election not a month away; and everything pointed to the melancholy truth that he had not the slightest thought of doing anything for the women. It had been foolish, really, to expect anything of him; his wife, who had supported him loyally all the way to Number 10, Downing Street, was naturally an ardent anti-suffragette. And so the WSPU, not bothering to wait for the inevitable, matured its plans, and on 18th November, when Parliament re-opened, it was ready for Mr Asquith.

Friday, 18th November, has gone down into suffragette history as 'Black Friday'. That afternoon, while Mr Asquith was telling the Commons that he had advised the Crown to order a dissolution, and that government business (in which no mention was made of women's suffrage) would take precedence at all the few sittings which were left – small bands of women began moving from the WSPU headquarters at

Caxton Hall. They carried little purple bannerettes, bearing such legends as 'Asquith Has Vetoed the Bill', 'Where There's a Bill, There's a Way', 'Women's Will Beats Asquith's Won't'; and they were headed, one and all, towards Parliament Square.

In Parliament Square, the police were assembled in great numbers. They had their instructions. Women were not to be arrested, except for extreme provocation, but they *were* to be kept away from the Houses of Parliament. In these simple tactics may be discerned the ingenious mind of Mr Churchill, who then presided at the Home Office and who had been, at one time, loud in his support of the suffragettes. His voice had sensibly diminished in the last year, until the WSPU was inclined to reckon him among the more subtle of its enemies; and certainly no enemy could have devised a more unspeakable ordeal than was implicit in the instructions of Mr Churchill to the police.

As the women advanced into Parliament Square, the police pushed them back; gently at first, and with laughter. But the skirted warriors were not so easily repulsed; their method was simply to push, with gloved hands, against the constabulary chest; and push they did, returning to the fray over and over again. The laughter of the crowd, and it was large, took on a coarser note; the police grew flushed and angry. Women should not behave in this unnatural way; and ladies (surely most of their tormentors were ladies) . . . it was inconceivable that *they* should so far forget themselves. Suddenly the atmosphere changed; and Jason and his argonauts could not have warded off the Harpies with more rage and despair than did those policemen in Parliament Square.

Bannerettes were torn and trampled; women were struck with fists and knees, knocked down, dragged up, hurled from hand to hand, and sent reeling back, bruised and bleeding, into the arms of the crowd. They were no longer demonstrators; they were monsters, their presence was unendurable. They were pummelled and they were pinched, their thumbs were forced back, their arms twisted, their breasts gripped, their faces rubbed against the palings: and this went on for nearly six hours.

The crowd, with instinctive sympathy for a loser, grew more in favour of the women as the dreary and indecent conflict dragged on, hour after hour; though, to be sure, only one onlooker seems to have dared to interfere with the police. But there was a certain number of tough characters who did not choose to let this opportunity slip, and some suffragettes were dragged away and miserably ill-treated; indeed, one woman is said to have died, a year later, as the result of having been indecently assaulted in a side street. The battle ended at last by lamplight. The Square was cleared. By the wall of the House of Lords, a number of anxious women kneeled around Miss Ada Wright, who had been knocked down a dozen times in succession, and was in a very bad way. A few torn bannerettes, a trampled hat or two, some fragments of clothing, remained on the field of battle until next morning – singular trophies of the Government's victory.

But was it a victory? Mrs Pankhurst, who had been admitted to the House of Commons in the afternoon, stayed for a while in the Prime Minister's room; but Mr Asquith did not appear. He had left the House. On Lord Castlereagh's moving an amendment, however, that the Conciliation Bill should be considered as part of the Government's business, he came hurrying back to his seat to ask that the amendment should not be pressed. But the temper of the House was against him. Member after member arose to beg him to receive the women's deputation, and put an end to the disgraceful scenes which were going on outside; and at last they dragged from him a promise that he would make a statement next Tuesday. As for Mrs Pankhurst, waiting miserably by the Strangers' Entrance, he made no attempt to see her.

In this he made his usual mistake; as he underestimated Sir Edward Carson and the Orangemen, so also he underestimated Mrs Pankhurst and the WSPU. He was very clement: the police had, in the end and in spite of Mr Churchill's strategy, arrested 115 women and 4 men and almost all of these were released. He was also very evasive. His Tuesday statement promised that the Government would provide facilities for the Bill 'in the next Parliament'; but the Bill must be framed on a democratic basis and admit of free amendment. Perhaps he thought that the women could be deceived for ever; that they would not see that 'the next Parliament' by no means implied the next *Session*, nor realize how little chance a women's suffrage Bill 'on a democratic basis' had of passing through both Houses without drastic and destructive amendments. But if he thought so, he was grievously mistaken: eager eyes searched every phrase of his illusory statement; it was pronounced unsatisfactory; and once again the WSPU prepared for action.

On the next morning, Mrs Pankhurst led a deputation to Downing Street; a deputation or an army – the words were soon to be synonymous. The police were caught unawares, and only a thin line of them, hastily summoned, barred the street's entrance. The Inspector attempted to parley: 'Push forward,' shouted Sylvia Pankhurst, standing on the roof of her taxi, and: 'Shove along, girls,' said Mrs Haverfield – a lady who had done rescue-work among disabled horses in the South African War, and who habitually wore a hunting stock and a small black riding hat. The ladies pushed forward, the police gave way, and Downing Street suddenly blossomed with tense faces and purple bannerettes.

At this precise moment, some malign fate prompted Mr Asquith to leave his house, and he was with difficulty rescued by the police – now reinforced by a mounted detachment – and hustled into a taxi, through the departing window of which an enraged female thrust her fist. Mr Augustine Birrell also chose this moment to wander on to the scene; but he was not so fortunate. Leaping in natural alarm for a taxi, he fell heavily and sprained his ankle.

When the street was cleared at last and with difficulty, for Mrs Pankhurst and her following put up a spirited fight, who should make *his* appearance but the Home Secretary! Only one suffragette remained, leaning in utter exhaustion against a wall. Mr Churchill, as usual, was unable to resist the dramatic gesture. He beckoned a policeman. 'Drive that woman away,' he said; though he knew her perfectly well to be a Mrs Cobden-Sanderson, his hostess on several occasions, and an intimate friend of his wife's family. The story went around London and made a bad impression, and a few days later, when the Home Secretary was travelling by rail from London to Bradford, a young man named Franklin very nearly got into his compartment with a horse-whip, and received six weeks' imprisonment for his pains.

The total number of arrests, from 'Black Friday' onwards, was now 280. Seventy-five women were actually convicted, among them Mrs Haverfield – whose offence was leading police horses out of their ranks in the course of what had come to be known as the 'Battle of Downing Street'.

And then peace descended again. The Liberals had been returned to power, the battle with the Lords had reached its final stage, and Mr Asquith appeared to be in a receptive mood. It was freely rumoured that when the Conciliation Bill, now re-drafted to exclude the £10 occupiers' clause, was introduced once more on 5th May, 1911, the Government would do nothing to block its passage. On census night – 2nd April – a large number of women refused to stay at home to receive the census officials, and spent their time in the streets or in one of the four all-night entertainments which the Suffrage Societies had got up for them; but apart from this mild remonstrance the suffragettes were quiet. On 5th May, the Bill passed its first reading by 255 to 88. Petitions in its favour poured in upon the Prime Minister; the Lord Mayor of Dublin, exercising an ancient privilege, appeared at the Bar of the House preceded by his Mace and his two-handed Sword, and put in a plea for women's suffrage; an ambiguous statement of Mr Lloyd George's was, on the Earl of Lytton's request, cleared up by Mr Asquith, who said: 'Government members are unanimous in their determination to give effect, not only in the letter but in the spirit, to the promise in regard to facilities.' What more could anybody want? The women had now become – as *The Nation* expressed it – 'in all but legal formality voters and citizens.'

Even the WSPU was content to wait until the Session of 1912 for the second reading of the Conciliation Bill. But then the Coronation ceremonies took place, and suddenly the suspicion grew that perhaps this shining truce between the women and the Government had been engineered for the simple purpose of preventing them from rioting until the King had been safely crowned. Mr Lloyd George was making a number of vague and disquieting remarks, and though the Prime Minister repeated his promises all over again, the WSPU became very uneasy. Nevertheless, it kept its part of the bargain; there were no demonstrations.

The year had almost passed. And then, quite without warning, the unrepentant Mr Asquith moved again. On 7th November, he received a deputation from an extremely shadowy organization known as the People's Suffrage Federation, which advocated equal suffrage for all adults, men and women alike; and to this deputation he declared that the Government, while abiding by its promises to expedite the Conciliation Bill, intended to produce a Franchise Bill of its own. This Bill, which had been held back since 1908, would do away with all existing suffrage qualifications, but it would apply to males only.

There was only one meaning to this. Nobody wanted a Male Suffrage Bill; but, if ever it were introduced, it would make a Female Suffrage Bill impossible. If a female suffrage amendment were tacked on to the Male Suffrage – or Reform – Bill, that would be nothing less than universal suffrage, with women in the majority of a million; and the House would not stand for that. Nor, on the other hand, could it reasonably accept a Bill which offered manhood suffrage for men, and then pass another one which offered the vote to women on a property qualification. The truth was out at last, so it seemed to the leaders of the WSPU.

From the moment that he had refused to see Mrs Pankhurst in the House on 'Black Friday', Mr Asquith had been secretly devising some means to thwart them.

A deputation composed of all the women's suffrage organizations waited on him the next day, but its members were already hopelessly divided. Mrs Pethick Lawrence and Miss Christabel Pankhurst of the WSPU declared that the Conciliation Bill was now worthless, and that they wanted an equal rights measure or nothing; Mrs Despard of the Freedom League seemed inclined to agree with them; Mrs Fawcett still preferred the Conciliation Bill; and Lady Betty Balfour and the Countess of Selborne were clearly of the opinion that anything more than the Conciliation Bill would be quite improper. Nothing could have pleased Mr Asquith more than the thought that these unpredictable opponents of his were now at odds among themselves, and he hastened to press home his advantage. How unfortunate it was, he said, that neither Party could take the matter up officially! But if a majority in the House approved either of an amendment to the Reform Bill or of the Conciliation Bill, he would keep his promise, he would not stand in the women's way.

Yet the notion that, somehow or other – though Mr Asquith himself, of course, could not understand how people could be so suspicious – an unasked Reform Bill had effectually ruined a widely demanded Women's Suffrage Bill, spread through the country. The Prime Minister had not broken his promises; he had merely seen to it that his promises would never have to be kept. 'For a naked, avowed plan of gerrymandering,' wrote the *Saturday Review*, 'no Government surely ever did beat this one.' Mrs Pankhurst, who was in America, was more explicit. 'Protest imperative,' she cabled.

The truce was over. The WSPU had given Mr Asquith every chance, and the slippery man had consistently evaded and out-guessed them. It was impossible to pit one's wits against England's greatest parliamentarian; especially when, with his admittedly high sense of personal honour, he always saw to it that it was Parliament which broke Mr Asquith's word, and not Mr Asquith himself. What could one do with such a contradictory creature? And as for Mr Lloyd George, he was even worse.

The day after the deputation (which he had helped Mr Asquith receive – 'scowling', so Sylvia Pankhurst said) he promised to assist the suffragettes; to move a Women's Suffrage amendment to the Reform

Bill; to advocate it 'inside and outside the House of Commons by speech and by influence'. But the suffragettes had grown wary. If Mr George were sincere, they argued, he would take the matter up in Cabinet, he would force it through there as a majority measure. What good would his speeches and his influence do, if they were to be neutralized by the speeches and the influence of other Cabinet Ministers? No, Mr George was simply helping Mr Asquith; or perhaps – how could you tell with such a man? – he was marking time, in the hopes that one day when the Suffrage Movement had grown powerful enough it would help him unseat Mr Asquith. In either case, the WSPU did not see itself as something which could be gulled perpetually. It was utterly tired of playing politics; the other women might do as they pleased, but for the WSPU all that was left was direct action.

On Tuesday, 21st November, Mrs Pethick Lawrence led another raid, the members of which, concealing stones and hammers in their bags, successfully shattered windows in the Home Office, the War Office, the Foreign Office, the Board of Education, the Board of Trade, the Treasury, Somerset House, the National Liberal Club, several post offices, the Old Banqueting Hall, the London and South-Western Bank, and the houses of Lord Haldane and Mr John Burns. Confronted with this new menace, the police acted as drastically as they could: 223 women were arrested, and 150 sent to prison for periods varying from five days to one month.

But prison, it seemed, was just what the suffragettes most desired. Motor cars were now driven to quiet country lanes where, under the cover of dusk, ladies could replenish their store of flints; and Sylvia Pankhurst remembers taking nervous recruits on reconnaissance parties through London, when she would point out likely windows....

The women were now clearly divided into militants and non-militants; and from the militants the country's sympathy ebbed swiftly away. Mr Asquith felt that his time had come. On 14th December, he told a deputation of the National League for Opposing Women's Suffrage that to grant votes for women would be a 'political mistake of a very disastrous kind'. He seemed to assume that the trouble was now almost over. But the WSPU did not see eye to eye with him. The next day a young woman called Emily Wilding Davison was arrested in Parliament Street; she held in her hand a piece of linen, saturated with paraffin and well alight, which she was trying to thrust down the pillar box of the Parliament Street Post Office.

VI

It may, indeed, be said that – from the moment Miss Davison was discovered with her paraffin-soaked rag and her matches beside the Parliament Street Post Office – the curious and irrational movement known as *militancy* really began. And it is by no means inappropriate that Miss Davison's should have been the hand which set it in motion. For the picture of Miss Davison which history has bequeathed us, fragmentary as it is and veiled in the mists of her subsequent martyrdom, is the picture of a very unbalanced girl. Among other things, she was much obsessed with the idea of death's being the greatest gift she could offer to the cause; but death, she discovered, was more easily sought than found. She had tried hunger striking in a Manchester prison as early as 1909, and the authorities had countered with that peculiarly odious form of torture known as 'forcible feeding'; whereupon Miss Davison barricaded herself into her cell, and clung weakly to her bed while a hose, thrust through the window-bars, deluged her with water until the cell floor was six inches deep in it. The memory of this ordeal did nothing to decrease her obsession. She was always in a fit either of gaiety or of despondency, and would do impulsive and sensational things (such as writing to the press in advance and warning it of her intention to attack the pillar box) entirely on her own initiative.

Two years afterwards her colleagues spoke with affection of her slight, awkward figure, with its too-long arms, and her narrow head crowned with red hair; and recalled how elusive and whimsical her green eyes were; and retrieved, from their memory of her quizzical thin lips, some resemblance to the mocking smile of Mona Lisa. But that was after she had died beneath the hoofs of the King's horse at Epsom. In 1911, she was suspected of trying to push herself too eagerly into the limelight, and of having an independent mind. And Miss Christabel Pankhurst – though she might have forgiven Miss Davison's nervous impetuosity, and condoned Miss Davison's rather uncomfortable desire for death – never had much use for an independent mind. By 1911, Miss Christabel was pretty convinced that suffragettes must only be impetuous on the word of command; and if they wanted to die – why, they would have to wait for the word of command before they did that, too. And the word of command, she was beginning to be certain, could only come from her or from her mother.

For if Emily Davison, so impulsive, so capricious, and so hysterical, represents – with something more than adequacy – the spirit of the militant rank and file, yet it is only the rank and file which she represents. She was merely one of those many ardent and irrational females whose long skirts, scuttling across Georgian history, invaded the most sacred places and disturbed the most respectable scenes; and what would these sheep have done without a shepherd, in what peculiar mountains would they have strayed, or perished, unremembered, in what ravines? Indeed, it is not too much to suppose that, without a powerful leader, they might not have been militants at all; they might have contented themselves with the gospel of Mr Wells and *Anne Veronica*, or strayed into the Fabian fold of Mrs Sidney Webb, or swooned among the candles and the incense of Mr Compton Mackenzie's Anglo-Catholic Church. But a powerful leader they had, and it was not so much Emmeline Pankhurst, as Emmeline Pankhurst's daughter Christabel.

By 1911, the cause of militant suffrage seems to have constellated itself around the attractive figure of this powerful young lady. The reasons for her supremacy are not very easy to state. She had none of her mother's fire, and none of her mother's infinitely moving oratory; but when she stood on a platform there was something in the smile on her broad and rosy face which, with its slanting olive-green eyes and high cheekbones, had a curiously Chinese look, something in the quick turn of her head on its slender neck, something in the graceful carriage of her body, something, above all, in the way in which she held her hands before her, inaudibly clapping them together, which inevitably captured, and sometimes converted, the most obdurate enemy. And yet, when those rather too supple lips smiled happily at an insistent heckler, and suddenly threw back the unanswerable retort, you knew – and even as you knew wondered how you could think it of so pleasant a creature – that there was a ruthless and intractable spirit behind this friendly appearance.

The secret of Miss Christabel's personality, that inexplicable combination of feminine caprice and masculine steel, became, as the months went on, the secret of the W S P U. It was not merely her strength which gave it sinews for the struggle; it was her private predilections which determined the course of its history. For Miss Christabel was the first to discover that Private Members were of very little use to the Cause, when the Cause appealed to Parliament. Some of these sympathetic M P's might, it is true, be respectable Conservatives; but what secretly irritated

Miss Christabel was the thought that, of all parties in the Commons, it was the Labour Party which was most friendly to the suffragette. Men like Keir Hardie and George Lansbury could be very useful at times; but the fact remained that they were men of the people, and that under their vulgar aegis the WSPU had first pushed itself into prominence. When she said, in the course of a speech at Queen's Hall, 'The Private Member is a rudimentary organ, like the buttons in the middle of a tail-coat's back,' she was doubtlessly stating a political truth; yet one cannot help thinking that those words were also aimed, and with a more profound conviction, straight at Mr Keir Hardie's peculiar clothes and the loud cockney accent of Mr George Lansbury.

What had happened, her sister Sylvia used to wonder, to those republican sentiments which Christabel had once cherished? The answer might be that it is difficult to cherish such sentiments when one can number among one's colleagues a Lady Constance Lytton, or can count on the sympathy of a Princesse de Polignac: for Miss Christabel had certainly begun to move in more exalted circles than would have been hers had she stayed in Manchester. But this is really only half the answer. The solidarity of women is possibly enhanced if there is blue blood in its composition, but – even without this desirable addition – it was the inevitable dream of a nature like Christabel Pankhurst's; and there was something altogether offensive to this growing solidarity – or so it must have seemed – in depending upon the uncertain help of individual MP's. And, then, with a nature like Christabel Pankhurst's, in which fastidiousness and snobbery were so oddly mingled, and which, for all its ability, was so preyed upon by delusions of grandeur, the thought that the most active and genuine of these parliamentary sympathizers represented the working classes was an added burden. All men, Miss Christabel was beginning to think, were coarse; but there was no escaping the fact that some of them were coarser than others.

And so the WSPU ceased to interest itself in the delicate, complicated, and patient game of working up a non-partisan majority in the Commons. Christabel Pankhurst had touched some profound instinct in every one of its members. The women must get together, they must fight shoulder to shoulder against the enemy; and what enemy was worthier, what body – once overthrown – would make a finer trophy, than that elusive and stubborn entity, the Liberal Cabinet? It was the Government they must aim at, and the Government was clearly most vulnerable on the question of property: property, therefore, must be threatened. 'The argument of the broken window pane,' Mrs Pankhurst declared, at a dinner given to released prisoners on 16th February, 1912, 'is the most valuable argument in modern politics.' And at this peculiar effort of feminine reasoning, the authorities groaned in spirit, thinking of London's infinite miles of valuable plate glass.

And well might they groan! At 4 p.m. on the afternoon of 1st March, a meeting at Scotland Yard deliberated on the best methods of protecting shopkeepers from the suffragettes, and at 4 p.m. on the same afternoon, little groups of women, expensively dressed and carrying large but fashionable bags, drifted with perfect nonchalance into the West End. Piccadilly and the Haymarket first resounded with the smashing of glass; thither rushed police and pedestrians, and women with hammers in their hands (flints, it had been discovered, were inclined to bounce off the best plate glass) were the centre of little groups, which accompanied them, in considerable excitement, all the way to the police station. But scarcely had the last offender been bundled safely inside, when, once again, the sound of ruined glass splintered the evening air. This time it was Regent Street and the Strand which suffered. The police hurried off to these new scenes of destruction, and no sooner had they rounded up the culprits than the windows of Oxford Circus and Bond Street crashed in their ears. Upon that crowded and brilliantly lighted quarter there descended a rattling darkness, as shutters were fitted and iron curtains came down on the run. Tall commissionaires peered out into the streets, gazing, with an angry but wincing eye, upon any unaccompanied female, if she happened to carry a bag or a parcel. But all these precautions were in vain. The tactic of ruining in relays worked perfectly and the ordered destruction went on until half-past six. Lyons and Appenrodt's, the great shipping firms in Cockspur Street, Cook's, the Kodak Company, Swan and Edgar, Marshall and Snelgrove, Jay's, Liberty's, Fuller's, Swears and Wells, Hope Brothers, the Carrara Marble Works – these, and other famous businesses, were visited by the relentless hammer, until the damage had mounted into thousands of pounds.

Meanwhile the indomitable Mrs Pankhurst had driven off in a taxi to Downing Street, where, at half-past five exactly, she and two colleagues succeeded in throwing four stones through the Prime Minister's windows, and disappeared, hustled but triumphant, within the portals of Cannon Row police station.

But was this to be all? The police thought not. Mrs Pankhurst was locked up, it was true; but Miss Christabel was still at large, and a great demonstration in Parliament Square had been threatened for 4th March. Early that morning, the British Museum and all the great picture galleries in central London were closed, the shops in Trafalgar Square were boarded up, and by nightfall as many as three thousand policemen were converging on Parliament Square, Whitehall, and the adjoining streets. There, with a vast assembly of onlookers, they waited and waited in vain. They had been out-manoeuvred and they knew it; the damage had already been done. For, that morning, as many as a hundred women had strolled singly up unguarded and glassy Knightsbridge, wrecking every window they passed; and almost all of them had escaped. As a result of these two raids about two hundred women went through the magistrates' courts, receiving sentences which ranged from seven days to eight months; and the next issue of *Votes for Women* came out so strictly censored that occasionally only the headlines were left; and phrases like HISTORY TEACHES and A CHALLENGE!, staring above blank spaces, spoke with what seemed – and still seems – a peculiar eloquence. . . .

When Mrs Pankhurst, Mrs Tuke, and Mr and Mrs Pethick Lawrence, who were considered the ringleaders, appeared before the Bow Street magistrate on 14th March, the proceedings, for the last time perhaps, were purely comic. Mr Archibald Bodkin – who, so his victims thought, looked really very like an egg – was the prosecutor, and he attempted to prove, in a resonant but humourless voice, that the WSPU was an underground organization of the most insidious kind. He quoted the suffragette code book, with the aid of which all telegrams and private communications were made, and with profound solemnity declared that even Cabinet Ministers were included, being 'designated by the name, sometimes of trees, but I am also bound to say of the commonest weeds as well'. (Laughter.) 'There is one called Pansy; another one – more complimentary – Roses, another Violets, and so on.' Every suffragette leader, every public building had its code letter, and he read out a telegram which had been found in the suffragette files. 'Silk, thistle, pansy, duck, wool, EQ.' For the benefit of the court, he would translate it. 'Will you aid protest Asquith's public meeting tomorrow evening but don't get arrested unless success depends upon it. Christabel Pankhurst. Clement's Inn.' (Laughter.)

But Christabel Pankhurst was no longer at Clement's Inn. On 5th March, substituting a close pink hat for the floppy one she usually wore, she fled to Paris, where she lived as Miss Amy Johnson, while the police combed London for her, and followed, with obliging perseverance, the false trails which feminine ingenuity laid for them. Miss Christabel's motives were presumably clear enough; a warrant for her arrest had been issued; and, with the Lawrences and Mrs Pankhurst already in the hands of the law, it was essential for one leader, at least, to be entirely free. But as one thinks of that young lady, with her strangely Chinese look, drifting gracefully through the Parisian spring; or writing her manifestoes and dictating her strategy while the foreign evening, scented and insolent, peers in at her window – what different ideas, unbidden but inevitable, crowd into one's head! Was it not, perhaps, even more essential for this militant movement, so rapturous and so irrational, to have its idol – a goddess who, with perpetual care, applauded from her remote and inaccessible shrine the labour and agony of her votaries? And was it not in this light that Miss Christabel saw herself?

But she was not altogether inaccessible. Close friends, thrilled with devotion and conspiracy, might creep over from time to time; and a regular go-between, a sort of Queen's Messenger, had to be found. And who else could be chosen for this exacting task but Miss Annie Kenney? Miss Kenney, it was true, never quite accustomed herself to the peculiar motion of Channel boats, but she was so enthusiastic, so faithful, so obedient. And well she might be. Only a few years before she had been condemned, supposedly forever, to the grinding monotony of a Lancashire mill town; but the Pankhursts and the Suffrage Movement had rescued her from that. From a mill-girl to a militant . . . it was very like the story of Cinderella, with Mrs Pankhurst for fairy godmother, and for Prince Charming . . .? Shortcomings Miss Kenney had, intellectually, but nobody ever accused her of ingratitude or indolence. Was somebody needed to dress up as a messenger boy, or creep, by heaven knows what cobwebbed ways, among the pipes of some Town Hall organ, Miss Kenney sprang to obey. And now, as the Channel steamer docked at Calais or Boulogne, you might see a little widow come down the gang-plank, shrouded in heavy black, and obviously still suffering from the effects of sea-sickness. She was clearly of a nervous temperament, poor thing; her thin and curiously knotted hands would tear at her gloves as she dragged them on. But if you could peer behind the black veil, you would catch a glimpse of golden hair, of slightly protruding blue eyes, and a mouth perpetually half open. Nerves or no nerves, sickness or no sickness, Miss Annie Kenney was on her way.

She remembered with peculiar distinctness her first visit to Paris. Christabel Pankhurst was staying at the Princesse de Polignac's house, and Miss Kenney, still in her widow's weeds, was ushered into the largest library she had ever seen – 'I felt so tiny!' she wrote in her memoirs – to wait there until her chief came back from an afternoon's walk. And she fell asleep at last – whether from weariness, or because she could not quite get the drift of what she was reading – over a translation of Sappho's poems, bound in cherry-coloured leather.

VII

The Bow Street magistrate committed Mrs Pankhurst and the Pethick Lawrences for trial at the Old Bailey, on the charge of 'conspiring to incite certain persons to commit malicious damage to property'; and the trial was postponed until 15th May, because of Mrs Pankhurst's health.

Politicians and the public in general considered that the militants had done their cause no good at all by these unseemly outbreaks. See what happened to the Conciliation Bill when that unlucky piece of legislation appeared for its second reading on 28th March! Liberal members canvassed against it, on the grounds that Mr Asquith would resign if it were passed; the Master of Elibank, Government Whip, protested that its passage would mean a Cabinet split; Mr Crawshay Williams (Mr Lloyd George's secretary) organized a round-robin against it, and swore that he was acting on his own initiative; the Irish members were known to be opposed to it to a man; and as for Mr Asquith, despite his promises of neutrality, he made an attack on it, for which he drew upon his considerable resources of dialectical finesse. It was therefore defeated by fourteen votes. Such, in the country's opinion, were the conclusions to be drawn from the argument of the broken window pane.

But the WSPU was indifferent to the fate of the Conciliation Bill; it might almost be said that it was growing indifferent to the fate of any Bill at all. A strange rapture seemed to have possessed it, a withdrawal from the world of men, that world in which legislation moved with such cumbered paces towards such insignificant ends. The conflict was beginning to lose touch with the uninspiring realities of ordinary life, it was a conflict in which the spirit yearned towards some ancient wisdom long withheld from women, though to women only it belonged, a conflict whereby, through unguessed tortures and as yet unconceived assaults, the encroaching and tyrannical presence of man could be conjured away.

In Holloway Gaol Mrs Pankhurst prepared for the nine months' imprisonment which Lord Justice Coleridge had imposed upon her at the Old Bailey. Or rather, she prepared to circumvent it by such means as lay in her power. Mr Asquith had relented sufficiently to suggest to the Home Office that Mrs Pankhurst and the Pethick Lawrences should be accorded the special privileges of what is known as First Division treatment. But no sooner was Mrs Pankhurst safely incarcerated than she discovered that the rank and file – whom she had been convicted of inciting – still languished in the comparative squalor of the Second Division. Here was her chance. She begged the Home Secretary to give other prisoners the same treatment as their leaders were receiving, and the Home Secretary – it was only to be expected – absolutely refused. Very well, said Mrs Pankhurst triumphantly, she would refuse to eat; and the news of this hunger strike reaching the other suffragettes in Brixton and Aylesbury gaols, they decided to follow her example.

Well might Sir John Rolleston declare that until a female prisoner being forcibly fed was displayed in effigy at Madame Tussaud's Waxworks, the history of these times would not be complete! It was to forcible feeding that the authorities now resorted, determined that the suffragettes should not escape them. It has occasionally been maintained that, if the victim does not resist, forcible feeding is no more than extremely unpleasant. But the suffragettes were determined to resist. And the consequences of resistance were apt to be revolting in the extreme. First the victim's jaws had to be forced open, and gags thrust in – sometimes they were made of wood, but often of steel which lacerated the gums cruelly; then, while she writhed on her bed in the grip of the wardresses, a feeding tube would – with infinite difficulty – be thrust down her throat, through which some nauseous fluid could find its way into her system. The victim's nerves, combined with a natural reaction to the tube, generally saw to it that this liquid food was immediately vomited up again....

Mrs Pankhurst, fasting in Holloway, had rather imagined that the authorities would release her as soon as they discovered her determination not to eat. But then, one afternoon, she heard the sounds of a struggle in Mrs Pethick Lawrence's cell next to her; and realized that she was not to be spared this final indignity. But, when the doctor and wardresses appeared at her door with the feeding tube, she threatened them with the heavy earthen water jug on her table; and the appearance of Mrs Pankhurst, tense with agony and despair, was such that they actually went away without molesting her. Perhaps they, too, had been sickened by their work in the next cell. When Mrs Pankhurst, on her peremptory demand, was allowed to visit Mrs Pethick Lawrence, she found her friend in a terrible condition; for Mrs Lawrence was a large and determined woman, and it had taken nine wardresses to overpower her. The two were released, on medical grounds, forty-eight hours later; but the hunger strike went on.

In Pentonville, Mr Pethick Lawrence was forcibly fed for five days. In Holloway, the rank and file still waited, with mounting horror, for the time when the door would open and the feeding tube would be brought in. And they still refused to eat. There was one doctor in Holloway so brutal in his methods that his very appearance called forth shrieks of anguish; and Emily Wilding Davison, utterly wrecked by her ordeal, flung herself from the gallery on to which her cell opened, in the hope of killing herself on the floor below. But death, as usual, avoided the advances of Miss Davison. A wire screen broke her fall, and she was merely badly hurt.

By 6th July the hunger strikers were all released; such was the state of their health and their nerves that it would have been dangerous to hold them any longer.

The echoes of this ordeal, as they reached Miss Christabel's ears, produced an effect of mounting exaltation. Aloof and adored, she issued her orders. Let the fight proceed! And now the members of the Cabinet, wherever and whenever they showed themselves, were certain to be harried by the suffragettes and their few men friends. At an India Office reception, Mr John Burns was reduced to picking up a struggling female and carrying her out in his arms. 'There is no door that way,' a waiter called to Mr Burns, as he staggered past with his burden. 'There shall be a door,' was the answer. At Kennington Theatre, Mr Lloyd George was accosted by a certain suffragette sympathizer called Victor Gray, and, in the struggle to remove Mr Gray, both the Chancellor and his tormentor were thrown to the ground. Some ladies even had the singular courage to travel into Wales and heckle Mr George in his native village of Llanystymdwy. They had dressed themselves for the ordeal in strong, thick clothing, but the Welsh—a pertinaceous race—reduced at least two of them to absolute nudity. And so it continued.

The militants received occasional support. In a speech at the Albert

Hall Mr Tim Healy – that brilliant but untidy man, untidy in his clothes and untidy in his convictions, who was against everything, even the Redmondite Party to which by right he belonged – declared that the Government's attitude towards the WSPU was one 'of specious and continuous hypocrisy'. And in the House itself, Mr Healy produced more cogent reasons for attacking Mr Asquith and his colleagues. Some suffragette prisoners had petitioned for release, on the grounds that their relatives were ill; and the Home Office had most obligingly agreed, if they would just sign an undertaking never to commit acts of militancy again. The legality of this was, to say the least of it, dubious, and Mr Healy made it the subject of a question, which he fired off at the head of the Prime Minister. This was on 23rd June, while the feeding tube was still in action at Holloway, Brixton, and Aylesbury. Mr Asquith affected surprise. 'There is not a single prisoner,' he replied, 'who cannot go out of prison this afternoon by giving the undertaking asked for by the Home Secretary.' Whereupon Mr George Lansbury arose, choking with wrath. 'You know they cannot,' he shouted. 'It is perfectly disgraceful that the Prime Minister of England should make such a statement.' (Order! Order!) Mr Lansbury left his seat below the gangway, rushed up the floor of the House, and, planting himself before the Treasury Bench, waved his arms as if to assault the whole Cabinet. 'You are beneath contempt,' he yelled. 'You ought to be driven out of office.' As the cries of Order! Order! mounted, Mr Lansbury raised his tremendous voice in a successful effort to be heard above them. 'It's perfectly disgraceful,' he bellowed: 'It's the most disgraceful thing in England.' Advancing a step, he shook his fist in Mr Asquith's perfectly impassive face. 'You will go down to history as the man who tortured innocent women,' he howled, absolutely beside himself: 'That's what you'll go down to history as.'

With this, he returned to his seat, while the Speaker agreed that he should be suspended for 'his grossly disorderly conduct'. Whereat Mr Lansbury burst forth again. 'I am not going out while this contemptible thing is being done. Murdering, torturing, and driving women mad and telling them they can walk out! You ought to be ashamed of yourselves. You may talk of principle and fighting Ulster. You ought to be driven out of public life. You don't know what principle is. These women are showing you what principle is. You should honour them for standing up for their womanhood. I say, for the Prime Minister to say they could walk out is beneath contempt, and I shall stick to it. I tell him it is beneath contempt to tell the Commons of England that and to laugh at the sufferings of these women. You ought to be ashamed of yourselves!'

The Speaker remarked, in soothing tones – for Mr Lansbury was one of the gentlest souls in public life, and very popular in the Commons – 'I must point out to the Honourable Member for Bow and Bromley that, in refusing to leave the House, he is disregarding the authority of the Chair'. This had the desired effect, and Mr Lansbury, after repeating his argument in softened tones, prepared to obey. But he was still unversed in the customs of the Commons, and did not quite know what was expected of him. He stood pathetically by his seat, wondering whether he was to walk out or be escorted out. At last he went over to the corner seat of the next bench, where Mr Ramsay MacDonald sat. 'What am I to do, Mac?' he asked in a loud whisper. And, having received the correct information from that astute parliamentarian and secret anti-suffragette, he left the House.

VIII

This scene, though it provided – to say the least – some reasons for congratulation, could not have moved Miss Christabel to any great extent. It was true that when Mr Lansbury had finally retired, a lady called Isabel Irvine shattered a glass panel in the central lobby of the House of Commons, and a rumour ran round the benches that suffragettes, armed with hammers, had seized all the doors and would presently attack the Members. This was amusing, no doubt; but most of the credit went to Mr Lansbury, for whom Miss Christabel scarcely pretended to have any affection. No, the women must do the work themselves; and from that ecstatic and self-centred shrine in Paris must come the directions for the work they had to do. What could the women perform next? What fresh outrage? How, with these adoring and obedient servants to obey one's slightest whim, could the signature of Pankhurst be firmly inscribed on English history? In July 1912, Paris issued its orders: the signature of Pankhurst was to be inscribed in letters of fire.

A certain very attractive young lady, dressed in the height of fashion, took to strolling about London; she appeared to have nothing very much to do; but every now and then, in the most public places, she would stop for a chat with a friend. And very soon afterwards one or two young women would drive out into the country; they would leave their car by the wayside; loaded with heavy cases of petrol or paraffin, they would

struggle through hedges and toil over unfamiliar fields; and finally, if
they were fortunate, some empty house or idle church would go up in
flames. Their orders stated that they must escape from the scene
of outrage unnoticed; the fires, rising at unexpected moments and
in unlikely places, must produce the effect of a secret and stealthy
terror.

The first attempt on record was made against Nuneham House, the
lovely home of Lewis Harcourt, against whose ivied walls two women
were discovered crouching at one o'clock on the morning of 13th July.
They were armed with inflammable oil, pick-locks, and glass cutters.
One of them was captured, but the other – whom the police reported to
have been a 'silent woman' answering to the name of Smyth – wriggled
out of her captors' clutches and disappeared across the fields. (She was
not Dr Ethel Smyth, the composer, who had a watertight alibi.)

Meanwhile, during the necessarily difficult and protracted preparation
of inflammable materials, house-breaking tools, and other weapons for
this new offensive, Paris decreed a second form of attack. Pillar boxes
were the objective. Through the slits which were placed in these useful
contrivances for the purpose of posting letters, the militants were
instructed to pour or thrust red ochre, jam, tar, permanganate of potash,
varnish, and inflammable substances, such as phosphorus. The damage
that was done was not very extensive, however; by December 1912, the
Home Office was able to state that 5,000 letters had been slightly
mutilated, but that of these only thirteen letters and seven postcards
were actually destroyed.

And then – quite suddenly and all over the country – golfers going
out on their morning round would be confronted with the legend
VOTES FOR WOMEN burned in acid across their greens. One Sunday
morning, while the Court was at Balmoral, the golf links there was seen
to be fluttering, not with the usual flags on the pins, but with those terrible
and familiar little purple banners. It was perhaps at this point that the
sportsmen of England – who could not help regarding broken window
panes and such irregularities with a certain amused indulgence – woke to
the fact that they were threatened with a deep and inexplicable menace.
They were grieved, they were astonished, they were outraged; but
what could they do? Well, they could at least repay violence with
violence. On one occasion, Mr Asquith, pursued by two women on the
links at Inverness, took refuge behind his opponent, who happened to be
Mr Reginald McKenna, the new Home Secretary; and Mr McKenna

threatened to throw the creatures bodily into a nearby pond. He would have done so, too, if the suffragettes had not prudently retired.

But the policy of secret arson was, of course, the most profoundly disturbing; and its effects were far-reaching. Miss Sylvia Pankhurst confessed that she regarded it 'with grief and regret', and other members of the WSPU discovered, to their sorrow, that it was more than their consciences could stand.

And so Miss Christabel came over from Paris in secret. She had expected this crisis, and rather welcomed it, even though it meant the departure of Mr and Mrs Pethick Lawrence, whose signatures, along with hers and Mrs Pankhurst's, had hitherto adorned every major suffragette order. For Mr and Mrs Pethick Lawrence had not strained at the gnat of window smashing, but they could not bring themselves to swallow the camel of arson. Besides that, had they not shown for a period of months an inconvenient tendency to think for themselves? It was best that they should go. And, indeed, the journey involved in following Miss Christabel and her mother was rather more than could be undertaken by two intelligent married people: that dark journey into some feverish realm of the spirit where woman secretly communed with woman.

To have a man among the leaders of the WSPU was not only a hindrance and an embarrassment, it was also – considering the circumstances – unnecessarily comic. How could men play a serious part in this enraptured drama? They used to try, poor monsters; but it was always as though a Bottom had strayed into Titania's kingdom, or a Caliban had blundered, once again, over the enchanted shores of Ariel's island. There was the famous story of Mr Sheehy-Skeffington, an ardent suffragist of Dublin, who determined to heckle Mr Asquith at a Nationalist meeting in July 1912. Now the Dublin Nationalists had issued their tickets with special care; no suspect women were to be admitted; and as for Mr Sheehy-Skeffington, he had been warned that if he attempted to get in he would be severely handled.

But Mr Sheehy-Skeffington was not to be intimidated. He procured a ticket made out in a priest's name, and, with the help of Dudley Digges, disguised himself as a priest. His make-up was extremely effective except that he refused to shave off his red beard, of which he was inordinately proud; and beards, among Catholic clergy, are rather the exception than the rule. Arrived at the meeting somewhat late, owing to the fact that his cabby was completely intoxicated, Mr Sheehy-Skeffington presented his ticket with some trepidation; but in Dublin, a priest is a priest; and the bearded apparition was admitted inside. And so it came about that Mr Asquith, in the middle of one of his finest periods, was completely put off with a cry of 'Votes for Wee-men!' There was no mistaking that high, shrill voice: with a howl of 'Skeffy!' the enraged ushers started a man-hunt, discovered their priest, and – with shouts of rage and laughter – bundled him, bruised and dishevelled, out into the street.

But this was the very kind of thing – in an exaggerated form no doubt, for Sheehy-Skeffingtons are by no means common phenomena – which Miss Christabel would give much to avoid. If there must be men sympathizers, let them sympathize in a sober fashion. Otherwise, they were sure to make fools of themselves. Her mind was already crowded with ecstatic visions of a sex war.

The Pethick Lawrences left the WSPU without recrimination, and agreed to resume control of *Votes for Women*. A new and more flamboyant magazine called *The Suffragette* soon appeared on the streets, edited by Miss Christabel in Paris. And the WSPU, moving into luxurious headquarters in the renaissance building of Lincoln's Inn House, at Kingsway, became – to all intents and purposes – the obedient and fanatical slave of Christabel and Emmeline Pankhurst.

IX

With the departure of the Pethick Lawrences, Miss Christabel and her mother at last attained the long desired peak of despotic authority, and it seems more than a little unkind to remark at this point – as remark one must – that this final step carried them into a slavery more abject than any they demanded from their followers. The outward picture presents them in an almost heroic light. In Paris the seductive personality of Christabel, in London the indefatigable brain of Mrs Pankhurst dictated every move, and swayed every heart, of a growing army of intoxicated women: at the stroke of a pen, the raising of an eyebrow, at a secret command travelling by devious ways across the Channel, or a passionate phrase hurled from a London platform – the work of destruction would begin afresh. They had only to say the word and castles and churches went up in flames, pictures were slashed, windows shattered, the majesty of parliaments and kings affronted; and then, too, at the mere thought of their applause, women would endure the violence of mobs and the agonies of cell and feeding tube. The details gradually sort themselves out;

each falls into its proper place; the lurid picture is complete: and there, above everything, the forms of Emmeline and Christabel Pankhurst scour the furious scene like a pair of risen but infernal queens....

Infernal! The word has its peculiar application, but it is not, alas, an heroic one.

They were, indeed, the leaders, yet the movement which they led traced itself back, by a lengthy chain of complicated cause and effect, to a vast and unseen origin. It is surely one of the minor ironies of history that it was the unconscious desires of all Englishwomen, who abominated militancy, which made militancy possible; and that womanhood, half waking from its long Victorian sleep, so filled with unrecognized fantasies and unremembered nightmares, should have expelled, like a sigh or a groan – the Pankhursts. It is best to repeat this here; to recall, once again, that Christabel and her mother were under the dictatorship of this singular tyranny; and to realize that the millions of women who detested and feared them unconsciously supplied them with strength and compelled them to outrage. The Pankhursts were the slaves of a vital but timid desire for freedom; they were its puppets, its projections: and, as is sometimes the unfortunate habit of projections, they began to assume a more and more demoniac form. To follow their activities backwards into the obscure recesses of psychological theory would be impossible here, and undesirable; it would only confound confusion: but, even under the meagre considerations here advanced, the subsequent battles of the WSPU become full of interest to the observer.

Not the least of the Pankhursts' remaining difficulties was that which involved the behaviour of the second sister, Sylvia. Sylvia was the artist of the family, dreamy and affectionate. From her childhood she had resigned herself to a lower place in her mother's love than was held by the more attractive Christabel: or, as she herself put it, 'I was always so busy drawing, writing, copying the embroidery on a Japanese screen, watching insects and worms', that nothing else seemed to matter much. But now she obstinately refused to forget her father's principles, and, along with her secret distaste for the policy of stealthy arson, openly paraded her socialist opinions. Christabel and her mother, to whom the days when they had worked for the ILP were fading into an indistinct and regrettable past, regarded these symptoms with alarm. Sylvia was not merely showing signs of independence, which was bad enough; she was actually down in the East End, in a disused baker's shop, in the middle of the Bow Road, with its stench of soap-works and tanneries and its pervading grime. Above the shop doorway she had inscribed in gilded Roman letters, VOTES FOR WOMEN: and her mother and sister could not but feel that this exalted legend was very much out of place in such surroundings. And then the people who would come in to see Sylvia! All sorts of women in sweated and obscure trades – rope-makers, waste rubber cleaners, biscuit packers, chicken pluckers, women who made wooden seeds for raspberry jam, all the uninspiring varieties of hopeless slum! Logic suggested that these, of all women, were most in need of the vote: but logic did not play much part in the inner conclaves of the WSPU. Sylvia's particular kind of ordeal, too, scarcely lent itself to lofty treatment in the pages of *The Suffragette*; in her first public meeting, in Bethnal Green, she and her supporters had been pelted with fishes' heads and papers soaked in the public urinal.

Miss Sylvia very soon discovered that she and the WSPU no longer saw eye to eye. Towards the end of 1912, George Lansbury was obliged to contest his seat at Bow and Bromley. He had quarrelled with the Labour Party because of its somewhat half-hearted support of Women's Suffrage, and felt compelled to seek re-election as an independent candidate. Mrs Pankhurst and Christabel condescended to meet him at Boulogne, to discuss the details of his campaign, but the results can scarcely be described as satisfactory. Sylvia's headquarters in the Bow Road bakers-shop were suddenly invaded by a WSPU organizer, armed with instructions from France, who, so far from assisting Mr Lansbury in his efforts, appeared to see this election as a heaven-sent opportunity for making speeches, selling *The Suffragette*, and generally raising the by now familiar Cain. Disgusted but obedient, Sylvia stood by and watched this young lady and her assistants – all of them blandly unfamiliar with the neighbourhood – as they attempted to steal the limelight from Mr Lansbury. Was it Mr Lansbury who was seeking election, or was it the WSPU? The question was stubbornly debated, but only on the morning of polling day did the final differences of opinion show themselves. Mr Lansbury's organization had only a very few motor-cars; the WSPU possessed a small fleet of them, and its organizer sent a message to Joe Banks, local Labour secretary, asking for a list of voters to be carried to the polls. Mr Banks – a hardened campaigner, with no love for the women – replied that the WSPU motor-cars must be sent to him. The organizer was very indignant: 'Mrs Pankhurst would never allow the Union to work under the men,' she said; and the cars remained unused. When the results were announced, Mr Lansbury's majority of 863 had become a minority of 731. The organizer burst into a flood of tears: 'What will Christabel say?' she moaned to Sylvia. Sylvia could not help wondering what Mr Lansbury would say.

But it was not here, in the comparative decencies of a parliamentary campaign, that the W S P U could give vent to the new spirit which possessed it. At the Albert Hall, Mrs Pankhurst had already invested that spirit with the fiery garment of her peculiar oratory.

'There is something which governments care for more than human life,' she said, outlining Christabel's new policy, 'and that is the security of property, and so it is through property that we shall strike the enemy. . . . Be militant each in your own way. Those of you who can express your militancy by going to the House of Commons and refusing to leave without satisfaction – do so. Those of you who can express militancy by facing party mobs at Cabinet Ministers' meetings, when you remind them of their falseness to principle – do so. . . . Those of you who can break windows – break them. Those of you who can still further attack the secret idol of property' – such was her delicate reference to arson – 'so as to make the Government realize that property is as greatly endangered by Women's Suffrage as it was by the Chartists of old – do so. And my last word to the Government is . . . Take me if you dare!'

This speech – in which the raptures of the new cause were so oddly intermingled with the imagery of a forgotten socialism – was no idle threatening: and yet, in the early days of 1913, the Government made its final move; and the risen masculinity of the W S P U came face to face with the caprice of a fading Liberalism. The encounter was not without its significance. For though all the resources of parliamentary strategy, brought into play by a master mind, seemed at the moment to have won a resounding victory for the Government, who can deny that the women ultimately had the best of it, and that Parliament – which the Tories were already reducing to a worthless debating chamber – proved, once again, its inability to deal with the assaults which were being made upon it?

The opening stages of this important scene were quiet enough. Sylvia Pankhurst had arranged for a deputation of working women to be received by the Prime Minister – women, so she hoped, who would represent the cluttered and dismal life of London's East End, and whom she would lead in person. This valuable notion was modified by an order from Paris which (as a comment upon Sylvia's growing independence) gave the leadership to Mrs Drummond, the bright little bustling obedient 'General', and added that all the working women of England should be represented, in the slightly irrelevant gaiety of their local costumes. Sylvia did not resist. She got her women together, and sent them off to join what had ceased to be a deputation and become a circus. At the Treasury, Mrs Drummond and her flock were received by an indulgent Lloyd George and a friendly Sir Edward Grey – Mr Asquith had discovered other engagements. It was all very pleasant. Mr George promised that, when the Male Suffrage Bill went into committee, he would support the Dickenson amendment – which would enfranchise some five million women. If that failed to pass, he would switch to the so-called Conciliation amendment, by which one and a half millions of women would receive the vote. Sir Edward added his polite assurances. This was on the morning of 23rd January, 1913.

The members of the deputation, returning from the Treasury, could scarcely have thought the Prime Minister's absence worth comment. Knowing what little we do of their state of mind, it must have seemed as if the heavens themselves had opened and dropped into Christabel Pankhurst's lap the ultimate political prize; and who were they to question the mysterious justice of Providence? And then – just four hours later – the Speaker dropped his 'bombshell'. It was during a desultory discussion of business, that afternoon in the Commons, that Mr Bonar Law asked the Speaker whether the Male Suffrage Bill (due to enter its committee stage the next day) would have to be withdrawn, if any amendment materially altered its character and purpose. And the Speaker indicated that this, in fact, would be the necessary consequence.

The news, when it reached WSPU headquarters, was received first with consternation and then with all the fury of baffled hope. It was realized, for the last time, that even the women's present lofty attitude towards the Government – accompanied as it was with the powerful inducements of menace and martyrdom – would produce nothing but evasion upon evasion, insult upon insult. They knew already what the future of the Bill would be. The next afternoon, to be sure, it went into its committee stage with every appearance of sincerity. Sir Edward Grey's amendment – to delete the word 'Male' – was moved, in his absence, by Mr Lyttleton, and opposed by Mr 'Lulu' Harcourt, in a speech which – so Lord Hugh Cecil maintained – clearly indicated that Mr Harcourt had never got over the indignity of having been born of a woman. The subsequent debate was serious and, at times, passionate;

and when the House adjourned for the week-end at 11 p.m. no casual observer could have guessed that its participants had been spending their breath and their brains on what was, to all intents and purposes, a dead Bill.

On Monday 27th January, Mr Asquith, who had kept himself hitherto in the protection of a politic silence, asked the Speaker which, if any, of the amendments regarding what was known as 'Women's Suffrage' would so affect the Male Suffrage Bill as to force its withdrawal. The Speaker replied that he would state his views immediately, 'for the convenience of the House'. If the word 'Male' were deleted, as the first amendment asked, this would make no difference, for in Franchise Acts 'person' meant 'male person'; but if any other of the Women's Suffrage amendments were passed, he would advise the withdrawal of the Bill, '*it not having been designed to open the franchise to any fresh class of the community*'.

Mr Asquith accepted this ruling with alacrity – 'loyally', as he phrased it, 'and without reserve'. He went on to say – and his words were scarcely those of a man who had been taken by surprise – that, in view of the special pledges and undertakings involved in it, he and his colleagues did not consider it right to proceed with the Bill. And so, in the sorry confines of a verbal *cul-de-sac*, the question of Women's Suffrage came to a halt. Two years of unparalleled effort – and *this* was the result! And with what a perverse cleverness, with what an astounding exercise of prevarication and pretence, the Government had reached its foregone conclusion! In order to 'torpedo' – the word had been let slip by Mr Lloyd George – the Conciliation Bill, the Government had produced an unwanted Male Suffrage Bill, only to 'torpedo' that with Women's Suffrage amendments. Things were just where they had started. And now, with a complacency which could only be described as insolent, Mr Lloyd George, Sir Edward Grey, Sir William Byles, and other so-called 'friends' were talking, once again, of the singular virtues of a Private Member's Bill! 'Either the Government are so ignorant of Parliamentary procedure,' said *The Suffragette*, 'that they are unable to occupy any position of responsibility, or else they are scoundrels of the worst kind.' 'I am inclined to think,' Mrs Pankhurst has added in *My Own Story*, 'that the verdict of posterity will lean towards the latter conclusion.'

The question is not quite so easily decided, since few of us have acquired Mrs Pankhurst's faculty for seeing a vital problem in simple terms of black and white. When the vanguard of a vast female movement leaps, with disconcerting vehemence, at the rear of a political faith; when a freedom which springs up from the soul meets the faded 'freedom' of Victorian philosophy; when the unbridled energy of life clashes with the multiple whimsy of approaching death – the results of this encounter are not very amenable to ordinary considerations of right and wrong. Mr Asquith has his defenders. The latest of them – Mr D. C. Somervell in his *The Reign of George V* – protests that the Prime Minister, not being a mindreader, could hardly have known which way the Speaker would interpret those amendments: that another Speaker, in fact – Mr Asquith himself, for instance, if he had held that position – might have delivered an opposite ruling. But this, as a defence of Mr Asquith's personal honesty, lays itself open to the charge of being somewhat ingenuous. If he had been at all serious about either Bill, he would not have mingled them together in so uncertain, so ambiguous a fashion: his known respect for the niceties of language would have prevented him. The question, perhaps, revolves around a more delicate point. How far can a man's private character affect his public career? The personal life of Mr Asquith is one of the pleasantest chapters in English biography; and in his public life it cannot be said of him that he ever broke a sincere promise or betrayed an inconvenient colleague, and his temptations to do so were more numerous than generally fall to the lot of even a Prime Minister. But it is rather too much to expect that any human being will drag his personal honesty – like some kind of patent cleanser – through all the ancient grimed corridors of parliamentary procedure. And then there was in Mr Asquith – as in most honest lawyers – a fundamental incompatability between his temperament and his training. How could even his candour resist the fascinating complexities of political life? How could that unimpassioned mind, so long used to the endless qualifications of legal business, so sensitive to the nicest distinctions of phrase and the innumerable possibilities of ambiguity approach a distasteful problem with complete candour? And was Mr Asquith's candour, after all, so very candid? As one watches his later career, and sees his characteristic simplicity spend itself in a thousand hesitations, evasions, and compromises, one feels as though two men were occupying the same body. On the one hand, there is the kindly gentleman whom his friends loved and his opponents respected; on the other hand, there is a creature helplessly meshed in all the irresponsible notions of a declining Liberalism. His very regard for truth melts at last into a perversion of truth.

Such enigmas, which cannot be solved on this earth, may possibly be disentangled in Heaven. Meanwhile one has to say that Mr Asquith had deliberately cheated the women of a privilege which, in his heart of hearts, he thought quite improper; and had dishonestly broken a promise which he honestly believed should not be kept.

The results of this last constitutional encounter between the new life and the old respectability were – as was only to be expected – extreme. Mr Keir Hardie, deeply wounded by the Prime Minister's behaviour, prophesied 'real militant tactics'. And he was right. Mrs Drummond, leading her deputation back to Lloyd George, was arrested in Parliament Square for 'obstruction', and hurled to the ground, where, to the consternation of her followers, she lay for a while, stunned and breathing hoarsely. She was then taken to the police station, along with Sylvia Pankhurst; and Sylvia vented her rage on Superintendent Wells by upsetting his ink pot, dipping her hand in the ink, and marking his face with what the newspapers were pleased to describe as 'The Black Hand'. It was not an inappropriate description for the preposterous, the almost fictional campaign which now began. From one end of the country to the other a new militancy reared its desperate and comic head. Street lamps were broken, key-holes stopped up with lead pellets, house numbers were painted out, the cushions of railway carriages slashed, municipal flower beds wrecked, bowling greens scoured with acid; otherwise nice old ladies began to apply for gun licences, to the terror of their local magistracy; bogus telephone messages summoned the Army Reserves and the Territorials; telegraph wires were severed with long-handled clippers. A fresh window-smashing raid went forth to do its worst with the West End Clubs, and the façades of the Carlton, the Junior Carlton, the Reform and other solemn institutions grinned dismally with jagged glass. The glass of the Crown Jewel case in the Tower of London was broken by a Mrs Cohen, of Leeds, and the royal palaces of Hampton Court, Kew, Kensington, and Holyrood were immediately closed to the public. Thirteen pictures were slashed in the Manchester Art Gallery. In Kew Gardens the refreshment pavilion was reduced to ashes. Careless alike of opinion and expediency – for Parliament was now closed to them, and they were glad of it – the enraptured members of the WSPU sought diligently for empty houses and unattended buildings, to set them on fire, and among the many to suffer were Lady White's house at Staines (valued at £4,000) and a £10,000 mansion at St Leonard's. Crude bombs were discovered, unexploded, near the Bank of England, at

Wheatly Hall by Doncaster, and on the steps of the Dublin Insurance Office. One such bomb actually went off, and Lloyd George's new house, half-built at Walton-on-the-Hill, was badly damaged by it; nor could the police discover any clues except those that were provided by the tale of a motor-car passing through the village at 4 p.m., two broken hat-pins, a hairpin, and a feminine galosh. (The actual culprits – Emily Wilding Davison and some friends – took care not to be captured.) A mother and daughter, bearers of a famous name, took to travelling up and down the country, dropping pebbles between the sashes of railway carriage windows, in the hopes that the glass would smash when next opened. Chairs were flung into the Serpentine. *Votes for Women* was painted on innumerable park benches. In Miss Olive Hockin's studio at Campden Hill the police unearthed a 'Suffragette Arsenal' of clippers, bottles of acid, hammers, flints, and false identification plates for motor-cars. On one and the same morning, every member of the Cabinet received a letter filled with snuff and red pepper. From *diminuendo* to *crescendo* and back again, the strangely orchestrated outrage took its course. But always the hand of a Pankhurst directed its loudest and most furious passages or drew, as from some lonely and wayward flute, its little hushed moments of lunatic caprice. . . .

The du-umvirate which had established its rule over the WSPU divided its authority into two departments: to Mrs Pankhurst the sword, to Christabel the spirit. Precisely how Mrs Pankhurst endured the various ordeals to which she was subjected is a question for students of fanaticism to answer. Frail and fearless, she took full responsibility for what was being done. On 24th February, soon after the wrecking of Lloyd George's house, she was arrested, charged with conspiracy, committed to Holloway, and – after a hunger strike which seriously affected her health – was released on bail until her trial at the Central Criminal Court on 1st April. Her appearance in the dock, the little body so fiercely upright under the lined and shadowed face, was sufficient to compel the sympathy of everybody there; and yet something, some arrogance in the upward thrust of the head, something at once pert and perilous in the burning eyes, diminished that sympathy almost as soon as it began to grow. You might admire Mrs Pankhurst – it was very plucky of her to stand such a deal of punishment, and she had an able mind; but you could not be sorry for her. She positively seemed to dislike affection. There she was, calling no witnesses, offering no evidence, refusing counsel, and pouring out upon judge and jury an overwhelming stream of cogent argument: but, just as it seemed that, as reasonable men, they would have to let her off, the acrid creature started upon a recital of the dreadful things which had been done by men in high places, and was mid-way in the story of an eminent Judge of Assizes who was found dead one morning in a brothel, when His Lordship stopped her short. She was convicted, sentenced to three years' penal servitude, and disappeared from the Court amidst a mounting clamour of 'Shame! Shame!' from her supporters, followed by a spirited rendering of the Suffragette 'Marseillaise' – 'March on, march on, Face to the dawn, The dawn of liberty' – which the officials found themselves quite powerless to prevent. On 12th April, after a nine days' hunger strike, she was released from Holloway on a fifteen days' licence. Her subsequent movements explain in part and partly excuse the peculiarly mean, the dubiously constitutional methods which exasperated authority began to use against suffragette offenders. Broken in health, she retired to Dr Ethel Smyth's house at Woking but the thought of work to be done outside, combined with the wearisome continual presence of detectives, was too much for her. She decided to attend a WSPU meeting at the London Pavilion on 25th May, was arrested outside Dr Smyth's door, carried fainting to the police station, committed to Holloway, and released after yet another hunger strike, her third. On 21st July, she was arrested at a weekly meeting of the WSPU and released on 24th July after her fourth strike. On 11th October she sailed for New York, and was re-arrested at Plymouth on 4th December: on 7th December, she was released from Exeter gaol after her fifth strike. On 13th December, she was re-arrested on her return from Paris, and released on 17th December after her sixth strike. In her case, the authorities might congratulate themselves that they had behaved with becoming chivalry towards what they still tried to persuade themselves was the weaker sex. Of her three years' penal servitude, Mrs Pankhurst had so far served some three weeks. But what was the use? They had been kind to her because they were afraid she would kill herself with continual hunger strikes, and from the less humane motive that they did not wish to indulge her obvious desire for martyrdom: and yet, no sooner was she released, than the sick and half-crippled woman hobbling between her friends or speaking from a bath-chair, would appear at proscribed meetings and – with all the persuasion of her emaciated and suffering presence – urge the women on to further acts of militancy!

X

It might seem rather odd that, while Mrs Pankhurst endured the heat of battle, her daughter Christabel should have been content to linger in her Parisian hiding place, observing, with the sinister passivity of an idol at a human sacrifice, the ardours and agonies of the WSPU. Some more clear-sighted member of the organization, one might have thought, would have commented on this division of the leadership. Was it not – to say the least of it – rather unnatural for a healthy daughter to stand by while her mother was literally broken on the recurring wheel of imprisonments and hunger strikes? But no such comment seems to have been made; and the fact that it was not made shows, more than anything else, in what strange regions of female history the WSPU was now occupying itself. One might almost be watching a puppet show. The little stage is beaten upon by a fierce light, but around it, above and below, lie the clouds of an impenetrable darkness. The hand that pulls the strings, the brain that concocts the *farouche* and almost fabulous drama – to discover *these* you must make an impossible search in the depths of English womanhood. Jerked hither and yon by forces it could not understand, so deep they lay in a general female dilemma, the WSPU asked no questions: it was the blind and obedient instrument of millions of disapproving wives and sisters and cooks and countesses and governesses and spinsters; it was the suicide of Respectability.

Yet a comparison between Mrs Pankhurst and her daughter is worth making if only because it illustrates an eternal principle of human living – that an unconscious desire will force itself into conscious thought, by any means and in any shape. Woman's desire to recover her lost womanhood found the Pankhursts ready to hand, and used them. In the case of Mrs Pankhurst, it was the *energy* of this desire which took possession. By the end of 1913, she can scarcely be considered as a human being any more: she was a walking proposition, an embodied idea. Women must be free; they must fight for their freedom: health, propriety, even ambition ceased to matter. In the case of Christabel some more mysterious force seems to have exerted itself in a highly paradoxical fashion; in her the secret necessity for personal relationship found a convenient shape. To say that she came to represent the spirit of the WSPU is by no means an exaggeration; and yet it is one of those contradictions which so ironically manifest themselves in the world of the soul that this need for personal relationship – only to be attained, so it seemed, through the almost mystical communion of woman with woman – should have been incarnated in so egocentric a figure as Christabel Pankhurst. She, too, was in the grip of an idea; but somehow she was sufficiently detached to use this idea for the furtherance of her own ends. The passionate idolatry with which she was surrounded went to her head like the fumes of some exotic wine or the clouds of a dangerous incense; determined to establish herself more firmly in her shrine, she set herself up, not merely as man's enemy but as man's superior. And so it came about that woman's vital need for woman expressed itself – with all the inversions of a cynical comedy of manners – in the self-aggrandizement of Christabel Pankhurst. But small as she was, she could be used by life to express a meaning unknown to herself.

One of the strangest documents in pre-war English history was a pamphlet called *The Great Scourge*, which, bearing Christabel's name and reprinted from *The Suffragette*, was sold in England during the year 1913. In this, with a characteristic boldness, she discussed venereal disease and the sex excesses of men. Seventy-five to eighty per cent of men, she declared, were afflicted with gonorrhoea and twenty-five per cent with syphilis. The sources from which she drew these formidable statistics are unknown; but the fact that they were highly exaggerated is a matter of very small importance compared to the conclusions which – with a mounting excitement – she proceeded to draw from them. Not merely did she demonstrate that almost all women's minor ailments were due to gonorrhoea in the husband, and that childlessness could be traced to the same origin; not merely did she exclaim that syphilis 'is the prime reason of a high infant mortality'; but she made it pretty clear that the very act of sexual intercourse with a man was highly injurious to female susceptibilities. Woman – there was no avoiding her meaning – was purer and nobler than man, and would do well to avoid his embraces. The Vote, it appeared, was something between a prophylactic and a call to the higher life.

VOTES FOR WOMEN AND PURITY FOR MEN was Christabel's new slogan. Today the words resound with comedy, and one can only wish that an Aristophanes or a Plautus had been there to do justice to them in a typical scene or two; but, in 1913, not a few people took them seriously. Both the slogan and *The Great Scourge* became popular with evangelical clergymen, who took to distributing the pamphlet among the faithful; and many a Boys' Club and Men's Bible Class must have sat and shivered at the thought of unguessed contamination as Miss Christabel's amazing pages were read aloud. But what effect would they have upon the militants? There was, after all, a grain of good sense in *The Great Scourge*: and, more than that, did it not rise – unknown, perhaps, to its author, unknown to its readers – from the very heart of an awakening womanhood? How would they accept it? To what new excesses would it lead them? On the little stage the puppets begin to move in an even more agitated manner; and then, quite suddenly, the unseen hand gives an unexpected twist of the strings, and one of the whirling figures springs out of her place, and falls.

It was Derby Day, 4th June, 1913. The evening before, in London, Miss Emily Wilding Davison, in cheerful humour, had gone to lay a wreath at the foot of Joan of Arc's statue. The next morning she went up to Epsom Downs, and pushed her way into a good position on the rails at Tattenham Corner. There she waited patiently until the Derby itself came sweeping round, the King's horse in the lead. And then, once again, that all too well known phenomenon – the sudden scuttle of long skirts; and down came the King's horse, and the King's jockey, and Miss Davison, in a frightful kicking heap. Afterwards, the King inquired for the jockey, the Queen for Miss Davison; but Miss Davison, after a long pursuit and many disappointments, had caught up with death at last.

What had passed through her mind as she stood there in the last moment, in the roaring crowd, on ground shaken with approaching hoofs? Had she only intended – as some maintained – to wave a Suffragette flag at the critical moment? And had some sudden and fatal impulse sent her forward? Nobody knew for certain; and yet it seemed, from the WSPU colours found sewn in her jacket, that she had at least considered pulling down the first horse that came by, and that her obsession had worked itself finally to rest.

The WSPU had a martyr. No more words were heard of Emily Davison's independence, her love of showing off, her difficult temperament. And *The Great Scourge* – is it too much to say that Miss Christabel's pamphlet, with its twisted reasoning, its ill-repressed emotionalism, and all its peculiar implications, had found itself a victim? that the idol in Paris could now smile upon a human sacrifice? These questions were certainly irrelevant at the time. Every militant could assure herself that the blessed martyr – who, after all, *was* a little unbalanced – was happy at last: and it had really gone off very well, with front page stories in the press, and a solemn procession, when 6,000 women – some in black, with purple irises, some in purple with crimson peonies, some in white, with laurel wreaths – accompanied the body of Miss Davison through crowded and respectful streets to St George's, Bloomsbury.

XI

And all this was a matter of considerable grief to Mr McKenna, who had left the Admiralty for the Home Office, and probably wished – as he had probably been wishing these last eighteen months – that Winston could be dragged out of his dream of ships, and made to see what *he* could do with the women. Not that Mr Churchill – if 'Black Friday' were any criterion – had been exactly successful in his dealings with militancy; but the question now was whether any Home Secretary could handle it. Take forcible feeding. Ordinarily speaking, the feeding tube with its companion horrors did not find its way into prison cells; it was reserved for the somewhat more medieval atmosphere of lunatic asylums. But if every convicted 'outragette' were permitted to avoid the consequences of her crime by the comparatively simple process – (simple, if she were young and strong) – of refusing to eat for a day or two, you might as well have no law at all. But then the feeding tube was really rather horrible: worse still, it led to the most inconvenient questions in the House. Everybody remembered the story of Lady Constance Lytton who – disguised as Jane Warton, a poor seamstress – had been forcibly fed in Walton Gaol, Liverpool, without a medical examination, and then hurriedly released as soon as her identity became known; which was scarcely the sort of thing which ought happen under a Liberal Government. That was in 1910, but in 1913 a far more regrettable case became public knowledge. A Miss Lillian Lenton, committed to Holloway as a remand case on a charge of arson, hunger struck and was forcibly fed. On 22nd February, her solicitor reported her to be in good health, but the very next day she was hastily discharged, being – on the Home Secretary's admission – 'in imminent danger of death'. She had struggled with a doctor and seven wardresses, food had penetrated her lung, pleurisy had set in; and though she recovered, the incident left a very bad impression. On 18th March, Mr Harold Smith formally moved the reduction of the Home Secretary's salary by £100, because of the incompetence, the lack of firmness, the 'humility', which the Government had displayed in its dealings with the suffragettes. Mr McKenna might have replied that getting food into a woman's lung is an act not without its element of firmness; but there was no denying the fact that the possibilities of catching pleurisy from the Government had not deterred the militants from pursuing their campaign of outrage. What *was* to be done? Since Women's Suffrage was not a party question, the honour of the whole House seemed to be involved. Some members maintained that the women should be left to die; Lord Robert Cecil thought that deportation might answer: only Mr Keir Hardie suggested, as a logical solution, that women should be given the vote.

Within a week, the harried Mr McKenna produced a piece of legislation which he believed would better the situation incalculably. It was called The Prisoners (Temporary Discharge for Ill-Health) Bill, and was better known as the 'Cat and Mouse' Bill. It provided that hunger-strikers should be discharged when their health became affected, and then re-arrested as soon as they were well, thus prolonging the term of their imprisonment indefinitely, and giving them a fair chance of ultimately hunger-striking their way into the next world. As to the legality of the Bill, the learned Mr Atherly Jones – during the debate on the second reading – declared that it violated a cardinal principle of the country's law; adding, correctly, that its methods were 'cruel and capricious'. The House, however, was not persuaded by the arguments of Mr Atherly Jones, and the Bill passed its second reading by 296 to 43. (Among the minority was that flamboyant and gentle creature, Keir Hardie, who observed – with a misery which is said to have hastened his death – that fifteen of his Labour colleagues were voting in its favour.)

On 25th April, the Cat and Mouse Bill received the Royal Assent, and it has only to be added that no clause in it prevented the Home Secretary from exercising, if he pleased, his right of forcible feeding.

Other expedients occurred to Mr McKenna. On 15th April, he forbade all WSPU meetings. In this, perhaps, he was urged on by the thought of what had happened at one of these meetings in the Albert Hall, only a week before. £15,000 had been collected for the cause, and Mr George Lansbury – that forgiving soul – made a highly inflammatory speech, in the course of which he exclaimed:

'Stand shoulder to shoulder with the militant women; hold them up in the fight they are waging. Let them burn and destroy property! Let them do anything they will; and for every leader that is taken, let a dozen step forward to take their places. . . . This is a holy war!'

This sort of thing really couldn't go on, but the police were rather half-hearted about suppressing meetings, and the Home Office began to look elsewhere. On 30th April, police descended upon the Kingsway headquarters, and arrested all the office staff of *The Suffragette*, along with Mrs Drummond and Annie Kenney, who happened to be on the premises; and at Bow Street the next day Mr Archibald Bodkin, breathing threats against all and sundry, declared that *The Suffragette* must be put a stop to without delay. So S. G. Drew, manager of the Victoria House Press, was arrested, and only released upon giving an undertaking not to print either the offending magazine or any other paper of the WSPU.

The Union transferred its magazine to the National Labour Press, an organ of the ILP, but Mr McKenna pounced again, and within two days the Press's manager, a Mr Whiteley, was also arrested and forced to sign an undertaking. At this point Ramsay MacDonald intervened, in the cause of freedom: he would take over the management of the Press himself, and would personally censor the contents of *The Suffragette*; and Keir Hardie – fearing, no doubt, that MacDonald's dislike of the WSPU would produce a remarkably unreadable magazine – offered his services as assistant editor. But Christabel, already regretting this mild flirtation with Labour, hastily handed *The Suffragette* over to The Athenaeum Press, with lamentable results; for The Athenaeum Press was under the command of J. E. Francis, a literary martinet of the most extreme kind. Not only was no statement accepted without full documentary proof, not only were militant sentiments suppressed with extraordinary rigour, but anything which offended Mr Francis's literary tastes – and they were very punctilious – was immediately blue pencilled. For a little while it seemed as if Mr McKenna had won.

But other and more terrible eyes had been watching this singular campaign of suppression. The *Manchester Guardian* – whose opinions no Englishman, and certainly no Liberal, could afford to disregard – declared that the law had no power to suppress newspapers in advance; and what else was Mr McKenna doing, if not that? Mr Bernard Shaw was more wounding still. 'The Suffragettes have succeeded in driving the Cabinet half mad,' he wrote. 'Mr McKenna should be examined at once by two doctors. He apparently believes himself to be the Tsar of Russia, a very common form of delusion.'

The protests poured in. Mr McKenna began to weaken. And so, just as Christabel and her editorial associates were on the point of despair,

Mr Drew was released from his undertaking, on condition that he would print nothing which incited to crime. *The Suffragette* was home again, with the Victoria Press; and though Mr Drew was arrested in the next year for printing the Biblical phrase – 'And they that walk in darkness shall see a great light' – which the authorities suspected of being a deep allusion to a recent case of arson; and though the magazine's thunders had been reduced to a mutter, its lightnings to a pallid glow – still it was on the streets again, it could be openly sold.

The Government, in the person of the agitated Mr McKenna, now found itself in a legendary predicament. On the one hand, there stood the increasing devil of suffragette insolence; on the other, there surged the deep sea of Liberal opinion. When Miss Kenney, Mrs Drummond, and the staff of *The Suffragette*, convicted in June of conspiracy and gaoled, went on hunger strike and were released under the Cat and Mouse Act, they retired to a house in Campden Hill Square, from which – with much agility and more impertinence, in a variety of disguises and in spite of a cordon of detectives – they would make their escape from time to time. And if this were not enough (and what Home Secretary wants to be made a laughing stock?) the severity of their sentences – which ranged from six months' imprisonment to twenty-one months' imprisonment – was being severely criticized. And it was being criticized because Queenie Gerald, a lady who made her living out of the immoral earnings of young girls, had recently been rewarded with only three months in prison. If a madam only gets three months, asked an unusual but dangerous combination of Nonconformist opinion and the yellow press, why should a militant get more? Which was the worse offence? And was it not true that Queenie Gerald would have been more strictly treated if a number of prominent men had not been involved in her sinful career? Questions like these do not hold the public attention for any length of time, but they are scarcely calculated to do a Liberal Government much good.

And for all Mr McKenna's efforts, the suffragettes grew worse and worse. Cabinet ministers were so frequently heckled, by so many shrill, slippery, and offensive young women, that they took to cancelling their engagements by the dozen. Mr Asquith's car was held up at Bannock-burn, and he himself attacked with a horse-whip; while his visits to important cities were so invariably attended by false fire alarms, smashed windows, attacks on letter boxes, and other varieties of militancy that it grew to be positively unsafe to invite him. Members of Parliament never knew when their debates were to be punctuated from the galleries by showers of flour, handfuls of mouse-traps, or the firing off of blank cartridges. The King was embarrassed by having petitions thrust at him by insistent females, one of whom was so determined in her efforts that a royal equerry had to beat her off with the flat of his sword. As for the tale of arson, it increased by leaps and bounds, until £500,000 damage had been done by the end of the year. This incongruous battle between Parliament and Pankhursts, as it raged up and down the country to the mingled delight, discomfort, and fury of His Majesty's subjects, seemed likely to end in the ludicrous defeat of His Majesty's Government. What *could* poor Mr McKenna do? On the whole, it seemed best to persist. In spite of the *Manchester Guardian*, Mr Bernard Shaw, a dignified deputation of formidable Scots baillies, the Bishops of Lincoln and Kensington, Mr Nevinson, Mr Gerald Gould, Mr Harold Laski, and innumerable other protestants, the Cat and Mouse Act was not repealed.

And the Home Office had one weapon it did not propose to discard – it still had the feeding tube. On 5th October, the Misses Mary Richardson and Rachel Peace were arrested on suspicion of having burned 'The Elms', an unoccupied house at Hampton-on-Thames. They hunger struck while still on remand, and were forcibly fed in Holloway Gaol – an action not only highly questionable in the case of remanded prisoners, but one which suggested that the feeding tube might soon become, not just a measure of precaution, but a new engine of punishment. This thought seems to have occurred, with particular force, to Miss Zelie Emerson who caught the prison doctor as he came out of his house and broke a South African sjambok over his back: while the poor man, who had administered the tube on orders and sorely against his will, very gallantly took his beating without offering any resistance or preferring any charges. When Mrs Pankhurst heard of what had happened to Dr Forward, she grimly remarked that, if any beating were done, she 'preferred it should be a member of the Government'.

XII

But indeed, if any beating were to be done, Mrs Pankhurst would have much preferred that it should not be done by Miss Zelie Emerson. For in the past year a profound but inevitable change had taken place in the militant movement; it had all but openly split into two; and Miss

Emerson was on the wrong side. Once again the unseen hand, out of the darkness surrounding that little stage, delicately twitches the complicated strings; and another puppet moves forward to dispute the scene with Mrs Pankhurst and her daughter.

The united psychology of pre-war womanhood had already bewildered the British public and itself with – in Mrs Pankhurst – the energetic embodiment of an obsessive idea; in Christabel, with the alluring but utterly selfish will to a kind of sexual power. And now, occupying a position midway between her mother and sister, Sylvia Pankhurst emerged as the projection of a simpler desire – the desire of women to get in touch with the problems of other women. In this she commanded the allegiance of Miss Emerson and any number of others. Sylvia might have been allowed to pursue her way in peace, but for two perhaps inevitable drawbacks. She had the family *flair* for publicity, and she was a socialist. These grave offences Mrs Pankhurst and Christabel could not forgive her.

For Christabel, and this, too, was perhaps inevitable, inclined more and more in her politics to a kind of romantic super-Toryism. She wanted her followers to represent the flower of their sex; and her mother agreed with her: what could be more sustaining, what – considering their efforts – more appropriate, than to exact a rigorous obedience from the keenest brains and the best families of England? But Sylvia, in her Bow Road baker-shop, absolutely insisted on working for those poor, degraded, uneducated women of the slums, women who could add nothing mentally to the movement, and would probably give it a remarkably bad name among such desirable sympathizers as went to Buckingham Palace Garden Parties, frequented the Primrose League, had their name in the *Peerage*, or even – *gloria in excelsis!* – could be found among the ramifications of the *Almanach de Gotha*. It would, of course, be very unjust to Mrs Pankhurst and Christabel to suppose that they were moved by simple snobbery; there was the infinitely more important question of obedience. When, by some inexplicable effort of un-logic, they decided that the faithful Keir Hardie should be heckled with even more vehemence than his colleagues in the Labour Party, Sylvia could not agree. It would have been useless, of course, to protest that Hardie's clothes, which were a standing joke in *Punch*, or Hardie's social standing, which was non-existent, made him an undesirable champion; or to maintain that, since the Labour Party as a whole had signally failed the WSPU, its most prominent member must suffer with the rest. Sylvia – it was very troublesome of her – could only see him as a loyal friend. And then, to crown everything, there was Sylvia's infallible instinct for getting herself into the news.

It all began towards the end of February, when Sylvia with some of her regrettable friends – such as George Lansbury's son, Willie – held an open air meeting near Bow Church, and concluded it with a little window smashing. Sylvia threw a flint through an undertaker's window, Willie did violence on the Bromley Town Hall, little Zelie Emerson on the Liberal Club; and the three of them, together with a sweated machine worker called Mrs Watkins, appeared next morning in the Thames Police Court, and were sentenced to two months' hard labour.

In Holloway Prison, Sylvia and Miss Emerson – the fate of Mrs Watkins has not transpired – decided to enter on a hunger *and thirst* strike. The authorities countered with the feeding tube. Sylvia's nervous imagination had long horrified itself with anticipations of this torture, and she collected a variety of weapons – her outdoor shoes, for instance – with which to pelt the doctors when they arrived: but when at last the awful moment came, and the cell door opened, she was confronted, not with a group of doctors, but with what seemed to be a little army of wardresses. 'I could not use my missiles on them,' she wrote in the *Suffragette Movement,* 'poor tools!'

Yet her hand disobediently clutched one shoe, and threw it among the poor tools, grimly advancing. The usual scene followed – the struggle, the vomiting, the torn and bleeding gums. And so it went on, as the days lengthened into weeks. Where other women might have broken down, Sylvia held out. And the prison authorities showed no disposition to have mercy on her. Did they, too, agree with Mrs Pankhurst and Christabel; did they discover some difference between window-smashing in Knightsbridge, by an army of ladylike hooligans, and window-smashing in Bow, among the poorest of the poor? Sylvia took refuge from her climbing terror by keeping a diary – she had paper and pencils hidden in a bag round her waist. Then she started a play on the story of David and Bathsheba. Once she found herself with the prisoner's slate in her hand, making an illustration for Omar's:

> *Awake! for Morning in the Bowl of Night*
> *Has flung the Stone that puts the Stars to Flight*

– a quotation appropriately popular with suffragettes that year. But at last these expedients failed her; her nerves, incredibly long-suffering in so sensitive a body, utterly gave way. At night, she would get a little relief from the agonies of hunger and thirst and forcible feeding, but she could not sleep; with the first sign of dawn, she would be up, pacing her cell. At length she decided that she would walk up and down – five paces to the window, five back to the door – until they released her. All day long she walked, all evening, all through the night, constantly falling but dragging herself up again: by daybreak she was barely hobbling, but still on her feet.

This was more than the chief wardress could stand; tearfully she begged her terrifying prisoner – whose eyes were now two pools of blood sunk deep in a dead white face – to lie down. Sylvia consented. Within twenty-eight hours she had gained her release.

Before she left, she was permitted to visit Zelie Emerson. What had been done to Miss Emerson heaven and Holloway only knew. She was groaning on her bed with abdominal pains, and her wrists were bound up, for she had tried to slash them with a blunt pen-knife. . . .

Sylvia left in a taxi. There was nobody to meet her; it was Good Friday; her studio was empty. She dragged herself away to the Pembridge Gardens nursing home; and there, hours later, poised in a kind of mist, she remembered the face of Keir Hardie bending over her, haggard with grief and insomnia. Nobody, not even the most sober and unsentimental, has ever denied that this kind of thing was slowly breaking Hardie's heart.

But it only hardened the heart of Mrs Pankhurst. Was not Sylvia stealing the limelight from the adored, the infinitely deserving Christabel? And everybody knew that the sweated women workers of the East End were moving on their own; Mary Macarthur – whose sanity and compassion were naturally suspect to the WSPU – was already forming them into a Trade Union, and Miss Macarthur seemed actually to believe that collective bargaining was of more importance than the Vote. If that was Miss Macarthur's belief – and it was an obstinately strong and precise one – the WSPU could simply ignore her. But Sylvia – what did Sylvia mean by dragging the sacred cause, and the equally sacred name of Pankhurst, into such impossible, such alien surroundings? and why – above all, why – did Sylvia set herself up as a martyr?

But Sylvia persisted. For at length one purely practical issue had glided, by the most gradual degrees, imperceptibly, like a serpent, into the fantastic Eden of militant exaltation. What could be done for the working women of England? The question, apparently so simple and so inevitable, had been easily brushed aside by the WSPU: the Union was not – at the moment at any rate – at all concerned with the working women of England. It remained for Sylvia Pankhurst, in spite of the romantic and fantastical strains in her, to discover, with an unerring instinct, the sources of the country's most profound unrest. She carried the purple, white and green banner of militant suffrage into the great movement which – with its syndicalist tactics, and its oddly native strategy – was then surging against the bulwarks of organized Capital. It is hardly to be supposed that she saw the issue very clearly. The workers of England were not, at that time, very much concerned with the Vote; it was, in fact, because the Vote had done them no good that they were turning, with a peculiar rage, to the more practical questions of organization and solidarity: and with Sylvia the Vote remained the predominant demand. She must still have believed – for she was, then and always, the puppet of a great unconscious force – that the ballot, by some high magic, would do much to relieve the sweated women from the tyranny of their bosses. And certainly it would have done something; it would have made some little difference, and it gave to Sylvia's characteristic excesses the unexpected sanction of an economic purpose. At long last, and after a severe intestinal struggle, the militant suffrage movement had broken in two; and one portion of it was already tossing, like a highly coloured cork, among the dark waves of proletarian anger.

What ironic prescience had prompted the WSPU to adopt as its battle-song – the 'Marseillaise'? As the year advanced, Sylvia did not actually break away from the mother Union; but she had a Federation of her own, down there in the grimy East End, and she counted men as well as women among her supporters. The dock labourers particularly favoured her. One catches sudden glimpses of her – in the intervals between her frequent trips to prison – now inciting a vast crowd in Trafalgar Square to go and loot outside Asquith's house, now escaping from the police by crouching among the sacks of firewood in Willie Lansbury's firewood cart. She had left her studio and gone to live with a shoemaker's family in Ford Road, Bow, within sight of the sooty steeple of St Stephen's Church; and when she lit her candle on sleepless nights, for she was perpetually in a state of nervous exhaustion, she found that the walls were crawling with vermin. But then in the morning, the peace of an earlier life would come flooding back; she would look out of her window on to the yard below, where pots of scarlet geraniums hung on a whitewashed wall, 'and a beautiful girl with smooth, dark hair and a white bodice would come out to delight my eyes in helping her mother at the wash-tub.' (The *Suffragette Movement*, p. 478.) And in this tumultuous life – in which her allegiance to the family cause so continually fought with her mounting enthusiasm for the workers around her – her very appearance was changing. Her once gentle face, so deadly white, so drawn, and yet so oddly exultant, was almost, one might say, the face of one of those nameless women who shouted in the vanguards of the French Revolution.

All the year through, her mother and sister had, with considerable difficulty, withheld the punishing hand. But at last Sylvia went too far. On 1st November, a great meeting was held in the Albert Hall, to demand the release from prison of James Larkin, the Liverpool Irishman, who had tied up the city of Dublin with a series of blood-thirsty sympathetic strikes. And there on the platform, crowded with every kind of reformist and radical, and resonant with the fervid oratory of experienced agitators, stood Sylvia Pankhurst! A remark of the *Daily Herald*'s that 'every day the industrial rebels and the suffrage rebels march nearer together' put the finishing touch to what had already become an impossible situation. Now Sylvia might remember what Mrs Pankhurst had once said to the Pethick Lawrences – 'If you do not accept Christabel's policy, we shall smash you!' From the shrine in Paris rolled the clouds of Christabel's wrath: Sylvia must be taught a lesson.

Just how effective the lesson was, remains to be told. But one can hardly resist the conclusion that one of those puppets had whirled right off the stage, and escaped – with singular good fortune – into a larger, a more immediate, a more intelligible scene.

Chapter Four

The Workers' Rebellion

I

THAT Albert Hall meeting on the night of 1st November, 1913, presents us with a very convenient phenomenon, for on the speakers' platform sat, in serried ranks, the united grievances of England. For the first and the last time Irish Nationalism, Militant Suffrage, and the Labour Unrest were met together . . . for what? Simply to demand the release from prison of a messianic strike-leader whose mind – to say the least – was a trifle unbalanced, and whose methods were definitely not sanctioned by Trade Union leadership? Or was Trade Union leadership itself under fire? One thing, at least, is certain; the vigorous and passionate oratory, rising in increasing volume and a variety of accents beneath the roof of the Albert Hall, was not – as some people rather ingenuously imagined – merely the irritable expulsion of reformist steam. It resembled rather the gathering of a heavy cloud, caught up out of some teeming sea; for its strength was drawn from every factory, every workshop, mine, wharf and slum throughout the length and breadth of England.

But to suppose that in 1913 the working classes were, as a whole, *consciously* dissatisfied with Trade Union leadership would be to suppose far too much. Was it the parliamentary Labour Party, then, which evoked both their wrath and those violent speeches in the Albert Hall? Certainly the Labour Party, so coyly and inextricably tied to the apron strings of the Mother of Parliaments, had become little more than an inconspicuous and uneasy ally of the Liberal Government. The workers of England were rightly disappointed in it; but was this the cause of their unrest? Or was it the Liberal Government itself, so suave, so specious, so ready to carry performance up to the very point beyond which performance might perhaps begin to bring results? Or was it the fall of real wages, in a time of apparent prosperity? These questions, mingled as they are with the mysterious movements of gold, the fatal concentrations of capital, the doctrines of sociologists, and all the conflicting theories of economic thinkers, scarcely admit of a positive answer.

They seem to lead us back, as through a labyrinth, into more and more shadowy recesses of English life, until at last, in that baffling darkness, we are lost.

The workers of England, united neither in their politics nor in their grievances, with no single desire for solidarity, yet contrived to project a movement which took a revolutionary course and might have reached a revolutionary conclusion; and how is this to be explained? The pre-war English worker was no *doctrinaire*. He could not be expected to respond to impressive theories and visionary speculations. He was consciously respectable, law-abiding, even reactionary. And yet from that world of his, into which legislation entered with such reluctance, and where ninepence a week meant the difference between acute and normal discomfort, there rose such an assault upon Liberalism as put the two previous rebellions completely in the shade.

An assault upon Liberalism! If one dared approach a proletarian movement with an intuition instead of a theory, here would be the answer. For Liberalism, after all, implies rather more than a political creed or an economic philosophy; it is a profoundly conscience-stricken state of mind. It is the final expression of everything which is respectable, God-fearing and frightened. The poor, it says, are always with us, and something must certainly be done for them: not too much, of course, that would never do; but something. The poor might reasonably be expected to have their own opinions about this; and, indeed, in certain periods of the Victorian era they gave vent to these opinions in a most disconcerting manner. But they, too, had been infected with the same disease.

'Several toasts were given' (so writes an observer of a workmen's dinner during the prolonged erection, in the '70s, of the Albert Memorial) 'and many of the workmen spoke, almost all of them commencing by "Thanking God that they enjoyed good health"; some alluded to the temperance that prevailed amongst them, others observed how little swearing was ever heard, whilst all said how pleased and proud they were to be engaged on so great a work.' (v. *Queen Victoria* by Lytton Strachey, p. 324.)

Honest labour bears a lovely face. To do my duty in that state of life unto which it hath pleased God to call me. Was it against these complacent phrases, and all they meant, that the British workman finally revolted? Honest labour, the doing of duty, reverence towards one's betters – all these are the conditions of a certain kind of security; and these, too, have a fatal attraction for the independent mind. And what is Liberalism itself but something which preys upon the independent mind – Liberalism which proffers, at one moment, the necessary minimum of reform, and protests, at the next, that – such is the sanctity of contract – a workman has the right to sell his labour where he pleases and for any kind of wages that he can get? In the worst slums, the most underpaid districts of Victorian England, the doctrines of security and independence had twined their roots and grown large; and their seeds had been blown – by what unkindly winds! – into the less promising soil of the infant Trade Unions. The worker, too independent to believe that solidarity was his only hope, looked upon collective bargaining as almost a decent, almost one might say a humble, plea for better treatment. The contradiction could not be borne forever; a man cannot be simultaneously proud and prostrate: but on that contradiction was founded the respectability of the Victorian working classes.

Respectability . . . wasn't it *safe*, after all? How glibly could one maintain – with remarkable optimism, of course, but optimism is glib, too – that it guaranteed every man a living! Let a worker be honest, sober, God-fearing, industrious and – somehow or other, you could not say precisely how, but by some mysterious method of cautious interference – the State would see to it that he never went hungry. This was one of the chief articles in the Liberal creed, though it was unwritten and only whispered deep in the heart. And as the great Labour Unrest of 1910–14 unfolds itself, might one not see it as a profoundly unconscious assault upon respectability, a vital revolution in the world of the soul?

Economics, to be sure, are extremely uneasy with a generalization such as this. And though the whole complexion of the Labour Unrest – the sudden class hatred, the unexpected violence, the irrational moods – makes it an essential, a sanguine, part of pre-war psychology, yet the immediate causes of it have a very different look. Grim and grey as they are, they direct us not to life but to death – to the unpleasantly decaying death of Liberal democracy.

II

The date of the Unrest's beginning is, by general agreement, January 1910; and the most obvious cause of it was the continued drop in real wages. . . .

Back in 1890, with the opening of new fields in South Africa, the world's stock of gold began to increase at an alarming rate; by 1909 it had been swollen by a quantity very considerably greater than the total amount of bullion and coin previously existing in Europe, America, and the Colonies, a quantity more than half as much as the world's total previous stock in all forms. The mysterious metallic tide, flowing into England year by year, trickled into even the poorest houses; but – such was its nature – the shape it took there was scarcely an aureate one. It became a halfpenny more on the pound of tea, or three-pence more on a pair of boots; it became a general price rise. By 1910 the purchasing power of the pound, steadily declining, had shrunk to sixteen shillings and eleven pence.

This was the effect of cheap gold upon the workers of England, and it was an unavoidable effect. But there should have been a compensation. For an increase in prices means an increase in productivity, and an increase in productivity means an increase in wages. Yet wages, though they had risen a little, had not risen in proportion; in 1910 the English worker was a poorer man than he was in 1900. What was the reason for this? Were business men, filled with a joyful confidence, investing too much of the nation's resources in worthless undertakings? Were they growing careless? Were weak men remaining in the field, who, in less prosperous times, would have sold their concerns to more ruthless competitors? Any one of these reasons would have resulted in a lessened productivity, and a consequent fall in real wages.

Or was capital discovering more attractive fields for investment than the field of British industry? The Boer War and the Russo-Japanese War had absorbed their share, and more than their share, of the national resources; and, by 1910, one and a half billions of private capital were sunk in North and South America, and perhaps two billions were profitably scattered to the foreign ends of the earth. Was there consequently less capital available to co-operate with labour in the home field?

These questions lead us deeper into the sad mazes of the investing mind, which at each turn becomes more careless, more greedy, more vindictive, and more feeble. The rate of return to capital was visibly increasing, but where was that capital invested? What uncouth toilers, in what remote corners of the world, sweated and starved to bring to some comfortable little householder in Upper Tooting his pleasant five per cent? The comfortable little householder probably asked this –

not of his conscience, however, but of his prospectus and balance sheet, which always returned the most reassuring answers. And, besides, what else could he do with his savings? They were not his to control. The independent small *entrepreneur* – that dream of Liberal economics – had vanished from the earth; the great illusion of the middle classes was over; wealth was in the grip of other and fewer and more formidable hands.

Indeed, that tide of gold, rolling up out of South Africa, had deposited in the boardrooms and drawing-rooms and palaces of England a pre-posterous and powerful flotsam, which, arriving casually like seaweed, established itself with the instinctive adroitness of a barnacle. The new financier, the new plutocrat, had little of that sense of responsibility which once had sanctioned the power of England's landed classes. He was a purely international figure, or so it seemed, and money was his language, like a loud and glittering Esperanto; it was a language, more-over, which England's upper classes seemed unable to resist. Where did the money come from? Nobody seemed to care. It was there to be spent, and to be spent in the most ostentatious manner possible; for its new masters set the fashion, and the fashion they set was not likely to be a reticent one. Society in the last pre-war years grew wildly plutocratic; the middle classes became more complacent and dependent; only the workers seemed to be deprived of their share in prosperity.

The picture is hardly a pleasant one, yet it has to be rendered even more unpleasant by the added colours of fear. The British industrialist was definitely afraid. The infinite interacting veins of credit, which seemed to knit the world up into one vast organism, gave a specious promise of peace and co-operation; a radiant promise. And the world's financial map, studded with the inevitable concentrations of capital, was radiant indeed; but it was the radiance of acne. It was a creeping disease, and the first of its victims was British industrial supremacy. Already in-human hostilities had been proclaimed; foreign tariffs, foreign bounties, the restrictive commercial policies of foreign governments. The old world-empire of Free Trade had long since tottered to its fall. American Trusts and German *Kartellen* controlling their own home markets, were dumping their products in non-protected countries; and though the influence of this was hardly yet felt in England, the very existence of such tactics bred a secret terror. Wherever the English industrialist looked, he could not escape the presence of America and Germany. Technical inventions were now *their* speciality; they were admirably organized; they had discovered within their borders vast resources of iron, coal, and oil. In '95, England was the leading coal-producing country; now she was far behind the USA, and only just ahead of Germany: in the relative production of iron-ore, pig-iron, and steel she was an ignoble third. Where was it all to end?

True, in her exports of domestic produce she still led the world, but by an uncomfortably narrow margin, which dwindled every year. And she still had almost a monopoly of the world's sea-borne trade. Almost, but not quite. Japanese shipping, leaving its particular hunting ground in the China Sea and the Pacific Islands, was creeping across to the Pacific coasts of South America, and even supplying parts of the Indian Ocean. Germany was becoming a menace. Even America, no longer content with her modest coal exports to Cuba and Mexico, was making shipments to Mediterranean and South American ports. Scarcely had the thunders of Gettysburg and Sedan died away, than this new and more sinister warfare declared itself, whispering at last into the farthest corners of the seven seas. Its first effects upon England had been the depressions of '75 and '84; and now – and now – why were economists prophesying another depression, perhaps in 1916? Well, there was no use thinking about it; times were unusually prosperous, England was still the leading industrial nation. But steadily and irresistibly the fear grew.

It spread downwards through the various layers of society until at last it vented itself upon the working classes. A capitalist might understand, and even condone, the concentration against him of foreign capital, but under the circumstances he could only feel extremely uneasy about any sign of agitation among the workers, from whose labours, between 1900 and 1910, he had realized a considerable profit. By going slow on wages, he could store up something against a rainy day. It was really unfortunate that he himself was compelled to cut a dash in the world, but then people seemed to expect it these days, and one's prestige was a valuable asset. As for the workers, he did not expect them to see eye to eye with him, and the only method that suggested itself was to give them a black eye the moment they showed any disposition to see at all. This is what was done in the early years of the twentieth century – and as a feat it was generally applauded by the middle classes who – themselves deprived of economic power and reduced to a mere assortment of clerks, salesmen, officials and civil servants – looked upon the producers of England with a jaundiced, a fearful, a vindictive gaze.

III

The fall in real wages can be considered, at least in part, as an attack of Capital upon Labour: it could be construed wholly as such. But elsewhere another and more direct attack had been launched. In 1901, after a disorderly strike in the Taff Vale Railway Company of South Wales, the General Manager of that company sued the Amalgamated Society of Railway Servants before the highest court in the land, the House of Lords. Precisely what the Society's offence was it would have been hard to say. It had not fomented the strike, which had been started without its authorization: it had merely tried to bring it to a successful issue. The Lords, however, decided that any Union, whether registered or not, and though it was denied the privileges of incorporation, was none the less corporately liable for any injury or damage caused by any person who could be deemed to be acting as its agent; and this not merely in respect of criminal offences, but of any offences which might be declared actionable.

The blow was a crushing one. Not merely was the A S R S compelled to pay £23,000 in damages, but from henceforth any stoppage of work, however lawful, could be made the subject of heavy damages against the Trade Unions. Nor was this all. For how could anyone contend that the law lords, however meticulous their interpretation of the law in this case, had not been heavily biased against the principle of Trade Unionism?

And what had the Unions done to deserve it? Little enough; perhaps too little. Ever since the collapse of Chartism in 1848, they had pursued a policy of 'opportunism', of attempting, that is, to obtain for every man a fair day's pay for a fair day's work. And if the Taff Vale Judgement were to be the reward of such mildness, might they not argue that mildness deserved no less? The conclusion, indeed, was unavoidable. Very well, then; they must show their power.

In the elections of 1906, fifty candidates, pledged to reverse the Taff Vale Judgement, were put up by what was then known as the Labour Representation Committee, and twenty-nine were elected. To these could be added twelve miners, officially Liberals. The Liberal Government, crowned with the laurels of an unparalleled victory at the polls, seemed unaware that a new and uncompromising voice had been added to its deliberations. It produced a Bill which, designed to put the Unions on a legal footing, was based on the findings of a Royal Commission appointed by the previous government, and satisfied nobody but the lawyers and employers. But scarcely had the Bill received its first reading when, from one part of the House and another, men stood up to explain that they had pledged themselves to vote for the complete immunity of 1871. Conservative and Liberals alike were seized with consternation. Not even the findings of a judicial committee of the House of Lords, it appeared, could silence the Unions. It was incredible, it was 'monstrous'; but what could one do? Parliament, alas, was no longer the exclusive property of landed gentlemen. Hastily a Trade Disputes Bill was prepared, hastily enacted. It gave the Unions an astounding, indeed an unlimited immunity.

Labour was jubilant. The most powerful Government in history had been compelled, by scarcely more than a single show of power, to yield to the just demands of organized workers. But the mind of Capital is secretive and dauntless, and already a tremendous counterblow – tremendous in its effect, but even more tremendous in its lack of any trace of consideration – was being prepared with infinite care.

In July 1908, a certain W. V. Osborne, heavily financed from capitalist sources, took action against the Amalgamated Society of Railway Servants, of which he was a member. He wished to restrain it from spending any of its funds on political objects, declaring that this was beyond its powers as a Trade Union. For more than a year the Lords deliberated, and at last, in December 1909, the law lords emerged with what was afterwards known as the Osborne Judgement. The ASRS, they maintained, must not use its funds for political objects; it must not levy contributions from its members for the purpose of supporting the Labour Party, or assisting Members of Parliament. The Unions were declared to be legal corporate entities, and, to support this extremely problematical contention, their lordships had conducted an exhaustive search into the Trade Union Act of 1876. And there, very conveniently, they had discovered a definition, contained in an incidental clause, which nobody had bothered to take seriously, and certainly not in the sense which their lordships gave to it. But after a lapse of thirty-three years, quite suddenly, every Trade Union in the land was forbidden to do anything which could not be brought within the limited and disputable meaning of that highly incidental clause!

What could this be but prejudice of the most glaring kind? 'That it should be illegal for the salaried President or Secretary of the

Amalgamated Society of Railway Servants to sit in Parliament, when it is perfectly legal for the much more generously salaried Chairman or Director of a Railway Company is an anomaly hard for any candid man to defend.' So the Sidney Webbs have written in their *The History of Trade Unionism*; and their argument is irresistible.

At the heart of that legal web which their law lordships had spun, with such intricate cunning, to entrap the Unions, there lurked the greedy spider of organized capital. The combination was formidable and sinister. When Wealth and Law go hand in hand, where shall a man turn? Armed with the dubious majesty of the Osborne Judgement, employers were openly attempting to persuade Trade Unionists to bring actions against their Unions, actions which would restrain them from taking part in municipal elections, or from subscribing to educational classes, or from taking shares in a Labour newspaper.

Could Parliament help?

Considering the pretensions of political democracy, the question seems hardly necessary. After nearly a century of almost revolutionary reform, of stubborn and protracted internal combats, of the labours of high-minded men, of defeated prejudice and tempered passion, Parliament could at least claim to be a tolerable example of a representative institution. Or so the politicians maintained, not always with their tongues in their cheeks. And then, in the time of the Taff Vale Judgement, had not the Liberals yielded, and with scarcely a murmur, to an inconsiderable chorus of fifty Trade Unionist voices? And had they not come forward thereafter with a shining procession of social reforms – a Workmen's Compensation Act, an Old Age Pension Act, a Miners' Eight Hours Act, a Trade Boards Act? And yet – what *could* be the matter? – wages never went up. In fact, they continued to fall.

Perhaps the Osborne Judgement would send them into action. For here, enhanced by the lordly splitting of legal hairs, was a heavy, brutal, and unprincipled assault of Capital upon Labour. And the Liberals were traditionally the friends of Labour; in fact a considerable majority of Trade Unionists still voted for them at the polls. But it was all very strange; the Osborne Judgement did not send the Liberals into action. On the contrary, they seemed to avoid it – as though the Trade Unions had fallen among thieves, and they had no choice but to pass by on the other side.

Mr Winston Churchill, whose chequered career had entered a momentary stage of fervid radicalism, let fall an angry phrase or two;

and Mr Lloyd George peppered, with the silver pellets of his oratory,
the various hides of peers and brewers and landlords. That appeared to be
all. Taxes were going up, it was true – the rich were being forced to pay
for reform. But could it be that reform itself was insufficient? If, poised
on the revolutionary brink of 1910, the worker could have looked forward, what would he have seen? An Act conferring on every Member of
Parliament £400 a year, by which the fertile Mr George hoped to take
the sting out of the Osborne Judgement. This was in 1911. In 1911, too,
appeared the Health Insurance Act, which the Liberals produced after a
period of prolonged and difficult gestation, in the gritty and inscrutable
way of an oyster with a pearl. But neither of these pieces of legislation
could possibly have satisfied the foreseeing eye. They were not designed
to advance the worker, but to propitiate him.

The Liberal Government was extraordinarily difficult to understand.
It was dying with extreme reluctance and considerable skill; you might
almost consider it healthy, unless you took a very close look, and it had
erected such a fence around it of procrastinations and promises that a
close look was almost impossible to obtain. The workers were simply
dissatisfied with it, they could hardly tell why; and, indeed, that fine
Liberal Hegelianism of at once believing in freedom and not believing in
freedom was beyond the understanding of all but the elect. To interfere
in the question of pensions, health, strikes, education, conditions of
labour – ah, yes, this could be done; to destroy the absolute powers of the
Lords, to cripple the vast landed estates – such actions were highly
desirable: but to insist that employers should pay a living wage? That
was a frightful impairment of freedom.

Indeed, it was. But then freedom itself was an old-fashioned notion,
suited to the vital passions, the philosophical visions, of the nineteenth
century, but somewhat misplaced among the disillusions of the twentieth. It was almost impossible to resist the thought that political
Liberalism was attempting to stave off the inevitable with reform, and
that the day would come when reform could go no further. What *was*
reform, after all, but the skilful balance of incompatibles, the ingenious
expression of that middle class philosophy which believes in resisting at
once the aggressions of the rich and the pretensions of the poor? And
what were the middle classes, in 1910, that any vague Liberalism of
theirs should still hold good? In fact, if Liberalism were to be the
solution, then the workers could get an excellent brand of it from the
Tory Party, which had now become the party of sudden innovation, and

might well be persuaded to grant some of the demands of the working classes, so long as the working classes, in their turn, agreed to consider themselves as the pampered serfs of an eternal economic feudalism.

The last parliamentary hope – and it had been unconsciously the hope of all workers, whatever their political convictions – was the Independent Labour Party. There, at least, was the political counterpart of the Trade Unions. In 1906, on its first appearance in Parliament, it had triumphantly reversed the Taff Vale Judgement. And after that – what?

The Labour Party had become a sort of admonishing left wing of the Government, supporting its sick policies with all the fidelity of a slightly cantankerous nurse. If it had a programme, it did not put it forward with any conviction – with the noisy and intractable conviction, for instance, that the Irish Party had once shown under Parnell. But an examination of its membership would show why. All but a very few of the so-called Labour MP's were Liberals at heart, and as for their leader – Mr Ramsay MacDonald – that handsome and spirited young Scotsman seemed well content to be a Liberal three quarters of the time and a Socialist only when occasion arose, and occasions seemed to arise with extreme infrequency. An attractive and strong personality, Mr MacDonald was already betraying a certain parliamentary astuteness; he did not let his left hand know what his right hand was doing. For while with his left hand he composed pamphlets in which a noticeable literary skill was mingled with demands for the collectivist State, with his right he beckoned, coyly, kindly, and persistently – towards the hovering presences of fame and fortune. And this was due to no deep-seated duplicity in Mr MacDonald. He was a man of principles. But he was quite unable, except for his splendid opposition to war, to ignore the good in anything anywhere – an inability which subsequently led him through all the transmutations of his singular career to the no less singular post of Socialist Prime Minister in an aggressively Tory government.

As for the socialists in the Labour Party – Mr Keir Hardie was one, but he was old and romantic, Mr Snowden was another, and there was Mr O'Grady, there was Mr Thorne, there was Mr Jowett, and perhaps there were two or three more. Whether the workers of England, who simply had a grievance which nobody seemed able to remedy, would consciously have accepted political socialism in all its glory is exceedingly doubtful; and whether they would have accepted such socialism as was then evident in the Labour Party is, if possible, even more doubtful. For the socialism of the Labour Party was derived from the Fabians – once the hope of the reforming '90s but now a little stale – who expected, by cautious and indeed almost imperceptible degrees, eventually to achieve a beatific state of intolerable bureaucracy.

Such was the nature and constitution of the Labour Party, and the workers of England, whose political barometer was wages and nothing more, were very uninterested in it by 1910. And a party which appeared to be the result of a rather unfortunate *mésalliance* between the Fabians and the Trade Unions was not calculated to raise anybody's hopes unduly.

The Trade Unions! There, perhaps, is the key which may unlock the problem of the Labour Unrest. Only, when the door is thrown open and one peers inside, what swirling clouds and indeterminate vistas suddenly disclose themselves! The fall in real wages, the crude assaults of capitalism, the ineptitude of Parliament, these are only preliminary considerations. It was around the Trade Unions that the deepest grievances, the most vehement desires, ultimately gathered themselves.

And yet they gathered there rather in the manner of a swarm of bees which settles unasked on the bald head of a highly perturbed old gentleman. The Unions had made a show of power in 1906, when their very existence was threatened, but there was nothing in their leadership to indicate that they were prepared to take their case beyond the walls of Parliament. Their leaders were simply administrators of the old 'Lib–Lab' (i.e., Liberal–Labour) persuasion; and, whatever their individual organizations may have been, *as a whole* they were far too loosely united. They had no common policy; their yearly Congress, for all its vast membership, concerned itself purely with political questions; their Federation, the only visible central body, was a federation of the weaker Unions, which drained its treasury; and, last but alas not least, they were at odds amongst themselves. The nineteenth century, with its mechanization and its enormous development of land and sea traffic, had bequeathed to its burdened successor an increasing host of unskilled and semi-skilled labourers. Obviously, the Unions could no longer remain 'craft' unions – that is, unions of skilled artisans: they must become 'industrial' unions – that is, unions which comprised all labourers in one kind of employment. And yet to what Union should an unskilled labourer belong who worked, shall we say, for a railway company? To the Amalgamated Society of Engineers? to the Railway Servants? to one of the new General Labour Unions? Nobody could tell for certain; but belong to one or another he must, for the sake of solidarity. The fight for the possession of his membership seemed likely to be long and bitter; and though the distinctively 'craft' Unions – the Boilermakers, the Steam Engine Workers, the United Machine Workers, and so on – might turn up an aristocratical nose at such goings on, the position was exceedingly ominous. For what earthly chance had Labour, at this critical point in its history, if its most powerful Unions suddenly plunged into a complicated internal warfare?

And, indeed, if its acknowledged leaders had had any say in the matter, Labour might have lingered on until the War in a state of jealous and even snobbish disintegration, crippled by the Osborne Judgement, and deluded at every turn by the shining mist of Liberal promises and Liberal compromise. But it was not to be. There were other forces at work – in France, in America, and deep in the soul of the English people. Indefinite as these forces were, alien one to another, inarticulate at times, unconscious even – yet they turned the English Trade Unions into an astounding symbol of rebellious energy. And this symbol, once deciphered, spells out the death of the Liberal Party.

IV

It is impossible to say at exactly what date the doctrine of Syndicalism crept out of France across the English Channel. But it is generally conceded that it made this journey at some time between 1905 and 1910, and James Connolly, the Irish labour leader, is suspected of being responsible for its arrival. The journey was a short one, but it was difficult. Though Syndicalism means nothing more than 'Trade Unionism' in French, it indicated a rather peculiar sort of Trade Unionism, and none the less peculiar – in the eyes of English workmen – for *being* French. It advocated the complete supremacy of the Trade Unions, which should federate themselves locally and centrally – a federation of local unions forming the local Authority, and a standing conference of national representatives of all the Trade Unions forming the National Authority. The producers, in other words, were to control all industries and all services; and they were to gain control through a violent succession of continuous strikes, culminating in a 'general expropriatory Strike'. Nothing, of course, could be more opposed to the collectivist theories of the Sidney Webbs, the Fabians, and the socialist members of the ILP, who foresaw, through a series of deliberate steps more or less divinely predestined by the Webbs themselves, the gradual evolution of the State into a great organization of consumers; and who, to be sure, are still foreseeing it.

Syndicalism had been a faith full-grown in France since 1902, and it had taken root among the immigrant population of the United States. In France the General Federation of Labour, in America the I W W were in much the same position as the British Trade Unions had been in 1834 – 'a fearful engine of mischief,' Dr Arnold had called them in that year, 'ready to riot or to assassinate.' The *Syndicats* and the I W W did, in fact, inspire a great deal of terror, nor is it to be supposed that any doctrine they might evolve would be quite so constructive as terroristic. As for the philosophy of Syndicalism, it was rooted in the anarchism of Nietzsche, had branched out into the *élan vital* of the Bergsonians, and finally come to flower in the *Réflexions sur la Violence* of M. Sorel.

This strange philosophical growth could not – *qua* philosophy – have had the slightest appeal to British workmen. In the first place, they had probably never heard of Nietzsche or Bergson, and as for the *Réflexions sur la Violence* of M. Sorel they simply would not have understood them: in the second place, they were never very happy with a reasoned system of revolution. And yet, between 1910 and 1914, and against the wishes of their leaders, they plunged into a series of furious strikes which, but for the declaration of War, would have culminated in September 1914, in a General Strike of extraordinary violence. The exact prescription for a syndicalist revolution.

How could this have come about? Could native thinkers have assisted them, re-stating the propositions of M. Sorel with all the passionate common-sense of the Anglo-Saxon tongue? One glance at the journalism of the day will prove that this could not be the case. The *Daily Herald* was a kind of intellectual ostrich, swallowing any and every wild idea, and disgorging them all, undigested, in a very unappetizing condition. The *New Age*, appalled at the apparent expulsion of all non-labouring intellectuals from the syndicalist world, was attempting to bridge the gulf with Guild Socialism, a mysterious combination of consumers and producers which the editor, Mr A. R. Orage, may possibly have understood. The *Daily Citizen* still called for the old opportunist tactics. The language of the *Syndicalist* was vehement but obscure. The *New Statesman* preached, with a vigour which was highly laudable under the circumstances, the complacent fatalism of the Sidney Webbs. These may well have had their effect – a far from negligible effect – upon the younger intellectuals; but the mass of the workers they could not have reached at all.

Could it perhaps have been the agitations of Mr Tom Mann, that ardent syndicalist, who, realizing that British workmen are not very susceptible to ideas, was determined to practice the ideas first and preach them afterwards? Mr Tom Mann was one of the most successful and intelligent agitators in British labour history, but he was an effect rather than a cause of those four and a half strike years.

Or could it be that the air itself seemed full of agitated whispers, of echoes, and insinuations? From America and France there came, seaborne like a sound of bells, the reverberations of a violent attack upon political democracy. From the rare, cold upper regions of economic speculation there drifted down, as light as snow and scarcely comprehended, a disturbing rumour that conditions would never improve in a capitalist world, that indeed they must inevitably grow worse. And a question, airy but insistent, poised itself on the edges of conscious thought: had not a combination of science and reform, by insisting on healthier conditions of labour and life, made more workers physically 'available' for longer periods of their existence? made them, in effect, cheaper and cheaper commodities in the labour market? Already, though hardly visible as yet in the general activity, an increasing horde of the casually employed, the unemployed, and the unemployable drifted through the country.

These reasons are forcible enough, but they do not answer the main question – How did these strike years come to be conducted, tactically, on purely syndicalist lines?

The majority of British workers were involved in the strikes, sympathetically if not actively; there is no doubt of that: and yet the majority of British workers, in the two elections of 1910, obediently voted either Liberal or Conservative, preserved – in their political consciousness – an almost theological reverence for the operations of Parliament, and would have been dismayed at the very mention of the word 'revolution'. How could they express – as they did – an increasing, an unprecedented class hatred? how could they shake – as they did – the very foundations of parliamentary rule? how could they be at once syndicalist and not syndicalist, revolutionary and not revolutionary? The answer may be found in a phrase of Mr Fabian Ware's, a Conservative writer, who in *The Worker and His Country* asserted that syndicalism was 'an assertion of instinct against reason' – in other words, a convenient expression for a new energy. Women's Suffrage was also a convenient expression for a new energy and so was the slogan 'Ulster will fight and Ulster will be right.' . . .

The instinct of the British worker was very active in 1910. It warned him that he was underpaid, that Parliament – left to itself – would keep him underpaid; it told him that good behaviour had ceased to have any meaning; it asserted that he must unite at all costs. The only visible symbol of unity was the Trade Unions: to the Trade Unions therefore he turned.

And the Trade Unions became the not too willing repository for instincts, for feelings, for a kind of vital unreason.

V

The first steps into the Unrest seem straightforward enough – anger at the fall of real wages, at capitalist aggression, at the unwillingness of Parliament; anger fomented by agitators, and informed by vague fears, and leading to solidarity. One step more, and we reach the Trade Unions; and suddenly there lies before us, in darkness and confusion, a labyrinth of contradictory paths. Revolutionary methods appear, but not revolutionary intentions; distrust of and respect for political democracy are hopelessly intermingled; the Government is simultaneously attacked and defended, and by the same people; reason wars with instinct. Can one discern at last, after the dark journey through those complicated mazes, the deployment for a mighty battle – in which Capital, already organized through the operation of inhuman and infallible laws, is pitted against the Unions, the fallible armies of human beings?

It would be very convenient to think so. But the battle, though it had begun far back in the nineteenth century, though it proclaimed itself in every strike and from every platform, was reserved in all its fury for the post-war world. Between the two armies there interposes itself, waving a worm-eaten olive-branch, the complacent presence of the Liberal Government, combining in its person at once the majesty of Parliament, the allurements of reform, and the solid weight of constitutional respectability. Is it really an economic battle, then, which will be found at the heart of the labyrinth? or can one take one turn more, creep around one more corner, and discover an even deeper, an even more human, conflict?

For the assaults upon Parliament of the Tories, the women, and the workers have something profoundly in common. In each case, a certain conscious security was in question. As for the workers, it must be remembered that their life was not – in 1910 – at all invaded by despair, by the post-war certainty that things would never, by any chance, get very much better. The majority of people did not think in economics then, but in politics. In 1910, an industrious man might still believe that he had a chance of improving himself, and that his children and his grandchildren would climb higher rather than descend as the years went on. And yet that smothering security, implied in the phrase 'a fair day's pay for a fair day's work', had to be overthrown; it was the very essence of Victorian respectability, and the ultimate expression of it was parliamentary mediation. The workers did not want to be safe any more; they wanted to live, to take chances, to throw caution to the winds: they had been repressed too long. And so the deepest impulse in the great strike movement of 1910–14 was an unconscious one, an enormous energy pressing up from the depths of the soul; and Parliament shuddered before it, and under its impact Liberal England died.

In this way the instinctive tactics of the syndicalists and the instinctive desires of the workers came together; but not for a syndicalist purpose. The movement on the surface was not revolutionary but rebellious; it did not *consciously* aim, as some have contended, at the overthrow of the wage system and the destruction of parliamentary rule; the only revolution that can be discovered in it is a psychological one. Such revolutions, it is true, have strange endings, and – if the General Strike of September 1914, had ever taken place – nobody can say what the result would have been. . . .

The Workers' Rebellion naturally expressed itself in terms of economic necessity, a necessity which makes it at once more realistic and nobler than the other two rebellions. And then – in spite of the fearful scenes of poverty, and disease, and oppression which revealed themselves during the course of it, like a cancer in the tissues of democracy – it has a far more exuberant appearance than the other two. The workers of England did not suffer from the same repressions as their betters. Even in the drabbest periods of mid-Victorian propriety their nature, in which romance and humour and innocence were so oddly mingled with stolidity and common sense, constantly asserted itself; until it seems that in that sabbatical procession of gloomy years, theirs was the only laughter to be heard. And now they threw off their respectability with a certain gusto; in their darkest angers, their most explicit announcements of class hatred, you might occasionally think – just occasionally – that they were actually having a very good time. Perhaps that is why Mr Ramsay MacDonald wrote, in 1913: 'The labour world responded to the call to strike in the same eager, spontaneous way as nature responds to the call of the springtime. One felt as though some magical allurement had seized upon the people.' (*The Social Unrest*, p. 96.) Coming from a socialist leader, these meditations seem filled with a peculiar fatuity. And yet the disturbing thought remains that Mr MacDonald may have been right.

VI

On 1st January, 1910, the Coal Mines Regulations Act of 1908 was to come into operation in Northumberland, and the evening before the miners' leaders finally agreed with the owners as to the conditions to be observed under the Act – conditions which included the change from a two-shift to a three-shift system. Chiefly from domestic reasons – for if three male members of one household worked on three different shifts, the house would never be clean, nor the babies properly fed, nor the shopping well done – more than one third of the miners in the Northumberland and Durham districts went on strike. In spite of the threats of their executives – whom they called traitors and deceivers; in spite of the cajoleries of the Miners' Federation of Great Britain; in the face of their own Council – a stubborn minority refused to go back to work until the middle of April.

Philip Snowden protested that the strike had been a flagrant violation of Trade Union discipline; but there were others who asked themselves a more pertinent question. The miners of Northumberland and Durham were the 'aristocrats' of the industry, they had been the last to join the Miners' Federation, they were proud and aloof: and it seemed almost incredible that *they* should be behaving with such an unreasoned, such a bitter vehemence. Was there something, perhaps, behind all this which did not meet the eye?

And then again, in the early days of July, a favoured group of 10,000 railwaymen, employed by the North-Eastern Railway (which paid them particularly well and even condescended to recognize their Union) had suddenly struck over some insignificant little incident, held up all traffic for three days, and calmly gone back to work without offering any apology.

Such incidents seemed trifling at the time; and yet they were like ripples on the surface of that 'Industrial Peace' which – but for two or three major disturbances – had lasted from 1893 to 1910. They were little ripples, but they formed a curious, an impulsive, an irresponsible pattern; as though some creature were swimming, some meditative creature, just beneath the surface....

The strikes which occurred between these two incidents, of the miners at Nottingham and Doncaster and Wrexham, the Glasgow thread-workers, the woollen and worsted workers at Bradford; the swift disturbance in South Wales, when only the labours of Mr George Askwith of the Board of Trade prevented a general strike; the beginnings of trouble in the Lancashire cotton industry – all showed the same curious irritation, the same disposition to disregard Union authority.

But it was not until September that the trouble really began. On the ninth of that month the Federation of Master Cotton-Spinners decided that a general loc'.-out should begin in October, if a dispute which had been hanging fire at the Fern Mill, in the Lancashire town of Shaw, were not speedily settled. A certain George Howe – on instructions from the Card and Blowing Room Operatives' Association – had refused to 'pick', or clean, flats at the mill, saying that it was not part of his work as a grinder. He was dismissed. The whole mill went on strike. Informal conferences led to nothing. The question at issue between the men's association and the employers' association was an exceedingly difficult one, for it centred upon two clauses in the Brooklands Agreement of 1907, which governed a great part of the cotton industry, and which, having unfortunately been drafted in a great hurry after an all night conference at a wayside inn, had only been successful as long as there was no need for it. Were the employers to blame now, or were the men? Clause 6 of the Agreement pointed straight to the employers, clause 7 condemned the men. Mr Askwith, whom both sides had agreed upon as arbitrator, confessed that the point was a very nice one, and that it would take him some time to make his award. Meanwhile the feeling between the two associations, as he noted, was 'strong and bitter', but he hoped that something would come of a meeting which he engineered at Manchester on 30th September. Nothing came of it. The employers insisted that Fern Mill, idle since 7th June, should start at once, and without the offending Mr Howe; they would then agree to withdraw lock-out notices, and, if the award went against them, they would pay Howe the whole of his back wages. The operatives stood firm. Nothing would satisfy them but an immediate reinstatement of George Howe, or a complete stoppage at Fern Mill. On 3rd October, 102,000 workers were locked out.

Mr Askwith, with all the intelligence of the Board of Trade at his command, knew very well that the lock-out would soon infect the whole industry. He came hurrying up from London. He tried, as tactfully as possible, to steer the matter away from George Howe, and begged that the Brooklands Agreement – the hasty language of which had attained an almost venerable beauty in the eyes of both sides – should be re-examined; and, being a man of great address, he succeeded. Conference followed conference, but at every turn, just as some decision appeared to be within Mr Askwith's grasp, the casual mention of Howe would suddenly ruin everything. There was no escaping Mr Howe.

In despair, the employers agreed that the very next vacancy in the Shaw district should be Howe's. They went further. They would find him one at once. They besought owner after owner to exchange one of his grinders for Howe, and owner after owner refused, for that almost mythical figure had come to typify the considerable powers of the Card and Blowing Room Operatives' Association. But at last, when all seemed lost, the Duke Spinning Company agreed to take him in. The men went back to work. Almost immediately, Mr Askwith discovered a gap in the Brooklands Agreement, and stopped it with a clause which somewhat favoured the operatives. The first of many battles had been won.

There had been another lock-out in the North of England that September, where a number of fitful strikes in the Federated Shipyards and Ship-repairing Yards so enraged the employers that they declared the Boilermakers to have broken their agreement of March 1909. The Boilermakers had other views – views which they did not share with their own executives, who were only too eager to patch up a peace. Provisional agreements reached at Newcastle on 21st September, and at Edinburgh on 11th October, were turned down by the men in scenes of quite unprecedented rage – unprecedented, indeed, for the Boilermakers had long been known as the most peaceful group in the industry; and once again Mr Askwith was called upon. The Agreement of 1909 proved on examination to be a document so rich in clauses and qualifications that any dispute it was expected to settle might easily drag on until the crack of doom. The delegates of the Boilermakers' Society were summoned to the Board of Trade; the methods of settlement were revised and expedited, so that in future the Boilermakers' patience would not be tried beyond the bounds of endurance; and a report was forwarded to the employers who – in Edinburgh on 7th and 8th December – agreed to accept it. On 15th December the lock-out was ended.

But the real drama of 1910 was being played elsewhere, and though its conclusion was neither simple nor victorious, its effects were far-reaching. Had the owners of the Naval Colliery Company, in the Rhondda Valley of South Wales, foreseen these effects, it is just possible that they might have behaved differently. But then the owners of the Naval Colliery Company happened to be the Cambrian Combine which – through the Cambrian Trust, a holding company – had a controlling interest in it, and thought of nobody but its shareholders. The Naval Collieries had never been very prosperous, though they produced coal of the highest quality and price and sold it to the Admiralty; but the Cambrian Combine was determined to make them pay. Casting about for a possible opportunity, it lit upon the Ely Pit, which could certainly be worked remuneratively if its Upper Five Feet Seam could be opened out under labour piece rate conditions. But could that be done? The Combine seemed to think that with a cutting price of 1s. 9d. per ton of large coal it *could* be done to everybody's satisfaction; the colliers demanded 2s. 6d.

On 1st September, the Ely Pit was closed, and its 900 miners were thrown out of work.

On 5th September, the miners at the other two Naval pits – the Pandy and the Nantgwyn – struck work in sympathy; on 19th September, all the Cambrian Combine collieries – the Cambrian at Clydach Vale, the Glamorgan at Llwynypia, the Britannic at Gilfach Goch – were out on strike. Such were the results of attempting to work an unprofitable seam at starvation wages.

The question, however, did not revolve around the greediness, or otherwise, of the Cambrian Combine. More vital issues were at stake, and all the coalfields of South Wales were in a state of ferment. The Upper Five Feet Seam of the Ely Pit was undoubtedly 'abnormal' in places – it would be difficult for men, working at piece rates, to get a fair day's pay out of it; and it therefore served as a convenient focus for a highly inconvenient agitation. For the South Wales Miners' Federation was itself torn in two. On the one hand, some of its Executive demanded – and the demand was a revolutionary one in 1910 – that a minimum wage should be established for all workers in abnormal places; on the other hand, there was a party which declared itself content with the Wages Agreement then existing. The controversy had been carried on since early in the year; it was growing more bitter every month; and several collieries were already threatening to secede from the S W M F.

On the whole, it seemed as if moderate counsels would prevail; the Miners' Federation of Great Britain was known to be working to that end. On 22nd October, the South Wales Miners' Conciliation Board – where owners and workers met to settle their differences – agreed on a cutting rate for the Ely Upper Five Feet Seam of 2s. 1·3d. per ton, with ¼d. per inch over twelve inches for all labour dealing with clod and stone. In ordinary times, these intricate figures would have satisfied the miners: but times were not ordinary. Two days before a bitter strike had broken out in the Powell Duffryn Collieries of the Aberdare Valley, chiefly over the men's right to carry away broken props for firewood without paying for them. Negotiations between Mr Hann, the General Manager, and Mr Stanton, the Miners' agent, had concluded with a telephone conversation, in which Mr Stanton remarked, 'Further I would like to say that if there is going to be blacklegging over this, there is going to be murder. By God, I mean it!' It was obvious, not only to Mr Hann, perspiring at his end of the telephone, but to everyone re-motely connected with the South Wales district, that a new spirit was abroad: for the Powell Duffryn men and the Naval Colliery men had no specific grievance in common – they simply shared a distrust for the Miners' Federation of Great Britain, a scorn of their own Executive, and an increasing fondness for the principle of the minimum wage.

It was not surprising, therefore, that when the findings of the Conciliation Board came before the Naval Strike Committee they were rejected; nor that a deputation of the S W M F, gathered in the Thistle Hotel at Llwynypia, should have pleaded in vain with the committee to give the new rates at least a trial. That was on 29th October. Two days later the fever had spread to North's Navigation Company in the Llynfi Valley, and on 1st November, all the men in the Rhondda Valley were on strike. It seemed for a moment as if the stoppage would creep onwards irresistibly in and out among the steep black hills of southern Wales – and over what? Over 2s. 1·3d. per ton of large coal at the Ely Pit? or over the feeble spirit displayed by the Executive of the South Wales Miners' Federation? The Executive could not conceal the answer from itself, and on 2nd November its three leading officials – Messrs Williams, Onions, and Richards – issued a manifesto, warning everybody concerned that all such 'sudden and unconstitutional methods' would surely end in disaster. This had the desired effect. Mr Stanton, it is true, greeted the document with a characteristic salvo of undismayed abuse, but South Wales as a whole seemed willing to listen. Only the men of the Aberdare and Rhondda Valleys stopped their ears; and in these two valleys there grew, day by day, an atmosphere of extreme tension.

In London, meanwhile, on 8th November, there was a meeting of distinguished gentlemen at the Home Office. At 10 a.m. that morning a telegram had been received from Captain Lindsay, Chief Constable of Glamorgan, reporting serious riots in the Rhondda Valley, and requesting the immediate assistance of two companies of infantry and two hundred cavalry. Mr Winston Churchill then occupied the Home Office, and he was very soon closeted with Mr R. B. Haldane, graduate of Göttingen and Secretary for War, with General Ewart, the Adjutant-General, and with Major-General C. F. N. Macready, CB. As a result of their deliberations Captain Lindsay was promised his cavalry, also two hundred and seventy Metropolitan Police (a force which was soon increased to eight hundred and two), together with the personal assistance of General Macready. The infantry were to be held at Swindon, ready to descend at a moment's notice. In two days' time they descended.

From the subsequent flock of telegrams and letters which flew to and fro between the Home Office and the valleys – and which have been embalmed for the curious reader in a Government Report – several interesting facts emerge. The employers who, though they controlled both the local police and the local Press, were in a state of extreme terror, bombarded the Home Secretary with a simultaneous volley of gratitude and criticism; the Miners' Federation of Great Britain deplored, with a laudable agility, both the violence of the miners and the employment of military to prevent it; and Mr Churchill, torn between his native militarism, his desire to keep order, and an instinctive dislike of the Welsh owners, alternately hesitated to send soldiers and sent soldiers. In this confusion of passions and interests, General Macready rode up and down the valleys with a handful of cavalry, indicated in his first messages that the whole affair was overrated, and hastily withdrew his cavalcade when its presence seemed to provoke remarkably ugly feelings among the onlookers.

Between 12th November and 21st November, the rioting increased, cold descended, there was snow on the hilltops, and people began to shiver – but not because of the cold. Captain Lindsay declared that 'the strike is totally different to any one I have previously experienced'. There was terror in the air, which never appears quite to have taken shape. Rumours flew up and down. The strikers were armed with revolvers, they had looted quantities of high explosives, they planned to blow up the manager's house at Gilfach Goch – that, at least, and how many other houses, too? The owners begged to be allowed to protect their property with live wire; the soldiers played a football match with the strikers; nobody knew the truth of anything. General Macready met a deputation of Aberdare men, headed by the redoubtable Mr Stanton, and parted with them on the best of terms. General Macready had a soldierly ignorance of the rights and wrongs of the labour world, but if he had had to choose between Mr Stanton and any one of the owners, there is hardly any doubt of what his choice would have been.

For the owners were behaving in a most unlikeable fashion. They ordered the local press to publish the most lurid stories of outrage and horror. They cried for soldiers and more soldiers. They hurried a mobile force of 1,400 constabulary up and down the precipitous roads and for all sorts of reasons – on 11th November, for example, some ninety policemen were summoned to a narrow glen high in the Avon Valley, not to repel a riot, nor yet to protect property, but to supervise a highly dubious deduction in pay! The owners and their satellites seemed to think that these men were their property, to be used when, where, and how they pleased; and a certain Mr Percy Jacob, manager of the Tondu mine, incensed at the independent behaviour of a body of Metropolitan Police, actually complained that 'these men were sworn constables of Glamorganshire, and that I had made a special requisition for their services, *and that they were employees of mine as long as I wished.*' The Owners' Association had the temerity to forward this complaint to the Home Office, and was rewarded with a letter composed in Mr Churchill's best vein of chilling sarcasm.

But not the sarcasm of the Home Office, nor the independence of the Metropolitan Police, nor their own fears, prevented the owners from their objectionable course. The mines were in danger of flooding, and in some there were pit ponies still underground. Ah, cried the owners, what a pitiful story! What could be done? The strike committees, to be sure, offered sufficient men to keep the mines from flooding and to bring the ponies up; but this, of course, could not be countenanced. Blackleg labour was the only solution, and blackleg labour was consistently employed. At last, on 21st November, the threatened importation of eleven blackleg stokers by railroad from Cardiff resulted in rioting all down the line between Pontypridd and Llwynypia. That night there were bloody battles in Tonypandy and Penycraig, home of the Ely Pit. In Tonypandy some despairing police, slowly beaten down with nail-studded mandril sticks, pieces of iron, and flints ('Get some with sharp edges for the b—' was the cry), were only rescued by Major Freeth and the Lancashire Fusiliers. Inspector Anderson, Captain Lindsay, and the Metropolitan Police, charging up the cliff-like side streets of Penycraig were assailed from upper windows with flints, bricks, crockery, and chamber-pots. At midnight a squadron of Hussars, riding in cautiously on frosty roads through Tonypandy to Penycraig, found that the battles were over. Though every single policeman was injured, only seven were in serious danger, and these recovered; the casualties among the strikers were never published.

The next day rain swept down on the valleys. And from then onwards the rioting declined. By the first week in December there was not a soldier to be seen, the General had thankfully disappeared, the trouble was said to be over. But was it? The Aberdare and Rhondda men refused to go back to work. In spite of the persuasions of the MFGB, the efforts of Mr Askwith, the promises of the owners, nothing would satisfy them now but a minimum wage of 8s. for skilled and 5s. for unskilled labour. In this demand they were backed by their own Federation, which had undergone an inscrutable change of spirit. In February 1911, Messrs Ashton and Harvey, of the MFGB – which grudgingly supplied the strikers with £3,000 a week – went down into the valleys to look the matter over. At Tonypandy they were met by a half-starved mob which howled at them, 'No ballot; go back to England; keep your £3,000 a week; give us the twentieth rule.' The twentieth rule meant a general strike. In great perplexity, Messrs Ashton and Harvey went back to England; it was beyond their understanding.

On 15th May, 1911, the MFGB – its patience exhausted – agreed that the Cambrian price list arranged in the previous October should be given a year's trial – in other words, that the Cambrian men should have struck for precisely nothing. In June it withdrew its £3,000 a week. The Welsh Federation had no money to spare, but still the strike went on; until at last, on 1st August, the miners were literally starved into acceptance.

The results of their bitter and gallant fight had already discovered themselves in every corner of South Wales. Things were not as they had been. The cautious spirit of the SWMF had been shamed away, and from now onwards the gospel of the minimum wage was openly preached, not only in Wales, but in every coal field of Great Britain. And so a spontaneous and impulsive strike, begun by a handful of Welshmen against the advice of leaders, the findings of Conciliation Boards, and the downright disapproval of the national Federation, ultimately sounded its alarum in the stilled soul of a whole industry.

This, indeed, was the lesson of 1910. It was easy to remark – *then* – that the Welsh were an aggressive and disagreeable race: but had they not simply followed an example set them by such peaceful entities as the Northumberland miners, the N E railwaymen, and the Boilermakers? It was easy, too, to maintain that the number of strikes, and of workers directly involved in them, was not much in excess of previous years. But the statistics pointed to one very significant fact. Only 20 per cent of the strikes had been concerned with wages; the rest had arisen over conditions of labour, refusal to work with non-unionists, and other questions heretofore solved by peaceful methods.

At the Board of Trade, Mr Askwith remembered – as who had better cause? – the words which Mr Appleton, General Secretary of the General Federation of Trade Unions, had spoken in 1909. 'It is the duty of the Federation,' said Mr Appleton, a decent old gentleman of Liberal views, 'to prevent disputes in the future.' Mr Askwith perceived that the workers were now fighting on two fronts – against the owners, and against old-fashioned leadership. What could it mean? He shook his head in bewilderment. This was quite new – quite, quite new. He foresaw strange developments in 1911.

VII

Mr J. F. Moylan, the Board of Trade investigator in the recent Welsh trouble, had managed, like General Macready, to keep his head; and it was doubtless he who discovered that the Cambrian men had been inspired in their deeds by a small group of hitherto obscure young syndicalists. The fact was pretty generally known – among those, that is, to whom it meant anything – by the opening of 1911. It was due to the influence of Syndicalism that the Welsh Federation stiffened its spirit, and that the position of its elderly leaders – Mr Brace, M P, Mr Richards, M P, Mr Onions, and even the venerable and Right Honourable Mr

Abrahams, Privy Councillor – was being threatened from below. And it was in January 1911, that the Miners' Conference – which included every British Union, whether a member of the M F G B or not – declared that all districts should press for a minimum rate to apply to workers in abnormal places or under abnormal conditions.

These facts did not seem particularly ominous at the time. Syndicalism might be expected in Wales and parts of Scotland, whose workers were – not being Anglo-Saxons – particularly susceptible to European brain-storms. No, really, one couldn't worry about that. And as for the decision of the Miners' Conference, it had been left in the cloudy regions of discussion: nobody had mentioned a general strike.

And yet the Comptroller-General of the Commercial, Labour, and Statistical Departments of the Board of Trade – that is to say, Mr George R. Askwith – grew more and more uneasy. He watched the new strikes which sprang up and withered between January and June. Nothing to trouble one's head over; but still – what was it? Was it the spontaneity of these strikes? Or was it just something in the air? – he had a strange feeling that a storm was about to break.

On 14th June, it broke.

That morning, the seamen and firemen at Southampton declared a general strike; their example was followed at Goole on the 16th, and at Hull on the 20th. Other ports in the United Kingdom seemed likely to join in. The country at large could only spare the time to tell itself that this was very unthinking of the seamen and firemen. The Coronation itself was not two days off. But the seamen and firemen were perfectly unconcerned with the pleasantness or otherwise of those ceremonies in Westminster Abbey; they had suddenly discovered a national pro-gramme. It included everything from a minimum wage to improved forecastle accommodation, they were extremely pleased with it, and decided to have it recognized at once; and their enthusiasm was shared by the dock labourers at Hull, who, though they had no very definite programme of their own, struck work to a man.

The Seamen's and Firemen's Union was well organized; its claims were succinct. But the dockers? The dockers, sad to say, were either very loosely organized or not organized at all, their claims and conditions varied from port to port, it would be difficult to state exactly what they wanted. But at the very heart of their grievances there stirred a rising anger at being indifferently paid in a time of increasing profits and increasing prices; they were striking about money. (A strike about money is not at all the same as a strike about wages: for while a strike about wages demands either a definite rise or the restoration of a definite cut, a strike about money comes from a sense of injustice. It is not specific, but incoherent and ominous. It is a voice in the wilderness, crying for recognition, for solidarity, for power. Its echoes are innumerable.) And so, as in 1910, it was a spontaneous movement which started the great strike months of 1911. Mr Askwith's fears had been justified.

Looking forward, at this vital moment, from which the tide of strikes rolled darkly into 1914, it is impossible not to be surprised at the little physical violence that was done – only a few men killed, in Wales in 1912, and two or three in Dublin in 1913; in England itself not a death. Is *this* the effect of revolutionary methods, and, if so, do the methods deserve the word? Or was it that Englishmen, whose forefathers had endured and survived and thrived upon so many curious revolutions in the past, were spiritually vaccinated against the infection of terrorism and the plague of sudden wrath? Could their revolutionary methods almost be called peaceful? Perhaps this is so. Perhaps that golden mean so dear to the heart of the Church of England and the Constitution is, as some maintain, an essential expression of the national character. Or perhaps that psychological revolution which underlay the strike movement was reserving itself – under the guiding hand of some ironical providence – for the great years of bloodshed and destruction between 1914 and 1918. However this may be, it certainly seems as if, in the recurrent crises of the strike fever, when passions ran highest, and moods were incredibly ugly, something asserted itself; something peculiarly English. What was it? Kindliness, a sense of humour, a native respect for the opinions of an opponent? Or was it lack of enterprise, stolidity, phlegm? It would be difficult to say. Such are the contradictions of the English character that, even when it undergoes – as it did in these strike years – an amazing spiritual death and rebirth, it is certain to do so in a manner calculated to baffle the inquirer.

And there is still another consideration. It is the genius of the English people always to raise up an appropriate man to suit every crisis. If the Tory Rebellion had been carried to its logical conclusion in the horrors of a civil war, there might have emerged – who can say? – the graceful figure of F. E. Smith to guide the country, with cynical adroitness, back into the paths of peace. Unfortunately for that brilliant and tragic man, his was a less pleasing career. And then, in the ranks of the suffragettes, there may well have been – now forever unknown – some intelligent woman to wrest authority from the iron hand of the Pankhursts. These events have expired, unborn, in the enormous womb of history, and we shall never be sure. But at least, in the strike movement, whenever things looked particularly bad, when it seemed inevitable that the greed of capital and the rage of labour could have no other issue than bloodshed or worse, there was the figure of Mr George Askwith, gliding unobtrusively from one camp to the other, and somehow keeping the peace. It is not an heroic figure. There is nothing in Mr Askwith's character and intelligence to call forth exclamations of rapture or aston-ishment; indeed, there is something about the position of arbitrator in such a conflict which seems – to our different eyes today – singularly uninspiring. But Mr Askwith, so equable, so tactful, and so just, seems to have embodied, in a special manner, the spirit of Compromise, which is a very English spirit. One might almost say more. Was he not the personification of Liberalism, in its most persuasive form? Three things, at least, are clear in his handling of the situation. (1) He did the Govern-ment's job, far better than the Government could have done it. (2) He kept the peace, almost single-handed, for over three years. (3) By the middle of 1914, he was no longer capable of keeping the peace; the battle had gone beyond his control.

Now he appeared in Hull. 'One shipowner came to me and discussed the matter; he spoke of it as a revolution, and so it was.' (*Industrial Problems and Disputes:* by Lord Askwith, p. 149.) Mr Askwith per-ceived that the dockers of Goole and Hull had new leaders, men un-known before; that the employers did not know how to deal with them; that the only body of military in the neighbourhood was a company of Territorials, which was certain to be worse than useless. Meanwhile fires, looting, and riot had broken out and 'I heard one town councillor remark that he had been in Paris during the Commune and had never seen anything like this, and he had not known that there were such people in Hull – women with hair streaming and half nude, reeling through the streets smashing and destroying.'

It was, indeed, somewhat beyond the comprehension of a town councillor. As one experienced labour leader remarked to Mr Askwith, it was impossible to tell 'what has come over the country. Everyone seems to have lost their heads.' Mr Askwith, however, did not lose his. He had been unwilling to come to Hull in the first place; he represented the very spectral authority of the Board of Trade, as defined by the

Conciliation Act of 1896, and if the strikers would not listen to him, things could only become worse. But he attacked the problem with characteristic *sang-froid*. Obviously the seamen's claims, being the only definite ones, must be settled; and, after many hours of strenuous debate, settled they were, to the satisfaction, at any rate, of owners and leaders. And what was the outcome?

'A settlement had been achieved. It should be proclaimed to the people; and the men's leaders went out to proclaim it. It was estimated that there were 15,000 people there when the leaders began their statement. They announced their statement; and before my turn came an angry roar of "No!" rang out; and "Let's fire the docks!" from the outskirts, where men ran off. The crowd surged against the platform in a space before the hotel; women who had come there to see the show shrieked with alarm.

'I hastily told them to keep quiet and to their credit they did. It was necessary to act at once, and I stood up with raised arm. There was dead silence. In a windy open air meeting it was not possible to be heard by all; the sound of a voice could only reach a certain number; but if these were to keep calm the effect would spread. As clearly as I could I said the meeting was adjourned; the employers and their representatives were going to continue to negotiate. They must go home. With two constables in front we walked through that crowd back to the hotel, in perfect peace. . . .' (*Industrial Problems and Disputes*, p. 150.)

In perfect peace: but not in peace of mind. Safely in the hotel, and away from the crowd of agitated owners and officials in the lobby, Mr Askwith was inclined to be plaintive. He had not come there, he told himself, to quell riots. But he was not a man to give up. What was the *real* reason behind the seamen's stubbornness? He had been to Hull twice before to settle disputes, he knew the men, and the more he thought it out, the more clearly it seemed to him that the dockers were behind it all – the dockers with their innumerable unformulated claims and grievances, and their infinite capacity for raising Cain. He knew he must act at once. He called the dockers' leaders, and asked them to collect meetings, at which he himself would expatiate on the values of negotiation; and then the men must instruct their leaders at further private meetings on Sunday. It was, he felt, a pretty hopeless scheme; but by some kind of a miracle it worked. And the moment the dockers were pacified, the seamen agreed to precisely the settlement which they had rejected with such fury before: to it there was added, as a kind of rider, a halfpenny an hour increase for the dockers – the stevedores, that is, the lumpers, wharfingers, and anyone carrying direct from ship to quay or quay to ship. A halfpenny an hour, and a level head, in the purest traditions of Kiplingesque verse – with these slender instruments the riots in Hull had been quelled. Would they always be so effective? Mr Askwith returned to London.

He had scarcely opened his front door, when a message was thrust into his hand, saying that the Lord Mayor of Manchester had been telephoning Mr Buxton, the President of the Board of Trade. The Lord Mayor, it seemed, was almost frantic. He wanted Mr Buxton's arbitrator without delay. On 27th June, the dockers at the Ship Canal Docks had ceased to work; on 3rd July, the carters had come out in a body. All transport was stopped, and the Lord Mayor feared that other trades would soon be following. Mr Askwith hurried North again.

In the endless corridors of Manchester's Town Hall, he was to spend the next five days and most of the next five nights, gliding imperturbably to and fro. Eighteen Trade Unions had pledged themselves not to go back; and in eighteen different rooms owners and workers cursed and wrangled and debated. Mr Askwith might be on one floor, putting forth all his powers of placidity in the midst of some complicated debate, when the news would arrive that another group of combatants, upstairs or downstairs, was just preparing to break up in a rage. He knew that, by hook or by crook, he must hold these eighteen quarrels within the walls of the Town Hall; he would hurry off; he would persuade them to keep it up just a little longer. How he managed to retain the mass of claims and counter-claims separate in his head; or how he stayed sane among those clusters of practically certifiable human beings who, with sweat and tobacco smoke and the stale breath of oratory, had turned the Town Hall into a malodorous madhouse by the fifth day – this is a story upon which, with typical modesty, he refrains from expatiating in his *Industrial Problems and Disputes*. But by Sunday, 9th July, the beginnings of a settlement had magically appeared. Only the carters and the seamen were still unsatisfied; and at 10 p.m. the seamen reached a settlement. But the carters, alas, had to be told that nothing could be done for them; a message rendered no easier by the fact that their claims were – even after five days' discussion – still completely obscure, and that they were a set of mighty men in an ugly temper. Askwith and the leaders went to face them. For two hours the leaders wheedled, and exhorted, and even cursed the carters, who gave back better than they got. 'I have been to many meetings,' one leader, hoarse with shouting, croaked into Askwith's ear, 'but never in one like this. What am I going to do?' Askwith replied that he intended to stay until ten the next morning.

At 2.30 he was up on his feet, summarizing the speeches. He had little to offer and he knew it: he was also quite exhausted. The North Eastern Railway could not give the carters what they wanted, he said. The carters were under contract. They must keep good faith. He would see the General Manager, and try to get conditions softened. He would certainly move the Home Secretary to remit the sentences of some of their comrades who had been imprisoned for rioting. Such arguments were hardly forcible, but he had scarcely sat down before one of the carters was up. 'By God,' he said, 'give Mr Askwith a chance. Up with your hands.' There were only three against. Such were the effects of Mr Askwith's tranquillizing presence, and they were doubtless worth the knighthood he received at the end of the year.

At 7.30 that morning he was awakened from sleep by a sound outside his hotel window; a lorry was crawling along below, with a plain clothes detective walking beside it. He told himself that the settlement had failed after all, and got back miserably into bed. At 9.30 he was awakened again, this time by a noise like thunder. He rushed to the window. On one side of the large square opposite the Town Hall were riding out the Scots Greys, who had been garrisoning Salford; on the other side the Metropolitan and Birmingham Police were marching off to the station. 'And in the main street were mile upon mile of lorries laden with goods coming from the docks to be distributed in the city and to the cotton mills.'

It was a great victory for the method of arbitration; and yet – the military and police march out, the food comes in ... wasn't there something wrong with *that* picture? Would not arbitration have been a little more impressive – as a method – without this background of arms and truncheons? Mr Askwith would certainly have agreed. And he must have told himself – though he did not commit such thoughts to his book – that arbitration in this case had not ended in a reasonable exercise of the principle of give and take. Personality had decided it, and the effects of personality are not lasting.

But the country at large breathed a sigh of relief, and the newspapers congratulated their readers on the fact that the 'strike fever' had now abated, and that everyone might look forward to a peaceful holiday season. And then, on 1st August, there were rumours of trouble in the London docks. Nobody bothered; the scene was occupied with more stolid and more glittering figures; Mr Asquith had reached the last stage of his fight with the Lords, and Europe's royalty was sailing into Cowes. On 8th August, however, London awoke to the fact that something very serious had taken place.

The reasons behind the great transport stoppage are very difficult to disentangle. One has to wrestle with the reticence of the press, the caution of Mr Askwith, the dry rustling interminable statistics of Government reports, and the none too lucid enthusiasm of Mr Ben Tillett's *History of the London Transport Workers' Strike*. The origins of it may be discovered far back in 1910, when the Dockers' Union pressed simultaneously for the formation of a National Transport Workers' Federation and the establishment of a minimum wage. The Federation was brought into being, but, owing to an unaccountable lethargy of members and officials, the minimum wage began to rattle in the dockers' brains – the dry seed of a dead idea. It was often discussed, but nobody thought it would ever amount to anything. And then the transport workers of Hull and Goole, striking in June 1911, fired the faint heart of every port in England, and by the end of the month the Dockers' Union had presented the Port of London Authority, and its chairman, Lord Devonport, with a formidable list of demands. From its eight specific claims there was one which especially stood out, and around which the coming conflict was to rage – the dockers asked for a minimum wage of 8d. an hour for day work and 1s. an hour for overtime.

During the early days of July, both sides rallied their forces. The dockers inspired, as best they might, the somewhat dispirited Unions in the Transport Workers' Federation; the Port of London Authority summoned to its aid the Shipping Federation, the manufacturers, the short sea traders, the granary keepers, and the master lightermen. Preliminary conferences led to nothing. Lord Devonport presided, and Lord Devonport, a recently ennobled tea-importer, could by no stretch of imagination be called a man of the hour. And then the Shipping Federation and the master lightermen – with the dim obstinacy of their kind – refused to recognize the sailormen's and lightermen's Unions.

On 25th, 26th, and 27th July, the skirmishing ceased, the trumpets blew for battle, and both forces advanced. Their first hand to hand encounter was almost chivalrous; thwacking blows were dealt and parried with an old-fashioned courtesy; and grim death, scouring the field, wore upon his face an ever more and more amiable smile. But the conflict, none the less, was a matter of life or death. Four preliminary questions were discussed. (1) The cost of living. (2) The Federation Ticket – that is, the insistence of the Shipping Federation that all its employees belong to an employers' union. (3) The difference between a stevedore and a docker. (4) Payment for meal-times. As to (3), Mr Harry Gosling, of the Transport Workers, explained that a stevedore, who was employed in loading ships for export, clearly deserved more pay than a docker. The owners were all compliance. If that was the case, they would not dream of hurting the stevedores' feelings; they would pay *them* at the present rate, and reduce the dockers' wages by just a little. It was simple. They laughed kindly, and their opponents laughed back.

Clearly this kind of thing could not go on for very long. When a truce was declared on the 27th, the really vital question of the minimum wage had hardly been touched upon. Mr Harry Gosling and his colleagues brought some sort of a meagre settlement to their followers that evening, and with one voice their followers turned it down. On 1st August, the National Transport Workers' Federation called a strike in the London docks.

A strike of the Transport Workers' Federation was not as serious as it might sound; the Federation controlled only a very small percentage of dock labour which for the most part – casual, manifold, and disorganized – had not bothered its head about unionization and solidarity. For two or three days work went on almost as usual. And then it was noticed that men who had no union affiliations were beginning to discover claims and grievances and to come out; and a creeping paralysis, almost imperceptible at first, with the impalpable persistence of a low mist bred from the Thames, began to invade the ordinary bustle of the riverside.

What was the matter? What had happened? There was good Sir Albert Rollitt arbitrating the questions at issue behind the respectable façade of the London Chamber of Commerce in Cannon Street. Surely they could wait until he had made his award. Was it the heat – which, to be sure, had never been greater in the memory of any living man? Nerves are apt to be strained in the heat, particularly the nerves of people who must spend their nights in a stifling maze of narrow streets and decaying houses. Was *that* the answer? If so, it was not a consoling one. Had this leaderless unrest – the thought was not without its terror – been pumped, like some fevered blood, out of the beating dark heart of London's slums?

In mid-Victorian days one might almost have said, without risk of contradiction, that people who lived in slums had only themselves to blame. It was sad, no doubt, but it was foreordained; and who would question the mysterious workings of providence? The slum-dwellers themselves, in fact, seemed to think on very much the same lines, and they were supported in this thought by the catechism of the Church of England and the general sense of the community. But towards the end of the century the Right Honourable Charles Booth wrote his *Life and Labour in London* (1889); it was followed by B. Seebohm Rowntree's *Poverty* (1901); and in 1907 by Mona Wilson's and E. G. Hawarth's *West Ham*: and these books, which set forth in all their detailed horror the filthy conditions of life in the London slums, made a great impression upon the country. Not that anything very much was done: people, at most, were rather proud at being impressed. But unfortunately the slum-dwellers had been impressed, too.

Cockneys are naturally intelligent, and not a few of them had gone very thoroughly through the pages of Mr Booth, Mr Rowntree, Miss Wilson and Mr Hawarth. Lice and crumbling walls and foul sewers and greedy landlords become mysteriously more real when they have been embalmed in words; and the effects of a little reading will sooner or later spread through a whole district to breed, not argument, but anger. There were reasons more profound and more forcible; but this one had its cogency – especially in 1911, when London was climbing towards its peak of plutocratic splendour, and tales of ballrooms banked high with the loot of hot-houses, of champagne flowing like a sea, of bare backs and jewelled bosoms and fabulous expenditure, would fly – with the impetus of fact and the wings of fantasy – out of the West and into the East End.

There is no doubt that in August 1911, London's East End was in a state of seething discontent. And through its unspeakable, fantastical, overpopulated wastes of brick and grime there swept, like the crimson banner of revolt through some desert of Arabia, that famous demand for a minimum of eightpence and a shilling – drawing up behind it the congregated, the incoherent, the almost exuberant grievances of a much aggrieved people.

When finally Sir Albert Rollitt emerged – on 6th August – from the seclusion of the Chamber of Commerce, he awarded the Transport Workers' Federation its principal claim. The result was made known to a vast meeting in Trafalgar Square. 'I don't want to keep you a moment in suspense,' said Harry Gosling. 'I am going to make the announcement first and talk to you as soon as you will let me afterwards. You have won the 8d. and 1s.'

But the award had come too late. For Mr Gosling waited for silence to remind his hearers that, though the dockers might be satisfied, not a man of them could go back to work until all the other claims had been met. It was a beginning, not an end. Spontaneously, without the advice of leaders often, often without specific form, demands were pouring in upon the Port of London Authority and the allied employers.

The stevedores were out, the carters were asking a sixty-hour week, the lightermen wanted 10d. per hour per day, the tugboatmen, the enginemen, the crane porters had joined the strike along with the coal bunkerers and the sailing bargemen. Slowly on London came down that unreal Sabbath quiet—

when the great markets by the sea shut fast.

Everything began to die – coal and water service, gas and electricity, railway, road, and river transport. Vegetables and flour grew scarcer and scarcer; great piles of fruit lay perishing in the docks. As for the butter trade, the Danish butter came in casks and was not refrigerated: it was growing rancid in the mounting heat. The frozen meat from Argentina, the United States, and New Zealand – on which the city largely depended – was going bad, for there was a shortage of cold-storage accommodation, and the refrigerating ships themselves lay useless in the river without coal. Famine drew nearer hour by hour, the strike had spread out to Brentford and the Medway. It seemed as if the whole Thames Valley must shortly be affected.

It was very soon whispered about that the Home Office and the War Office were seriously thinking of bringing troops into the city. How else could the food be got out? it was asked. How, indeed? If the Metropolitan Hospitals needed supplies, or even if petrol was required to keep a skeleton bus service running, nobody thought of applying to the Home Office, or moving the police – the Strike Committee alone – headed by Mr Harry Gosling, Mr Will Godfrey, and Mr Ben Tillett – could give the necessary permission. For four days Messrs Gosling, Godfrey, and Tillett had the singular satisfaction of governing London.

And against them, a solitary opponent, was the mysteriously smiling figure of Mr Winston Churchill – Mr Churchill, who had once led a charge at Omdurman, and to whom the thought of dispatching soldiers on a difficult expedition through nine miles of East End streets was not without its fascination. It would lead to bloodshed, of course; and if the dictatorship of the Strike Committee were put down with blood – things would look very awkward afterwards. For a little while the soldier and the administrator in Mr Churchill fought a silent conflict, and the administrator won. It was just after this happy victory that Mr Ben Tillett paid a visit to the House of Commons, uninvited, to call upon the Home Secretary and beg that troops should not be loosed upon the docks. He and his colleagues had come to think of Mr Churchill as a kind of modern Nero, with an awful lust for gore; but no – 'the bloodthirsty one looked as lamblike and as amiable as the gentlest shepherd on earth. . . . If patience and courtesy, if anxious effort and sincerity count for respect, then Winston Churchill is entitled as a man to gratitude.' (*The London Transport Workers' Strike*, p. 35.) Mr Tillett, it might almost seem, had come just too late to see another side of Mr Churchill – a side that was not, perhaps, quite so anxious and sincere. Then in 'those mobile features, ready for boyish fun', on that 'good sized brow', in those eyes 'sparkling with a wistfulness almost sweet', which had inspired such contradictory emotions in Mr Tillett's breast, there might have been observed another look – the slightly speculative look of the gifted amateur strategist. There were others, besides Mr Tillett, who came just too late. One merchant, in particular, begged Mr Churchill to bring his meat away by force from the docks. It was worth £100,000, and it was growing green and musty. What did he propose to do with it? Oh, he was going to sell it to the Government. And what might the Government be expected to use it for? For the soldiers of course. 'Indeed', said a quiet voice, whose owner the merchant had not condescended to notice: 'Musty and nearly green meat to the men risking their lives for your cargo and at your suggestion? Surely you don't wish me to tell that to the country, or the Minister to explain the bargain in Parliament.' It was the voice of Mr George Askwith.

For once again, inevitably, unobtrusively, Mr Askwith had intervened. Sir Albert Rollitt's arbitration had come to nothing; claims were increasing; the city was on the edge of starvation. The strikers, too, were growing more and more dangerous, and down where the heat quivered against the great, black, closed dock gates police and pickets faced one another, sullenly, all day long. On Tower Hill, where the Strike Committee had established a virtual government over the ten million inhabitants of the Thames Valley, nightly meetings summoned the men to close their ranks. 'O God!' cried Mr Tillett on one of these occasions. 'Strike Lord Devonport dead!' Lord Devonport, had he been present, might have added a fervent Amen; for things could not have been more uncomfortable. And yet – in those critical four days between the 8th and the 11th – there was Mr Askwith, quietly gathering and separating and rearranging the innumerable tangled threads. By 11th August, most of the settlements had been made, with substantial gains for the strikers in every case but two. That evening the strike was called off.

For seven days more, it seemed as if Mr Askwith's almost magical labours would be fruitless after all. Sometimes because the owners broke their promises and refused to reinstate their workers, more often from a new feeling of independence in the whole dock district – trouble flared up again and again. The public and the press, aroused, began to mutter about military and gunboats. And then Mr John Burns appeared upon the scene; and he who had once been the hope of the embattled dockers of 1887, now endeavoured, as a Liberal Cabinet Minister, to soothe and to satisfy. These efforts were ironical, but they were also successful; and at the Home Office, on the 18th, a final settlement was signed by the Strike Committee, the employers, Mr John Burns, Mr Winston Churchill, and Mr Askwith.

The great London transport strike was over.

Looking back upon it, the transport workers might well claim that they had won a great victory. Wages had been raised, hours reduced, the Unions recognized. The Port of London Authority and the Shipping Federation, those solid figures which bulked so largely in the doorway to freedom, had been forced to retreat. And, more important still, the Transport Federation had immeasurably increased in numbers and importance. Nor had it increased through any cautious display of opportunist tactics; the milder sort among its Executive had been overruled; it had made a show of strength – more strength, indeed, than it actually possessed – and immediately there had gathered to it, as if it had been some kind of a magnet, all the fragmentary grievances of a vast port.

And not of a port only. The reader who turns the pages of Mary Agnes Hamilton's *Mary Macarthur* will discover the strike there in a more curious aspect. The story of the Bermondsey women seems almost to have isolated – with its mingling elements of unreason and necessity and gaiety and rage – the various spirit of the whole Unrest. One stifling August morning, while the strike was at its height, the women workers in a large confectionery factory, in the middle of Bermondsey, in 'the black patch' of London, suddenly left work. As they went through the streets, shouting and singing, other women left their factories and workshops and came pouring out to join them. They could not tell why they were doing this, but they were afterwards to swear that a fat woman had appeared in one place after another, calling the girls out or threatening the employers. Nobody had actually seen her, but everyone believed that she was true: she passes, like some collective myth, through that strange morning, and disappears.

Very soon the streets were filled with women, and fetid with the smells of jam, glue, pickles, and flesh. It was then, when they were all out, that the women discovered what they had come out for. Their average wages were 7s. to 9s. a week for women and 3s. for girls: they wanted an increase.

At the Bermondsey Institute Mary Macarthur, president of the National Federation of Woman Workers, opened a strike headquarters. Day by day the enthusiasm increased. Processions passed through the streets with collecting boxes. Fifteen thousand women, seething with rage and excitement, cheered Ben Tillett in a meeting at Southwark Park. Within a single week four thousand recruits joined the NFWW; and within twenty days the employers had yielded in eighteen of the twenty strikes which Mary Macarthur was conducting. The total gain was over £7,000 a year, in wage increases of from one to four shillings a week.

Mary Macarthur was never to forget the scenes at headquarters, where she had undertaken the dual problem of feeding and organization. Long queues, waiting in the blazing heat for bread and milk, filled the Institute with vermin and the vile smell of stale jam. And why not? The women were underpaid and over-crowded. She choked down her nausea. Yet they were oddly light-hearted, too. Many of them, dressed in all their finery, defied the phenomenal temperature with feather boas and fur tippets, as though their strike were some holiday of the soul, long overdue.

VIII

While Ben Tillett laboured in London, another agitator – the only leader who was really acquainted with the theories of M. Sorel – had been putting his syndicalist notions into practice in the North, and with great success. His influence upon the movement as a whole it would be difficult to gauge. He has certainly not over-estimated it in his *Memoirs*. And yet, combining the powers of a demagogue with the precision of a student, passionate, sincere, kindly, self-sacrificing – his presence pervaded the strike years in an extraordinary way. Men who disagreed with his longer views – such as socialist Sunday Schools or the necessity for converting the Army to class warfare – would applaud him instinctively the moment he got on a platform; and would afterwards discover that – such were his gifts for organization – they had not only been persuaded into striking, but had every chance of getting what they wanted.

A most impressive instance of his powers was now to be given. On 5th August, some thousand union and non-union carters, in the employment of the North Eastern Railway at Liverpool, ceased work – declaring, with justice, that they could get no satisfaction in their demands for increased wages and shorter hours. By 7th August, the railwaymen themselves were coming out in large numbers. There were riots between the Catholic Irish and the Protestant Irish, always a sign, in Liverpool, of extreme tension, and the Lord Mayor wrote to the Home Office, asking for military help.

The Home Office had troubles enough in London, and probably did not ask itself what spirit was flitting – what agile, elusive spirit – in and out among the transport workers of England. But the answer, in this case, was simple enough. Tom Mann was in Liverpool.

It was a matter of great satisfaction to him that the railwaymen's executive had not expected its men to come out; under such circumstances he worked best. By 14th August – in spite of the best endeavours of the police, the Scots Greys, the Warwickshire Regiment, and a small committee sent down by the Labour Party – rioting was so frequent, and the city's transport so thoroughly tangled up, that the Liverpool shipowners declared a lock-out of all men engaged in cargo work. In triumph, a general strike was called of all the city's transport workers.

But something else was happening – something which, with his strange prescience, Tom Mann seems to have expected. In one centre after another throughout England, little groups of railwaymen were coming out; by 15th August, it was pretty clear that nothing would satisfy them but a general stoppage. The executives of the various Railway Unions, caught unawares, could only put a good face on things. Meeting hurriedly in Liverpool they issued an ultimatum to the Companies, protesting that the men would never get their grievances settled with dispatch unless the Companies recognized the Unions, and giving the Companies twenty-four hours in which to frame a satisfactory answer.

Between the 15th and the 18th negotiations went through seven distinct stages. At the end of the first, Mr George Askwith had brought representatives of the Companies and the Unions to London. At the end of the second, the Companies had agreed to communicate with the Unions through an interchange of notes. At the end of the third, the Cabinet had decided to offer the services of a Royal Commission. At the end of the fourth, it had hastily changed its offer to a Commission of Three. At the end of the fifth, the Companies and the Unions, still interchanging notes, had disagreed on the structure of the Commission. At the end of the sixth, they had almost agreed on the structure of the Commission, but had come to a deadlock on the question of recognition. At the end of the seventh, the Companies had refused to recognize the Unions, and negotiations broke down.

It was during the fourth of these stages that Mr Asquith interposed himself between the two parties. The Prime Minister – there is no doubt of it – was a sorely tried man. The last two months of continuous striking had severely shaken him, and this new stoppage, coming on the very heels of the London strike, found him angry and bewildered. He could not understand exactly what it was all about, and nothing was so calculated to irritate him as not being able to understand. He realized, however, that his Government was being seriously threatened from a new quarter; he intervened in person; and the results of his intervention were to leave things far worse than they had been before.

On the morning of 17th August a Cabinet meeting at Downing Street agreed that a Royal Commission should discuss the railwaymen's grievances. Now Royal Commissions are notoriously slow; their deliberations have been known to last for two or three years, and their findings, though just in the main, usually appear long after the need for them has passed. The Cabinet, therefore, had scarcely hit upon the likeliest means of appeasing a group of men who happened to be in a hurry. None the less the Prime Minister, accompanied by Mr Askwith, hurried off to the Board of Trade to inform the Unions' officials of this luminous solution. It was perhaps unfortunate that the language he used was threatening from the start; he seemed to be offering them either a Royal Commission or immediate reprisals. At three in the afternoon they returned with their answer. It was a curt refusal. Alas for Mr Asquith! Hardly waiting to hear them out, he stalked from the room, muttering –

audibly, inexcusably, to Mr Askwith's intense dismay – 'Then your blood be upon your own head.'

Such was the first meeting, face to face, between the Prime Minister and the people. Within the next half hour some two thousand telegrams began flying to all parts of the country. This was their message. 'Your liberty is at stake. All railwaymen must strike at once. The loyalty of each means victory for all.' Though they lingered at the Board of Trade for another day, the Union executives ceased to pretend that anything would satisfy them but recognition; by 18th August, the railways were practically at a standstill.

'Your blood be upon your own head.' What did the Prime Minister mean? Was he bluffing? And if not, where did his words lead? Unhappily enough, they led back into the excited brain of Mr Winston Churchill.

Ever since the 16th, the Companies had been promising 'limited but effective service', and Mr Churchill – casting aside that administrative forbearance which had so touched the heart of Mr Tillett – began to send soldiers hither and yon with a scarcely concealed alacrity. At twenty-seven different centres the troops appeared, sometimes because there was serious rioting, sometimes because there *might* be rioting. On 19th August, telegraphic instructions from the Home Office stated that 'General Officers Commanding the various military areas are instructed to use their own discretion as to whether troops are, or are not, to be sent to any particular point. The Army Regulation which requires a requisition of troops from a Civil Authority is suspended. . . .' And was it rioting alone which the soldiers had to repel? Or were they being used for the protection of blackleg labour? The official correspondence proves that had the Companies not attempted their 'limited but effective' service, there would have been no riots. And it proves something else. Behind the guarded language of the Home Office communications, there lurks – it is hard to think otherwise – an increasing desire to militarize the railways. There were rumours abroad, which even found their way into *The Times*, that the Government intended to use Royal Engineers to run the trains. . . .

The troops were, on the whole, far milder than the Liberal Minister who dispatched them. At Chesterfield, for example, where the Midland Station was partially wrecked and 'covered with blood', as the Mayor put it, and where the Riot Act was subsequently read in a hail of stones at the bottom of Corporation Street, a half company of West Yorkshires was standing by. Part way through his reading, the Mayor took refuge behind a fence, and, crouching there, 'I ordered the Officer in Command to fire on the mob.' Captain Cooper-King, however, wisely refrained.

But Mr Asquith's threat of the 17th was to be realized one day later in Llanelly, with a certain wantonness which even the discretion of official language has not entirely concealed. On the afternoon of the 18th, so runs a telegraphic report from the Chief Constable of Carmarthenshire:

'Attack made on train which had passed through Llanelly Station, under military protection, at railway cutting sloping on either side to considerable height near station. Troops under Major Stuart quickly on scene, followed by three magistrates. Troops attacked on both sides by crowd on embankment hurling stones and other missiles. One soldier carried away wounded in head and others struck. Riot Act read. Major Stuart mounted embankment and endeavoured to pacify mob. Stone throwing continued, crowd yelling defiance at troops. Shots fired as warning' – (This last statement, as the inquest subsequently proved, was untrue. A rifle was discharged by mistake.) – 'No effect, attitude of crowd threatening and determined. Other shots fired, two men killed, one wounded, crowd fled.'

Thus the Chief Constable of Carmarthenshire. One might perhaps inquire whether a train 'under military protection' was not in itself a provoking circumstance; or whether Major Stuart might not have done better either to withdraw his men or to fix bayonets. The fixing of bayonets – a fact which can be gleaned from the arid acres of the official correspondence – had elsewhere a quietening effect upon even the most ardent throwers of stones. Meanwhile, to pursue the Chief Constable a little further, the results of this little massacre appear not to have been too pacific. At two in the afternoon:

'On line above railway station, trucks looted and set on fire. Very considerable loss in property and damage. Trucks containing two cylinders of detonators caused violent explosion resulting in death of four people and injury to many. . . .'

Once upon a time, when Mr Asquith was Home Secretary, two men were killed in a strike. Mr Asquith was not to blame in this instance, but hecklers used often to remind him of the affair. 'When you murdered those men in 1892,' someone yelled at him once in a political meeting. The answer was afterwards quoted as a pleasing instance of the Prime

Minister's wit and of his exact memory – 'I didn't murder them in 1892; it was in 1893.' Would he remember 18th August with the same facility? He was not responsible, to be sure. And yet – he was Prime Minister, head of a government ostensibly devoted to the cause of peace and the cause of reform. Soldiers up and down the country, generals directing the traffic on the railways, shootings, explosions, the strange inconsistencies of Winston Churchill. . . . Poor, temperate Mr Asquith! *Que diable allait-il faire dans cette galère?*

By 19th August, there were at best a few trains on the move, crawling with difficulty from point to point. The country was seriously alarmed, and such news as came through was hardly reassuring. London itself was almost an armed camp, and each regiment in England had been mobilized at full strength, with every unit equipped under service conditions. The Government, clearly, had decided upon a policy of repression, and what the next few days held in store – who could tell? Mr George Askwith, that very morning, had brought about an agreement on the structure of the Commission of Three; but, try as he would, he could not persuade the Companies to recognize the Unions. No – let the worst happen – that they would not agree to. That union agents should attend all future meetings of the Conciliation Boards? Impossible! What had the soldiers been summoned for, if not to show that the Government itself was determined to have no more of such demands? In despair, Mr Askwith turned to the Chancellor of the Exchequer.

Could Mr Lloyd George do something? He certainly could. The Agadir crisis was still at its height, and Mr George's part in the early period of that crisis had been at once extremely fortuitous and highly important. It had also gone to his head. He approached the Companies. Did they not realize that a stoppage on the railways would seriously hamper the Government in its dealings with Germany? The Companies confessed that they had not thought of *that* before (nor had Mr Lloyd George); and – somehow or other – it sounded like very good sense at the time. Reluctantly they agreed to meet the Union representatives; to reinstate the strikers; to allow Union officials 'under the special circumstances' to attend the next Conciliation Boards; to give every assistance to the Special Commission of Inquiry, upon whose structure they had just agreed. This was 'recognition' of a sort, enough to satisfy the leaders, who were secretly alarmed at the violent turn which events had taken. Would it satisfy the men? At the moment, at any rate, it seemed so. A manifesto, calling the strike off, was generally obeyed, and by the end of the next day most railways were running on a full schedule again.

As for Mr Lloyd George, this successful intervention came as the climax of a glittering year's achievement. The world, and the kingdoms thereof, seemed to be at his feet.

IX

On 19th August, 1911, he appears to have been at the very peak of his pre-war career. On the slopes behind him there rose, like monoliths, the legislative victories for which he held himself alone responsible. And before him? The triumphs and the disgraces alike were mercifully hidden.

And yet those monoliths were not made of very durable stone. Time itself, and the weather of opinion, has dealt hardly with them, and they are crumbling things today. The Parliament Bill – Mr George might well congratulate himself on that. His budget and his oratory had undoubtedly driven the Lords to madness; it was he, surely, who had engineered their downfall. But was it? Somehow or other the Constitution, that mysterious and powerful ghost, has taken all the credit – purloining with imponderable fingers the very laurels from his brow. And then there was the Bill which bestowed £400 a year upon every Member of Parliament; that was Mr George's work, and his alone, and today it seems like a very ingenious piece of timely double-dealing. Ah, but there was one triumph more – the Health Insurance Act, that monument *aere perennius*, upon which no small part of his fame depends.

Health Insurance was enacted in 1911, and began to mean something in the last month of the year 1920, and then only because of its appendix – or Part II – which originally appeared as an experimental scheme of unemployment insurance, only applicable to certain trades. Mr Lloyd George, in fact, had not been at all eager about unemployment insurance in 1911; he had thought it a dangerous innovation; and had only consented to put it in at the instance of Mr Churchill who – with characteristic *clairvoyance* – foresaw its necessity when he was still President of the Board of Trade and still considered himself a radical. It was on Part I of the Act that Mr Lloyd George prided himself – Part I, which was to come into operation in July 1912, and which compelled every worker, for the small payment of 4d. a week, to accept the conditional gifts of medical, sickness, disablement, maternity, and sanatorium benefits.

The theory behind all this, which was German, and the emotion, which was Mr Lloyd George's, were both highly laudable; and he would be a carping sort of a man who tried to impugn either of them today. But theories, unfortunately, must be judged by results, and emotions – in what scales are we to weigh emotions? The Liberal Government had gone out into the highways and hedges and compelled them to come in: but into what? An illimitable feast of health? So Mr Lloyd George believed with all his heart, but the answer today might justify one in thinking him a little optimistic. 'When Mr Lloyd George published his scheme,' writes Dr Harry Roberts (*The Nation & Athenaeum*, 1st June, 1935),

'I had a slum practice that was, numerically, enormous. . . . I had the good fortune to be young, to have gone to the slums from choice, to be interested in people, and to have strong Socialist sympathies. But . . . it would have been unfair to expect all my professional neighbours, not in possession of these physical and psychic assets, to put into their work the same measure of enthusiasm. To begin with, most of the men who practised in my area were not there from choice, but from necessity – whisky or other alleviator of worldly difficulties having made mores remunerative practice for them impossible. . . . Mr Lloyd George's new Act [the doctor continues] was, however, after a lot of squabbling and haggling, brought into operation. It was to do wonderful things. Every poor man was henceforth to have at his disposal all the medical and surgical science and skill that had hitherto been at the service only of the rich. There was to be a bottle of "real medicine" on every tenement mantelpiece. . . . When the Insurance Act was introduced, the bottle of medicine was just about to settle down on its deathbed. The Act rejuvenated it, and today there can hardly be a working-class home in the land without a partly consumed eight or ten ounce bottle of bitter or sweet, brown or pinkish, mixture, composed of ingredients in the efficacy of which not one doctor in fifty has the slightest faith. . . .'

The medical profession, Dr Roberts adds, and he is borne out by Dr Christopher Addison in his *Politics from Within*, was furiously opposed to the new Act; it was the servant of Aesculapius, not of Mr Lloyd George. Swathed in innumerable regulations, it thought its new duties, as laid down by Act of Parliament, 'so much useless drudgery', and settled down to do as little of them as it possibly could. The feast of health had been prepared, indeed, and the people compelled to come in;

but when they arrived were they to find, after all, spread out upon those shining legislative tables, nothing more substantial than row upon row of bottles of pinkish medicine?

These considerations are too complicated for a layman to pursue, and they are possibly unfair to Mr Lloyd George, who can hardly be expected to have foreseen the reactions of the medical mind; moreover they are quite irrelevant to the situation in 1911. In 1911, the workers were interested in wages, not health; and whatever may be said for or against the Insurance Act, one cannot maintain that it raised anybody's pay. Indeed, except for the Trade Boards Act of 1908 – which was devised to bring wages in sweated industries up to, but not beyond, the standard, and which sometimes did so – had Liberal legislation ever raised anybody's pay by so much as a penny?

But Mr Lloyd George was a friend of the people. That was still being said, and by nobody with more conviction than Mr Lloyd George himself. What an orator he was! Here, it seemed – wages or no wages, legislation or no legislation – here was the very embodiment of progress; here was the prophet of plenty. His words, filled with the instinctive music of his race, lit up by the most alluring of imaginable smiles, pointed with sudden pantomime, had all the mysterious drama of a shower in the sunshine – and, like a shower in the sunshine, bred rainbows. At the end of every rainbow there lies a crock of gold – but who has reached the rainbow's end? It is always ahead, just a field away, just across the hedge; maybe no more than ten yards of common turf separate the pursuer and pursued. . . . So with the promises of Mr Lloyd George.

Had the workers already discovered this and retired from the chase? Certainly, they greeted his Insurance Act with no great enthusiasm, but news of that kind travels slowly, and he was not aware of it. He believed in his promises, and no one could have followed them – just one leap behind – with a more gleeful, a more indefatigable zeal than he. One day, he was sure of it, there would be gold for all.

Meanwhile into this shimmering world of his there crept a German gunboat, called the *Panther*. Actually it crept into the sandy bay of Agadir, in south Morocco, an empty and impoverished bay, in which a few palm-trees, bedraggled in the bright eye of the July sun, seemed mutely to claim a unique interest. Unhappily, however, the German Brothers Mannesheim also claimed an interest in Agadir and its hinterland. It was an excellent excuse for a nation, greedy for Morocco and jealous of French development there, to stage a scene, and perhaps emerge from it with something gained. But why on earth should Germany send a gunboat there? Was it stupidity or calculated menace? Neither England nor France could be sure, but they both knew that anything might, at any moment, hurl all Europe into war. From 5th July to 21st July, a silence of extreme tension, as brittle as a dome of cheap glass, covered that strip of water where HIMS *Panther* – sometimes alone, sometimes accompanied by another lean black warship – protected the interest of the Brothers Mannesheim.

On 21st July, the silence was broken, and by none other than Mr Lloyd George, who, in a speech at the Guildhall, took occasion to remark – with all the flamboyant accompaniments of his most excited rhetoric – that should there be war, England would fight – and fight on the side of France. Such words, coming from such a pacifist, could not be neglected. Would Germany yield before Mr George's challenge? Would she protest? Would she demand his resignation? And if she did, would England, in her turn, give way? Four days later, the German protest arrived; but it had been worded so insolently that the Foreign Office disdained to reply. And – very, very gradually – the tension relaxed. Had Mr George's speech done the trick? Or could it possibly be that the discreet endeavours of diplomacy had already forestalled him when he made it? The country, at any rate, was in no doubt. He was a statesman in the highest sense of the word, for he laid aside his most cherished habits of mind to save Europe from disaster.

It had been a critical four days. The German fleet was concentrated off the coast of Norway, ready for a sudden lunge across the sea. Mr McKenna had sent out a warning to the British fleet – or, as Mr Churchill put it with characteristic relish in *The World Crisis*, 'the Admiralty wireless whispers through the ether to the tall masts of ships'.

But another message had been whispered, under circumstances no less romantic, through another ether. Something began to tell Mr George, with startling conviction, that he was a diplomatist to the manner born, that his words had echoed through the chancelleries, and had brought Imperial Germany to her senses. He had never thought of himself in such a way before – Liberal ministers were traditionally indifferent to foreign affairs. If he could deal with Germany, he could certainly deal with the North Eastern Railway Company and its fellows; he would trail the glory of his Guildhall speech along the dusty ways of the Labour Unrest.

But diplomacy in the world of labour has none of the glamour of its counterpart in the world of international affairs, and the politician who adventures upon it must be very careful. Mr George's sudden discovery that a continuation of the railway stoppage might start another European crisis rebounded upon his head in a curious way. At the moment it seemed that he had intervened on the side of the strikers, that he had forced the companies to behave. But the strikers were not satisfied; somehow or other – it was very contrary of them – they went back to work with the distinct notion that they had been cheated. If only they could have continued the strike – with all the possible consequences of bloodshed and death implicit in Mr Churchill's military tactics – if only they could have continued it just three days more – they might have won a clear victory! Now they must wait, and they must wait because Mr Lloyd George had intervened at that critical moment on 19th August.

The fact that their leaders had somewhat let them down, or that a Minister has certain responsibilities towards the public at large, did not affect their feelings. When political democracy itself is being questioned – blindly, perhaps, and instinctively – and when so anomalous a figure as David Lloyd George thrusts itself into the debate, a simple conundrum will very likely be asked. When is a friend of the people not a friend of the people? And the answer would appear to be: when he is a Cabinet Minister.

It is difficult to resist the conclusion that at this moment – at the height of a triumphant career – Mr Lloyd George began to lose the confidence of at least one section of his numerous public. He who had hitherto preserved a delicate distinction between himself and his colleagues was now being forced – now, by the inexorable pressure of events – back into their ranks. He would emerge again – as a Coalition Prime Minister first, and then as the discredited leader of a little clique: but he was never to emerge – never, never again – as the messianic friend of the working classes. It was not his fault. The cards were against him. They had turned against him finally when he persuaded the Railway Companies to remember Agadir, on 19th August, 1911.

X

Mr George Askwith used the Agadir argument again, on 23rd August, in Liverpool, where 70,000 dockers threatened to stay out indefinitely over the Corporation's refusal to reinstate 250 tramwaymen. But this time, strange to say, Agadir meant nothing to the Corporation. What seemed to matter was that Tom Mann was still in Liverpool, demanding, with the familiar accompaniment of riots and assaults upon the military, a national strike of all transport workers. So Mr Askwith resorted to his own more persuasive tactics, and the tramwaymen got back 'as and when satisfactory to the General Manager' – a phrase which smoothed the Corporation's feathers and did not noticeably delay the tramwaymen. The 70,000 dockers also returned to work. Tom Mann was soon to disappear into prison on a charge of incitement to mutiny. The great strike months were over.

All the really important strikes, so the press told the public, which agreed, could be attributed to the phenomenally hot weather. Mr Askwith might have told another story, but with the characteristic reticence of a civil servant he refrained from doing so. Even when the October elections of the South Wales Miners' Federation resulted in the retirement of Messrs Onions, Brace, and Richards in favour of three young syndicalists, the general confidence was unshaken. How could the public be expected to know that South Wales was an industrial barometer? that the weather for the next year, as those elections indicated, was to be 'Very Stormy'? And why should it tell itself that any new movement in the South Wales district was due – not to the heat of 1911 – but to those chilly weeks of 1910, when General Macready rode in the Rhondda Valley, and Messrs Onions, Brace, and Richards refused to call a general strike? Such thoughts were far too obscure to appear in the newspapers.

It was in October, too, that the Special Commission produced its findings, and these were of so ambiguous a nature that the Railway Companies accepted them immediately, while the men, with no less alacrity, offered to go on strike again. If they did, would the South Wales miners come out in sympathy, projecting the issue of a national minimum wage into the complicated argument on the railways? Parliament, thoroughly frightened, passed a unanimous Resolution, insisting that the Companies should meet the railwaymen. They did so, and, after a long and bitter argument which lasted until 11th December, finally agreed to recognize the Unions. And what had the summer heat to do with this? or with a bitter quarrel between the Shipping Federation and the dockers of Dundee, which was only settled on 24th December, *in solstitio brumali?* or with the weavers' lock-out in Lancashire which began on 28th December?

The heat had doubtless assisted the passions of 1911, given them a dark and sullen strength; but for the origin of such passions it is hardly sufficient to search the records of the weather bureau. Nor are statistics themselves so very helpful. From January to December, 961,800 workers were involved in stoppages – a number exceeding by 300,000 that of any previous year. The total number of working days lost was 10,319,591 – or about one day per head over the whole industrial population; but this total, when you deduct from it the days lost in strikes which were carried over from 1910, is considerably less than the 1910 total. The figures argue back and forth among themselves, and he who wishes to take a part in their inhuman dialectics can emerge with any victory that suits him. But then we discover that Trade Union membership, in 1911, was swollen by 600,000; and what does *this* figure stand for? Does it mean a new desire for solidarity among the Unions themselves? Had they gone forth to fish for souls, like an economic St Peter? Or had the process been reversed – had the souls gone fishing for them?

The questions, if they can be furnished with a true answer, are essential to a real understanding of what had taken place in 1911. And the true answer, conveniently enough, is easy to find. The great strikes almost invariably began in the seaports, among non-union labourers, who, once the battle was joined, would flock to the Unions as soldiers might flock to an idle fortification, and force its somnolent commanders to do their bidding. The Union leaders, trembling for their power, hastened to obey. Those who were agile enough pushed their way to the fore, just as if they had always been there; others stood apart, bewildered, mortified, and helpless, while unknown leaders took their place in everything but name. And at last – it was inevitable – a movement which had started impulsively among the obscure and the unskilled suddenly revealed itself in all its infinite promise: here was power. Here was something which all the respectable diplomacy of earlier years could never have achieved – power. In the Trade Union Congress that year, a hitherto moderate old leader suddenly declaimed, 'Let those strike who have never struck before, and those who have always struck strike all the more.' The Unions had not gone forth to convert the disorganized and the underpaid; it was the disorganized and the underpaid who had converted them.

XI

The gospel of Syndicalism, preached among the unskilled workers in the mines of South Wales, and flaming up among the skilled miners in the Cambrian pits, was gradually softened the further it spread. By the end of 1911, it had worked upon every Miners' Union in the country to this extent – that every Union recognized the vital necessity for organization and solidarity. But the abrupt and revolutionary demands of Syndicalism had become simply a demand for a minimum wage for all workers in abnormal places; and this in itself was so reasonable in theory that the owners could only advance against it the complexity of fact.

A joint national meeting of the Miners' Federation of Great Britain and the Coal-Owners' Association was held on 29th September, 1911. It had been achieved with great difficulty, for the MFGB – negotiating nationally for the first time – had found no Coal-Owners' Association or federation of associations which corresponded with itself. The Mining Association of Great Britain, for instance, said that it had nothing to do with wages, and that if there had to be a meeting, it must be with the coal-owners in each district. But when the meeting did at last take place and the workers insisted that an agreed and understood day-rate should be paid to men in abnormal places, whatever the district, the owners replied – with suspicious mildness – that they were willing to take into account not only the character of the place *but the ability of the man employed there.* And, thus replying, found that they had stirred up a hornets' nest.

In every other industry in the country the doctrine of the 'common rule' had long been established – that for doing the same kind of work all men shall receive the same pay. It is the very corner-stone of Trade Union policy; but, somehow or other, it had never been built into the coal industry. Why was this? Were the Miners' Unions to blame, or were the coal-owners too obstinate and evasive? Or could it be that in the coal industry no two men ever can be said to do the same kind of work? Such were the intricacies of the question that it was not until 1912, many years after it had been settled elsewhere, that the 'common rule' became a vital issue in the coal-fields of England.

For indeed, in the depths of a mine, working in perpetual midnight by the meagre glimmer of a lamp, a man is alone – as nowhere else – with all that is mysterious and inscrutable in this planet we live upon.

Between himself and a death which some of us have vaguely experienced in nightmares there is nothing but his own skill and experience and good luck. A few wooden props support the vast weight of unknown *strata*; the flame of his lamp, burning blue, warns him of the escape of some ancient imprisoned gas, deadly and without smell; brackish damp threatens his health or dry air charged with innumerable particles of dust and stone: there are no precautions, no regulations, no devices known to man, which can give him protection against these unpredictable treacheries. He is working, not in a charted and civilized and historical world, but in some angry fragment of a timeless universe; against that he pits his small strength.

Certainly, in 1912, there was something extremely individualistic in a miner's work. How could the 'common rule' operate when two men, at work in neighbouring stalls, might find a different problem awaiting them in the very same seam of coal; when a little more skill in one or the other would make a difference in the day's pay; or when – the skill being equal but the coal not equally easy to 'get' – only a complicated system of 'considerations' and adjustments and bargainings could bring the earnings of one up to the earnings of the other?

The system of a miner's pay, and the nature of 'abnormal' places, must both be examined before it can be understood what a strange accumulation of minor frictions, of human and inhuman influences, of prejudices and customs and beliefs resulted in the great coal strike of 1912.

The Cambrian strike of 1910 was a very fair instance of the bitterness which could arise over the question of a pit 'price-list'. A 'price-list' had a pleasant domestic sound, and even those who stopped to think how close to the grim margins of life a worker lived might wonder at the fury and despair which it had caused in its time. They forgot, or they did not know, that it had a social as well as an economic reference. Briefly, it was a list of piece-rates or prices (the hewer was always paid by piecework). Apart from the cutting price, or standard rate per ton paid for 'getting coal' from the face, there were countless prices for 'deadwork' – all the work, that is, which was not actual hewing, and which varied from cleaning the stall to extending the tram-lines.

Each colliery had a price-list and no two price-lists were alike, for every one was a matter of bargaining, and the bargaining might go on for months. The first step after a new pit was opened was to try out a number of working places, the hewers doing their work on day-wages.

The idea was that their average output over a number of weeks would indicate, with fair accuracy, the productivity of the pit or seam; but this idea was subject, in the course of weeks or even months, to a series of very natural qualifications.

The miner contended that the management had only opened the more favourable working places – the management replied that the miner had not been doing his best. Sooner or later, the manager went below and did a day's work, his object being to double the average output. He produced his results in triumph, whereupon the men said that he had chosen an easy place, or that any hewer, if he chose to exhaust himself, could do as well. Argument and counter-argument, accusation and counter-accusation, were part of the game; and at last the price-list resolved itself into a matter of bargaining skill, with the miners' district agent pitting his wits against a whole Board of Directors. And once the list had been made it was practically impossible to unmake it. It was somebody's charter – either the men's or the owners', and whoever had won the battle of wits would not allow it to be altered without a mortal fight. Owners in South Wales had been known to sell their pits rather than face the struggle that was bound to follow the alteration of a price-list, and the new buyer reckoned the expense of strike breaking in with his purchase price. Cory Brothers, in 1910, closed their Gelli Pit because the men refused to submit to an altered price-list, and it stayed closed until the war, for not a member of the South Wales Miners' Federation would work there.

And for that there was sufficient reason. Upon the making or altering of a price-list there might hang a very sordid drama. If the men had not held their own with the management, if the wages for a new pit were low – and variations between neighbouring pits with identical seams had been as high as 20 per cent – then a special kind of labour would be attracted there. High pay brought steady and skilful workers; to low pay came the nomads and the ne'er-do-wells of the industry; and the very destiny of each little town of five or six thousand depended upon the quality of its miners. In South Wales, for instance, there was little to be expected from the foreign miners, the unlikely immigrants who drifted in from the older North England pits, or the unskilled labourers from the pastures and ploughlands of Devon and Somerset: and a cheap price-list, in years of normal employment, meant just such foreign labour; it meant casual lodgers in the cottages, men without families; it meant public houses, and drunkenness, and dirt. A price-list was something more than a matter of pence and shillings – it might be the death warrant for a whole community.

From this it may perhaps be understood what the Cambrian Combine had to face when it attempted to open the Upper Five Foot Seam in the Ely Pit at less than reasonable pay.... Nor was it from mere perversity, or from lack of self-control as some imagined, that the miner – that proud and independent man – had punctuated the history of industry with hundreds upon hundreds of small and bitter strikes.

A series of moves by Parliament – the Coal Mines Act (1896), the Workmen's Compensation Act (1897), the export tax on coal (1901), and the new safety regulations of the Home Office (1902) – had considerably increased the cost of production. Now wages in the coal industry were 60 per cent to 70 per cent of production, and it was to wages therefore that the owners turned in an effort to retrench. Yet how were they to do it? Price-lists are based on a standard, to which a variable percentage is added, and in the twentieth century, with the sliding-scale in operation – whereby wages varied automatically with the price of coal – the selling price of coal was the equivalent of a standard wage. The system was a cruel one, causing wide fluctuations in wages, but at least the owners could not tamper with a standard which was set by forces beyond their control. Could they, perhaps, lower the percentage which was added to the standard? They tried; but with the Conciliation Boards in operation, they discovered that the miners were strong enough to resist them. But there was one respect in which neither standards nor Conciliation Boards offered the miner any assistance: workers in abnormal places still bargained with the management individually. Upon abnormal places, then, the owners concentrated their attack.

An abnormal place was a place from which, by circumstances beyond his control, the hewer was unable to get a subsistence wage. The seam might be thin, or crushed into small coal (small coal was not paid for at all in South Wales, and but meagrely elsewhere); or an exceptional amount of timbering might be required to prop up the roof against murderous falls; or stone might occur in the coal, with a consequent loss of time in sorting it out; or the working place might be too damp or too dry. Even in 'normal' places the management did not always supply the hewer with a regular number of 'trams' or tubs into which to load his coal, or with sufficient timber for props and sleepers.

For years these drawbacks had been dealt with by a system of 'considerations' or allowances: 3d. a ton, say, for a soft roof or 2d. a yard for ripping of roof, and so many pence extra for 'clod' – loose stone in or above the coal. It was not until Parliament's action had increased the cost of production that these allowances – which ranged from 6d. to 4s. a day – became unsatisfactory; for it was the allowances alone which offered the owners a real opportunity for retrenchment. Their methods, to say the least of them, were dubious. They began to keep elaborate cost accounts of each district of a mine, and would set the under-managers competing against each other as to who could produce the lowest average expenditure per ton in allowances and dead-work. Sometimes the management was even restricted to a lump sum for such allowances, irrespective of what the men's claims might be. And the management was not behindhand. Once a fortnight a 'measuring up' party would traverse the mine, prepared to hear the men's claims: and very soon complaints came pouring in from half the mines in England and Wales that, unless a man kept a sharp look-out, the measuring-up party would get past his working place unnoticed. And even when he did attract its attention, the bargaining that went on was likely to be far more severe than formerly. If, when an agreement was finally reached, the clerk took it down, all might be well; but sometimes the clerk did not take it down; the miner had to content himself with a verbal promise, and the promise was not always kept. Such were the results of parliamentary mediation and the greed of owners. What could be done? Could anybody help the individual miner but himself, since there was no one but himself with sufficient knowledge to make the claim? Would the law perhaps, extend itself into that dim-lit, that fabulous underworld where the measuring-up party and the hewer struck their bargain? It was worth trying; and in 1907 a skilled miner named Walters, of Ynysbwl, brought a case against the Ocean Coal Company for non-payment of an allowance, contending that such an allowance was customary. The County Court judge ruled against Walters, saying that allowances were not specifically provided for in the price-list (as if they could have been!) and were therefore gratuities not recoverable at law.

Thereafter the colliery companies reduced allowances to the exact point beyond which the law might be tempted to interfere on the miners' behalf. And all the worker in an abnormal place could do was to try and make up for it by working longer and harder than he had before. Then came the Eight Hours Act which from 1st July, 1909, restricted the miners of Wales – to take one example – to 8½ hours instead of the customary 10 or 10½ hours. Under the old régime, bad as it was, a man in a normal place took his work fairly easily, and only put forth all his exertions when he was in an abnormal place – with the worst possible consequences to his health. Under the new Act, a man in a normal place somewhat increased his speed – so long as he could get trams to clear the coal; and a man in a bad place lost money however hard he worked.

Such was the state of affairs when the miners and the owners came into conference in September 1911. Already it was clear that nothing but a minimum wage for workers in abnormal places would satisfy the miners; and when the owners responded with what was, in effect, an announcement that the old system of individual bargaining should remain, the battle, so long impending, could scarcely be delayed for very much longer. The owners might argue that the 'common rule' could not operate when conditions varied from district to district and pit to pit; when individual working places required individual attention; when the very difference of skill in each miner was a matter of vital interest: they might argue until the walls 'grew weary of their reverberations', but they had been driven into a corner and they knew it. Whether they could fight their way out again, the year 1912 would show.

XII

Before Christmas 1911 the labours of Mr George Askwith were rewarded, and he received a knighthood. He spent the first month of 1912 settling a weavers' lock-out of 160,000 men in Lancashire, which had frightened the country almost out of its wits, and a serious dock dispute on the Clyde. Both these crises, he noted, turned on the question of Union labour. In February, he and his department concentrated their attention on the gathering dispute in the coal-fields.

The miners had been moving with extreme rapidity since that inconclusive meeting with the owners in September of 1911. A month later, the MFGB, meeting at Southport, adopted the principle of an individual district minimum wage for men and boys, *without reference to abnormal places*. A further conference on 14th November reported no settlement. The owners, it appeared, were not interested in the district minimum wage; nor did they see that, in the back of the miners' heads, the dream of a national settlement was already assuming a formidable clarity. A national settlement – a national minimum wage . . . in 1911 such things were too improbable even to be worth a thought; and the owners, together with the public as a whole, refused to bother their heads.

On 20th and 21st December, the miners balloted on the question: 'Are you in favour of giving notice to establish a minimum wage for every man and boy working underground in the mines of Great Britain?' Answer: Yes – 445,800; No – 115,271.

Could this *really* be serious? The public still refused to believe so. But the owners, observing, with justifiable alarm, the speed with which the question of abnormal places had disappeared from the miners' argument, began to wonder. A national coal strike was inconceivable for the beautifully simple reason that it had never happened before. And yet ... notices had been served in every district, terminating at the end of February 1912. And then on 2nd February, they received the miners' demands which, amidst a great deal of complex circumstance, put forward the claim that all underground workers should receive not less than five shillings a shift for men and two shillings a shift for boys – a claim which speedily became known as the 'five and two'. There could be no doubting any longer; unless something were done before the end of the month every pit in England would be on strike.

At a meeting with the miners on 7th February, the owners made one last attempt to conjure away this dreadful ghost of a national minimum. They went back to the September argument, and said that they were now prepared to discuss special terms for abnormal places. Prepared – they should have been prepared before: the miners answered that they would discuss nothing less than a minimum wage, and the two parties separated in considerable heat. There was just a vague possibility that the Federated Area – which included North Wales and all England except Northumberland and Durham – might reach a settlement; but on 20th February even that possibility disappeared. The cry for action came swelling up out of South Wales. A general strike was just six days off.

It was at this point that the Prime Minister intervened.

The curious and unfortunate pilgrimage of Mr Asquith through the subsequent negotiations proved that, in the pre-war world, it was extremely unwise for political power to meddle in economic battles. The coal industry was unknown to Mr Asquith: and, what was more to the point, Mr Asquith was unknown to the coal industry – unknown, that is, until he decided, on 20th February, to invite both parties to a conference at the Foreign Office. It took place two days later. With an ingenuous eagerness, Mr Asquith, Sir Edward Grey, Mr Lloyd George and Mr Buxton listened to arguments which everyone else had heard *ad nauseam*, and with which – it was all too plain – they had hitherto not acquainted themselves. Hours were spent while the owners' representatives and the miners' representatives and Sir George Askwith carefully explained to the Ministers the rudiments of this national question. At last the Ministers seemed to understand. They suggested district conferences with a Government representative presiding at each. If a decision were not arrived at within a reasonable interval, the Government representatives should themselves decide upon the outstanding points in dispute. In other words – though this thought had not as yet occurred to Mr Asquith – the Government had now entered the battle – not as a referee, but as a third fighter.

On 28th February, miners and owners returned with their answer to this proposal. Of the owners, all but the Scotch, South Welsh and Northumberland gentlemen seemed ready to agree with it. The miners were frankly opposed. They would not negotiate, they declared, except on the straightforward question of an individual minimum wage for all underground workers; but they would meet the owners to discuss a complicated chart which they had with them, and which set forth the minimum rates for each district. This was reasonable enough. The Government and many districts had indicated at least a willingness to discuss the district minimum: but Mr Asquith, grasping what appeared to be a conciliatory hand, discovered that he had grasped too soon. What about safeguards? he asked. Safeguards? The miners tossed the notion aside. Safeguards against workers' abusing the privileges presented them in a minimum wage? It could not be thought of; too much time had already been wasted in fruitless talk. And suddenly Mr Asquith realized that the miners were not in the least interested either in the district minimum, or in any form of negotiation. And why should they be? How could one negotiate about an irreducible minimum such as the 'five and two'? And then Mr Asquith realized another thing. The miners' blank refusal to consider the question of safeguards was an ultimatum – an ultimatum presented, not to the owners, but to the Government itself.

Too late he had discovered his mistake. For the first time in English history the Government and not the employer was directly under fire: and it was he who had manoeuvred it into that comfortless, that unprecedented position. He could not withdraw now. Already the notice to cease work had expired; hour by hour mine after mine, district after district, grew idle; by 1st March about a million men were out.

After four days of desperate conference, Mr Asquith had to admit that nothing could be done. Obstinately the miners insisted upon their 'five and two'; obstinately the owners refused to countenance such a scheme: and both parties – was it from obstinacy, too, or was it because the truth was out at last? – both parties seemed to think that the Government had made matters infinitely worse. Meanwhile industry all over the country began to limp, to hesitate, to shut down. Pig-iron, steel, tin-plate, sheet steel, pottery, bricks, glass – these industries were practically idle by the end of March. Railway servants were forced to take their annual leave, or put on half time, or simply thrown out of work. Seamen, coal trimmers and teemers, dock and waterside workers, coal exporters, and casual labour in all its forms felt the growing paralysis. The fishing industry was badly damaged, especially at Hull and Grimsby, where all but a few trawlers were laid up. And the expense to the country – who dared compute that?

The public was angry and frightened, and would have been more than willing to believe the words – had it been privileged to hear them – which John Dillon, the Irish politician, spoke to Wilfred Scawen Blunt. 'The country,' said the oracular Mr Dillon, 'is menaced with revolution.' Perhaps this was going too far; but the mere fact that the miners, whom everybody had trusted to keep the peace, were actually responsible for this sudden dislocation, was too much for all but very sober and unemotional people. 'Of course I'm feudal,' said a Mrs Frankau to Arnold Bennett. 'I'd batten them down. I'd make them work. They *should* work. I'd force them down.' Mr Bennett set these phrases down in his Journal, with a characteristic lack of comment, but, making some allowance for the lady's feudal leanings, they were typical of what was being said in all the drawing-rooms and parlours of England. Would Mr Asquith have agreed with them, in his secret heart, had they been spoken to him and not to Mr Bennett? Did he share the public's sudden hatred? Few men had more reason; for the miners had only deprived the public of its regular supply of coal, of its transport facilities, and its peace of mind – but *him* they had deprived of his self-respect. It was not to be borne; yet it had to be borne. Through the first weeks of March he laboured to bring the stoppage to an end by the only means he really understood – discussion. Words were his special province, and he used them unsparingly: but it was very disconcerting – the miners' representatives seemed to think him insincere. At last he knew that Parliament itself must bow to the miners, and Parliament was of the same mind. A Bill was hastily prepared 'to provide a minimum wage in the case of workers employed underground and for purposes incidental thereto'. Considering the short space of time in which it had been drawn up, the Bill was a very creditable piece of work, except in one particular – it made no mention of the one thing the miners wanted: the 'five and two'. It passed its second reading by a large majority, and the strike continued.

An amendment which specifically wrote the 'five and two' into the Bill was rejected by 326 to 83, and the strange, equivocal document became law on 29th March. Would it satisfy the miners? Would they content themselves with having humbled Parliament, as Parliament had never been humbled before? Would they think it sufficient that, while their chief demand was refused, the *principle* involved in that demand was now embodied in an Act? Nobody could tell.

When the Bill went through its third reading, a curious scene took place, and Mr Asquith was the chief actor in it. He was on his feet, speaking, not so much to the apprehensive faces before and around him, as to the miners themselves. He begged them to stay the havoc with which the country was confronted; he recited once again the efforts which had been made, how hopes had risen and hopes had been shattered. 'We laboured hard,' he said. He turned to the packed Labour benches. If their case for the five shillings and the two shillings was strong, would they not trust the district boards to provide these rates? Must the country be subjected to further hardship? 'I speak under the stress of very strong feeling,' he went on; and hesitating between words – he, who was always so impassive, so lucid – begged Parliament to pass the Bill. 'We have exhausted all our powers of persuasion and argument and negotiation,' he concluded, in low thick halting tones. 'But we claim we have done our best in the public interest – with perfect fairness and impartiality.' He stood there, struggling for words; and they would not come. The House watched him, fascinated and appalled: something was taking place before its eyes which not one of its members had ever expected to see.

The Prime Minister was weeping.

XIII

This singular drama deserves a little further investigation. The spectacle of Mr Asquith in tears was, after all – as Mr Tim Healy once remarked on a very different occasion – about the greatest miracle since Moses struck the rock. Was it mortification which produced this curious display? Was it weariness? Or was it a sudden, an unexpected encounter with an overwhelming reality? Another encounter, no less unexpected, provides us, at least, with the evidence that for many days there had been an atmosphere of excessive uneasiness at No. 10, Downing Street.

Mr Robert Smillie was Vice-Chairman of the M F G B in those days, and Mr Smillie has recorded in his autobiography – *My Life for Labour* – what is by all odds the strangest little comedy of all the strike years. He was staying in London, at the Westminster Palace Hotel, where the Federation had made its headquarters, and on 15th March he went to luncheon with Sir George Askwith. He was a busy man, but like most labour leaders, he was very fond of Sir George. Before luncheon he was introduced to two ladies, whose names he did not catch, and one of them 'promptly got hold of me . . . and began to talk with extraordinary animation'. It was some few minutes before he discovered that she was Margot Asquith.

At luncheon, too, Mrs Asquith sat next to him. She plied him with questions about the strike and about social conditions, to which he answered mostly with 'Yes' and 'No'. Mrs Asquith was not daunted. Could she meet Mr Smillie again? Mr Smillie was very busy, but he would see her two days later at the Westminster Palace Hotel, if she found that convenient. Shortly after luncheon Mrs Asquith left with her friend, 'and we had then', Mr Smillie comments, 'a pleasant talk with our host and hostess'.

The next day he received the following missive:

> *10 Downing Street*
> *Whitehall S.W.*
> *16th March 1912*

DEAR MR SMILLIE,

I was pleased to meet you yesterday. You will keep your promise of being at the Westminster Palace Hotel at 3.30 tomorrow, where I shall meet you. The big question I long to ask a man of your ability, sympathy, and possibly very painful experience is: What do you want?

I don't, of course, mean for yourself, as I am certain you are as straight as I am, and are disinterested. It would be on far higher grounds than this that I would ask it.

Do you want everyone to be equal in their material prosperity? Do you think quality of brain could be made equal if we had equal prosperity? Do you think in trying or even succeeding in making Human Nature equal in their bankbooks, they would also be equal in the sight of God and Man? Equal in motive, in unselfishness, in grandeur of character?

I am a socialist, possibly not on the same lines as you. . . . People who get what they want at the cost of huge suffering to others I would like to understand more perfectly.

Just now I suspend judgement, as I don't really comprehend. I don't care what creed a man holds, but the bed-rock of that creed should be Love, even of your enemies, which is a hard creed to put into practice.

Having suffered greatly yourself, I expect you don't want anyone else to suffer, and this is what makes you a socialist. It is also my point of view, but I am only a woman. I don't like to see my husband suffer in his longing to be fair, just, and kind to both sides in this tragic quarrel.

I know what you said was true. For seven years, or even more, you and your best and noblest friends have foreseen this coal strike, and doubtless it could have been avoided by the mine-owners.

But keep your blood warm. Don't let it get cold. Use your great power for an honourable settlement. Destruction is a sad exchange for construction. Help my husband. He is a self-made man like yourself. He is courteous, understanding, infinitely compassionate, and courageously patient. He is also straight.

No doubt the other side will do their best to make political capital out of this. They are bitter over his policy. They are narrow and ignorant, and would love, just now, to make all the mischief they can. I only write this in advance of our talk tomorrow, as a fair appeal to a perfect stranger, in favour of a man who, though he is my husband, is as liberal as yourself and wants to act fairly by all men.

You have great power. See that you use it for good. I know nothing of the Bill beyond what I read in the papers. I have not seen my husband since I saw you. (He had left for the country when I got back from golfing with my little girl.) I shall see him tomorrow morning. I am alone here today and I am thinking deeply of you and the strike and what is the true and right thing to do. Don't bother to answer this. I shall see you at 3.30 tomorrow and look forward to having a real quiet talk.

Yours,

MARGOT ASQUITH

These sentences, so oddly compounded of condescension, sincerity, ignorance, and courage were, in any case, scarcely distinguished by a nice sense of tact. Nor was it exactly discreet for a strike leader to meet the wife of the head of the Government, at a time of extreme tension, and in the temporary headquarters of the Miners' Federation. It was doubtless this latter notion which prompted Mr Smillie to reply that he would be unable to keep his engagement with Mrs Asquith. Mrs Asquith, however, thought that one more blow should be struck for her husband; and it was perhaps inevitable that this blow should have widened, like some unfortunate stroke with a pick-axe, the fissure which already yawned between her mind and the mind of such as Mr Smillie.

I don't see why [she wrote on 18th March], *anyone should know we have met. I am afraid I vexed you in my letter, which was written quite freely. (Perhaps you did not get my letter?) Do the masters and the miners live at your hotel? Do let us meet again. I don't want to talk about the strike at all. It is only for the pleasure of discussing abstract ideas with a man whose temperament and views interest me.*

I am sorry you have thrown me over. I've never been afraid of any individual, or any situation, or rumour, or gossip in my life; but can assure you that I would meet you at 3 Queen Anne's Gate, Sir Edward Grey's house, at 3.30. Even he need not know. I would just ask him if he would allow me to have a private talk with a friend for fifteen minutes. He would say 'Yes' and never even ask, nor would I tell anyone. If you won't do this, do answer my letter.

Yours,

MARGOT ASQUITH

'I did not meet Mrs Asquith again,' is all Mr Smillie has to say by way of comment.

XIV

This correspondence, at once pathetic and preposterous, throws some light upon Mr Asquith's state of mind – which must have been pitiful indeed to have driven his wife to such extraordinary pleas for help. Nor is it entirely irrelevant to the whole situation. Were the Ministers themselves, after all, any less at sea than Mrs Asquith in their dealings with the miners? They had certainly not shown as much courage as she, and it cannot be said that they had made themselves much more intelligible. Mr Smillie complains that in all his conversations with the Prime Minister he never could understand exactly what that gentleman meant. Mr Asquith might have returned the compliment; in the persons of Mr Smillie and his colleagues he had come face to face with a side of the national life which was altogether beyond his comprehension. Those tears which he shed in the Commons seem more and more like a tragic confession, not merely of a personal failure, but of the failure of Liberalism itself.

As for the miners, they had won a moral victory, and had the times been less uncompromising, with a moral victory they might have contented themselves. But the railwaymen had won a moral victory in 1911, and the railwaymen were notoriously not content. Meanwhile, with infinite reluctance, the strikers went back to work. On 6th April, they actually balloted against a resumption, and only a decision of their leaders that a two thirds majority was necessary to prolong the strike, saved the country from an indefinite continuance. By the middle of April, the coalfields were normal again.

The effect of the Minimum Wage Act was threefold. (1) The wages of unskilled underground day-wage men were materially increased, though rarely to the 5s. demanded. (2) District negotiations, provided for in the Act, secured for the skilled hewers a minimum day-wage, when they were employed in abnormal places. (3) The principle of a national minimum wage, which had seemed but a year ago so very Utopian, had now been established by Act of Parliament. Such gains were worth fighting for. And yet – there was no denying it – both owners and miners were eager to renew the battle whenever circumstances were favourable. Parliament, moreover, which had once enjoyed the respect of both sides, was now powerless to prevent them from creating what havoc they pleased.

And Liberalism . . . Liberalism, with its fatal trust in compromise, had evaded the issue once again. But, slide and wriggle as it would, there was a doom which it could not evade. The millstones of Capital and Labour, the upper and the nether, grind slowly but exceeding small, and Liberalism was caught between them. It might put off the evil hour, poor slippery old faith, but they would crush it in the end.

XV

The miners were back at work; and, as is always the case, the production of coal immediately increased. For, while mines lie idle with no human hand to work them, the vast weight of earth is itself in labour, leaning upon and loosening the coal in the seams, so that it becomes for a time twice as easy to 'get'. The coal-fields were busy. Peace descended upon industrial England. How long would it last?

How long *could* it last, when the very air was congregated with discontent? In May, fresh trouble threatened; and, once again, the transport workers of London were involved. It was on 21st May that the Society of Watermen, Lightermen, and Bargemen came out on strike, about 6,000 strong; nor, from the outset, could there be any doubt that the whole port would soon be affected, for the stoppage was clearly designed to strengthen the hand of the Transport Workers' Federation. The owners, with an odiously polite passivity, had refused to discriminate between Union and non-Union labour. It was not their business, they said. As far as they were concerned, the transport strike of 1911 might never have been.

The Federation bided its time, and at last it discovered, in the employment of the Mercantile Lighterage Company, an elderly watchman by the name of James Thomas. Once upon a time, Mr Thomas had been a foreman; he was one of the original founders of the Association of Foremen Lightermen, a freak Trade Union, designed in part 'to protect the property of our employers', and possessing a membership of 250 worthies. To the Association of Foremen Lightermen Mr Thomas still belonged when his case was brought to the attention of Harry Gosling, general secretary of the Amalgamated Society of Watermen, Lightermen, and Watchmen of the River Thames; and Mr Gosling perceived that the gods had, as it were, dropped Mr Thomas into his lap.

He invited Mr Thomas to join the Amalgamated Society of Watermen, Lightermen and Watchmen of the River Thames, and Mr Thomas refused. Perhaps he wanted to remain, in spirit at least, the foreman he once had been; or perhaps, as seems more probable, he was opposed to such Trade Unions as Mr Gosling's. He was a respectable old body, more than a little plaintive at this intrusion upon his private life – more than a little frightened, too, for he had been threatened once before during the great dock strike in the previous year. But he stood his ground. On 30th April, therefore, a member of the Amalgamated Society refused to work with him, and appealed to the Mercantile Lighterage Company, which expressed itself perfectly indifferent to what was, in its opinion, a quarrel between two Unions. On 16th May the Association of Master Lightermen and Bargemen – in the belief, as they put it, that otherwise 'their heads were to be chopped off one by one' – decided to do the offending lighterage company's work, and discharged such Union men as refused to obey. On 21st May, all the lightermen were out.

Two days later the Executive of the National Transport Workers' Federation called upon all transport workers 'to cease work tonight', a command which succeeded only in London and on the Medway, where work slowly came to a standstill.

It was at this point that certain members of the Cabinet, headed by Mr Lloyd George, were seized with a fatal notion. Mr George himself could not forget that he had once handled a railway strike; the others were possibly dissatisfied with Mr Asquith's behaviour in the recent coal stoppage; and Mr Asquith himself was away, conveniently cruising in the Mediterranean. Circumstances were favourable for Government intervention on a grand scale, and the Ministers were not behindhand. They would teach Mr Asquith a lesson; they would try their hands at running the country without any interference from above; they would restore the battered fortunes of their afflicted party; they would be hailed, in headlines, as saviours; and, in general, they would have a wonderful time. If there was any lesson to be learned from the Government's recent interference with the coal strike, some of Mr Asquith's colleagues, it was plain, had not bothered to learn it.

The sorrows of these amateur arbitrators (Mr Lloyd George, Sir Rufus Isaacs, Mr Reginald McKenna, Mr John Burns) began almost immediately with their choice of Sir Edward Clarke, KC, as the right man to conduct an inquiry into the whole affair. For two days Sir Edward listened to a confusion of claims which, as must always be the case in a dock strike, seemed to conjure themselves, hour by hour, out of the thin air. It was clear from the outset that not merely the master lightermen, but the short sea traders, the wharfingers, and the master carters had not kept their agreements of the previous year; it was clear, too, that Sir Edward was being asked to decide upon a question of whether or no all workers should belong to a Union. He did his best to confine the inquiry to specific agreements, but, try as he would, that dread spectre of unionization arose to confound him at every turn. Hours were spent discussing, in acrimonious detail, the wrongs of one Captain Fitch, who, refusing to take his tug to the assistance of the *Lady Jocelyn*, a notorious blackleg ship, during the dock strike of 1911, had been dismissed by his firm after fifty years' service. Then Mr Thomas, supported by a friend named Reekie, insisted upon airing *his* complaints. And so it went. And when it was all over, Sir Edward had no suggestion to offer. He had simply discovered that the owners and employers in the Port of London were extremely elusive: some of them were banded together in associations, some were not, some were affiliated to the Board of Trade, some were not. About the only way in which they could be made to keep their agreements was by Act of Parliament. Thus Sir Edward.

These conclusions were not likely to pacify the employers. As for the men, they declared that it did not satisfy their main contention. But what was their main contention? During the inquiry, Sir Edward had a distinct impression, which happened also to be a correct one, that a compulsory Union ticket for all dock workers was the vital issue. But one of the features of a dock strike is that it has no permanent features; it will change its face from day to day. The ill treatment of Captain Fitch, the lamentations of Messrs Thomas and Reekie, were as if they had never been; the vast and complicated toil of the London docks had come to a standstill, it now appeared, upon nothing more substantial than the obstinate behaviour of a certain Mr Bissell and his two carters. Upon inquiry it was discovered that Mr Bissell had once been a member of the Master Carmen and Contractors' Association, and that he had broken the agreement of 1911 by employing two carters at less than the 1911 award. Unfortunately, Mr Bissell had since left the Association; more unfortunately still, his two men stuck by him. Nothing less than an Act of Parliament could compel Mr Bissell and his men to behave.

Around the person of this remote and indifferent employer the battle of charge and counter-charge raged furiously, while one hundred thousand men stood idle. Meanwhile, Mr Lloyd George and his colleagues, poring over Sir Edward Clarke's report, seized upon his statement that the employers were too scattered and diverse to be dealt with as a body. The implications of this were obvious. If there had been a federation of employers, there would have been no strike. To the forming of a federation of employers, therefore, the Ministers turned their attention. Their first effort was scarcely successful; the shipowners remarking, with a contemptuous finality, that if they were to be held responsible for a dispute about a master carter they would have to look after every contract made by every employer in every hole and corner of the port. And this, the shipowners said, they were not prepared to do. The Ministers, however, were not easily discouraged; their solution was clearly an inspired one, and, with a simple-minded alacrity which would have done credit to an African missionary, they proceeded to importune every employer who could be discovered and would listen. At length, a fairly representative body of these gentlemen was prevailed upon to give an answer.

'a. Under existing circumstances such a scheme is impracticable.

b. The employers desire that it should be distinctly understood that, whilst they are willing to discuss with His Majesty's Ministers at all times any suggestions made by them, no such suggestions, however acceptable in other respects, will be adopted until work is resumed throughout the Port. Further, they will not under any circumstances consent to any recognition of the Union or Transport Workers' Federation ticket, or to any discussion for such recognition. . . .'

This was final; it was also unflattering. Indeed, if the employers had given the ministerial faces a shrewd slap, they would scarcely have made their point clearer. But the unhappy Mr George and his friends realized that they were too far in to stop. They searched their minds for suggestions. Could not something be run up on the lines of the Brooklands Agreement? The employers turned a deaf ear. Very well, then – why not an Appeal Court? Most certainly an Appeal Court, with representatives from both sides, and powers to inflict penalties for breaches of agreement. The employers were silent.

But not the men. Once again, the Cabinet's interposition had left behind it a twofold impression – that the Government was ignorant, and that it could be bullied. Mr Harry Gosling, expressing an extreme enthusiasm for the Appeal Court, added that if the employers did not agree to it within twenty-four hours, he would declare a national strike. This was on 7th June. The employers, asking for three days' grace, countered, on 10th June, with a flat refusal. A telegram was immediately dispatched to all ports – 'Employers' point-blank refusal to accept proposal for settlement. National Executive recommend general stoppage at once.'

That zealous little Cabinet clique could hardly have found much cause for congratulation in this. Instead of settling the question, as it had hoped, by a subtle display of administrative wisdom, it had simply presented an already weary country with another general strike. And then, at the last minute, it was saved by the refusal of the ports to join in the strike; their funds were depleted, and they had not recovered from their efforts of 1911. Outside of London, only twenty thousand dockers ceased work. Mr Lloyd George and his fellow-conspirators, heaving a sigh of relief, made preparations to disappear from the scene as unobtrusively as possible.

And well they might. For Mr Asquith was on his way home, and Mr Asquith's anger, though rarely stirred, was not a pleasant thing to face. Immediately upon his arrival, he summoned Sir George Askwith to his house, and asked for a full explanation. Sir George did not mince his words: he offered no criticism, but as the tale of ministerial intervention unfolded itself, with all its naked implications of self-advertisement and conspiracy, the Prime Minister grew more and more angry. At last he burst forth – 'Every word you have spoken endorses the opinion I have formed. It is a degradation of Government.' He paced up and down the room, his hands in his pockets. 'Can't you suggest *anything?*' he said at last. Sir George thought there was nothing for it but that the employers should declare their intention of keeping all agreements. The employers, however, were not of the same mind. They would make no promises, they said, until the men had all returned to work; and this was their attitude all through the month of June and well into the middle of July.

The Port of London got along as best it could with the inefficient assistance of 19,000 imported blackleg labourers. There were riots, of course, but somehow the spirit of 1911 had not returned to aid the strike of 1912. The hospitals reported only seventy-eight cases of minor injuries among the strikers. . . . No more than six policemen were hurt. . . . A Miss Ada Molesley, of Mucking, had to be treated for an injured collar-bone, caused by a stone hurled from a railway train. . . . No, if the hospital statistics were any indication, the warlike spirit of 1911 was definitely absent; the Federation, it was clear, was not yet strong enough to carry through two strikes in successive years.

But, as the stoppage proceeded from June into July, and the employers still obstinately declined to consider any proposals without an unconditional return to work, famine came closer and closer to the dockers' families. In vain the Industrial Council – that respectable but futile aggregation of old-fashioned labour leaders and elderly capitalists –

urged a new inquiry. The employers were obdurate. Let the workers be starved back. Others were more compassionate: one Bishop opened a relief fund, three more tried their skill at mediation, prompted no doubt by the example of Cardinal Manning, who had settled the dock strike of 1887 almost single-handed. But, alas, the Bishops were no Cardinal Mannings. It was not for them to stand up, as that grim and powerful old man had done, before a packed assembly of dockers, and beseech them to remember their wives and children. A luminous mist had seemed to swim then – was it a trick of light, or emotion in his hearers, or something more? – about an image of the Virgin and Child behind the Cardinal's head. But the Anglican bishops could not speak before such an image, and, if they had, it is doubtful if any mist would have swum for *them*. They had 'butted in' – the words were Sir George Askwith's – and that is to be their memorial. Help for the strikers' families came, when it did come, from a very different quarter. Lord Devonport suddenly confessed himself willing to promise that all agreements in future should be kept. Would he see the leaders personally? He would. And would he be sure not to mention the Federation ticket – a smouldering issue, ready to burst into flame? Lord Devonport was very eager never to hear of the ticket again, let alone speak of it. And so, one morning, Sir George and two leaders appeared at Lord Devonport's door, Sir George waiting just long enough to see that they were admitted. The subsequent conversation seems to have gone off amicably enough, and Lord Devonport published, in the press of 18th July, a specific denouncement of all breaches of agreement. On 27th July, the strike was called off. And then, at the last minute, after two months of striking, the men refused to go back to work; and it took all Sir George's suavity to get the port open by 6th August.

Indeed, the end of the strike – that final flame of insubordination – was more typical of the Unrest years than any other part of it. For when the leaders began anything, when a movement was not forced upon them from below, when – as in this instance – a reasonable attempt was made for the cause of unionization, success was not likely to follow. The Unrest was irrational, it was unconscious, it came hurtling up from the soul of the people; and unless the soul of the people was involved, Mr Harry Gosling and his colleagues might talk the weightiest common sense, and talk until they were hoarse, and nothing would come of their words. Such were the lessons to be learned, for those who chose to go to school to it, from the London stoppage of 1912.

Mr Asquith had learned his lesson, too, and he was determined that the Cabinet should have the benefit of it. He issued an order that no Minister was ever again to meddle in an industrial dispute, and the order was obeyed.

Nobody was exactly happy when work was resumed on 6th August. It would have been idle to pretend that either side had gained anything. But everyone knew that when the National Transport Workers' Federation moved again, it would move to more purpose. At the moment the workers were weary after the privations and the efforts of 1911, and the disappointment of 1912: but as soon as they had rested and recovered their spirits . . . It was more comfortable not to think what would happen then.

The total number of disputes in 1912 had been 857; the workers directly involved numbered 1,233,016; the aggregate loss in working days was 38,142,101. In the pre-war world such figures were staggering; but they were even more staggering when one stopped to consider that most of the strikes had been concerned with Trade Unionism, and that the greatest of them all had been fought over the establishment of a principle. But the most staggering thing of all, as one looks back into those far years, is to realize that only through the putting forth of an unparalleled, an inarticulate, an irrational energy did the principle of Trade Unionism and the principle of the Minimum Wage pass so swiftly from the realm of formula into the realm of fact.

XVI

The disputes of 1911 and 1912 had followed, with singular fidelity, such tactics as were prescribed by the syndicalists: they were bitter and frequent, they had convulsed the country, they had humbled Parliament, and they were leading – with a disconcerting speed and directness – towards the final assault of a General Strike. One by one, the transport workers, the miners, and the railwaymen had come out; one by one they had returned, not merely with a sense of grievance, but with a sense of power: it was simply a question of time before they joined forces.

Time, indeed, decided the question otherwise; but the most insidious of all the enchantments of history lies in those parts of it which cannot be written, where the premises only are given, and their implications may be followed any way one pleases.

The winter, spring, and summer of 1913 must have seemed, to the casual observer, a time of peace in the industrial world. Mr Ramsay MacDonald's *The Social Unrest* appeared – a little book which, while hinting at fresh developments in the future, ingeniously contrived to suggest that the trouble was now over: wish-fulfillment, one can only suppose. The railways, the ports, the coal-fields gave every outward appearance of activity and order. Business prospered. The polite world indulged itself in an orgy of spending in which vulgarity, hysteria, and mounting dividends were inextricably intermingled. And who could have told that more strikes were taking place than had ever been recorded before by the Board of Trade? They were such little strikes, sometimes they involved less than a thousand men; and yet their fever flitted to and fro through all the counties of England, raising a rash of class hatred which would have surpassed all records, too, if records of such inconvenient phenomena had also been kept by the Board of Trade.

The public, however, interested itself in other matters. It had never cared to startle itself with unnecessary speculation as to where the industrial trouble would end, having, for the most part, a touching faith in what it liked to call the good sense of the working classes. The perturbations of the Balkans, the vaulting mind of Wilhelm II, the possibilities of espionage among German waiters, Ulster, Post-Impressionism, Mrs Pankhurst, the Russian Ballet – these and kindred subjects occupied its attention. And then it began to lick its lips over a savoury little semi-political fracas which came to be known as the Marconi Scandal.

The details of this affair, so often debated, are not worth repeating in full; but a swift *précis* of them may possibly show to what unseemly lengths, down what bemired by-paths, politicians were capable of dragging their cause. Nor can one help adding that, in the prevailing state of the working class mind, a more unfortunate controversy could hardly have been aired within the walls of an already discredited Parliament.

Early in 1912, the Marconi Company had been invited to tender for the establishment of a chain of state-owned wireless stations within the Empire. Its tender was accepted, subject to ratification by Parliament, and immediately the most disreputable rumours began to creep about the country. The Managing Director of the Company happened to be Mr Godfrey Isaacs, who was also brother of the Attorney-General, Sir Rufus Isaacs; and Mr Cecil Chesterton started accusations in the *Eye Witness* and the *New Witness* (of which two weeklies he was editor) that certain Ministers – to be specific, Mr Lloyd George, Sir Rufus, and the Master of Elibank – had been dabbling in the Company's shares. Mr Chesterton's motives, never very clear, appeared to be anti-Jewish, for it was upon Sir Rufus Isaacs that he concentrated his attack, persecuting that unfortunate gentleman with the most lurid posters, which, hung about the shoulders of sandwich-men, haunted the Attorney-General on his walks abroad. Accusations of ministerial corruption being practically unknown in England since the eighteenth century, Mr Asquith had no choice but to appoint a Select Committee of fifteen to look into these charges. Meanwhile, in a full-dress debate in the House on 11th October, the Ministers roundly denied that they had had any dealings in the shares of the English Marconi Company. With this everybody seemed satisfied, and it was not until February 1913, that the scandal was heard of again. In that month *Le Matin* published a paragraph in which it repeated the accusations, naming Sir Rufus Isaacs and Mr Herbert Samuel, the Postmaster-General, as the culprits. The two Ministers instituted a libel action, and it was in the course of these proceedings that Sir Rufus made a very sad confession. He had not dabbled in English shares, but he had, at the instance of his brother Harry, a ship and fruit broker in the City, purchased 10,000 shares in the American company, and some of these he had resold to Mr Lloyd George and the Master of Elibank. Now the American Marconi Company had no concern with the English Company and could not benefit by its recent transactions; but none the less it was clear that Sir Rufus and Mr Lloyd George were in for a very bad time of it.

In the first place, they had obviously wanted for candour in not revealing these purchases during the debate in October; in the second place, this was no time to give the Tory Party even the slenderest opportunities to make itself unpleasant. It was on Mr Lloyd George's head that the Tories now began to spend their venom. Insinuations of the most disgraceful nature were put about – that he had mansions in Surrey and Wales and a villa in the South of France; and that you really couldn't keep this sort of state up on a salary of £5,000 a year. Nor could you. Mr George explained to the Select Committee that he had exactly one house – in Wales; that his mansion at Walton – which the suffragettes had partly exploded – was somebody else's property and he was to have the lease of it; that he had never possessed a villa in the South of France; and that his total investments from savings might amount to £400 a year. But the Select Committee was frankly partisan, and its Tory bloc, headed by the revengeful Lord Robert Cecil, managed to convey the impression that the Chancellor had been indulging in a highly dubious flutter, and observed with pleasure that their victim's hair had gone distinctly grey and that he was obliged to use spectacles for the first time. The majority report, of course, completely exonerated the two Ministers; a vote of censure, on 18th June, was defeated by 346 to 268; and though Mr Asquith who had, with characteristic loyalty, stuck to his colleagues, ventured to remark that they had broken one of the 'rules of prudence', and though Mr Balfour and Mr Bonar Law gently accused them of impropriety and lack of moral courage, it was obvious that Parliament had washed its hands of the whole affair. The Tories realized that they had done Mr George's reputation a good deal of damage, and they saw no point in turning him into a martyr.

But that unfortunate phrase 'There's no smoke without a fire' continued to dog Mr George's footsteps. Innocent as he was, those mythical villas and mansions were held against him. People began to wonder if, in spite of his low sympathies, he might not be something of a capitalist on the sly. He rallied as best he could. In a speech on 3rd July, he declared that he was a petrel which had ridden the storm; he also likened himself to a Samson, and to a Sebastian whose hands were tied behind his back while arrows were shot into him from all sides. Pursuing these sacred analogies a little further, he announced that his Health Insurance Act was 'doing the work of the Man of Nazareth'. But even this sublime comparison, strange to say, did him no good. His prestige had been severely shaken, and he knew it. Nor was he quite sure where to turn. His Health Insurance Act was being so severely assaulted by the whole medical profession, and so apathetically received by the poor themselves, that it could be of no assistance to him in the recovery of his good name. His recent interference with the London dock strike had taken on the colours of pure farce. The Home Rule question presented too many dangers for a man with a strong Protestant following. Where *could* he turn?

For some time he had been playing with the idea of land reform, and now he adopted it in earnest. But what sort of reform did he propose? A change in the land laws and in land taxation, with further reform of housing, and State control of the railways? Mr Lloyd George did not say. His opening speech at Bedford proved to be little more than an attack on the game laws. 'We have complaints from farmers in every part of the country,' he said, 'that their crops have been damaged by game. Here is one farmer who was sowing his crop – it was a field of mangolds. The man assured me that there was not one mangold out of a dozen which was not pecked by pheasants. Where you should have got thirty-five tons, you could not have more than ten tons. It was not worth the trouble of carting.'

The only reply to this, of course, was that nothing in the world would induce a pheasant to peck a mangold-wurzel, for which unappetizing vegetable it has a very proper distaste. But, in any case, Mr George's land campaign did him no good. The agricultural labourer was either uninterested in land reform or obstinately on the side of the landlord and the game laws; while the urban workers could only wonder what had happened to the man who had once set himself up as their champion. What, indeed? In what causes, when you came to examine it, had his famous eloquence spent itself? There was that notable passage of his in the course of a debate on the Welsh Disestablishment Bill in May 1912.

'The Duke of Devonshire issues a circular applying for subscriptions to oppose this Bill, and he charges us with robbery of God. Does he know – of course he knows – that the very foundations of his fortune are laid deep in sacrilege, fortunes built out of deserted shrines and pillaged altars.... What is their story? Look at the whole story of the pillage of the Reformation. They robbed the Catholic Church, they robbed the monasteries, they robbed the altars, they robbed the almshouses, they robbed the poor, and they robbed the dead. Then they come here when we are trying to seek at any rate to recover some part of this pillaged property for the poor for whom it was originally given, and they venture, with hands dripping with the fat of sacrilege, to accuse us of robbery of God.'

This was in admirable vein. But then the Disestablishment of the Welsh Church was an unimportant issue in 1912. And it seemed more and more that most of Mr George's redoubtable energy was absorbed in attacking the great, in hacking at the branches, as it were, and not at the root of economic evil. It was all very well to assail the Dukes, but did he also assail the drains? Did he demand, with equal vehemence, the suppression of coronets and the clearance of slums? Had that persuasive voice once raised itself, for so much as a syllable, in behalf of the 'five and two'? The answers were not calculated to reassure those workers who still believed in him. It almost seemed as if this firebrand, this hope of the

Liberal Party, this uncompromising friend of the poor and oppressed, was now – with his greying hair, and his spectacles, and his bruised reputation – disappearing from the political scene. For surely no event could have been more ironically, more precisely inopportune than the intrusion of that wretched Marconi Scandal into the life of a Liberal demagogue at a time of extreme industrial unrest.

And yet one thing was more ironical, and that was the public attitude towards the Unrest itself. On 1st August, *The Times* was able to remark: 'The general interest in the subject has died away. Strikes are no longer of interest except in so far as languid attention may be given to events 6,000 miles away on the Rand.' Just one month later, the following brief announcement appeared. 'Dublin. 1st September. Killed 1; injured 460; arrested 210.' Another strike was in full swing, a strike more serious, in its way, than any that had gone before. . . .

XVII

From the sordid and somewhat bloodstained complexities of the great Dublin transport strike, two figures emerge – those of William Martin Murphy and of James Larkin. Mr Murphy was a man of enterprise. His financial interests had extended themselves in many directions since he had taken over his father's contracting business at a comparatively early age: he had carried out a great many railway and tramway undertakings in Dublin, Belfast, Cork, Ramsgate, Margate, Scotland, and West Africa. One of the achievements upon which he doubtless looked back with most satisfaction was the construction of a tramway line from Vauxhall to Norwood, which became almost derelict, and was sold to the public authority at a handsome profit. He owned the *Independent* and a chain of Irish newspapers, and he had once refused a title from Edward VII. It need, perhaps, only be added, to complete the picture, that he had an interest in a large drapery business and that he looked like a solicitor of the old school – tall, spare, stooped, with masses of silvery hair, and a face the general benevolence of which was occasionally confused by a pair of deep-set, penetrating, cold grey eyes. Such was the man whom Mr James Larkin described from time to time, and with legitimate hyperbole, as 'an industrial octopus', a 'tramway tyrant', and a 'pure-souled financial contortionist'.

As for Mr Larkin, his gift for words was considerably less questionable than his background, the obscurity of which not even the researches of his enemies had altogether illuminated. That he came from Liverpool was certain, but whether he was actually the illegitimate son of a Phoenix Park informer, who could say? Not that it mattered very much, for the personality of the man was sufficient for all but the very particular. The *fact* of Larkin was enough.

It was this personality, rather than Mr Murphy's, which dominated Dublin during the closing months of 1913. Preposterous and powerful, half genius and half lunatic, with his strange moments of sheer courage and stranger moods of childish pride, cruel, criminal, tender, inspired – James Larkin will neither be altogether dispraised nor altogether forgotten. Those who ever had dealings with him are certainly not likely to forget. 'You cannot argue with the prophet Isaiah,' said one Dublin employer after an unprofitable exchange of words with Mr Larkin. Mr Larkin's opinion of himself was not very different. 'I have got a divine mission, I believe,' he said, 'to make men and women discontented.' He rather welcomed abuse, and the hatred of eminent men was meat and drink to him. 'I knelt down in Sligo cathedral,' he told an audience once, 'at the feet of a bishop when he said, "Anti-Christ is come to town: it is Larkin" '; and one cannot help feeling that he found the comparison a flattering one. And yet – tall, slim, athletic, with blue-black hair and burning eyes – the impression he made upon some people was of another kind. 'He is a great man,' said William Orpen.

Larkin had imbibed his social doctrines from no less a source than the *New Age*, for whose editor, the persuasive A. R. Orage, he had a profound regard. Whether he actually comprehended Orage's mongrel and mysterious Guild Socialism is another question; but the tactics of Syndicalism he understood well enough, and these were invested with an extra fascination by the dialectics of Orage. And what better field for the practice of syndicalist manoeuvres could possibly have been chosen than Dublin – Dublin having, among other likely features, the worst slums in the world, and a considerable minority of almost eighteenth century workers who would much rather fight than work?

And, to tell the truth, it was with men who had never worked and who never intended to work that Mr Larkin's nature expanded to its utmost. When speaking to them, his eyes would burn with an ever more and more prophetic light, his figure would seem to grow visibly, and his voice – taking on something of the gigantic resonance of an African elephant-tusk trumpet – would seem to populate the normal world with living images of contorted violence.

His ambition was to raise his Irish Transport Workers' Union to a position of pre-eminence; and his methods were somewhat unconventional. The Health Insurance Act, for instance, which insisted that all workers should belong to some kind of approved society in order to receive their benefits, had put the disposal of a good deal of sickness benefit into the hands of Mr Larkin and his Union. One day – it was 8th February, 1913 – an advertisement appeared in the *Irish Worker*, expatiating upon the singular generosity with which the Union dispensed these gifts, and appending a few Tennysonian verses which set forth how a representative Sick Hundred charged up the steps of Liberty Hall, the Union headquarters.

Homeward those sick ones went (ran the last verse of 'The Charge of the Sick Hundred'),

> *With money to pay the rent*
> *Which Lloyd George had kindly lent,*
> *Happy sick hundred!*
> *And tho' they are badly crushed,*
> *Into the pub they rushed,*
> *Later with faces flushed,*
> *Homeward they went.*

Such methods were persuasive, but it is hardly to be supposed that they found favour either with the authorities or with the English Trade Unions. But Mr Larkin's activities did not stop with the handling of benefits. He began to instil into the practice of the sympathetic strike certain logical refinements which did him credit. The sympathetic strike had appeared, in a rudimentary form, in the great English transport stoppages of 1911 and 1912; but under Mr Larkin's hand, it became a weapon of extraordinary flexibility.

If a shipping company, for example, met with his disapproval, he would insist that any firm dealing with that company must either cease to deal with it or take the consequences. Now ships carry a great variety of cargo, and it is clear that the effects of resistance would be far-spreading: indeed, if Mr Larkin had possessed a respectable fund of capital and enjoyed the backing of the English Unions, there is no telling how far the thing might have gone. Meanwhile, not enjoying these advantages, Mr Larkin contented himself with exercising upon his immediate surroundings what was swiftly becoming an unparalleled power. Such was his influence over the workers of Dublin, and such the ramifications of his Transport Union, that, by the middle of August, both the building trades and the shipping industry were very reluctant to cross him, and he was approaching – rapidly and inevitably – a final tussle with the Dublin Tramway Company. At the head of the Dublin Tramway Company was Mr William Martin Murphy.

People on both sides of the question had been looking forward to this encounter – besides which the other battles seemed a mere preliminary skirmishing – with considerable relish and for many weeks. It was a meeting of giant and giant; of a stone image and a savage Indian; of Pecksniff and – one had almost said Quilp.

Since July, the tramwaymen had been demanding an increase in pay. Very well, said Mr Murphy, no man wearing the Red Hand – this being the pleasant badge of the Transport Workers' Union – should in future find employment with the Tramway Company. The challenge was a rude one and it could only be met in kind. Larkin determined to wait until Horse Show week and then strike the Company, 150 of whose 750 employees were Unionists, and the rest either sympathetic or easily intimidated. On 26th August, therefore, at 9.45 in the morning, the tramway cars were deserted by conductors and drivers alike. Mr Murphy was not to be caught. He ordered the clerical staff to run an emergency service, which they did, all day long, and amidst nothing more dangerous than showers of abuse. That evening Mr Larkin announced that the workers should arm to protect themselves, since what was legal for Sir Edward Carson and his Ulstermen was legal for them. 'My advice to you,' he shouted, 'is to be round the doors and corners, and whenever one of your men is shot, shoot two of theirs.' Two days later he was quietly arrested, released on bail, and borne in triumph from the police court to Liberty Hall. On the next day a meeting of 10,000 workers was held in Beresford Place, and a Government proclamation forbidding the meeting was publicly burned. 'I care as much for the King,' said Larkin on this occasion, 'as I care for Mr Swifte, the magistrate. People can make kings, and people can unmake them. . . . If they want a revolution, well then, God be with them.' And certainly the arrest of Larkin and the subsequent ban on his meeting were acts of monumental stupidity, for which, presumably, one would have to blame Mr Augustine Birrell, Chief Secretary for Ireland – a genial little gentleman, of a literary turn of mind, who treated the problems of Ireland with such engaging levity that he was known in that island as 'The Playboy of the Western World'.

Serious trouble, it was clear, could not be far away. At eight o'clock on the evening of the 29th, a large crowd assembled in Beresford Place, staring at the dark and silent façade of Liberty Hall, from which Mr Larkin was expected to speak. There was no sign of Mr Larkin, nor from Liberty Hall so much as a glimmer of light. The crowd, too, seemed peaceable. After waiting a little while, the officer in charge dismissed all but ten of his policemen.

At this moment a window was thrust open in Liberty Hall, and a single bottle fell among the unsuspecting ten. The crowd surged forward. The police flourished their batons. Within a few minutes, Beresford Place was cleared, and Liberty Hall resumed its former enigmatical silence.

But now, as if by magic, a vast mob appeared in Abbey Street, well armed with bottles. It was charged, injuriously; it disintegrated; it reappeared in Store Street, hurling glass and brick; retreated down Mabbott Street; and there made its stand. A large body of police went in again and again, and was beaten back with heavy injuries. At last the street was cleared. Some hundreds had been injured, and two rioters, Nolan and Byrne, died of fractured skulls.

Larkin, meanwhile, had disappeared. All night he was hunted, but neither in Liberty Hall nor any of his accustomed haunts was there any trace of him. And yet he had promised to speak in O'Connell Street, in the heart of the city, the next morning; and he was not a man to break his word. As if to increase the difficulties of the police, the next morning, which was Sunday, dawned bright and warm, and by midday O'Connell Street was filled with loitering crowds, tasting the good day and visibly thrilled by the unexpected presence of imported constabulary. And here and there among the passers-by were some five hundred men, wearing the Red Hand, who, as the hour approached to one o'clock, began edging towards a point of vantage opposite the Imperial Hotel. Uncertain what to expect, but expecting nothing good, the police spread out in a long line from the Post Office to the O'Connell Monument. The crowd of onlookers grew denser and more gay.

At half-past one precisely, a window on the hotel's first floor was thrown open, and out upon the balcony there stepped an imposing figure in a frock coat, an immaculate high silk hat, and a false black beard. It paused, it gazed dramatically upon the crowd: the crowd stared back. This singular apparition – it couldn't be! – but it was – it was Larkin! A great roar of mingled delight and laughter travelled the length of O'Connell Street. Larkin stepped forward – 'I am here today,' he boomed, 'in accordance with my promise to address you in O'Connell Street, and I won't leave until I am arrested.'

He got no further. The line of police wavered, paused, hurled itself forward. The crowd scattered in a panic, onlookers and Larkinites alike. The batons rose and fell without mercy under the bright sky. Part of the fleeing crowd was bottled up in Prince's Street, where advancing reserves hurled them back upon their pursuers. It was all over in a few minutes – the horrid crack of wood, the shouts of terror and pain, the cries for pity. All down O'Connell Street the injured writhed and crawled, men and women, their faces covered with blood.

From melodrama to tragedy and back again, to and fro, this strike was to take its course. Nor were the omens absent. On 2nd September, like some fearful, some prophetic comment on the situation and its actors, two tenement houses collapsed in Church Street, and seven corpses were dragged from the rotting débris; the injured were uncounted. To look at that outrageous pile of filthy brick and plaster, festered with the ancient accumulations of dirt and neglect, was almost to look at Dublin as it had been when Jonathan Swift wrote his *Drapier's Letters* and rhymed, with furious mirth, upon 'Liffey's stinking tide'. Liffey's tide stank no more; but otherwise had the city's slums changed so very much since that almost incredible, that starved and savage eighteenth century? Little rooms, sixteen feet by sixteen, housed families of nine; one hundred and nine people, crowded within the infested confines of one house, shared the conveniences of two water closets: such were the conditions. Of the 5,322 tenement houses exactly 1,516 were structurally sound and fit for habitation; 2,288 were on the border line of unfitness; 1,518 were impossible. As for those murderous ruins in Church Street, they had been 'inspected' in August and passed! It was often from such tottering and terrible habitations that Larkin's following came forth to riot, and small blame to them.

A few hours after the collapse, the body of Nolan was carried to Glasnevin Cemetery for a 'martyr's' burial. Liberty Hall was draped in black: 'To the Memory of Our Murdered Brother' stared from a huge placard on its front. The funeral cortège was immense and mournful. A long line of striking tramwaymen, bandaged and battered; the Lord Mayor, for the Corporation had condemned the police; labour leaders, with Mr Keir Hardie; thousands of citizens; two bands. As it wound into O'Connell Street, a rumour spread like lightning that the police were going to attack, and such was the miserable terror inspired by their recent barbarisms that mourners fled in all directions, and the hearse was left alone in the middle of the street. At the cemetery, in the absence of the imprisoned Larkin, Keir Hardie preached the funeral oration.

Mr Hardie's presence was due to the fact that the English Trade Union Congress had at last decided to intervene. The Congress leaders did so reluctantly, but they knew that their followers were whole-heartedly in support of Larkin; and if Larkin were ever to become – as he might – a prophetic hero to the English unionists . . . The leaders shuddered at the thought.

But for the delegates of the TUC the suppression of Larkin became a matter of extraordinary difficulty. They tried to make agreements with the employers on their own; but when the employers asked for an assurance that Larkin would keep such agreements as were made, the delegates had to confess themselves beaten. How could one be sure of anything where Larkin was concerned? 'Those who know Jim,' said Mr Hardie, cautiousl ', 'like Jim. But you know the old saying that "the man who never said a foolish thing never did a wise one" and that is especially true of a man of Jim's temperament.' On 15th September, the delegates returned to England.

Larkin had preceded them thither by exactly three days, the moment, in fact, that he was released from prison. Things were going so well in Dublin – a lock-out by the Coal Merchants' Association, another by Messrs Jacobs, the biscuit manufacturers, the port closed by order of the Lord Mayor – that he felt he could take the time to stir up English opinion. For two and a half days he whirled from town to town, giving vent to any fancy which happened at the moment to be galloping through his head. 'I prefer to go to the seventh pit of Dante,' he told the workers of Manchester, 'than to heaven with William Martin Murphy. Better to be in hell with Dante and Devitt than to be in heaven with Carson and Murphy.' But at times he could talk to the point. The Irish question, he said, 'is not a question of Home Rule. No, it is an economic question – a bread-and-butter question.' The Trade Union leaders observed with alarm that he was extremely popular with all his audiences.

And he left behind him a legacy of sympathetic strikes, which threatened for a day to close the great port of Liverpool.

In Dublin the Builders' Association declared a lock-out. The Farmers' Association followed suit. Larkin hurried across the sea again, and was thundering in the ears of the delighted workers of Glasgow, when news came that another riot had broken out in Dublin. On this

occasion a procession of some three thousand strikers had run foul of the
mounted police: horse and baton had been pitted against pieces of
concrete, iron nuts, bottles, and bricks – mostly bricks. Thirty-six
mounted police had been injured. In Glasgow, Larkin hurled the last
brick – 'The Dublin Cossack,' he roared happily, 'that dirty brute in
blue clothes.'

Hunger stalked among the Dublin tenements. On 27th September,
when the Trade Union Congress food ship, *The Hare*, came up the
Liffey with £5,000 worth of provisions on board, Larkin exclaimed in
triumph, 'The starvation boom is broken!' But was it? How much help
could he expect from the TUC? The TUC, indeed, was so engrossed
in its own problems, and its leaders were secretly so opposed to Larkin,
that it preferred to wait for the results of a Court of Inquiry at which Sir
George Askwith was to preside. If anybody could handle Larkin – the
opinion seemed to be – Sir George was the man.

But Sir George, with all his powers, was unable to cope with a
situation such as this: in that clinging network of sympathetic strikes
even the finest arbitration was doomed to flounder. On 1st October,
Tim Healy – one of William Murphy's nearest friends – appearing for
the employers, drew a graphic picture of the effects of the strike. 'If you
go into the country for ten miles,' said Mr Healy, 'you will not find a
single labouring man in employment. The very harvest is rotting, and
farmers are going about with revolvers, and all in the name of the
"divine mission to create discontent".' The last five words were uttered
with such excellent mimicry that even Larkin joined in the laughter. On
3rd October, Larkin himself cross-examined the employers. But not for
nothing was Mr Healy known as The Wasp. His interruptions were
frequent, pointed, and informed with that special unfairness of which
only an astute lawyer is capable. In the end Larkin could stand no more.
'I am not going to submit to you or anybody else bulldozing me,' he
burst out. 'I am only a wage-slave,' replied The Wasp, stinging meekly.

In his summing-up on 4th October, Larkin declared that Christ
would not be crucified in Dublin any longer by the employers: adding,
as if to clinch this interesting argument, that anarchy was the highest
form of love. It was in such an atmosphere that the Court of Inquiry
adjourned for a fortnight, and even the most sanguine observers hardly
expected anything to come of its deliberations.

As for the TUC delegates, they produced their report on 6th
October, which praised Larkin's Union for having 'considerably

raised the wages of the various sections of industry which it had organized', and condemned the employers for attempting to crush out Unionism. Such words were mere formality – the delegates could have said no less; the question was what action would the TUC take upon them? The TUC seemed to think that a grant of £5,000 a week for ten weeks would be sufficient, and, having bestowed this pittance, appeared to wash its hands of the whole affair. Larkin rushed to London. On 10th October, at the Memorial Hall in Farringdon Street, he made a violent attack upon the National Union of Railwaymen for frowning – as it had – upon sympathetic strikes. The NUR disdained to reply that at this moment, when it was consolidating its forces and its funds for a second attack upon the Companies, it could not afford to get itself involved in every dispute in England. But Larkin had made a formidable enemy. There could no longer be any pretence of comradeship between him and the TUC.

And then another enemy, colder than Mr Murphy, more stubborn than the TUC, an enemy with whom it has never been considered advisable to tamper, arose to hinder the progress of the strike. Mr Larkin had angered the Catholic Church. A quarrel with a group of pious nuns, who managed a laundry and did not see the necessity of joining in a sympathetic strike, started the trouble; Larkin increased it by roundly abusing every priest who spoke against him in the pulpit. With these minor irritations, however, the Church might have borne. It was when Larkin hatched an ingenious scheme for sending strikers' children to stay in the homes of English artisans, that its wrath descended upon him. What Catholic mother – asked Archbishop Walsh in an agitated letter to the press – could possibly fall in with James Larkin's scheme? How could she tell that her child would be sent to a Catholic home? How, indeed? Larkin hastened to reply that it was a poor religion 'which could not stand a fortnight's holiday in England'. But the Archbishop's query was unanswerable. The Press took it up, and within a day or so the strangest reports were being circulated among the faithful.

The first batch of children was due to leave on 22nd October. They were actually being cleansed in the Corporation Baths by an agile Englishwoman named Mrs Montefiore, when a posse of priests descended, seized all but nineteen of them, and hastened off, daring Mrs Montefiore to move a step. Mrs Montefiore, however, departed to Kingstown with what was left of her charges. Ten more were captured on the way; the other nine seized from the deck of the packet boat. The baffled Larkin could only protest, that evening, that it was well known that priests had shares in the Tramway Company.

For the next two days, the docks were carefully picketed by priests, and every child who went on board a cross-channel steamer had first to submit to a thorough scrutiny. Miss Delia Larkin, attempting to smuggle some of this human contraband off to Belfast by rail, was confronted in the station by a group of furious clerics, and forced back to Liberty Hall. That night, it was the night of 24th October, a party of strikers on the one hand and of priests and faithful on the other were only prevented from coming to blows by the interposition of the police. . . .

To such a war there could only be one ending. All but the most spirited of Larkin's followers had no heart for a battle with the Catholic hierarchy; the majority confessed themselves beaten. And it was then – at this particularly opportune moment – that Mr Augustine Birrell fluttered into action once again. 'In this country,' Mr Healy had said but three weeks before, 'when any agitator, labour or political, is in trouble, the Government always comes to his assistance by locking him up.' This was precisely the course pursued by Mr Birrell. Larkin was suddenly arrested for sedition, sentenced to seven months' imprisonment, and hastened away to Mountjoy Gaol, protesting obscurely that he took no count of a verdict 'by a packed jury of Jews and Gentiles'. Other protests were more intelligible. The Dublin dockers came out to a man, the whole press of England shouted that such an imprisonment was both illegal and unwise, and in the Albert Hall was held that vociferous meeting, for attending which Miss Sylvia Pankhurst finally cut herself off from her mother. The Government was alarmed by such a sudden outburst, and bewildered by this iteration of its inability to deal with labour questions. On 13th November, Larkin was released.

He came booming out of Mountjoy into Beresford Place. 'The Government made a mistake in sending me to prison,' he declaimed, 'and they have made a greater mistake in letting me out.' The *Standard* was of the same opinion. 'It is a shameless prostitution of the prerogative of mercy,' it said. Larkin himself could hardly wait before carrying to England what he was pleased to call 'the fiery cross'. In Manchester's Free Trade Hall, putting forth all his powers of vehement and suggestive rhetoric, he had a packed audience groaning, cursing, and dripping with tears. Elsewhere, his efforts were no less successful; only the Trade Union leaders turned a cold shoulder. At Swindon, on 17th November, Mr

J. H. Thomas made a veiled attack; on 18th November, the Parliament-ary Committee of the TUC protested that it could have nothing to do with sympathetic strikes. But Larkin was still in England, and still propounding his objectionable principles to enthusiastic audiences. Something more must be done, and on 3rd December another TUC deputation crossed the Irish Channel to confer once more with the Dublin employers. It was not very hopeful; it objected impartially both to the employers and to Larkin. Sir George Askwith had felt the same way, and had he not tactfully retired from the scene? As for Larkin, he did not so much as bother to come back to England; he committed his opinions of the deputation to paper, and sent them to the *Irish Worker*. 'Certain well-disposed gentlemen,' he wrote, 'are prepared to settle this difficulty by hook or by crook – mostly crook. The lines upon which they are working is to get the bloodsuckers to withdraw the ban against our Union, they will then go their way.' And shortly afterwards the well-disposed gentlemen went their way, with nothing settled at all.

For, indeed, Mr William Martin Murphy and his associates had a champion whose arguments were more conclusive than those of the TUC. This champion was Starvation. Gaunt and listless, the workers were beginning to straggle back. The benevolent Mr Murphy had prepared a little paper, a kind of declaration of dependence, against this hour of victory. 'I HEREBY UNDERTAKE to carry out all instruc-tions given to me by or on behalf of my employers, and further I agree to immediately resign my membership of the Irish Transport and General Workers' Union (if a member); and I further undertake that I will not join or in any way support this Union.' One by one the workers signed.

Larkin, realizing at last that the ground was cut from under his feet, made one final attempt; at a special meeting of the TUC, on 9th December, he denounced 'the tactics of our false friends in the Trade Union movement'; and he was hissed down. It was the end. He went home to Dublin, to find his followers drifting back by dozens, by hundreds. What else could they do? The TUC grant had expired, there were no more doles at Liberty Hall, there were families to feed. Shamed by this dismal finish, and by the manifest triumph of Mr Murphy, the TUC sent over one more deputation to the employers: and Larkin desperate, dauntless, with that strange nobility which never altogether deserted him, strode into the conference and shouted it down.

But the actions of the TUC were not quite so half-hearted as it might seem. Looking back to the Congress of 1st September, one perceives that something had happened then which was of far more importance than the failure or success of Jim Larkin. For at that Congress it was agreed that the newly formed National Union of Railwaymen, the Miners' Federation of Great Britain, and the National Transport Workers' Federation should combine in a Triple Alliance. Each party to this agreement had its grievances. The railwaymen were being treated with extreme asperity by the unforgiving Companies; the transport workers had not forgotten the London strike of 1912, and were burning to revenge it; the miners, baulked of their 'five and two', were also enraged by the continued refusal of owners to abide by the safety regulations prescribed by Act of Parliament. At the slightest excuse, the Triple Alliance was prepared to go into action, and proclaim a General Strike for nothing less than a national living wage. Clearly, it could not afford to have its plans upset by indulging Jim Larkin in his desire for sympathetic strikes. If it did, its funds and its energies would be frittered away in a series of minor disputes, ubiquitous, interminable, and – what was worse – dictated from Dublin. Between its own leadership and that of Jim Larkin there could be no choice, and Larkin was thrown overboard. But perhaps he might refuse to remain there; perhaps he would clamber back. There were some who, analyzing the statistics for 1913, wondered whether even a General Strike would be the end of the business.

Certainly, with the formation of the Triple Alliance, the Trade Unions had discarded once and for all that respectable policy of opportunism which had hitherto hampered them in their dealings with capital. But there was something else in the country – a nameless energy, a new life – which had little to do with Trade Union leadership. The figures showed that there had been no less than 1,497 separate disputes in the course of the year; disputes which had started up without reason, suddenly, instinctively, and as suddenly disappeared. What did they mean? How had they come about in a time when employment was expanding and wages, at last, had taken an upward turn? Why had Jim Larkin been received, in the face of heavy disapproval from headquarters, with such enthusiasm by the rank and file?

In the mist of these questions, the future seemed to take shape – vast, impending, terrible, obscure. The Government had proved itself helpless to resist any pressure from below. And suppose the pressure were put on from another quarter? Suppose the efforts of Sir Edward

Carson and the Orangemen and the Tories resulted in a civil war? Would it remain just a civil war? Between Larkin and the Irish Nationalists there was one link, and that link was James Connolly, who had drowned his Syndicalism in the dearer cause of the Irish Volunteers. If Ulster and Southern Ireland ever came to blows, it was far from inconceivable that Larkin would join in, to give this domestic bloodshed the deeper colour of revolution. And if Larkin joined in, how would the English workers behave? One thing was certain – the Dublin transport strike had completed a fatal circle: the Tory Rebellion and the Workers' Rebellion were no longer separate. To that small minority to whom these thoughts presented themselves in all their implications the prospect for 1914 was anything but hopeful. 'Within a comparatively short space of time,' Sir George Askwith said to the members of the Cavendish Club in Bristol, 'there may be movements in this country coming to a head of which recent events have been a small foreshadowing.' And Sir George had never yet been accused of overstatement.

PART III

The Crisis

January – August 1914

Chapter One

Mutiny at the Curragh

I

THE words of Sir George Askwith to the Carlton Club lead us, once more, into the multiple confusions of Liberal politics. That these words contained a more awful prophecy, neither Sir George nor his hearers could possibly have been aware: the diplomatic horizon was singularly unclouded at the beginning of 1914. But the domestic horizon? In spite of the pleasures of high society, the complacency of the middle classes, and the sudden peace which, at the beginning of January, laid its unexpected salve upon an irritated industry, the domestic horizon was ominous and autumnal. The sunlight, golden and pervasive, fills the scene; and yet – upon the far, low edges of the sky – there is a growing stain, like the stain of dead leaves; dampness curdles the clean air; and already – a creeping whisper, no more – some mournful and mysterious wind blows upon the faces of men. Such, one might say, was the condition of Liberal England in January 1914; the long season of bourgeois respectability was drawing to its close, but the storms had momentarily passed, the high sun walked the world. Shutting her eyes and her ears to the sights and sounds of trouble to come, England took her last fill of peace.

In Craigavon, meanwhile, surrounded by a score of self-conscious henchmen, Sir Edward Carson kept royal state; and nobody laughed any more. That long, dyspeptic face – stiffening day by day into a mask of humourless authority – effectually defied laughter. 'The King of the Bluffers' was becoming – what? Nobody cared to think; it was enough to know that at the moment he was doing nothing, and would do nothing until Parliament re-assembled in February. In the War Office, Sir Henry Wilson diligently spun his web of plots; but who on earth could be expected to bother about the disloyal activities of the office of the Director of Military Operations? Even the Secretary for War himself seemed oblivious to what was being done beneath his very nose. Quietly, with the wrapt and ordered efficiency of an intelligent child, Sir Henry set about the disaffection of His Majesty's forces.

As for Mr Asquith, he was like a figure painted, in some posture of formal indolence, upon this scene of unreal peace. An extraordinary quietism seems to have suggested itself to him. Now a private man may be quietest without doing very much harm; but this is hardly the case with a politician, particularly when he happens to be the head of the Government. Never very assertive, Mr Asquith performed his duties with a more and more gentle indifference. What could be the matter with him? Even a threatened Cabinet split over the question of Mr Churchill's Naval Estimates left him comparatively unmoved. It was not unusual for people to say that he was a tired man, but this was something more than ordinary weariness. Could it be that the spiritual castigations which he had undergone for the last three years had bruised him into a kind of insensibility? That, having seen his most cherished reforms, his sincerest efforts thrown back at him with mockery, insolence, and suspicion, he felt he could do no more? That he was the victim of accumulated disillusion?

This may have been the case. Very few Prime Ministers in history had been afflicted with so many plagues and in so short a space of time. The only consolation, the only refuge for a man of his temperament, lay in the careful observation of parliamentary punctilios, and the exact performance of all the outward duties attendant upon his high office: and here Mr Asquith did not fail. It was not a spirit within, but tradition without, which upheld him; and, at a time when some enormous activity, some feverish final effort, was the least that could be expected of him, he turned upon the world an expression of vacant and venerable calm.

For at length – in February – the crisis, so long expected and so often averted, cast its tall, approaching shadow over England and Ireland. The Home Rule Bill still assumed that Ulster, along with the rest of Ireland, was to be subject to its provisions. The Tories and the Orangemen still insisted that nothing but total exclusion would satisfy them; that unless Ireland were divided, by Act of Parliament, into two nations, there would be Civil War. Was this the bluffing of 'desperate and dispirited men', of 'defeated men trying to cover their retreat'? Mr John Redmond would gladly have believed so; those, indeed, were *his* phrases: but nothing in the appearance of Sir Edward Carson and Mr Bonar Law indicated that they were correct. At the opening of Parliament on 10th February, Sir Edward and Mr Law and the whole Tory opposition assumed an air of scarcely concealed triumph. What could this mean? Was it because they knew that Mr Churchill's £51,000,000 naval programme was threatening to split the Liberal Party in two, that a section of the Cabinet, headed by Mr Lloyd George, had offered to resign over it? Or was there some other reason, more sinister and far more discreditable?

The imperturbable Mr Asquith, at any rate, was in no doubt. What Mr Asquith suspected, so he told Mr Redmond, was that the Tories would create such a disturbance in the Commons when the Army Annual Bill came up there, that no business could be done. Now the Army Annual Bill was a pure formality, it was passed without question year by year: but if it were not passed, then the Army would simply cease to exist. And without an Army, how could the Government hope to keep the peace in Ireland? Such were Mr Asquith's suspicions, and one would like to know more about them than one is ever likely to know. Was Mr Asquith aware that this almost incredible plot was the fruit of an interesting alliance between Sir Edward Carson, Mr Bonar Law and Sir Henry Wilson? that the War Office, in effect, was openly intriguing with the Opposition? And if he *was* aware, why did he not demand Sir Henry's resignation?

However this may be, there is no doubt that Mr Asquith intended to forestall this plot by making concessions to Ulster. He was prepared, he told Mr Redmond, to offer (1) The Post Office. (2) Local administrative control. (3) That a majority of Ulster members in the Irish Parliament could appeal to the Imperial Parliament against the application to Ulster of certain pieces of legislation 'to be defined and set forth'. As the prospects of an unamended Home Rule Bill began to vanish, before his very eyes, in this cloud of Asquithian compromise, Mr Redmond became extremely uneasy. Nothing but destructive criticism, he protested, would result from such a course, for the concessions were such that neither party could agree to them. Mr Asquith was unmoved. In his opinion the way was now clear to a Bill which 'would pass by consent'. 'I am to see the King again on Thursday,' he added.

This was hardly reassuring, for – more than Tory plots, and Liberal concessions, and the peculiar passivity of Mr Asquith – it was George V whom Mr Redmond feared. Around the figure of that conscientious monarch, the most extraordinary rumours were astir. It was said that he might exercise his constitutional powers and either dissolve Parliament, insist upon a referendum, or dismiss his Ministers; and that some of the

most responsible opinion in the country was urging him to do so. Mr
Asquith himself had expressed some misgivings on this subject, and how
was Mr Redmond to know that George V was, at this moment, far more
to be relied upon than his Prime Minister? Only a very few people
knew anything about the King at all, and Mr Redmond was not one of
them. George V had – it was only too true – been subjected to the con-
sistent pressure of some very imposing personages, but he had resolutely
declined to yield: that unique capacity for doing his duty, which has
since been recognized by the world, was never more bitterly tested than
in 1914, when nobody recognized it at all.

Beset by fears, poor Mr Redmond had very little time in which to
make up his mind. The Home Rule Bill – having twice been passed
through the Commons and twice rejected by the Lords – was due, in
March, to receive its Second Reading for the third time. He must either
agree to concessions, or . . . he must put Mr Asquith out. The dilemma
was an odious one. He went into hasty conference with his leading
colleagues, Mr Dillon and Mr Devlin.

II

But everybody knew that concessions would have to be made, sooner
or later; to make them was to choose the lesser of two evils. In Parliament, the Opposition leaders altered their tone; they knew that their
position was immeasurably stronger than it had been, and for a while
they became almost friendly. Did not Sir Edward refer to Mr Redmond
as 'my fellow-countryman'? Sir Edward, to be sure, observed in almost
the same breath that Mr Redmond wanted nothing more of Ulster than
its taxes, but for the saturnine Orange leader to permit himself so much
as an amiable gesture was considered something of a miracle. Perhaps –
was it too much to expect? – perhaps the Opposition would actually
accept the concessions, if they were good enough!

But the Post Office, local administration, or any offer which did not
altogether wreck Mr Redmond's single demand of 'an Irish parliament,
with an executive responsible to it, together with Irish integrity' – Mr
Asquith had admitted to his Cabinet, as early as 9th February, that he
was 'sick' of such poor expedients. Clearly nothing less than exclusion
would satisfy Sir Edward, and it only remained to find a form of
exclusion which would satisfy Mr Redmond. At last, Mr Lloyd George
hit upon an ingenious idea. Let every Ulster county be given the right to

contract out of the Act for a space of five years; which would mean that it would still be 'out' at the next Elections when, if the Unionists were returned, Parliament would doubtless confirm its exclusion forever. At first Messrs Redmond, Dillon, and Devlin could not see this at all. Conference succeeded conference. And then, with infinite caution, step by step, the Nationalist leaders began to retreat. They would accept a three years' exclusion for the Ulster counties. They would accept five. They would – at last the bitter pill was swallowed – they would actually agree to six. This final agreement was made on 7th March: 'It is the extremest limit of concession,' said Mr Redmond. It only remained to be seen whether anybody would accept it. How did the Nationalists feel about it, for instance? The more extreme Nationalists, it seemed, were somewhat uneasy. 'When God made this country,' said *Sinn Fein*, 'He fixed its frontiers beyond the power of man to alter while the sea rises and falls. . . . So long as England is strong and Ireland is weak, England may continue to oppress this country, but she shall not dismember it.' 'Ulster is Ireland's,' was the comment of *Irish Freedom*, 'and shall remain Ireland's. We will fight them [i.e., the Ulster Unionists] if they want fighting, but we will never let them go, never.' James Connolly, in the *Irish Worker*, called for the 'bitterest opposition'. And as for Cardinal Logue, the Primate of all Ireland, he confessed that he found it rather hard to consider becoming, even temporarily, a foreigner in his own Cathedral City of Armagh – for Armagh, strange to say, was an Ulster city. On the whole, what with the perturbations of Irish patriots and the paradoxes of Irish geography, it rather appeared as if Mr Redmond were in for a little trouble.

None the less Mr Redmond – it was very simple of him – believed that he could manage Southern Ireland. What worried him was the attitude of Sir Edward Carson and the Opposition. Would they accept his 'extremest limit of concession'? They did not leave him long in doubt; on 9th March, during the debate on the second reading, Sir Edward characterized the whole business as 'a sentence of death with a stay of execution for six years'; he would have absolutely nothing to do with it. And then, at last, something impressed itself upon the Ministerial intelligence which should have left its mark upon that unimpressionable organ at least a year before. No matter what happened in Parliament, however decisively, nor what schemes were advanced, however subtle – neither the Orangemen nor the Nationalists intended to pay the smallest attention. The quarrel was beyond the control of the English electorate;

it was also – though he did not realize it as yet – beyond the control of Mr Redmond.

Well might Mr Asquith have repeated the words he had once used to Sir George Askwith – 'It is a degradation of government.' Parliament was now helpless, unless . . . Might a show of force, at this last minute, prove to those stubborn Ulstermen that a Liberal Cabinet was not to be trifled with? What other expedient was left? Already the Ulster Volunteers were showing a more and more insolent front, posts and telegraphs were tampered with, arms were being smuggled in all along the coast, there was talk of raids upon military stores: worse still, in the Catholic Ulster counties of Tyrone and Fermanagh the Nationalist Volunteers were daily increasing. As for the Opposition, having first promoted this rebellion, and then discovered that it was powerless to prevent it, it sat back, with a smile which was half complacent, half confused, and altogether infuriating, to see what Mr Asquith would do next. Mr Asquith had decided to take action, but even his decisions, these days, were indecisive. Orders were sent to General Paget, Commander-in-Chief of the army in Ireland, that troops should be moved to Armagh, Omagh, Enniskillen, and Carrickfergus – the four strategic points for an investment of Ulster. But the orders were so worded that General Paget found it easy to misunderstand them; instead of moving troops, he removed stores. Sending a letter ahead of him, explaining that any other manoeuvre 'would create intense excitement in Ulster and possibly precipitate a crisis', he hurried over to London. The War Office then telegraphed General Friend to carry out the orders which General Paget had bungled, and General Friend replied that he greatly feared the Northern Railway would not allow his troops to move northward. The Army, obviously, was not at all disposed to take part in what Ulster loyalists were already describing as a 'horrible plot' to subdue them by force of arms.

How to overcome the doubts of General Friend and the Northern Railway? Left to himself, Mr Asquith would probably have done nothing. But there was one member of his Cabinet upon whom the merest hint of military action worked a powerful spell. Mr Winston Churchill came out of his seclusion with a suddenness which caught everyone by surprise; ordered two cruisers to Kingstown (whereupon General Friend and the Northern Railway found no difficulty in coming to terms); dispatched the Third Battle Squadron, with eight destroyers of the Fourth Flotilla, to Lamlash; and sent HMS *Pathfinder* and HMS

Attentive to Belfast Lough, with orders to defend Carrickfergus 'by every means'. Nor did he stop short at these extremely suggestive manoeuvres. At Bradford he made what was, by all odds, the best Liberal speech of a decade:

'If Ulstermen extend the hand of friendship,' said Mr Churchill by way of peroration, 'it will be clasped by Liberals and by their Nationalist countrymen in all good faith and in all good will; but if there is no wish for peace; if every concession that is made is spurned and exploited; if every effort to meet their views is only to be used as a means of breaking down Home Rule and of barring the way to the rest of Ireland; if Ulster is to become a tool in party calculations; if the civil and Parliamentary systems under which we have dwelt so long, and our fathers before us, are to be brought to the rude challenge of force; if the Government and the Parliament of this great country and greater Empire are to be exposed to menace and brutality; if all the loose, wanton, and reckless chatter we have been forced to listen to these many months is in the end to disclose a sinister and revolutionary purpose; then I can only say to you, "Let us go forward together and put these grave matters to the proof".'

Mr Churchill's methods of going forward were, it must be admitted, forceful enough. The movements of troops and ships suggested nothing less than an offensive campaign of unmitigated severity. Or were they, perhaps, the effects of some more subtle plan? Mr Churchill had accused the Ulstermen of 'preferring shooting to voting and the bullet to the ballot': did he hope now to provoke them into making the first attack, which would certainly alienate them from Unionist sympathy in England? But whatever his hopes and his plans, it was plain that they depended upon the absolute obedience of the Army. And the Army? If the emotions of General Paget were any criterion, the Army was not in a very reliable mood. For the whole of 18th March, the General sat at the War Office arguing with Colonel Seely, the Secretary for War: could not some concessions be made to those officers who felt that they could not operate against loyalist Volunteers? The question was, to say the least of it, an irregular one, and any other man than Seely might have felt that the only answer to it was a sharp rebuke and an order to the General to go about his business. But Seely, besides being possessed of a kind heart and a pliable disposition, was remarkable, even among Secretaries for War, for an extreme ineptitude for the office he held. In the end, he presented Paget with a guarantee that all officers actually domiciled in Ulster should be permitted to 'disappear'; which, under the circumstances, was about the most lunatic concession that could possibly have been made.

While this was going on in the War Office, a very different scene was taking place in the House of Commons. Sir Edward Carson, attacking Mr Churchill's Bradford speech, declared that he ought not to be in Westminster but in Belfast. He accused the Government of provoking an insurrection in Ulster. 'You will no longer be cowards,' he declared, giving to each word a brutal value. 'You will have become men. The cowardice will have been given up. You will have become men in entrenching yourselves behind the Army. But under your directions they will have become assassins.' And, followed by the faithful Craig, he strode bleakly from the House.

That same evening, General Paget left for Dublin. As to the nature of his instructions, he was not very clear; but he had Seely's guarantee in his pocket, and the best course seemed to be to go into immediate conference. He did so. The results of that conference were to give the whole problem a new and sinister colour.

III

General Paget's position was rendered none the easier by the fact that he was the clumsiest of talkers. In the conference with his general officers, on the afternoon of 19th March, he gave those gentlemen a distinct impression that he was offering them a choice between 'active operations against Ulster' and 'dismissal with loss of pension'. Now the picture which immediately leapt to the mind of the Generals was one which a series of Orange orators had for some time been impressing upon the public imagination: it was a picture of English soldiers conscientiously annihilating a Citizen Army which advanced against them under the Union Jack, singing 'God Save the King'; and this rhetorical oleograph, with its several qualities of farce and tragedy, of cheap theatre and overwhelming fact, was not merely ridiculous, but bewildering and beastly. The Generals went away to their own officers, and, before midnight of the 19th, two telegrams had reached the War Office from General Paget.

'Officer commanding 5th Lancers,' ran the first, 'states that all officers except two, and one doubtful, are resigning their commissions today.

I much fear same conditions in the 16th Lancers. Fear men will refuse to move.'

'Regret to report,' ran the second, 'Brigadier and fifty-seven officers Third Cavalry Brigade prefer to accept dismissal if ordered north.'

This was mutiny. General Gough, who commanded the Third Cavalry Brigade at the Curragh, knew that it was mutiny. After the war, he saw fit to explain that his orders were either to undertake active operations or to leave the Army, and that, in obedience to these orders, he decided to leave the Army. The explanation is ingenious; but one cannot help inquiring whether an officer can be given orders to disobey orders. In any case, the Government was hardly less to blame than General Gough and the officers at the Curragh. What it had expected General Paget to convey was this: that the Cavalry were to descend upon Ulster simply as a 'precautionary' measure. Whether a concentration of warships along the coast, and of troops in the four strategic positions inland, could possibly be described as 'precautionary', admits, at least, of some debate; to the officers, at any rate, it seemed like the beginning of an intensive campaign, and they made their decisions accordingly.

But these decisions were rankly mutinous; and upon no one did the blow fall more heavily than upon Mr John Redmond. He had always believed that Parliament was paramount. He had always believed that the deliberations of a few hundred gentlemen of various faiths, classes, and races, would – eventually, through the exercise of some mysterious prestige – grant Ireland the freedom which had been withheld from her for centuries. When the news from the Curragh reached him, he knew, at last, that nothing could be expected from constitutional action; that His Majesty's Government, for the first time since the Revolution of 1688, had lost the allegiance of His Majesty's forces; that it was powerless. 'The Ulster Orange plot is now completely revealed,' he cabled to his supporters in Australia. '... The plan was to put up the appearance of a fight and then, by Society influences, to seduce the Army officers, and thus defeat the will of the people.... The issue raised is wider even than Home Rule. It is whether the Government are to be browbeaten and dictated to by the drawing-rooms of London.'

In the War Office itself, all was consternation and conspiracy: while Colonel Seely gave orders that General Gough and the three Colonels who had resigned their commissions should repair, in secret disgrace, to London, Sir Henry Wilson was surrounded by an increasing group of high officers, protesting that the Army was unanimous in its determination not to fight Ulster, and asking what on earth they should do. Sir Henry's suggestion was that the screws should now be put upon what – with characteristic delicacy – he described as 'Asquith and his crowd'. On Sunday, 22nd March, Gough and the colonels arrived, and went straight to Wilson's house, where there was a constant coming and going of Unionists – the most noticeable of these being no less a personage than Mr Bonar Law, who might have had the decency to keep away. On Monday, General Gough breakfasted with Wilson. A little later in the morning, the two met again at the War Office; not as guest and host, but as mutineer and censurer, and this meeting was further graced by the agitated and ineffective presence of the Secretary for War.

This confusion was now to be worse confounded by a complete misunderstanding between Colonel Seely and the rest of the Cabinet. 'Asquith and his crowd' were determined that Gough should not escape without at least a promise that he would assist in the maintenance of law and order in Ulster. They would gladly have done more; but to dismiss the General was to invite the resignation of every ranking officer in the Army. On Tuesday, 24th March, they prepared a document setting forth their conditions, but Seely was absent at the time, trying to explain matters to the King. When he returned from Buckingham Palace, he found that the Cabinet meeting was over, and that the document contained none of the promises which Gough and Wilson had bullied out of him at the War Office – promises which assured the general that he would never have to move his cavalry against Ulster, and which Seely had refrained from communicating to Mr Asquith. He therefore embellished the document with two further paragraphs, completely justifying the mutiny, had them initialled by Generals French and Ewart, and gave the whole screed to Gough, who departed in triumph for the Curragh.

The fat was now in the fire. In the House of Commons on Wednesday, in a debate which was marked with extreme animosity – ('Don't bite, don't bite,' shouted the Opposition. 'Gladly, gladly,' Mr Churchill was heard to groan, 'would I assume that responsibility') – Mr Asquith announced the resignations of Generals French and Ewart, and of Colonel Seely: he himself would assume the office of Secretary of State for War, and would leave the House until his constituents had approved his position.

He departed amidst cheers, and with a certain complacency which circumstances hardly justified. The screws had been well and truly applied; the Army was now in control. As for the Opposition, having encouraged and supported the mutiny, it began to see itself for what it was – a notable traitor to the Constitution and the Crown. It remained for Mr F. E. Smith, that brilliant and wayward young politician, to put on, for a brief moment, a mantle of gravity and wisdom which he knew so well how to wear, and the wearing of which he unfortunately found so tedious.

'Nobody can ever persuade us on this side of the House,' said Mr F. E. Smith, 'that we have not been justified in the things we have done, and no one will ever persuade the honourable gentlemen opposite that they equally on their part were not justified in what they have done. These events will be decided by the historian, and he will care very little to hear us complaining with a loud voice that the beginning and end of all these difficulties has been merely your subjugation to the Irish Nationalist Party. He will care less to hear you say that the principal responsibility rests upon the shoulders of those who inculcated and preached the doctrine of insurrection. What he will say is "The whole House of Commons – all of you – who ought to have been trustees, not for any party, but for the nation as a whole, inherited from the past a great and splendid possession, and where is it now?" '

A moment later, Mr Smith twitched his mantle of gravity, and moved into more congenial pastures. He began to describe the Government's recent attempt to occupy all the strategic points in Ulster. 'The scheme was Napoleonic,' he said: and, waiting for a meditative moment, added gently, 'But there was no Napoleon.'

Sir Henry Wilson himself hurried to Paris, where he attempted to assure a sceptical General de Castelnau that the British Army's recent disobedience to the civil power did not imply an equal unreliability in the event of war. It was a pity that his engagements to France did not permit his making the same assurances in Berlin, where every scrap of Curragh news had been devoured with an extraordinary relish. Sir Henry, it appeared, was not to suffer the fate of Generals French and Ewart: he was not to lose his Directorship of Military Operations. Why was this? Was it because – as Mr Asquith subsequently implied (*Memories and Reflections*, Vol. II, p. 154) – he was too good a soldier? Or was it perhaps that the Cabinet was now extremely frightened of him? that

'Asquith and his crowd' had meekly endured the last insufferable turn of the screw?

There was certainly little love lost between the Government and General Wilson. In the pages of Mr Asquith's *Memories and Reflections*, otherwise so remarkable for the kindness of their memories and the urbanity of their reflections, there occurs this embittered description of Wilson. 'He was voluble, impetuous, and an indefatigable intriguer. As his Diaries, which the misplaced devotion of friends has disclosed to the world, abundantly show, he was endowed by Nature with a loose tongue, and was in the habit of wielding a looser pen' (Vol. II, p. 185). Might not this be considered the General's memorial? Or was it perhaps that spatter of Irish bullets which, in 1922, mowed him down on the very doorsteps of his London house?

IV

The prospects of a little blood-letting in Ireland – which the conspiracy just related brought appreciably nearer – seem of little importance when one thinks of the terrible slaughter which the world was soon to endure and, at the moment of writing, seems about to endure again. Beneath that past and this impending shadow, the tale of the Curragh Mutiny shrinks away; and yet, though it is diminished indeed, it is not destroyed. For its significance was not military but constitutional. Not since 1688, when James II lost his crown, had the Army refused to obey its orders, as it now refused to obey them; not since 1688 had it controlled the country: this was the first time, since that violent year, that an Opposition had promoted a rebellion, and the first time in all history that a Liberal Government virtually ceased to govern. In the constitutional history of England the events of March 1914 have a place all of their own, and it is a very important place. Indeed, if a war tomorrow were to do away with the last vestiges of Imperial England, if that country were to explore the *pulvis et umbra*, the dust of Athens, the shade of Rome, the story of General Gough's mutiny might well remain as a perpetual reminder, not merely of the petty treacheries and follies of man, but of the strange ways in which a great political philosophy can come to grief, and the Government of a great country can be put to shame.

Chapter Two

The Guns of Larne

I

THE words of Winston Churchill, the movements of the Fleet, had come to nothing; no more was heard of the 'investment' of Ulster. But the Government had to make some pretence of doing its duty; and to Mr Asquith fell the immediate, the delicate task of doing as little of it as he conveniently could.

In his new office of Secretary of State for War, therefore, the Prime Minister appointed Major-General Sir Nevil Macready, the WO Director of Personal Services, to assume command in Ulster. The appointment was a fortunate one: it might even be called a wise one, except for the fact that every other General Officer in the Army, at that moment, would have refused point-blank to undertake such a task. And why not? Gough's disobedience had been all too successful. The alternative of resignation had now been invested with the glory of genteel martyrdom.

But Macready's conception of duty was considerably less extravagant than that of Sir Henry Wilson and his friends. The Director of Personal Services, strange to say, still believed that politics were one thing and that military affairs were another: he was willing to go wherever he was sent, and entertained no more definite opinions about the rights or wrongs of Ulstermen than he had about the ethics of the Cambrian coal strike.

When this equable and efficient officer arrived in Ulster, the state of affairs in that province – he was obliged to confess – was enough to make anyone rather uneasy. His own mission was not very clearly defined; Mr Asquith had seen to that. The best he could do – the best he could hope to do – was to try to keep the peace. But then he discovered that the Government had made peace almost impossible; that ninety per cent of Ulstermen, thinking their Volunteers had intimidated Mr Asquith's Cabinet, were in a mood of mounting belligerence; and that the Royal Irish Constabulary, badly housed in indefencible barracks, were either hopelessly lazy or violently for Carson. He also perceived that, if it came to fighting, the bloodshed would be appalling. The Volunteers, it was only too obvious, would not hesitate to fight the Army, should the Army be asked to overthrow Carson's Provisional Government, and the Volunteers heavily outnumbered the Army in Ulster. Well-trained men, when heavily outnumbered, are forced to kill in merciless fashion....

Such meditations were scarcely consoling. But still another thought presented itself. Would the Army, by any chance, refuse to fight? Macready had not taken Gough's mutiny very seriously; but he realized, when his own Staff was subjected to constant and seditious pressure from the War Office, that he had sadly underestimated the perseverance of Sir Henry Wilson and his *clique*. What *would* happen if trouble broke out? Macready had a soldierly notion that commands, given without hesitation, were apt to be obeyed; if it came to fighting, he thought, he could give a good account of himself; but even he could not be sure.

The dim, bleak airs of Ulster did nothing to relieve these forebodings; and it was in such rare moments of comedy as the situation presented that the general took refuge from the dispiriting interactions of climate and Carsonism. On his arrival he went to pay a courtesy call at Craigavon, Sir Edward Carson's headquarters. He drove up with his A D C; sentries of the Ulster Volunteers presented arms; a small army of photographers took his snapshot; he was ushered into a little anteroom by no less a personage than Captain James Craig, who appeared to be something between a major-domo and a Prime Minister, and who informed the general that Sir Edward would see him 'directly'. Nobody had ever accused Sir Edward of an undue sense of humour – and now, his heavy features composed into a look of portentous majesty, the head of the Provisional Government of Ulster was clearly not insensible of his high position. General Macready, in fact, watching that dyspeptic countenance brooding above its high collar, while the conversation consumed itself in more and more awkward trivialities, could not help thinking of the Grand Lama of Tibet, and with difficulty kept his face straight.

He found it amusing, too, when the Ulster press described him as a 'Home Ruler' and a 'Roman Catholic'; or when his own chauffeur, who spent off-duty nights in gun-running, expressed a conviction that the Pope would leave Rome, in the event of Home Rule, and establish himself in the Irish capital. The general advised him to invest his savings in a Cook's tour to Italy, in which case he would realize that His Holiness would hardly leave the Vatican for 'such a god-forsaken hole as Dublin'. As for the famed Carsonist Secret Service, its attentions were persistent and preposterous. The dining-room of Macready's hotel looked out upon a railway platform, and the General and his staff, taking their meals at a table by the window, were subjected, mouthful by mouthful, to the piercing glances of an extremely shabby individual, who, after watching them through the various courses, in the apparent belief that he was unobserved, would disappear with mysterious suddenness into a telephone booth. At last Macready's patience was exhausted. One morning, he sent out an aide-de-camp with the menu, and a message that, if it would make his work any easier, the spy could have it sent him every day.

With these distractions, Macready passed the heavy time until 24th April. In the forenoon of that day, in London, Sir Henry Wilson was closeted in a conference with Mr Bonar Law. It was through such unconventional meetings with the Director of Military Operations that War Office secrets, with which Mr Asquith himself was unacquainted became the general property of the Opposition leaders. In this instance, the activities of a certain Major Crawford would appear to have been under discussion. Major Crawford was an Orange fanatic, who had signed the Covenant in his own blood, and had long been an active gun-runner. The major was dissatisfied with the speed of the running, the number of guns run, the occasional invasions of Ulster customs officials, the pertinacity of Scotland Yard in searching out his various London *caches*, and the fact that Volunteer officials – who were not as a rule very realistic in such matters – refused to take him seriously. He decided, therefore, that a bold and spectacular attempt must be made, and in February went off to Germany to explore.

It was in Hamburg that he discovered a benevolent and upright Jew, known as B S, who was prepared to sell 20,000 modern rifles, 10,000 bayonets, and 3,000,000 rounds of ammunition. The Major was over-joyed. The Volunteer Committee could hardly turn up its nose at this. But, to make quite sure, he stopped on his way back to pay a call upon Sir Edward Carson, who had been forced, for parliamentary reasons, to abandon the delicious solemnities of Craigavon for the lesser amenities of his London town house. The Major, who had all the innocence of a child and a fanatic, was unwilling to transport those rifles and bayonets to Ulster, without some assurance that the venture would be considered a matter of life and death. In Carson's library he struck an attitude. He was prepared to lose his life, he asserted, so long as Carson backed him to the finish. Carson's answer was in the highest degree satisfactory: he rose from his chair, advanced, shook his fist in Crawford's face, and intoned in a voice which the major afterwards swore he would never forget, 'Crawford, I'll see you through this business, if I have to go to prison for it.' 'Sir Edward,' said Crawford, 'that is all I want. I leave tonight. Good-bye.'

These necessary preliminaries accomplished, the Major set out upon his dangerous mission. What with the connivance of the German Government, the convenient blindness of the English fleet, and the nonchalance of Mr Augustine Birrell, the guns could have been landed upon the Ulster coasts, with perfect safety, in less than three weeks. But Crawford was not as other men. From the beginning of February to 24th April, he delighted himself with a series of extraordinary man-oeuvres. The chartering of a boat was not very difficult: the SS *Fanny* was discovered in Bergen, where she had just discharged a cargo of New-castle coal; friends in the Antrim Ore Company provided a skipper, a mate, and two engineers. Nor were the arms trans-shipped with any of those melodramatic accompaniments which Crawford yearned for. The German authorities, unhappily, were far too efficient. A tug-boat, towing two lighters filled with B S's guns, went quietly through the Kiel Canal at the cost of exactly £10; and Crawford could only console himself with the fact that she flew a black flag, and that liners of ten to fifteen thousand tons were obliged to make way for her. But, once beyond the sober reach of Germany, Crawford gave his romantic fancies full play. He and the *Fanny* rushed hither and yon with all the violent aimlessness of a water beetle. They appeared in Danish waters, in the English Channel, off the Tuskar. They disappeared. Suddenly, the Major materialized on dry land, in Belfast, threatening to run his cargo ashore if the Committee did not show more enthusiasm. He returned to Hamburg; he dashed over to London. He lost the *Fanny* altogether. He fled from London to Holyhead and back again, besieging the telegraph offices with inquiries for her. He raved, he tore his hair, he discovered her again: but it was no use. Try as he would, neither Mr Birrell nor the Fleet would pay the slightest attention.

At last he had to admit to himself that the game was up: the guns must be landed without any more ado. Even the Volunteer Committee, realizing that the *Fanny*'s expensive cargo might actually be captured if it were subjected any longer to the precautions of Major Crawford, had decided to act. On the night of 24th April, a triple cordon of Volunteers surrounded the coastwise town of Larne; the police and the coastguards, locked into their various barracks and strongly guarded, slept; the roads to Belfast were alive with Volunteers and noisy with the constant coming and going of motor-bicyclists: it would have been difficult not to perceive that a plot was afoot. The Government, however, preferred to be caught unawares. The guns were landed – at Larne, at Donaghadee, at Bangor. The long-suffering *Fanny*, lightened of this burden and of Major Crawford, disappeared into the night and from history.

The Committeemen's reluctance to support Major Crawford was only equalled by the Government's unwillingness to prevent them from doing so: timidity, it appeared, was pitted against timidity, and it is only surprising that in the course of this strange duel the gallant Major did not contrive to spirit himself and his cargo off the face of the seas. But, now that the plot was, somehow or other, achieved, the rejoicings in Ulster (whose Volunteers, to be sure, did not share the faint heart of their leaders) were vociferous, and vehement was the wrath of Southern Ireland. Sir Edward Carson's feelings were more obscure. He had done nothing to stir the lethargy of his Committee. Did he perhaps regard the affair with less enthusiasm than he had shown to Major Crawford? Was it possible that, as a prominent lawyer and a candidate for high honours in some future Tory government, he preferred to surround himself with menaces rather than with Mausers? That the famous 'Bluff' was, after all, no more than bluff? Whatever the answer, there could be no turning back now. The enthusiasm with which the news was greeted in high quarters was more imperative than flattering. He had scarcely received the code telegram 'Lion' on the morning of the 25th, than who should appear upon his doorstep but Field-Marshal Earl Roberts of Kandahar, primed with congratulations! Mr Bonar Law, Mr F. E. Smith, Mr Austen Chamberlain were only less delighted. This was scarcely reassuring, since the final responsibility – should those rifles ever be put to use – rested upon his shoulders: his future, and not theirs, was in the balance. But then it began to dawn upon him that, such was the docility of Mr Asquith and his colleagues, the rifles never *might* be put to use. In the Commons that afternoon, it is true, the Prime Minister denounced the gun-running as a 'grave and unprecedented outrage', and threatened 'appropriate steps'. Two days later, a note from the Cabinet to the King promised 'instant and effective action'. But nothing was done.

Deserted by the Army as a whole, dubious even of Macready's power to control his troops, the Government was helpless. At this moment, perhaps, swift and forthright action might have saved the day and reasserted over Ireland an accustomed control. But Mr Asquith had already decided to yield. He would pass the Home Rule Bill through its subsequent stages, and would bring in – almost simultaneously – an Amending Bill, aimed at that elusive target 'settlement by agreement'. He made this announcement on 12th May. The urgent invitations of Mr Bonar Law failed to drag any information from him as to what the terms of the second Bill would be, but everybody knew that Ulster had won her demand for exclusion. It was in vain that Mr Churchill characterized a Tory motion for an inquiry into the Curragh mutiny as 'audacious', and 'impudent', 'like a vote of censure by the criminal classes on the police': the time for words was long past. The Government had been beaten to its knees.

And now, just as the Opposition, congratulating itself upon this happy result of its treasonable activities, adopted an almost benevolent tone; just as Mr Asquith informed the King that a 'better political atmosphere' prevailed; the spirit of Ireland – so long forgotten, so alien to the rivalries of English politicians – arose to confound both the hopes of Sir Edward Carson and the plans of Mr Asquith. The Ulster Nationalists were on the move at last.

II

Bishop O'Donnell of Raphoe, in a letter written to Redmond on 9th May, prophesied a terrible 12th of July (the day when Orange drums beat, and Orange tongues abused the Pope) in the Ulster counties of Tyrone and Fermanagh, in North Monaghan and East Donegal. The Ulster Protestants and the Ulster Catholics, the Bishop said, were highly inflamed against each other. As for the Nationalist Volunteers, they had increased from 10,000 to 100,000; and of these one third were in Ulster. What was to prevent the two Volunteer armies from coming to blows?

Indeed, the Curragh Mutiny and the Larne gun-running had done their work all too well. No matter what happened now, whether Ulster was excluded or whether she was not excluded, one side or the other would plunge Ireland into Civil War. Sir Edward was just as much the loser by this as Mr Redmond; for Sir Edward, so long as his only visible opponent was the Liberal Government, could flatter himself that he was in control. But the Liberal Government had, to all intents and purposes, vanished; and instead of that indolent foe there now appeared, along the borders of Ulster, an unpredictable force of angry Catholics. And could he be sure of defeating these? He had to confess that he could not. For the moment, at any rate, fear rather than fury dominated the Orange camp. The Lord Mayor of Belfast, almost beside himself, declared that at any moment fighting might break out in the city. Even the imperturbable Macready was of a like mind, and hastened to London for fresh instructions.

But Mr Asquith looked upon these new developments with a lacklustre eye. If fighting broke out between Unionists and Nationalists, he told the General, troops must not be asked to intervene: they must simply isolate the area of fighting until reinforcements arrived. If Carson proclaimed his Government, the only course 'was to remain on the defensive and do nothing'. If the Lord Mayor called on the Ulster Volunteers to protect Belfast, that was the Lord Mayor's responsibility. If special companies of the Ulster Volunteers were dispatched, fully armed, to outlying districts, Mr Asquith gave it as his opinion – both as Prime Minister and as Secretary of State for War – that there was no power to prevent them. 'With notes of these heroic instructions in my pocket,' was Macready's comment, 'I returned to Ulster.' (*Annals of an Active Life*, Vol. I, p. 191.)

As for Mr Redmond, the spirit of the Nationalist Volunteers filled him with alarm and disgust. At first he refused to recognize its existence. He plunged his head once again, ostrich-like, into the desert sands of parliamentary business, and in this illusory refuge was understood to declare that he feared nothing more than isolated disturbances in Ulster – 'local irresponsible outbreaks', so he told Mr Birrell, who gladly agreed. But at last he could no longer stop his ears to the growing mutter of revolt. It was not simply that the Nationalist Volunteers were hurrying him, like some dilatory general, into a campaign for which he had no taste. That would have been disagreeable enough. But the sad truth was that he could not be at all sure that the Volunteers wanted to hurry him anywhere; a fair proportion of them, it seemed, would be only too glad to throw him away, like so much unnecessary baggage. Duty and ambition, conscience and self-interest, united to warn him that, now or never, he must exert himself; that talk of party discipline and parliamentary leadership must yield to more forcible arguments; that, in brief, he must become a leader of men. He groaned in spirit, and cast a mournful eye backwards at those happy days when things were decided in the comparative peace of Westminster: then he settled himself down to examine his prospects. The more he looked into them, the more apprehensive he grew. It was just as if, in the place of some temperate landscape, whose roads and fields were all familiar, and whose very flaws were pleasant to contemplate, there suddenly writhed the incredible fecundity of a tropical jungle. The track that led through was clear enough; but it was overhung with such forbidding festoons, such violent flowers leered from the marching twilight, and the whole place was filled with such a murmur of unknown life, that it would take him all his courage to make the journey.

What *was* the composition of the Nationalist Volunteers? He could not be sure. The relics of Larkin's Citizens' Army seemed to have joined in; and they had not acquired any taste for discipline nor any distaste for looting and riot. And how did James Connolly, leader of the Irish Labour Party, fit into the picture? Was he a Nationalist or was he a syndicalist? Was he recruiting for the Volunteers – who were now increasing at the rate of 15,000 a week – or was he still dreaming of a revolutionary army? If the unthinkable event took place – if Ireland were hurled into Civil War – if Ulster were beaten – would Mr Connolly be satisfied with the mild reward of Home Rule? And then there were those inconvenient young men – Professor Eoin MacNeill, Padraic Pearse, and Lawrence Kettle. Pearse was a Republican, and though MacNeill and Kettle were strong constitutionalists the fact remained that MacNeill was now hand in glove with none other than Sir Roger Casement. Sir Roger's belief in freedom, which he had cultivated as a youth in the glens of Antrim, had been considerably increased by two appalling investigations in the Congo and the Putumayo which he had undertaken as a member of the British consular service. He now hated England. For Carson he had a passionate admiration, even though Carson was on the wrong side: had not the Orange leader taken up arms in defence of his cause? and if one Irishman could do this in the North, why not other Irishmen in the South? These arguments appealed, with equal force, to Professor MacNeill: the only trouble was that they did not appeal to Mr Redmond.

Nor did they appeal to Arthur Griffith, the founder of Sinn Fein, and yet there was a strong element of Sinn Fein in the ranks of the Volunteers. Griffith himself held aloof. His movement – founded partly upon a belief in passive resistance, partly upon a reverence for the Irish Constitution of 1782, partly upon the economics of List – had now, after rashly contesting an election in 1908, settled down to a journalistic solitude. When Mr Redmond described it as 'the temporary cohesion of isolated cranks', he spoke for most of Ireland; and yet – in 1910 – it had suddenly split into two, and its new half was frankly republican. With the publication of Seaghan MacDiarmada's *Saoirseacht na h-Eireann* (Irish Freedom), an eight page fortnightly, Mr Griffith's perverse high Tory demand for an Irish King, Lords, and Commons was openly repudiated by men who still believed in other Sinn Fein principles, in non-recognition of English authority, law, justice, or legislature. The only thing wrong with such men, in Griffith's opinion, was (apart from their unaccountable dislike for the Constitution of 1782) the fact that they were revolutionaries, who wanted to achieve their ends by force. It was these young revolutionaries – men like Padraic Pearse and Thomas Macdonagh – who brought the name of Sinn Fein into the ranks of the Volunteers – and into Irish life.

Such were the contradictory forces with which Mr Redmond had to deal. On the other hand, some fifty per cent of the Volunteers – backed by that venerable machine, the Ancient Order of Hibernians – still believed in him, and he had the support of public opinion as a whole. Griffith might call his policy 'half bluster and half whine', Connolly might describe his Home Rule Bill as a 'Gas and Water Bill', designed to reduce the Irish Parliament to the status of a municipal council, Pearse might talk of revolution, and Casement hint of the tactical advantages to Germany of friendly Irish harbours – but in the end they would have to bow to his authority. They would not dare, speaking, as they did, always of a United Ireland, to split the Volunteers in two.

And yet – in spite of these assurances – he grew daily more uneasy. It was not merely that in Pearse and Connolly and MacNeill he had at last been brought face to face with an Ireland which he could not hope to understand. It was the *fact* of the Volunteers which distressed him. They had come into being without his consent. He could not forgive that. Nor was this all – for if they obeyed him, it would only be upon the condition that he allowed them to fight: in that respect, they were all agreed. They were, perhaps, not so well agreed upon the question of *why* they should fight. Pearse, for instance, declaring he loved the Ulster Volunteers like a brother and shared their hatred of the Liberals, was all affection and fratricide; whereas Redmond's followers professed a loathing for Ulster, and vowed that they were fighting for Liberal principles against a Tory plot. These motives were certainly confusing; yet the truth remained that one and all had caught the fever which burned along the Ulster borders. Civil War was not far away. Mr Redmond, it seemed, must either take his place in the Nationalist vanguard, or abandon forever his claim to be the Irish leader. It was in vain that he recited to himself the pacific creed of O'Connell and Parnell; there was no consolation to be had there. From the middle of May onwards he began to scheme for the control of the Volunteers – as though, piece by piece, with shaking fingers, he were putting on the whole armour of unrighteousness.

III

On 21st May, the Home Rule Bill came up for its third reading, and was shouted down by the Opposition. 'The demonstration,' wrote Lord Ullswater, 'had been recommended, I believe, by the *Observer*, on the previous Sunday.' (*A Speaker's Commentaries*, p. 151.) But the Bill was scarcely worth the effort; it had ceased to have any meaning. On 25th May, when the third reading was again attempted and with success, Mr William O'Brien made the most satisfactory comment. Mr O'Brien had refused to vote with the Nationalists, on the grounds that Mr Asquith's Amending Bill would make any vote worthless. 'The Government,' said Mr O'Brien, 'are determined to pass this Bill. Yes, but they are equally determined not to put it in force in its most vital particular. The Prime Minister confessed only a few minutes ago that this Bill is only a first instalment and that the second instalment is to nullify the first. . . . The Member for Waterford [Mr Redmond] spoke as if the technical passage of this Bill will be a joy-day for Ireland as a nation. On the contrary it will be one of the grossest frauds ever perpetrated on a too confiding people. It will be little short of a cruel practical joke at expense of their intelligence as well as their freedom.' Mr O'Brien was generally at odds with Mr Redmond, but rarely – very, very rarely – for reasons as sound as these.

The echoes of those voices, fading across the years, still sound a note that is at once ironical, futile, and angry. As long as there is history, they must always sound that note, and however faint it grows, the hearer will always respond to it with alarm, first, and perhaps with laughter. In the spectacle of a helpless Parliament there is something frightening and something funny; it is like a South American football game which breaks up because the spectators have begun to burn the stands. And Parliament, in May 1914, was quite helpless. Its Members, Liberal and Conservative, glared at one another with the concentrated venom of enemies who discover – too late – that they have been fighting about nothing at all. The foolish pretence of responsibility which kept them still talking in their narrow chamber, still passing with pointless diligence through the division lobbies, brought with it nothing but hatred. Beyond their walls, careless of their deliberations, England settled her own affairs as best she could: the violent reality outside left a vicious unreality within. The two parties were no longer on speaking terms. Their leaders communicated with one another only through liaison officers. Tory treason and Liberal weakness had worked themselves out at last.

The battle raged furiously through London, where people dined against each other in the deadliest fashion, and where drawing-room met drawing-room in mortal combat. This singular warfare, with its accompanying rattle of cutlery and popping of wine corks, grew in intensity as the season advanced. Entrenched behind acres of flowers and miles of table linen, hostesses gave battle; rival orchestras moaned and thundered through the nights; on neutral ground, there was constant exchange of snubs and shrugs and cuts direct. The Marchioness of Londonderry would not enter a house without first inquiring if there were any Home Rulers there. Lord Curzon, too, plunged into the fray with a characteristic pomposity. In May he gave a great ball to which, since the King and Queen had consented to attend, no political significance could be attached. And yet it was very soon known in London that the Prime Minister, Mrs Asquith, and Miss Elizabeth Asquith were not to be invited. When Mrs George Keppel brought this news to Number 10, Downing Street, Mrs Asquith could hardly believe her: but no invitation arrived, and now, upon the faces of the Tory ladies in the Speaker's Gallery, she observed a look of 'icy vagueness'. She was to be ostracized, and at the instance of a man who had once enjoyed with her the delightful intimacies of 'The Souls'! Mr Balfour, another Soul, still invited her to his dinners; but then Mr Balfour's philosophical detachment, so impervious to Tory humours, deprived this gesture of any consolation. When the Curzon ball was over, Mrs Asquith wrote a letter of protest to her former friend. Curzon replied that it 'would be impolitic to invite, even to a social gathering, the wife and daughter of the head of a Government to which the majority of my friends are inflexibly opposed'. Their entrance, he added, would probably have caused a painful scene. Mrs Asquith seized her pen. She could imagine no scene, she wrote, provoked by 'Elizabeth and myself going into a room of any sort', and cordially looked forward to the day when her daughter would not be regarded as a bomb. (*More Memories:* by Margot, Countess of Oxford and Asquith, pp. 179–83.)

Of course, Mrs Asquith added with tearful frivolity, the suffragettes who had been invited to Lord Curzon's ball *might* have objected to her presence there. But was the suggestion, after all, so *very* frivolous? Was there any place, however exclusive, where the votaries of Mrs Pankhurst and her daughters might not be found in May 1914?

Chapter Three

The Pankhursts Provide a Clue

*'These things, these things were here, and but the beholder
Wanting.'*

I

ON the evening of 18th June, a motor-car, filled with women, drew up
near Richard I's statue in Parliament Square. Out of it there was carried,
with mournful care, the body of a young lady who was clearly in the last
stages of exhaustion, if, indeed, she could have been said to be alive at all.
She was borne to the Strangers' Entrance of the House of Commons. 'I
stood beside her, very helpless,' writes one of the few observers of this
curious incident, 'while she lay on the steps, apparently dying, and the
police, perhaps in pity, hesitated to drive her away.' The observer was
H. W. Nevinson and the young lady was Sylvia Pankhurst.

The police might have been tempted to lay hands upon Miss Sylvia,
whose second hunger and thirst strike had left her so much at their mercy;
if George Lansbury and Keir Hardie had not come running out with a
message which they communicated to the little group on the steps. The
Prime Minister had consented to receive, at some future date, a suffragette deputation of six working women. Handkerchiefs were waved,
voices raised in a sparrow-like huzza. 'We are winning, we are winning!'
Even that helpless figure on the ground betrayed, with a turn of the
head, some sign of understanding and even, it may be, of enthusiasm.

This scene deserves to be recorded on canvas and hung in a Town
Hall or a municipal Gallery or wherever it is that such pictures belong.
It is one of the more important moments in English history. It would
look well, in oils, executed (as is usually the case) by a conscientious
artist of moderate attainments. At any rate, it would look as well as
Drake's game of bowls or the Archbishop on his knees before Queen
Victoria. It might even look better.... The late summer evening drifts
out of Parliament Square, putting its pleasant style, at once vague and
high, upon everything there – as if:

293

there does some soft
on things aloof, aloft,
bloom breathe . . .

A momentary gleam, perhaps, could be made to light upon that little group of people, as they bend over the recumbent Sylvia with expressions of solicitude and agitation and triumph. Departing from the strictest verisimilitude, the artist might depict, upon the faces of the police, some mingling traces of admiration and shame: and for his necessary touch of historical irony he could suggest in his background the dusk-draped statue of Oliver Cromwell.

Oh, yes, the scene is important enough. *We are winning!* That shrill cry in Parliament Square has a deep significance. Nor is it only the significance which attaches to every movement of the militant suffragettes: the significance, that is, of new life in the soul of woman. It is curiously enough the small voice of all England in its last year before war. The only question one has to inquire into is whether anyone heard it correctly.

II

For some time it had been the opinion of Europe that English democracy was in a swift decline; in 1914 it was generally considered that this decline had turned into a galloping consumption. While the Army refused to move against Ulster, the Government persisted in its intention to clutter the Statute Book with the meaningless provisions of an amended Home Rule Bill. The situation, farcical enough as it was, was rendered even more so by the violent speeches of eminent men. Now was the time, too, to recall the no less violent speeches of men to whom eminence had been denied. Major Crawford, for instance, had told the people of Bangor that 'if we are put out of the Union, I would infinitely prefer to change my allegiance to the Emperor of Germany': and then there was the prediction of that remarkable loyalist, Captain James Craig. 'There is a spirit spreading abroad which I can testify to from my personal knowledge, that Germany and the German Emperor would be preferable to the rule of John Redmond, Patrick Ford, and the Molly Maguires [The Ancient Order of Hibernians].' These words meant nothing in fact, perhaps; but were they not straws in the wind? Could one honestly say that a country, into whose ear such fantastical hints were being dropped with such immunity, was anything but extremely vulnerable? What could be expected of a liberal democracy whose Parliament had practically ceased to function, whose Government was futile, and whose Opposition had said enough to put lesser men in the dock for treason? Mr Gerard, the US Ambassador in Berlin, might protest that Carson's 'gigantic political bluff... has no more political or revolutionary significance than a torchlight parade during one of our presidential campaigns'. This was not the opinion of the German Falkenhayn or the Austrian Conrad. (*Aus Meiner Dienstzeit*, p. 676.) Such gentlemen, watching the Tory Rebellion with an increasing solicitude, inclined more and more to the opinion that England's day was over.

From our vantage point in history, we are able to assure ourselves that they were wrong. The reasons for their mistake, however, are not quite so apparent. Was it through some magnificent, some miraculous assertion of an historical vigour that a united England answered the call of war, when war came? Or was there another reason, not less miraculous, but scarcely so magnificent? The England which the world had in mind, during those early months of 1914, was a country which, behind the solid figures of Victoria and Edward, had established and with difficulty retained a certain ascendancy over the rest of the world. For all her arrogance, her seeming perfidies, her perplexing moments of gaiety, carelessness, and romance, she had enjoyed a pre-eminence among the nations which deserved – above all others – the epithet 'respectable'. In her damp green corner of Europe, behind her impregnable barrier of rains and seas, she had put forth her unique powers of superior decency. And now... look at her! If the events of 1913 and 1914 could be followed to their logical conclusion, what would one find there but the weariness, the decadence of a great democracy? It might be argued, of course, that no logical conclusion was evident in the events of 1913 and 1914: that they twisted and turned upon themselves like the baffling paths of a maze. But the hostile observer must have felt that in politics he had a clue which, if carefully followed, would lead him to the centre, and that he would find there – as one who comes at last into a weed-grown, melancholy clearing – the same reassuring elements of decadence and weariness. Or, if politics were insufficient, he could follow the thread of commerce: the end was the same.

But there was one clue which – perhaps because it was too obvious, too scarlet, or because it seemed to go plunging off along the wrong turnings – he had altogether neglected. Yet anyone who followed it with sufficient perspicacity might well have discovered himself, at the end of his wanderings, in a very different surrounding. He would, in fact, have discovered that in the midst of death there was life, the kind of life which those who fondly imagined that England had ceased to count among the fighting nations, would have done well to consider. As for the clue itself, we can pick it up at any point we please, and follow it backwards or forwards as the fancy dictates: we can pick it up, for instance, at the point where Mrs Asquith, thrusting a little barb into the hide of Lord Curzon, suggested that only the suffragettes could have rendered her entry into his ballroom inopportune. . . .

The record of suffragette arson for the first seven months of 1914 was an impressive one – no less than 107 buildings were set on fire, and among the instances of total destruction were the venerable Whitekirk, in East Lothian, with its priceless Bible, and the lovely ancient churches at Wargrave and Breadsall. Mrs Pankhurst's record was no less impressive. Between 9th March and 18th July she was imprisoned four more times and endured four more hunger strikes. This raised her record of strikes to ten, and reduced her health to a point at which most women would gratefully have slipped from the world. But not Mrs Pankhurst. With the agility of a ghost, her emaciated body hastened, between imprisonments, from rally to rally. Her appearance was terrifying; it seemed as though the idea within, like a fire, had all but consumed her flesh and her bones. Indeed, it would hardly be too much to say that, at this moment in her career, she was as good as disembodied.

That, unfortunately, would be too much to say of Miss Christabel Pankhurst. In Paris this healthy young lady wrung from her followers the last exquisite drop of adoration and something more than the minimum of comfort: nor, gazing upon her female empire with an increasing *hauteur*, could she discover any rival there but one. That one was her own sister. Ever since her appearance on the platform at the Larkin meeting, Sylvia Pankhurst had been proscribed for exile from the intoxicated, high-Tory world of the Women's Social and Political Union. In January 1914, a peremptory order came, bidding Sylvia to report immediately in Paris. She did so, and in Christabel's apartments the three of them met for the last time.

They must have made a curious picture as they sat there in conference – Mrs Pankhurst so fragile and so weary that she looked as if she could scarcely bear the fatigue of sitting upright; Sylvia with the marks of sleeplessness and imprisonment drawn down her face; and the slim, firm body and broad, abundant, rosy face of Christabel. It was Christabel who announced that Sylvia's organization – the East London Federation – must withdraw from the WSPU. She made this long-expected remark quite casually – she might almost have been talking to the little Pomeranian dog which she was nursing. But it was final. Sylvia pressed her sister for reasons, though she knew them well, and Christabel told her that her speech at the Larkin meeting was contrary to the policies of the WSPU. Had not the faithful George Lansbury been there? 'We do not want to be mixed up with him,' said Christabel. And then the constitution of the East London Federation was democratic – 'We do not want that.' It was worse than democratic, it was composed almost exclusively of working women. 'We want only picked women.' Then came the final, the damning accusation. 'You have your own ideas; we do not want that. We want our women to take their instructions, and march in step like an army.' We want, we do not want; we do not want, we want. Sylvia was too tired to argue. The conversation frittered itself away in tedious recriminations, each sister accusing the other of appropriating moneys which did not belong to her. 'You can't need much in your simple way,' said Christabel haughtily. At last Mrs Pankhurst intervened. She did not love Sylvia as well as Christabel, and may even have thought that Sylvia had betrayed her: but she was her daughter. 'Suppose I were to say we would allow you something,' she said gently: 'Would you . . . ?' 'Oh, no, we can't have that,' Christabel cried: 'It must be a clean cut.'

When the news reached England, both the press and the Home Office agreed that the movement had broken up; and yet, in May, it was apparent from Mrs Asquith's letter that nothing of the kind had happened. The press and the Home Office might be excused for jumping to conclusions – they shared the common opinion that militant suffrage was a crazy attempt to gain a political end. They did not see it – how could they? – as so vital, so energetic a part in the evolution of woman that family affections counted for nothing. Woman would hardly refrain from evolving because the Pankhursts were no longer a united family: on the contrary, she would probably continue the process at a dizzier speed. The energy which had separated the Pankhursts was greater than they; it was greater than militant suffrage: it arose from all the women of England.

The unconscious turning from respectability – here, with all its implications, was the force which had twisted pre-war England into a maze of conflicting violence. In the case of woman, the improbable, the essential, the living expression of this force was the militant suffrage movement: here is the clue which leads to the heart of the maze. If one can permit oneself the alarming hypothesis that Sir Edward Carson was a woman, he would probably have burned churches and hurled bricks and heckled Ministers with all the abandon of an Emmeline Pankhurst. Fortunately for the peace of the London constabulary and the wardresses of Holloway, Sir Edward was a man. But had *he* not thrown away that restraint which becomes an eminent barrister? Had not the Trade Union Congress discarded its traditional decorum? Had not the Army sunk its professional pride in a chivalrous and excessive disobedience? These events might have been considered the signs of weariness and decadence in English democracy, but for the energetic accompaniments of militant suffrage.

Those devoted women whirled, it is true, like straws in the wind. But it was not that melancholy low wind which blows at evening, like a ripple before the prow of night; it was a morning wind, which announces the sun. It was life and not death. What *had* become of the England of Victoria and Edward, the respectable England whose sickness was being watched with such flattering solicitude by the observers of Europe? Perhaps it was not sick any more; perhaps it was dead. Between 1910 and 1913 it went through all the contortions of a man who has swallowed too much strychnine, which is only beneficial in small doses. It died of a sudden attack of too much energy; and since the energy was generated by itself, one might almost say that it had committed suicide. And since one likes to provide such acts with an appropriate finale, one might go so far as to say that Gough's mutiny was the precise moment of Liberal England's death, the end of pre-war history, the occasion upon which – suddenly, stealthily, unknown to itself – a new and terrible England took the place of the old. Terrible, indeed. Given the time, it might have destroyed itself – in civil war, in revolution, in the raptures of martyrdom. But it was not given the time. War, when it came, was nothing more than a necessary focus: political furies, sex hatreds, class hatreds were forgotten; with all the simulations of patriotic fervour, the united energy of England hurled itself against Germany. Could it be that, looking back into its past, England should be grateful to General Gough and the officers at the Curragh? That it should mark their mutiny as one marks a birthday? That this ultimate constitutional folly, engineered by a remarkably disreputable Conservative Opposition, was actually a sign of health? History is so full of paradoxes that one more need not come amiss.

The contemporary observer, however, was both obliged and happy to content himself with what he saw. The wind blew, the straws whirled in the wind; and one can hardly blame him if he thought that the wind, with its playthings, was blowing backwards upon the past, instead of on into the future.

III

When Sylvia returned to the Bow Road and the consolations of her East London Federation, the *Daily News* proclaimed: 'There could scarcely be a more crushing condemnation of militancy than its formal abandonment by all save one of its inventors.' Christabel was furious; had Sylvia pushed herself so far into the foreground that *she* alone was considered a militant? And then the Home Office, in a Memorandum officially given to the press, declared that the movement was now broken up. This was tempting Providence which, in the shape of the fulminating Christabel, struck back with ferocious alacrity. The record of arson and the activities of Mrs Pankhurst, as has already been shown, were not those of a broken movement. On the contrary, the offensive, it appeared, was to be resumed in the most savage fashion. In that respect the disillusioned authorities, in their turn, were not backward. Once more the feeding tube was carried from cell to cell. In the case of Miss Ethel Moorhead, its employment was particularly striking. Miss Moorhead, imprisoned in Calton Gaol, Edinburgh, on a conviction for arson, refused to touch her food; and the prison authorities, with a delicacy which was very touching, declined to administer the tube themselves. Instead, they called in an expert from the criminal lunatic asylum at Perth who, by pushing hot wires into her ears, with one or two other tricks of the same order, persuaded Miss Moorhead to take nourishment; and these methods were continued until, one day, food entered the lady's lungs, and she had to be released with double pneumonia. On the whole, however, the tube was administered with no more than the ordinary accompaniments of sickness and terror. Stories like Miss Moorhead's were, from a governmental point of view, very inopportune. None the less, mistakes occurred from time to time. Miss Mary Richardson, committed to Holloway on 10th March for having slashed the Rokeby *Venus* – (if there was an outcry against her deed, said this enterprising vandal, 'let everyone remember that such an outcry is hypocrisy so long as they allow the destruction of Mrs Pankhurst and other beautiful women') – was released on 6th April and again on 20th May under the provisions of the 'Cat and Mouse' Act. Miss Richardson had not taken kindly to the tube. There was something wrong with her; nobody could be quite sure what it was. But at last, after her third re-arrest, she had to be let out of Holloway and hurried to a hospital, where her appendix was found to be much inflamed and diseased, with other signs of recurring inflammation. Nor was this all. For Dr Flora Murray, who examined her, declared that her mouth was scarred and sore from the finger nails of prison officials, that there were cuts and scratches all over her body, and over her appendix one large bruise. Miss Richardson recovered. But it is not surprising that, after this ordeal, she should have plunged into speculations of a somewhat disordered kind; and that, when last heard of, she should have been contemplating the founding of a house of Communist nuns, dedicated to social and religious service.

Undeterred – indeed, encouraged – by the sufferings of her followers, Mrs Pankhurst taxed to the very utmost both her own strength and the resources of the police. She took to appearing on the balconies of private houses in London from which – with an organized bodyguard of Amazonian women to protect her from arrest – she contrived to make one or two very telling speeches. She was, of course, still under sentence of three years' penal servitude, and liable at any moment to re-arrest. At last, in Glasgow, she went too far. She had been advertised to speak in St Andrew's Hall on 9th March, arrived on the platform, and discovered that the front rows were packed with a gratifying concourse of police officials, all anxious to claim the honour of capturing her. Her departure from Glasgow was very flattering; a large body of detectives accompanied her on the train to London, and an even larger body – a positive army – guarded every approach to Holloway Gaol until she was safely inside. She then served another five days of her three years' sentence: she served them on her back, on the cell floor, fully clothed, and refusing either to get up or take food. The Holloway officials, however, had tried their usual enticements; for when she was released, so ran the doctor's report, her body was marked with 'various bruises and abrasions, all evidencing the marked degree of violence to which she had been subjected'.

IV

The energy of the whole movement – of which the split between Christabel and Sylvia was profoundly, as these other activities were superficially, an instance – increased in the most infuriating manner. The country now detested militancy. And yet – it was very peculiar – the more outrageous these militants became, the more support their cause received. The W S P U might be considered an organization of intolerable lunatics, but the same could hardly be said of the United Suffragists. The United Suffragists, it is true, were an object of scorn and loathing to the W S P U, but their arguments – backed up by such people as George Lansbury (at length a convert to non-militancy), Gerald and Barbara Gould, Laurence Housman, Evelyn Sharp, and H. W. Nevinson – were almost as forcible as arson and picture-slashing. To these reasonable voices were added those of Lord Selborne and the Bishop of London. Could it be that – in spite of those odious Pankhursts – women's suffrage was actually to be achieved? Many a modest lady and respectable gentleman shook a bewildered head. It might be difficult – it might be very difficult – to keep women in subjection much longer.

V

The W S P U itself, however, had almost lost sight of its political objective in the ecstatic conduct of a sex war. Wherever it looked there appeared – with delicious convenience – a new enemy. It now turned its attention to no less a figure than Sir Edward Carson. That grim rebel – in 1913, when his need for allies was still a pressing one – had made some half promise of the franchise for all Ulsterwomen. In 1914, however, Sir Edward already suffered from an embarrassment of allies, nor was his cause – or any cause for that matter – likely to be enhanced by the support of the W S P U. The Union urged him for a repetition of his promise. Sir Edward was silent. At length, besieged in his house by a group of determined women, the Orange leader blandly denied that he had committed himself in any manner whatsoever. This was early in March, and within a very few days amateur bombs began mysteriously to explode in Ulster, buildings went up in flames, and the very hospitals set aside for Volunteers in case of civil war suddenly caught fire. The battle was carried to London where, on 4th April, the militants attempted to confound a vast Hyde Park meeting of Carson's followers with a counter-demonstration of their own. An unauthorized procession – suffragette meetings were still officially forbidden – headed by the indomitable Mrs Drummond in a dog-cart, was actually allowed to enter the Park. But the sight and, above all, the sound of 'General' Drummond, whose voice was a commanding one, were too much for the police. Dog-cart and orator were pushed towards a side exit, and separated one from the other; and in the subsequent mêlée, which was vigorous, the General was to be observed, held aloft in the arms of her supporters and talking with laudable persistence for as long as fifteen minutes at a stretch. She continued these tactics in Marlborough Street police court on the following Monday. The question she had to ask – and it was a pertinent one – was this: why should *she* be in the dock, and not Sir Edward Carson and the militant Unionists? Since she repeated this question with monotonous regularity and at the top of her voice, the magistrate's answer, if any, has not been recorded. She was removed from the court three times and finally, when Mr Muskett, the prosecutor, confessed that he could not make his voice heard above hers, the evidence was taken in her absence. She was brought back again on Wednesday. She had been hunger-striking for two days. Her voice had not lost its power, however, nor her arm its cunning: she engaged in a hand to hand struggle with the policemen attending her, threw one of their whistles at the magistrate, shouted Mr Muskett down, and was with difficulty brought to hear her sentence of 'forty shillings or one month'. The fine was paid anonymously, the General retired in triumph, and still – unanswered these many years – the question remains: why *was* she in the dock, and not Sir Edward Carson and the Unionists?

The WSPU had now declared war upon anything and everything masculine – Liberals, Labourites, and Tories were alike its enemies. There remained, perhaps, only one place where its influence had not been sufficiently felt, and that place was Buckingham Palace. What could be done to the King? Christabel had already declared that the Royal name and office were 'dishonoured', and in December 1913, during a performance of *Jeanne d'Arc* at Covent Garden, three young ladies addressed His Majesty through a megaphone, having taken the precaution of locking and barring themselves into their box. The substance of their discourse, which was none too audible above the oaths of the audience and the crash of weighty shoulders against the box door, was that women were fighting as Joan of Arc had fought centuries before, and that they were being tortured and done to death in the King's name and the Church's. But George V, the WSPU noted with distress, showed no sign of conversion to its cause. Perhaps he had not heard clearly enough. At a matinée at His Majesty's Theatre, therefore, a young lady, inextricably chained to her seat, addressed him for a considerable period as 'You Russian Tsar!' But even this argument failed to make any effect.

Women began chaining themselves to the railings of Buckingham Palace. A portrait of the King in the Scottish Royal Academy was badly damaged. At a Drawing-Room in 1914, Miss May Blomfield dropped on her knees before the King and Queen crying, 'For God's sake, Your Majesty, put a stop to this forcible feeding,' and was immediately carried from the Presence, which, we are told, 'remained serene'. Could it be permitted to remain so? Mrs Pankhurst, at any rate, thought not. She had already petitioned the King in February for an audience, and had received an answer from the Home Office, saying that the petition had been laid before His Majesty, and that the Home Secretary had been unable to advise His Majesty to comply with the prayer thereof. Such were the disadvantages of dealing with a constitutional monarch. The only way of getting round the Home Office, it seemed, was to lead a deputation to the Palace, and this was the course which Mrs Pankhurst now proposed to adopt. The date she set was 21st May, and on the afternoon of that day, while a vast crowd gathered around the Palace in the pleasant anticipation of a lively fight, a procession of women came up Constitution Hill, and pressed with dignified zeal against a stubborn barrier of mounted and foot police. Except for a few Indian clubs, one horsewhip, and a few packets of red and green powder, the ladies were unarmed; the only weapon they used was the weight of their bodies. The police, unfortunately, used their truncheons. A scene of considerable brutality was witnessed, not merely by the crowd below, but by a large number of interested spectators on the roofs and at the windows of the Palace itself.

Another procession, attempting to approach by way of Admiralty Arch, fell in with a horde of youths, each bearing a suffragette in effigy on his walking stick. Shouting, 'You ought to be burned', these gallant young men sorted out the more buxom ladies with a discriminating eye, and proceeded to rip their clothes off their backs. Perhaps the most edifying scene of all was that of a young woman, facing her tormentors with her back to the wall, while one of the Palace sentries beat her with his fists.

Mrs Pankhurst herself lingered, unobserved, until the Wellington Gates were opened to admit police reinforcements; then she slipped through with a number of spectators, made her way to the very gates of the Palace, was seized at the last minute by a huge Inspector, and carried bodily into a taxi. In Holloway Gaol she entered upon her eighth hunger strike.

The following day, sixty-six suffragettes appeared at Bow Street. Here, following the example of General Drummond, they kept up an incessant shouting. Some refused to stand up, some turned their backs on the magistrates, two or three threw powder about, and one lady removed her boot and hurled it at Sir John Dickenson, the presiding magistrate, who caught it with dexterity. Though the defendants refused to be bound over they were almost all discharged – it was generally supposed that the King had asked for leniency. One or two of the worst offenders were remanded until the London Sessions, two or three days later, where similar scenes occurred, with this exception – that, having spent the interval in hunger-striking, the defendants were only able to utter their protests in a very enfeebled voice. They were sentenced; they were removed to Holloway; they refused to take off their clothes or be examined by doctors; they entered upon a hunger and thirst strike; they were released within a very few days. So ended the great deputation.

VI

One of the few prominent suffragettes who had not taken part in this peculiar and peculiarly gallant demonstration was Miss Annie Kenney, who had been reserved, on orders from Paris, for a more eccentric manoeuvre. The Church was to be Miss Kenney's objective. On 22nd May she was to present herself at Lambeth Palace, demand sanctuary of the Archbishop of Canterbury, and stay in sanctuary until the vote was won. The Archbishop's powers of extending sanctuary were at least as dubious as the King's powers of altering the policy of the Home Office. Miss Kenney was undismayed. She had received her *ukase* from Christabel, she had been told to see the Archbishop, and see him she would. She also brought her luggage with her. An unsuspecting servant showed her into the study of Dr Davidson, who, after hearing her request and observing those hysterical protruding blue eyes and uneasy hands, hastily sent for his chaplain and Mrs Davidson. The three of them begged her to go, but arguments were lost upon Miss Kenney, who further endeared herself to her hosts by disagreeing with His Grace on a matter of Church history. They gave her lunch, they gave her tea; the Archbishop, she noted with satisfaction, grew 'hot and irritated', the hour grew late. Long after dark, at last, the door opened and 'there were my old friends of Scotland Yard and Holloway'. It cost Miss Kenney a six days' hunger and thirst strike before she was sufficiently low in health to be released from prison: but such was her pertinacity that, as soon as she was strong enough to walk, she made a similar attempt upon the Bishop of London, who only got her out of Fulham Palace by pleading his unmarried state. People might think it odd, said the ingenious Bishop, if Miss Kenney spent her sanctuary with him.

VII

The fantastic expedients to which the Union now resorted were soon to be emphasized in a somewhat unfortunate manner. It so happened that while the 'raid' on Buckingham Palace was taking place, the police themselves raided a flat in Lauderdale Mansions, Maida Vale, where they arrested two young suffragettes called Grace Roe and Nellie Hall. The Misses Roe and Hall, charged with being 'loose, idle, and disorderly persons, suspected of having committed or being about to commit a felony, misdemeanour, or breach of the peace', were eventually convicted of conspiring together to commit malicious damage to property. Their trial, which continued on and off for seven weeks – owing to the ladies' methods of obstruction, such as flinging themselves on the ground, trying to jump from the dock, shouting, and throwing things at the Judge – was rendered unusual by an incident which prefaced it. Miss Roe was caught in an attempt to get a drug smuggled in to her. The drug, it is true, was nothing more than a powerful emetic, and the smuggler none other than a lawyer's clerk: but the country preferred to believe the worst. If Miss Roe protested that she wanted her emetic for the purpose of vomiting after forcible feeding, then was it not true that the suffragettes' much publicized sufferings from the tube were due to drugs rather than to hunger or brutality? And if one kind of drug were smuggled in, why not another? Who could tell but that the whole militant movement was positively riddled with drug-fiends? Indeed, considering the fantastic and indecent demonstrations which had lately been witnessed, what other conclusion could be reached? So argued the country. The spreading of these insinuations (to which the WSPU could only oppose that most ineffective of weapons, its innocence) was hardly diminished by the inopportune suicide of a rather notorious young militant called Joan Lavender Baillie Guthrie. The reasons for this act have never transpired, but anyone who has read Vera Brittain's *Testament of Youth*, with its revelation of the strange fancies whisking round in the heads of even the most ordinary young ladies of that day, will not be surprised at the extravagances of one who had been subjected to the triple enticements of Fabianism, militant suffrage, and the *New Age*. Miss Guthrie was very much a victim of the times she lived in; but she was a militant, and her death – which might with equal justice have been attributed to the doctrines of the Sidney Webbs and the arguments of Mr Orage – was laid at the door of the WSPU, which discovered that it was now being populated in the public imagination not merely with a large number of habitual drug-takers, but with an even larger number of potential suicides.

In these circumstances it is not surprising that the Union should have redoubled its activities; that it should, in fact, have been seized with the final exhilaration of outlaws and martyrs. Its members burned, smashed, slashed, heckled, hooted, and hunger-struck with a terrifying enthusiasm. Indeed, things grew so bad that a second motion to reduce the Home Office vote by £100 was put forward in the House of Commons on 11th June. In the course of the debate Mr McKenna gave a curious picture of the state of the public mind; the suggestions he had received, he said, for dealing with the suffragettes might conveniently be summarized into four divisions:

(1) To let the prisoners die.
(2) To deport them.
(3) To treat them as lunatics.
(4) To give them the Vote.

The last solution, he thought, was scarcely the right one; his remedy was 'patient and determined action'; and at this point his words were punctuated, in a singular fashion, by a muffled explosion from the direction of Westminster Abbey. A suffragette bomb had gone off beneath the Coronation chair, slightly damaging that venerable piece of furniture, and making something of a dent in the walls of Edward the Confessor's Chapel.

Thunder itself could not have been more appropriate. 'Patient and determined action' – against these words, with their familiar, their fatal Liberal ring, the heavens themselves might have uttered their voice. The situation had passed far beyond the control of Mr McKenna. The barricaded picture galleries of London (the slashing of the Rokeby *Venus* had been followed by the mutilation of Sargent's portrait of Henry James), the ruins of church and castle, bore witness, no less than the cells of Holloway Prison, to the increasing energy of the suffragettes. And then – just as the country's rage and loathing reached its highest pitch, just as the first of Mr McKenna's suggestions seemed actually to have become the most popular – then, with a suddenness which still takes one's breath away, symbol yielded to symbol, the old bowed to the new.

Mr Asquith and his Cabinet gave up the battle.

VIII

The importance of this incident has not been stressed either in suffragette history or in the minds of its survivors. Sylvia Pankhurst played the chief part in it, and around her figure there lingers, even to this day, the obscure atmosphere of jealousy and prejudice. But it was *her* deputation which, on 18th June, the Prime Minister consented to receive. It was she – a prisoner under the Cat and Mouse Act, a discredited woman, officially barred from the precincts of Parliament – who, lying *in articulo mortis* on the steps of the Strangers' Entrance, had wrested from the head of the Government this vital concession.

Two days later the working women's deputation waited upon Mr Asquith. The WSPU refused to have any part in it. 'As for my daughter,' Mrs Pankhurst wrote to Norah Smyth, while Sylvia was still in prison, 'tell her I advise her when she comes out . . . to go home and let her friends take care of her.' The meaning of this was obvious – Sylvia must drop her idea of a deputation. But Sylvia persisted. She could not go with them herself, but she saw her six women off the morning of 20th June. They were headed by a brush-maker called Mrs Savoy, who suffered from dropsy, palpitations, and the grumbling attentions of an elderly eccentric husband, and who – we are told – was nevertheless invariably gay. Confronted with Mr Asquith and Mr Lloyd George, these six workers developed their argument – 'we do not get a living but an existence' – with a skill which was only marred by a momentary hitch at the outset. Mrs Savoy, in order to emphasize her opening sentences, suddenly produced from her reticule a brown paper parcel. The two Ministers, with undignified alacrity, made for the door. Mrs Savoy chuckled: it wasn't a bomb, she said, unwrapping it, but part of a brush. It was full of holes, and perhaps the gentlemen would care to see the number of holes there were and the number of bristles she had to put into them. For this she earned a few pence. The Ministers, reassured, came back to experience – with unfeigned attention – what was clearly their first meeting with the actual facts of sweated labour. Nor were the other women's arguments less convincing. The unmarried mother, prostitution, white slave traffic, the wrongs done to widows and deserted wives – these were the realities of their existence and they spoke of them with profound knowledge and almost heart-breaking simplicity. And they were suffragettes, yet speaking with the authentic voice of the lower classes. Mr Asquith's previous encounters with the lower classes, in the strikes of 1912 and 1913, had not been very fortunate; but these women, humble and courageous and appealing and proud, made a very different impression. He felt that he could understand them; his diffidence vanished; and when he answered them it was to say that, in his opinion, women's suffrage could not be long delayed. Now Mr Asquith had often made this statement in the past. But he was not the man to break a sincere promise, and there was something in his voice which – for the first time in his questionable dealings with the suffragettes – was beyond question sincere. On the next day the Liberal press echoed his assurances in the most positive manner. Sylvia Pankhurst, also, dragging herself from her bed, had interviews with Mr Lloyd George and other members of the Cabinet. There could be no doubt about it. The Government was now prepared to support a Woman's Suffrage Bill.

This victory, so swift and so unexpected, is open to two or three rather contradictory considerations. The Government was already so battered that it may have thought that one more concession scarcely signified; it may simply have been bullied once again. Or it may have been persuaded by the fact that working women, upon whose sympathies it depended, or hoped that it depended, were joining in the suffrage movement. The voices of radicals may have moved it, or the knowledge that the Labour Party, discarding its previous neutrality, had now decided to make Adult Manhood and Womanhood Suffrage its chief plank at the next elections. Any one of these reasons would have been sufficient. But there is one more which the curious inquirer can hardly neglect. Is it possible that governments, even democratic governments, respond not merely to the opinions but to the deepest, the most hidden feelings of the countries they govern? That those sudden decisions, which so often surprise us in history, are due less to ministerial whimsy than to some unconscious and almost unimaginable prompting of the whole people? Could it be that representative governments actually *represent*, and represent in a most subtle and mysterious way? The decision of the Asquith Cabinet, in this particular instance, may have been the effect of indifference or the effect of wisdom. But its very swiftness, its sudden and unpredictable descent – like a ray of sunlight – from the very midst of such piling clouds of public disapproval – leads us on to quite another conclusion.

Militancy – whatever sins may be urged against it – can scarcely be accused of insignificance. Militancy was the living symbol of the reassertion of a great female principle. And militancy had now reached its peak. It must either consume its energy in wearisome reiterations of outrage and suffering, or give that energy back to the source from whence it came. The first of these two alternatives runs counter to every example of history; and the second – what effect would the second make upon the hidden life of the Englishwoman of 1914? Perhaps she was involved in the agitations of those puppets of hers – the Pankhursts and the WSPU; perhaps her deepest instincts were reaching out to the Vote, which promised, among other things of almost equal necessity, both an impersonal goal in life and the right to possess children legally as well as naturally. If this were indeed the case, then the decision of Mr Asquith and his colleagues takes on a very different look. Woman, one might almost say, had pulled the strings again; and while, in one corner of the little stage, those militants whirled through their abandoned paces, the other corner was occupied by no less a puppet group than the Liberal Cabinet, nodding its ministerial head in dignified and helpless acquiescence.

At this point, where even the biographer – who is the artist of history – might founder, the historian must scramble back to the solidity of fact. Sylvia had been warned by Mr Lloyd George that victory would be achieved with far more dispatch if militant tactics were now abandoned. She herself was inclined to agree. She would like to collect a more and more imposing body of supporters; to consolidate the position she had won: and for this she needed peace. She said as much in a letter to Christabel, adding that she hoped very soon to come over to Paris and report progress. The letter was friendly and tactful, for it assumed that Christabel was still head of the movement, still titular goddess of the East London Federation. But the answer, when it came, took the shape of a telegram to Norah Smyth: 'Tell your friend not to come.'

In *The Suffragette*, Christabel's attitude was even more intransigent. 'The WSPU,' she wrote, 'desires to receive no private communication from the Government or any of its members.' The Union, clearly, had received the news of this approaching triumph with something like chagrin. It was, of course, jealous of Sylvia and her despised federation of working women, whose deputation had delivered the final assault. But, more than that, it was furious with Sylvia for suggesting an abandonment of militant tactics. What? Throw away one's arms in the very hour of victory? It was absurd. People might say that the support of peaceable folk like Nevinson and Barbara Gould and Evelyn Sharp had done some service to the cause of women's suffrage; that the voices of Lord Selborne and the Bishop of London, who had actually argued for the Vote in the House of Lords, had not been without their effect. But which was more persuasive – a speech by His Lordship of London, or the explosion of a bomb beneath his lordship's throne in St Paul's? The WSPU was in no doubt at all. And then it was questionable whether, lost in the ecstasies of a sex war, the Union at all cared for some trumpery victory over the Cabinet, for so small a thing as the Vote. 'The militants will rejoice when victory comes,' Christabel wrote in *The Suffragette*, 'and yet, mixed with their joy, will be regret that the most glorious chapter in women's history is closed and the militant fight over – over, when so many have not yet known the exaltation, the rapture of battle. . . .'

The words are revealing. No less revealing were the actions of Christabel's militants. During the whole of July they committed outrage after outrage, as though they were actually defying the Cabinet to give them suffrage. The police hunted them from Lincoln's Inn House to new headquarters in Tothill Street, from Tothill Street to Campbell Inn Square. In Perth, Miss Janet Arthur was subjected to the final indignity of rectal feeding. In London Mrs Pankhurst, suddenly announcing that she intended to return to Lincoln's Inn House, was arrested at its very doors, taken to prison, and there stripped and searched – the Grace Roe incident had given the authorities their opportunity. Mrs Pankhurst was released after her ninth hunger strike, but on the 15th she was arrested again – the tenth time since her sentence to three years' penal servitude in April 1913 – and underwent her tenth hunger strike. 'They must give us the Vote or they must give us death' was her new slogan, and she meant every word of it. But it seemed that she much preferred death.

And then, in the middle of these battles, there fell the extinguishing shadow of the World War. What would the suffragettes do? How would they behave? Which was the greater enemy – man or Germany? On 11th August, Mr McKenna announced that all their sentences would be remitted. 'His Majesty is confident,' said Mr McKenna, 'that they can be trusted not to stain the cause they have at heart by any further crime or disorder.' Trusted! Certainly they could be trusted! They turned patriot to a woman. Those 'defiant and insolent lawbreakers' – so *The Times* had called them at the beginning of 1914 – whose insolence had been so necessary to the good of women and whose work, so vital and so extravagant, was completed, with results which could only appear in time, now made the last comment upon themselves. It was inevitable that it should be a humorous one. Forces which are thrust up from the soul contain within themselves the mingling elements of tragedy and comedy. So now those hands which had smashed windows, and lighted the stealthy fuse, and poured jam into letter boxes, gave out white feathers to civilian youths and wounded soldiers in mufti. The mouths which had uttered the extreme language of rebellion now made recruiting speeches. The breasts which had shuddered from the feeding tube, and endured the rough hands of policemen and toughs, now bore a placard 'Intern Them All'. In September, Christabel, the Parisien outlaw, returned to London to give a discourse on 'The German Peril'. Mrs Pankhurst, with a characteristic enthusiasm, sounded the same note. So, in loyal fervour and jingoistic enterprise, ended the great Woman's Rebellion.

Only Sylvia, the single realist among the suffrage leaders, maintained that war was a disaster. She alone continued to call for the Vote, and to declare that women should stand for peace, not bloodshed. But what was the use? The East London Federation of working women could not exist in solitude. For even the proletarian movement, the Workers' Rebellion, which had carried its semi-revolutionary banner on to the very ramparts of Capital, now threw that banner aside, and hurled itsel. forward, in a new direction, against a more visible enemy, and beneath the Union Jack.

Chapter Four

The Triple Alliance

I

APART from a serious coal strike, in Rotherham, in the spring of 1914, when 15,000 men came out over the district minimum wage, the workers of England, from January to July, presented an appearance of deceptive calm. Alone of the three rebellions, theirs seemed to have come to an end. The members of the Cavendish Club of Bristol must have recollected, with satisfaction, the words which Sir George Askwith had addressed to them in November of the previous year – 'Within a comparatively short time there may be movements in this country coming to a head of which recent events have been a small foreshadowing.' Such words – it must now have seemed to the Cavendish Club – were clearly disproved: nothing was coming to a head in the industrial world. The country as a whole was certainly of that opinion. It was weary of the very word 'strike', and only too glad to take the appearance for the reality. But in well-informed quarters – in the Statistical Department of the Board of Trade, for instance – very different ideas prevailed: it was noticed there that a positive fever of small strikes – so small as to be almost imperceptible – was spreading through the country. Exactly the same thing had happened in 1913; and the conclusion of that irritated succession of minor stoppages – whether it was the Dublin transport strike or the formation of the Triple Alliance – was anything but reassuring. Sir George and his assistants, following the little strikes of 1914 with a practised eye, began to wonder just how soon the storm would burst and from what quarter it would come.

Sir George was not saddled with an excessive imagination, always an inconvenient burden for a civil servant. He still believed that the Unrest could be attributed to low wages. But there were other thoughts which, though he entertained them with reluctance, he was too honest to conceal from himself. That desire for solidarity among the rank and file could not be denied: but whether it was due to the Eight Hours Act, which

gave the workers more leisure for thinking, or whether to better education, which gave them something to think about, he could not be sure.
Nor was this all. Anyone who reads that interesting book of his,
Industrial Problems and Disputes, will discover, sandwiched with
considerable finesse between slabs of politeness and impartiality, a vast
contempt for the Liberal Government which, for all its protestations of
friendship and prescriptions for reform, was so entirely ignorant of
conditions in the labour world. And he will discover something else. Sir
George did not especially concern himself with literary excellence: he
was no Winston Churchill, to invest his weightiest facts and most
formidable statistics with the rich colours of prose. But his brief account
of 1914 conveys, almost in spite of itself, a pregnant atmosphere of
bewilderment and mystery. Something was stirring which – try as they
would – his reason could not elucidate nor his imagination apprehend.
It was not simply a desire for shorter hours, better wages, and improved
conditions of labour which threatened once again to convulse the
country's industry; it was a fever, an effervescence; and the causes of it
were hidden from him.

He noted, however, that 'a network of associated employers and
federated Trade Unions' was spreading over Great Britain. He noted,
too, that the employers – from indifference, or fearfulness, or greed, he
was not prepared to commit himself as to the exact reason – were unwilling to meet their men half-way: something was sadly amiss with the
upper classes. But for an elaboration of this latter discovery we must
turn to a more partial observer. It was in 1913 that Mr Ramsay Mac-
Donald published *The Social Unrest*, a little essay which expressed both
a veneration for aristocracy and a hatred for the *parvenu*, and which
leaves one uncertain whether its author was a Tory with Socialist
leanings or a Socialist with a Tory imagination – an uncertainty which is
increased rather than diminished by one's knowledge that, at the time,
he was the leader of the Labour Party. 'The age of the financier had
come,' wrote Mr MacDonald, reviewing the past few years. '. . . The
rich – gathered from all quarters of the earth, from American millionaires
seeking vainglories that a republic could not offer, to the scum of the
earth which possessed itself of gold in the gutters of the Johannesburg
market-place – received the homage of every dignitary in society. To
the drawing-rooms and into the families of the ancient aristocracy, as
to the Parliament of the people, they bought their way.' Such people 'did
not command the moral respect which tones down class hatreds, nor the

intellectual respect which preserves a sense of equality even under a régime of considerable social differences, nor even the commercial respect which recognizes obligation to great wealth fairly earned'. This was certainly unfortunate, since 'the sentiment of "respect",' in Mr MacDonald's opinion, 'has often enough been subversive to the State, but that it corresponds to real instincts in the human mind cannot be denied'. (*The Social Unrest*, by J. Ramsay MacDonald, pp. 36–38.) The lamentations of Mr MacDonald are supported by Mr Stephen McKenna who, in the pages of his *While I Remember*, remembers from time to time the sad effects upon society of the invasion of industrial millionaires and Rand magnates and Jews and American heiresses, who found their way into the most sacred enclosures of Cowes, Ascot, and Covent Garden. And there is one more consideration. The reader who goes through the bound volumes of *Punch* will suddenly find himself arrested, in the most startling way, as he passes from 1913 to 1914. He will seem to have moved from a world in which there lingers some of the enchantment of antiquity, and where – could he be carried back there today – he would be a perfect stranger. The clothes, the furniture, the talk already bear the impress of history; and upon the physiognomy itself there is that timeless look which one encounters, with equal certainty, in an indifferent eighteenth-century portrait or the lovely faces that dream from the walls of Chartres. 1913 has slipped into the past. But 1914? It remains for *Punch*, which has always shared with the late Queen Victoria a profound response to the moods of the English middle classes, to record, by a kind of instinct, an extraordinary change. It is not merely the 'plus fours', the one piece bathing suits, the low lean automobiles; nor yet the recognizable dialogue in the pleasant little stories: there is something in the facial expression which – there is no denying it – is oddly contemporary. You begin to ask yourself what scene this is that you have wandered into. It is not very different from our own, only fresher and more fortunate. And at last you feel an extraordinary gratitude to that group of humorous artists, which, working under an editorial system of unparalleled efficiency, had made itself so sensitive to the changing times. For you have had an experience–not unpleasant – of intellectual midwifery. You have been assisting at the birth of a new world.

The social history of the last pre-war years cannot be written yet. The memoirs of that time – such as they are – have a certain diffidence. One can turn the pages of Lady Asquith or Lady Rhondda or the

Princess of Pless or Sir Almeric Fitzroy or Mr Blunt or Lady Keeble or of any one of a hundred raconteurs and diarists and still receive no lasting impression of the truth. Nor is there much consolation to be had from the society magazines of the time; nor yet from the brittle pages of fading newspapers. The facts are important, but the impressions are fugitive and unreal. The intimate correspondence of eminent people is still, for the most part, unpublished; and documents of incalculable importance lie in heaven alone knows what domestic archives, waiting for the day when they can be used with safety. But what an exciting day that will be, when it comes! The chief actors in the drama are, in some cases, still very much alive, and the social historian has to wait until they are no longer able to trouble him with libel suits or confound him with eye-witness accounts: then, and only then, can he make them live. Facts are not the only, nor the most important, consideration with him. Social history, like history itself, is a combination of taste, imagination, science, and scholarship; it reconciles incompatibles, it balances probabilities; and at last it attains the reality of fiction, which is the highest reality of all. At present one can only say that pre-war society was changing in a remarkable manner: one can detect, in that confusing assembly of dances and night clubs and extravagance and vulgarity and emancipation, some evidences of death and of rebirth.

Rebirth. There is the sign-post, pointing the way to that yet undiscovered reality. It is customary to think of that society as a doomed thing, calling in the traditional doomed manner 'for madder music and for stronger wine', and plunged at last, with no time to say its prayers, into the horrors of war. The scene may even be given some of the qualities of a pre-Raphaelite canvas. The sky is massed with tall black clouds; but one last shaft of sunlight, intolerably bright, picks out every detail of leaf and grass; and in the midst of it those little figures go through their paces with the momentary precision of a dream. There is, too, a satisfying irony in this: the spectator knows what is going to happen, the actors do not; they are almost in the happy condition of Oedipus and Jocasta, before the news arrived which made the unhappy gentleman remove his eyes. And the conception is, above all, a convenient one. It is easier to think of Imperial England, beribboned and bestarred and splendid, living in majestic profusion up till the very moment of war. Such indeed was its appearance, the appearance of a somewhat decadent Empire and a careless democracy. But I do not think that its social history will be written on these terms. As has already been shown in the activities of politicians, and women, and workers, there was a new energy which leavened the whole lump of society from top to bottom. You can see this energy flitting, in 1914, across the faces of those middle class people, as they are portrayed by the ingenious pencil of *Punch*; and you believe that you can hear it, winding its discordant horn amidst the costly merriment of the upper classes. And you know that the abandonment of respectable punctilios and worn conventions, which was such a feature of society after the war, had already begun before the war. It is worth repeating once again that it was not death which gave Imperial England such a disturbing appearance in the spring and summer of 1914: it was life.

It is time to return to the meditations of Mr Ramsay MacDonald. The Unrest, he said, was 'peculiarly liable to sink into an angry class conflict' and society, in its new plutocratic form, was 'unprotected against such an attack'. If, given these premises, one were to follow Mr MacDonald's argument to its logical conclusion, it would appear that under a different régime – the régime, say, of Mr Lloyd George's hated Dukes – the English worker would never have entertained so low a sentiment as class hatred, or, if he had, would speedily have been cured of it. This conclusion may have been true, though it hardly applied to the Social Unrest of 1910–14; and, in any case, its appearance in Mr MacDonald's book must have produced a disturbing effect upon the Socialistic conscience of some of his followers. Class hatred existed; it was one of the chief features of the Unrest. No doubt the behaviour of a handful of plutocrats was an irritant; no doubt the inhuman system, which brought those plutocrats into being, was much to blame: but what was the element in this hatred which so bewildered Sir George Askwith and which seems to have eluded the grasp of Mr MacDonald? Could it be that the worker – like the plutocrat and his satellites – was overturning the conventions and punctilios of *his* world? that the energies of rich man and poor man ran, not counter, but parallel? Wherever one looks in the history of the strike years, the worker's conscious assault upon capitalism seems to have been reinforced by an unconscious rebellion against himself. It was the Trade Union leaders, and the members of the parliamentary Labour Party – his own creations, his own particular symbols of law and order – against whom he turned; as though, by denying that 'sentiment of respect' which 'corresponds to real instincts in the human mind', he was at last permitting himself to come alive.

II

Certainly the Triple Alliance of miners, railwaymen, and transport workers was the result of agitation among the rank and file of the Trade Unions. The Trade Union Congress, left to itself, would never have forged so potent a weapon. There remained the question of when and how the weapon would be used.

If we could borrow the wings of imagination, and hover among the various departments of the Board of Trade, during the first seven months of 1914, we should probably observe an expression of considerable uneasiness upon the more responsible faces there. Between January and July there were no less than 937 strikes. The origins of most of them were extremely obscure, and even unreasonable. Perhaps – though of this we cannot be sure – the senior officials of the Board of Trade were struck by the singular resemblance between the swiftness of these small strikes and the tactics of Syndicalism; but if they were, they doubtless comforted themselves with the reflection that the British worker cared nothing for the philosophy of M. Sorel. Had not Mr MacDonald dismissed the whole question with his comment upon 'a temporary toying with syndicalism, not as movement, but as a temper'? How true this was! And yet there was something rather ominous about that word 'temper'. The philosophy of M. Sorel, after all, was based upon the *élan vital* of M. Bergson, and, whatever else one might or might not say of the strikes of 1914, they certainly showed an inconvenient amount of *élan vital*. Could the workers possibly be getting themselves into the mood for a General Strike?

It might be possible to exorcise from the strike statistics, as they came in month by month, the spectre of that troublesome French philosopher, but not the spectre of the Triple Alliance. Here was something ready to materialize on the slightest provocation, as soon as the workers' 'temper' was sufficiently aroused. Indeed, quite apart from the general irritation in the country, the three allies had reason enough already to start their strike. In the first place, the Trade Unions Act of 1913, which the Cabinet had produced only after a severe internal struggle, gave the Unions the anomalous position of outlaws upon whom the law could no longer revenge itself; and, while it removed from their shoulders the burden of the Osborne Judgement, yet contrived to do so with an air of condescension and unwillingness which was, to say the least of it, provocative. And then each separate ally had his grievances. The miner could not forget that his great strike of 1912 had ended only in the establishment of a principle: the minimum wage was trembling like a ripe fruit on its stalk, and another shaking was necessary before it would fall. And he was forever reminding himself that when strikes or legislation raised the charges upon coal getting, it was the consumer who had to pay, and pay in a manner which guaranteed the owners a profit of several hundred per cent. Nor were such incidents as that of the Senghenydd mine likely to soften his sense of injustice. In October 1913, the mine exploded, with a loss of 439 lives. It had long been known as a 'fiery' mine, but neither the provisions of the Coal Mines Act, nor a circular from the Home Office, had made much impression on its manager. There was no apparatus for reversing the current of air, nor for dealing properly with coal dust; the electric signalling wires, on the covering of which the Home Office was particularly insistent, had been left uncovered. Prosecuted before the local magistrates on seventeen different counts, the manager was fined exactly £22! 'Miners lives at 1s. 1¼d. each' said the district Labour paper; and it was true. If legislation could do no better than this, it was clear that the Government needed another lesson, for many other mines were hardly better protected.

The railwaymen's grievances were chiefly concerned with Union questions. In spite of their strike of 1911, as a result of which the railway Unions had been virtually 'recognized', their employers were behaving in a most vindictive manner. 'A series of dismissals and punishments on one of our chief railways,' wrote Mr MacDonald in *The Social Unrest*, made it abundantly clear:

'that someone in authority is punishing men for the offence of being active Trade Unionists. A day porter is degraded permanently because some luggage is delayed, though it has been proved that he was not responsible; another is suspended because he cannot perform duties given to him by two independent foremen at the same time and because he asked for his usual supper-hour; men interfered with in their usual work are accused of trivial offences against those who interfere with them, and are dismissed; in violation of the terms which ended the strike, unionists are not advanced when vacancies take place, and non-unionists are promoted over their heads; accusations of theft proved to have been false, are made and the accused dismissed; certain men have not been paid their usual advances in wages and others are being paid less than colleagues employed at exactly the same work and having exactly the same qualifications; unexplained dismissals and degradations are taking place. In every case the victims of this policy are members of their Union. Who can wonder that unrest is spreading and that there are rumours of fresh troubles passing up and down the railways? Men are being goaded into revolt' (p. 46).

The strike of 1911, moreover, had cost the Companies some £1,000,000 in increased wages; whereupon the Companies had announced their intention of raising merchandise rates by 4 per cent and passenger rates by 5 per cent – thus assuring themselves an additional annual income of £2,000,000.

As for the third member of the Alliance, the National Transport Workers' Federation, it was still smarting over its inability, through lack of funds, to support the London strike of 1912. It was from the ports, with their natural disposition to strike, their growing armies of unskilled and insubordinate workers, and their endless variety of possible grievances, that the Federation drew its strength. And the influence of Jim Larkin had moved, like a spirit troubling the waters, over every pool of casual labour in every port in England. The transport workers, clearly, were in no pacific mood.

Such was the condition of the Triple Alliance. Its leaders, urged forward by specific grievances and by that nameless agitation which – to the consternation of the Board of Trade – appeared to be spreading through all the districts of Great Britain, were standing with characteristic reluctance on the edge of a precipice. At the bottom of that precipice lay a General Strike. It remained to be seen whose hand would push them over.

By July 1914, it became very apparent that hands would not be lacking. There were disputes in the London building trade and electrical industry. The Marine Engineers' Union was in a state of ferment. The shipbuilding and engineering trades were demanding an eight hour day. The engineers and boilermakers were engaged in a complicated battle with the Great Western Railway. The General Labourers' Union was moving for shorter hours, increased wages, and improved conditions. And from one and all, says Sir George Askwith, there rose and increased the alarming cry of 'Wait till Autumn'.

Sir George's worries were emphasized, in a very significant manner,

by a direct action strike, in a Government department, without the
sanction of labour authority. On 4th July, the munition workers of
Woolwich Arsenal downed tools over the dismissal of a single workman.
The affair could be adjusted no doubt – it actually was *not* adjusted until
the very outbreak of war – but Sir George could not help feeling that it
had arrived at a very inopportune moment. There was that trouble in
Serbia. True, it might come to nothing – probably *would* come to
nothing – but it was just as well for one's munition workers not to
choose this particular moment for ceasing work. He recollected the
rather too anxious interest which, for the past year, Prince Metternich
and Baron Marschall von Bieberstein had shown in the progress of the
Unrest. He had told them, not long before, that none of the strikes was
'anti-governmental', but neither the Baron nor the Prince had seemed
particularly convinced. Indeed, as he settled down to the difficult task
of pacifying the munition workers, it occurred to him that, of all the
German diplomats, only Prince Lichnowsky, the Ambassador, had
remained indifferent to the course of the strikes. But Prince Lichnowsky,
as it afterwards transpired, was a victim of that powerful delusion
known as Anglophilia.

And now the leaders of the Triple Alliance, balancing so precariously
upon the edge of their precipice, began to totter, to sway forward. . . .
And the hand that urged them from behind was that of the Scottish
coal-owners. In July, the coal-owners declared that they could no longer
pay their district minimum day-wage of 7s. – that they would be obliged
to reduce it, in most localities, to 6s. To the miners' rank and file this was
the final challenge. It was evident that the Miners' Federation of Great
Britain would take issue with the Scottish coal-owners; that the transport workers and railwaymen would join in; and that – in September or,
at latest, October – there would be an appalling national struggle over
the question of the living wage.

III

The great General Strike of 1914, forestalled by some bullets at Sarajevo
has slipped away into the limbo of unfinished arguments. But there is a
certain fascination in pursuing it thither and watching it perform, after
the manner of Barrie's *Dear Brutus*, a fantastical drama of the might have
been. The spirit of the workers in 1914 has never since been equalled.
In the past four years, their Trade Union membership had increased

from 2,369,067 to 3,918,809; and the same energy which (with the unwitting assistance of the National Insurance Act) had swept them into the Unions, now filled them with enthusiasm for the struggle ahead. The employers, on their side, were equally determined. Never again would they listen to the persuasions of Sir George Askwith. Like Mr Redmond, they had reached 'the extremest limits of concession', and, rather than agree to a national minimum wage, were ready and even willing to fight to the death. As for the Government, it had gone as far as it could go – that is to say, it had lost the confidence of both parties; nothing remained for it but the melancholy duty of keeping order.

But could it keep order? In this respect, it was fortunate in its Home Secretary; that *entraînement* which carried Mr Churchill away whenever there was a chance of employing soldiers was not likely to possess Mr McKenna. But soldiers, sooner or later, would have to be used; for democratic governments are, strange to say, always on the side of the employers, employers are solicitous for their property, and property is safer when ringed about with bayonets than it is behind barbed wire or police. The strikers would inevitably have been either starved or shot into submission – except for one thing, and that is the coincidence of their activities with those of a Civil War in Ireland. In that case the shooting would be heavier and the submission longer delayed; for though the TUC had abandoned Mr Larkin in 1913, the workers as a whole had a fondness for him, as they had for Mr Connolly, and – should Orange Ireland and Nationalist Ireland come to blows – the followers of both Larkin and Connolly would be prominent in the Nationalist ranks. And if the cause of the minimum wage were mingled with the cause of Home Rule; if bloodshed on one side of the Irish Channel were supported by revolution on the other. . . .

History has supplied the premises, and if the propositions to be discovered at the end of them are fantastic, at least they have the merit of being logical. They had already occurred, it would seem, to Prince Metternich and Baron Marschall von Bieberstein and their superiors in the Wilhelmstrasse; they had occurred to Sir George Askwith; Mr Lloyd George touched upon them in a speech which he made to the bankers on 17th July. A conflict between Capital and Labour (before which that tired General Strike of 1926 pales into insignificance) could not be averted. The only question that remained was this – could anything possibly be done to prevent a Civil War in Ireland?

Chapter Five

Sarajevo

I

SINCE, when war was declared, the Scottish mine-owners withdrew their demand for a reduction, and the Triple Alliance suddenly forgot about the minimum wage, and labour and capital joined hands in a frenzy of patriotic enthusiasm, and the Prince and the Baron and the Wilhelmstrasse were utterly crestfallen – it will be seen that the limbo into which the General Strike of 1914 has vanished is about as remote as the limbo of Milton and about as fantastic as the limbo of Pope. Moreover if the public had been aware of an approaching industrial catastrophe, if the situation had been presented, with all its implications, in the most forcible language, and in every newspaper, it is doubtful – even then – if there would have been a great deal of alarm.

The public was now so accustomed to thrills – from motor-cars and aeroplanes to the cinematograph, ragtime, and the menace of Germany – that, so far from bothering its head about a national stoppage, it declined to take even the palpable prospects of an Irish Civil War with any sort of seriousness. Civil War was a game, it was a dangerous and exciting game, in which Sir Edward Carson, with his 30,000 Larne rifles and his 3,000,000 rounds of ammunition and his £1,000,000 war chest was threatening . . . whom? The Irish Nationalists? The Government? Or the British public? Nobody seemed to care.

Indeed the confusions of 1914 are hardly more curious than the detachment of the public. The loudest cries, the most lamentable predictions, failed to arouse in its bosom any stronger emotion than one of pleasant excitement. 'The public', of course, is a brittle expression which, the moment one examines it, offers to break into numberless fragments—

> *Quicquid agunt homines – votum precor, ira, voluptas,*
> *Gaudia discursus. . . .*

These are its parts – these conflicting desires and incompatible emotions:

'Public' is a very chimera among words. Perhaps it signifies nothing more than a nation caught off its guard, like a human face asleep. Then its odd jumble of features – its political creeds, its various classes, its different moralities – are momentarily composed into an appearance of unity. And it was in some kind of a sleep that the great British public put forth those mysterious energies which, by the end of 1913, had effectually destroyed its old-fashioned respectability, and which now threatened to hurl it into domestic chaos. A prey to excitement and to lethargy, now frivolous, now flaccid, it resembled, in 1914, a man who is approaching a nervous breakdown; it turned towards everything but reality. But when it came face to face with reality – with reality in its simplest and most terrible form – it accepted it with a vigour which still surprises one, pursued it with fortitude, and retains to this very day a sanity which seems to have been denied the other nations of the world. Such has been the effect of the Three Rebellions.

II

It is not to be supposed, therefore, that the manoeuvres of Mr Redmond excited any attention whatsoever. For the whole of May that unhappy gentleman, with the reluctant assistance of Mr Dillon, forced himself gradually and painfully upon the Nationalist Volunteers. The question at issue was whether the Provisional Committee of twenty-six, controlled by MacNeill and Casement, should suffer the addition of twenty-five members, all satellites of Redmond. Week after week, MacNeill and Casement wriggled in the grasp of their opponent. They accused him of withholding money; they swore that he was diverting arms from Southern Ireland to the Hibernians in the North; they threatened, they flattered, they cajoled. But it was of no use. In June, at length, they admitted defeat. Without Redmond's leadership, they had to agree, the Nationalist army would break into two. In private, however, their thoughts were less direct; they had already matured their plans for a gun-running of their own, on the principle that 'those who provided the arms would control the Volunteers': and of this Redmond was ignorant.

If it is true that only an Irishman of genius will ever write an acceptable life of Swift – (and who else could interpret the author of *The Drapier's Letters* and *A Modest Proposal?*) – it is equally true that no one but an Irishman of genius can do justice to Mr Redmond. These two biographies have an extraordinary, an opposite fascination: the mystery of character in the one is balanced by the mystery of circumstance in the other. It is true that Mr Redmond does not lend himself to biography; he was reserved and correct, he was unimaginative, he was uninspiring. But the Ireland whose leader he tried to be! The Ireland whose various spirit – renascent, violent, romantic – mocked his efforts, as it might have mocked even those of a Parnell!

It was melancholy indeed that his last few years should have been spent adventuring in such a country; that the spiritual exile in Westminster should have been forced to return home. But the Volunteers were, after all, the realities of this new Ireland, beckoning him back; and he could not resist. His subsequent adventures, when they come to be told in full, will have the mingling qualities of tragedy and fairy tale: and the scene will be populated with figures, some of them very noble, some of them very singular, and all repaying investigation.

It was useless for him to count up on his fingers the number of political parties represented in the Volunteers, to weigh the influence of one against the influence of another, and the influence of all against his own. For who could reckon the weight of the Abbey Theatre, of the Gaelic League, of Yeats's lyrics? Who could positively declare that a play like *Thomas Muskerry* or *The Shuiler's Children* had not at least as much reality as a rank of Volunteers? or that the immortal voice of a non-political poet did not count for more than all the clamour of the Irish benches? It was the Irish Revival which Mr Redmond had to deal with, for Ireland is one of the few countries – perhaps the last – where the boundaries between politics and art have never been fixed. The last days of Mr Redmond became the first days of Mr Redmond's country, and the biographer who re-creates them – with all that is fascinating in them, all that is fatal, eccentric, singular, sordid, passionate – will have written a great book. Nor is the central figure, perhaps, so unamenable. Behind that grave and cold exterior one sometimes catches a glimpse – a momentary glimpse – of mysterious passions, of vaulting ambitions and human jealousies. And then, too, his end was a tragic one. He died towards the close of war, in the full knowledge that Home Rule was a dead thing; his death was hastened by the furies of Sinn Fein and the hideous mistakes of his former allies in the Government: he had been forced to resign his presidency of the Volunteers, and the high destiny which he had once foreseen for himself as Ireland's parliamentary leader descended to that cold doom which was Parnell's. He died in humiliation and defeat; perhaps of a broken heart.

Such was the end of the man who, in June 1914, imposed the prestige of his leadership upon the Nationalist Volunteers. At first he was far more highly thought of in English political circles. He was Carson's equal now: he had but to lift his hand and – there might be an end of Carsonism. But Mr Redmond, unfortunately, could not play the rôle of a militarist; as the days passed, it became clear that he would keep his inconvenient warriors in control for as long as he could. The Liberals may have been thankful for this attitude, but it was not in them to respect it.

For the better part of June and July, there was a good deal of what Mr Asquith had once described as 'reckless rhodomontade' from Orange pulpits and Nationalist platforms; Protestant bishops and Presbyterian dignitaries went about blessing Ulster flags with exemplary *sang-froid*; and in certain border counties the Volunteers of either side shared drill grounds and targets, without relaxing for an instant their eager desire to assassinate one another in the event of war. On 23rd June Mr Asquith's Amending Bill – which proved to be nothing more than his March proposal for county option – went up to the Lords and was immediately pounced upon by Lords Milner and Lansdowne, while Earl Roberts took occasion to remark that any attempt to coerce Ulster would result in the utter ruin of the Army. But these were just preliminaries. It was when the Bill came into Committee that some of the Conservative 'wild men', it was feared – Lord Willoughby de Broke, for instance – would give vent to language of such ferocity as to force the rival armies into battle then and there. And the Bill was, at the most, nothing more than a feeble brake, to keep the Constitution from crashing immediately downhill into ruin. Were there other expedients? Could some stout shoulder, at this last minute, push it back into safety?

There was the Speaker, there was Lord Murray of Elibank, and the Archbishop of Canterbury. The Speaker tried, in vain, to get Carson and Redmond to meet in his library. In vain Lord Murray went nimbly between the parties, now threatening Mr Redmond – 'He informed me,' Mr Redmond noted at the end of their first interview, 'that Lord Northcliffe, the editor of *The Times*, the political editor of the *Daily Mail*, and a number of other journalists, started this morning [30th June] for Ulster, and that he is very uneasy, as he does not understand what this move means' – now bringing offers from Carson and Bonar

Law. They were (1) Ulster's right to vote her exclusion every six years; (2) Sir Edward's promise to attend the opening of the first Irish Parliament. But Mr Redmond found even the latter proposal insufficient. As for the Archbishop, he was much disturbed by the hardness of Carson's heart; but what really distressed him was the softness of the Prime Minister's. He complained to the King's secretary of Mr Asquith's 'serene optimism' and 'pulseless attitude'. But alas he was not the man to play Bossuet to Mr Asquith's Fénélon, and even a sad letter from the King failed to disturb the unruffled weariness of Number 10 Downing Street.

It was into the midst of these rather desperate interviews that news arrived – on Monday, 29th June – of that successful murder in Sarajevo the day before. The slain Archduke Franz Ferdinand loved to slaughter game, and in the basement of his Bohemian castle he had gathered, for one reason or another, the world's largest collection of statues of St George; of his other tastes and characteristics little was known. But he was an intimate of the German Emperor, and a fortnight before, among the roses of Konopischt, they had pledged their friendship. The crime that June morning of a printer's devil and a schoolboy stripped off the diplomatic covering, and laid bare certain iron facts to the eyes of the world. (*The People's King*, by John Buchan, p. 84.) Among the world's eyes, however, could not be included those of Sir Edward Carson and Mr Redmond, who concentrated their gaze upon each other with an unrelenting severity. Mr Lloyd George's vision was also impaired. As late as 17th July, he was able to say to a group of bankers at the Guildhall – 'In the matter of external affairs the sky has never been more perfectly blue.' And the bankers were not displeased.

III

The story of Sarajevo entered, with a more ironical precision, upon a very different meeting. On Saturday, 27th June, there were great festivities at Kiel, where the German and English fleets lay side by side, with the Kaiser in the midst of them. There had been races and salutes and fraternal strolls; and banquets in which ward-room after ward-room had risen to the toast of 'Friends now, friends forever'. The next day, hearing that his friend of the Konopischt roses was no more, the Kaiser fled the scene. But that evening the two fleets prepared to renew their friendship, with all the circumstance of an old and fated world.

As far as we are concerned, those dinners can be left untasted; the sun has gone down upon the last of many pageants, and the few days that are left will be dark, aimless, and bitter. Now the gracious, the terrible twilight absorbs, minute by minute, the low German coast, and seems, in the mind's eye, to creep reluctantly westward. It has passed the never peaceful, the shallow grey North Sea. It covers Lindisfarne, and fingers the rocks of Bamburgh, and Warkworth keep, and the headlands at Tynemouth; at Whitby the lovely ruined abbey is folded up; the crumbling cliffs of Southwold go under before it; it webs with mist and darkness the Essex flats. In one minute it has travelled everywhere inland, from north to south. It is already staining the long Atlantic waves; it crosses the Irish Channel, and invades the haunted seas above. And now the half light fades away altogether, and on the splendour of Imperial England there falls, at last and forever, an inextinguishable dark.

Chapter Six

Buckingham Palace
to Bachelor's Walk

I

In the month that was left them of world peace the politicians contrived to throw the domestic affairs of England into such extreme disorder that nobody made much pretence any more of being able to correct it. A war between Irishmen, backed on the one side by the Government, on the other by the Opposition, had infamous possibilities; and one might have thought that, in the year of grace 1914, the hand of any Cabinet, however feeble, would have stretched itself forth and hurled one final thunderbolt in the name of decency and common sense. For one short moment, indeed, the clouds seemed to gather, there was a pale flicker of lightning; and then the skies cleared, and the familiar, serene incompetence reasserted itself.

The words of Lords Milner, Lansdowne, and Roberts conjured from the obscurity of his land campaign, like a genie from a bottle, the figure of Mr Lloyd George. And like a genie, whose size is purely a matter of emotion, Mr George began visibly to swell. He assumed the proportions of his Budget days – those happy days when Dukes were 'prancing proconsuls' and it could be said of noble families that 'the older they get the higher they get', like cheese. He told Mr T. P. O'Connor that Asquith was compromising altogether too far. At this suggestion of Cabinet opposition to the Amending Bill, Mr O'Connor was filled with joy, but it was a very short-lived joy: for almost in the same breath Mr George remarked, unhappily, that he did not think the King would sign one Bill without the other. And with this remark he began to shrink, his tremendous shape collapsed, he disappeared into his bottle. Within a few days he was once again instructing an indifferent country on the habits of pheasants and the wickedness of landlords.

Lord Murray and the Archbishop also gave up their attempts at intervention. Only Mr Asquith remained, still smiling, still at the helm, and still – with the rocks now just ahead – turning it gently in the wrong direction. He rather thought that a few more concessions – that Ulster, for instance, should be given a perpetual option to exclude herself – would settle the business. He dismissed with a sigh the simple fact that one more concession from Redmond would set the Nationalist Volunteers in an uproar. Such intemperate people! It would not have set *him* in an uproar. And then there was that pitiful Amending Bill of his – still among the Lords. Something might come of that – he could not be sure – one must wait and see.

Over Ireland, as over central Europe, there hung a silence. Not a shot was fired. But the proclamation of the Ulster Provisional Government, and Sir Edward's progress to Belfast on 12th July, were so provocative and so royal that the Cabinet turned in despair towards the Throne. The movement, a weak one at any time, was rendered even weaker by the fact that during the past six months the King's name had been bandied to and fro, among the extremists of either party, in a manner the scurrility of which was only balanced by its total lack of common sense. To the Tories George V was a 'cipher'; to the Liberals a 'kind of second-lieutenant to Bonar Law'. During the Curragh mutiny, both sides had accused him of favouring the other; the backstairs of Buckingham Palace had been freely populated by rumour with seditious generals and whispering Nationalists; his movements had been questioned in Parliament: such were the results of His Majesty's efforts – and they had been persistent efforts – to keep the peace. If he intervened now, he would lose what little remained to him of a never very noticeable popularity. But the Cabinet was dauntless.

'16th July. It has been decided,' Mr Asquith wrote in his Diary, 'that I should advise the King to intervene with the object of securing a pacific accommodation, through a conference of the representatives of all parties concerned – both British and Irish.

'17th July. I found the King in a tent in the garden. He was full of interest about the Conference, and made the really good suggestion that the Speaker should preside.'

And in a letter to the Prime Minister, dated 18th July, the King concluded: 'I shall feel confident that . . . a great advance will be made towards a friendly understanding which please God may result in averting the dangers which threaten the welfare not only of the United Kingdom but of my whole Empire.'

The Lords, therefore, postponed their debate on the Amending Bill, and on Tuesday, 21st July, the Conference assembled at Buckingham Palace – for the Government, Messrs Asquith and Lloyd George; for the Tories, Mr Bonar Law and Lord Lansdowne; for Ulster, Sir Edward Carson and Captain Craig; for the Nationalists, Mr Redmond and Mr Dillon. The meeting was held in the large Council Room which overlooks the Palace gardens, and the King, who appeared to be nervous and unhappy, opened its proceedings as follows:

'Gentlemen:

'It is with feelings of satisfaction and hopefulness that I receive you here today, and I thank you for the manner in which you have responded to my summons....

'For months we have watched with deep misgivings the course of events in Ireland. The trend has been surely and steadily towards an appeal to force, and today the cry of civil war is on the lips of the most responsible and sober-minded of my people.... Your responsibilities are indeed great. The time is short. You will, I know, employ it to the fullest advantage, and be patient, earnest and conciliatory in view of the magnitude of the interests at stake. I pray that God in His infinite wisdom may guide your deliberations so that they may result in the joy of peace and honourable settlement.'

This speech, having unfortunately been published, was received with a storm of abuse from the Liberal press. Upon what lips was the cry of Civil War to be heard, if not upon Unionist lips? The Unionists, then, in His Majesty's opinion were 'the most responsible and sober-minded of my people'. And what could this mean, pray, except that George V was openly inclining to the Tory cause? These arguments were reinforced in a striking manner by Mr Keir Hardie who set forth his views in the *Labour Leader*. They were of a somewhat more comprehensive nature than those of the Liberal papers, for Mr Hardie was piqued at the Labour Party's exclusion from the Conference: the King had now 'cast in his lot with the reactionary peers and the rebellious Ulsterites'; the 'royal crowd' had been visiting the workers of Merthyr and other industrial centres during the past two years for the purpose of 'riveting the chains of their iron rule more firmly upon them'; and this was intolerable because, had George V been born into the working classes, he would undoubtedly have become a street corner loafer. 'But Democracy,' was Mr Hardie's dark conclusion, 'will accept the challenge.'

As for the Conference, it followed in a reverse direction His Majesty's advice of employing its time 'to the fullest advantage'. The vital question was this – should Ulster be excluded simply for a period of years, or should it be excluded forever? But Mr Redmond could not bear to face immediately a problem which, if its solution went against him, would saddle him ever afterwards with the crime of having partitioned Ireland. He protested that an area to be excluded must first be decided upon; his opponents agreed; and it was on this interesting but secondary issue that the Conference expended the rest of its time.

Two considerations presented themselves. Should Ulster in its present shape be taken as the proper area? or should only those counties be excluded which were predominantly Protestant? The former alternative clearly favoured Mr Redmond, for the whole of Ulster could not be excluded forever; but the mere idea of depriving the northern Nationalists, even for a year or two, of their rights under Home Rule was too much for him. He proposed county option. Under that scheme, he thought, the counties of Down, Derry, Antrim and Armagh, and the Borough of Belfast, would vote to keep themselves in the Union; the counties of Cavan, Donegal, Fermanagh, Monaghan, Tyrone, and the Borough of Derry, would ask to be included in the rest of Ireland. In the four excluded counties, there were 293,000 Catholics, while the five included counties contained only 179,000 Protestants. Obviously Sir Edward and the Unionists, so Mr Redmond argued, would gain by this division. But Sir Edward and the Unionists had hitherto looked at the question of county option backwards and sideways and upside down: they had never encountered it face to face. Four counties for five? It was impossible. They refused to have anything to do with it.

On the 22nd, the Conference tried to break up, and was only prevented by the forceful tact of the Speaker. It lingered for two days more, and gradually reduced its differences to a point where – if only a suitable boundary line could be drawn through the County of Tyrone – it could proceed to the vital discussion of permanent or temporary exclusion. But the line was never drawn, for the fair faces of 'Protestant' Tyrone and 'Catholic' Tyrone were liberally pock-marked, the one with Catholic, the other with Protestant communities. Only an earthquake or a general conversion could have settled the problem: and the sorrows of the Conference were due to the fact that it was attempting to decide by Act of Parliament what could only be effected by act of God.

From these futile deliberations the spirit of Ireland alone seems to have emerged with any credit. Both Nationalist and Orange leaders had pursued it, like some tall stag, through the complexities of the last four years, and had brought it to bay at last in the middle of Tyrone. Yes, it was a stag, antlered and gallant. It planted its feet in the soil of Tyrone, it lowered its head, it invited them to tear it in pieces. And they crept away.

On the morning of 24th July, the Conference broke up. One by one the members went in for an audience with the King. Mr Redmond was particularly impressed by his reception: the worried man, whom he was meeting for the first time, protested – with an agitation which could not be suspected – that he sympathized with the Nationalists just as much as with the Unionists, that he was a constitutional monarch, and that the welfare of Ireland was all that he cared about. As the members prepared to leave, Mr Redmond made a last, a rather lovely gesture. He went up to Carson and asked him 'to have a good shake-hands for the sake of the old days together on the Circuit'. And Carson could not refuse.

There was literally nothing left now but an appeal to force. How long could the Civil War be delayed? Would it wait until the Amending Bill had been dealt with? All afternoon the Cabinet sat, surveying the hopeless prospect. It was about to separate, wrote Winston Churchill,

'when the quiet grave tones of Sir Edward Grey's voice were heard, reading a document which had just been brought him from the Foreign Office. . . . He had been reading or speaking for several minutes before I could separate my mind from the tedious and bewildering debate which had just closed . . . but gradually as the sentences followed one another, impressions of a wholly different character began to form in my mind. . . . The parishes of Tyrone and Fermanagh faded back into the mists and squalls of Ireland, and a strange light began immediately, but by perceptible gradations, to fall and grow upon the map of Europe.'

Just before five o'clock the Cabinet filed into the Commons from behind the Speaker's chair. A dreary debate was coming to a finish on some Housing Bill brought in by Mr Runciman, the President of the Board of Agriculture. The House was full, but not for the pleasure of hearing Mr Runciman's views on the cottages of agricultural labourers: it was waiting to welcome, with the now customary 'scene', Mr Asquith's opinions on the Buckingham Palace Conference. But something on Mr Asquith's face and on the faces of his colleagues – some look of deep solemnity – projected upon those packed benches a corresponding silence. The Speaker put the motion – 'that this House do now adjourn'. The Prime Minister rose to announce that the Conference, having been unable to agree in principle or in detail upon the possibility of defining an area for exclusion from the operations of the Government of Ireland Bill, had brought its meetings to a conclusion. The Government's Amending Bill would be taken the following week. That was all. He pronounced every word in the manner of a man whose thoughts are already occupied with graver things, and his colleagues on the Treasury Bench stared straight ahead of him, as though they could see, shaping themselves above the Opposition's heads, the clouded features of a fearful reality. Reality, indeed, had entered that quarrelsome little narrow chamber, thrusting upon it the first dignity it had known for months. Slowly, very slowly it emptied. Within a short time the details of the Austrian Note to Serbia – whose presence, unheard, unknown, and scarcely guessed at, had just compelled them to peace – were known to the members of the House of Commons.

Surely it was impossible – *now* – for the loyalists of Ulster to carry their Union Jacks into some disintegrating Civil War! But was it? Was anything impossible for the loyalists of Ulster, except – perhaps – loyalty? Mr Asquith told General Macready to return to Belfast and keep the peace, if he could, just a few days longer. The General went back with a heavy heart. He had the utmost contempt for Carsonism and the Provisional Government, but he knew that Sir Edward's game was full of danger, and he feared – as he was afterwards to write – 'lest the blood of the soldiers for whom I was responsible should be shed in a useless encounter with fanatical enthusiasts'.

But another sort of blood was to be shed in Ireland, by British soldiers, and in just two days' time.

II

One April afternoon in 1914, a bearded gentleman, with a haggard and rather beautiful face, stood by a window in Mrs J. R. Green's house in the Grosvenor Road, and stared out at the Thames, where a sunless mist glided on the ebb-tide, and the muddy banks, uncovering themselves, wore the sleekness of fish scales. At such a time the river has a kind of dejected magic; and there was something dejected in the face of Sir Roger Casement as he gazed at it from Mrs Green's windows. Behind him the voices of Eoin MacNeill and Darrell Figgis argued to and fro, until at last 'Let's buy the rifles,' Figgis shouted, 'and so at least get into the problem.' Casement turned gratefully from the window and the Thames. 'That's talking,' he said. And his face was quite radiant.

The situation, as Mr Figgis has outlined it in his *Recollections of the Irish War*, was not very promising. The three conspirators had neither money nor information. Yet if Mr Redmond was not to gain complete control of the Nationalist Volunteers, rifles were necessary: as for money and information, MacNeill, who was to travel to Dublin that night, hoped to get both from a gentleman called The O'Rahilly, chief of an ancient clan, a man of scholarly habit, a clear head, and a romantic temperament, whose obscurity in Irish life Mr Figgis has done little to illuminate. While MacNeill was absent, Figgis and Casement tried to discover how their guns could be transported from Germany to Ireland – if there should ever be any guns to transport. Steamers could only be chartered by Ulstermen with Tory wealth to back them, but at last they lit upon an English publicist named Erskine Childers who was willing to lend his yacht; and then The O'Rahilly – swearing that he had been pursued thither by detectives – arrived in London with information and promises of money. Figgis and Childers set out for Belgium.

The merchants of Liége were expensive and impossible. The O'Rahilly, however, had also mentioned the names of the brothers Magnus of Hamburg, and the brothers Magnus – Michael and Moritz were their names – proved far more accommodating. The German Government – the Larne affair was not two days old, and England must not be irritated – had forbidden any further selling of arms to Irishmen; but the brothers had the practical character of 'their compatriot, St Peter', and when Figgis and Childers represented themselves as two Mexicans, Michael and Moritz confessed that they had a few rifles – about 1,500 all told – lying in a Liége warehouse, which they might be persuaded to sell. While Figgis set about the chartering of a tug – a sadly expensive business, for Crawford and his Tory guineas had been there before – Childers hurried over to Dublin to ratify their arrangements. He returned with exciting news – the rifles were to be landed, in broad daylight, on 26th July, at Dublin's port of Howth.

On the last day of June, as near as he could remember, Figgis was in Liége, where he superintended the packing of his rifles by a number of jocose but ancient men and women, who, having all stripped to the waist for that purpose, presented a singular appearance of withered agility. By 4th July, the whole consignment was put on rail for Hamburg, and on 10th July, after bidding farewell to the agitated Magnuses (whose consciences had been severely pricked by some inquiries on the part of the Hamburg police), Figgis saw his arms on board the tug. At the last minute, however, a new harbour regulation threatened to ruin all his plans: a Customs official would have to examine his cargo before he could leave. Figgis was at his wits' end. Even his character of a wealthy Mexican would hardly account for the presence, not merely of 1,500 rifles, but of case after case of dum-dum bullets which the brothers Magnus had cleverly unloaded upon him. Dum-dum bullets are said to be very effective in stopping the more insensitive kind of savage, but they had long been condemned as inhuman, which indeed they were, being blunt, and more or less tearing their victim in two. But at last, hunting in desperation through the regulations, Figgis discovered a clause which permitted a pilot to act as a Customs official; secured an amenable pilot; bribed him with three English bank notes and a cigar; and set out peacefully with his rifles and his dum-dum bullets for the mouth of the Scheldt.

Here, at midday on 12th July, near a certain lightship, he was to meet Erskine Childers in one yacht and Conor O'Brien in another. Midday came. The tug, rolling in a golden mist, was alone. Hour after hour it slid up and down the tarnished waves, until the mist, lifting, turned to silver; and out of the silver came O'Brien's small black yacht. It was 5.30. They loaded O'Brien with 500 rifles, and as he cast clear and lurched away, Childers' yacht loomed up in the dusk. Childers took the other 1,000 and the ammunition, and this contraband, as it afterwards transpired, he carried comfortably through the whole British Fleet at Spithead. . . .

On 25th July, O'Brien landed his rifles safely at Kilcoole, in County Wicklow, while Figgis cleverly removed HMS *Forward*, lying in Dublin Bay, by spreading abroad the false news that Joseph Devlin's guns were to be landed at midnight near Wexford. (Devlin, Mr Redmond's friend, was endeavouring to run some antiquated Italian rifles, in which, since he had not bothered to provide them with ammunition, he presumably had little faith.) The *Forward* steamed away. By 9.30 on Sunday morning, the 26th, Childers was cruising within sight of Howth Pier and the anxious eyes of Figgis; by 10.40 a force of seven hundred Volunteers, under Bulmer Hobson, had reached Raheny, eight miles away, and was advancing rapidly. At 12.40 the Childers yacht, piloted by Mrs Childers in a bright red jersey, slid alongside the Pier, while Hobson's breathless men came out of Howth on the run, lined up beside the yacht, and burst into tears as the first rifles were brought to light. The coastguards, outnumbered, fired a rocket for the *Forward*. But the *Forward* was far south, hunting Mr Devlin's Italian relics along the coasts of Waterford.

Nothing could have been more punctual. While the Police-Inspector at Howth telephoned to Mr Harrel, his superior in Dublin, the Volunteers set out for that city in triumph. They included, it might be mentioned, both Mr Arthur Griffith, the pacific leader of Sinn Fein, who seems to have undergone a change of heart, and a troop of the Countess Markievicz's Boy Scouts with a trek-cart – which that lady had thoughtfully provided with 150 heavy oak batons, in case the police should be tempted to intervene. But it was not the police who intervened. Owing to a curious misunderstanding between Mr Harrel and Sir James Dougherty, the Under-Secretary at Dublin Castle, a battalion of the King's Own Scottish Borderers was most illegally dispatched to meet and disarm the Volunteers; and the two forces, amateur and professional, came together at the Malahide Road. Exactly what happened afterwards we shall never know, since Hobson and Figgis have both written their accounts in which, quite naturally, each tries to claim the credit for himself, with some consequent damage to the truth. The troops may or may not have fixed bayonets; a Volunteer may or may not have fired his revolver; either Hobson or Figgis or both together engaged Mr Harrel in such a vehement and protracted argument that the men behind them were able to straggle off, by ones and twos, across the Christian Brothers' Park and into Dublin. But one thing is certain – the Volunteers escaped to a man. Angry and empty-handed, the soldiers marched back to their barracks.

As they entered Dublin, they were pursued along the quays by a large crowd, justifiably enraged, and armed with stones and brickbats. Bayonets were fixed, the rearguard was constantly changed to avoid trouble: but the stones and brickbats flew thicker. At last, in Bachelor's Walk, Major Haig ordered his bruised rearguard to block the narrow road; and the rearguard lost its head. It fired, indiscriminately. Three people were killed, and thirty-eight were injured.

In this little spatter of blood and bullets an end was written to the Civil War. Tory rage, Liberal procrastination, and the muddled oratory of Ulster pulpits were to produce . . . three civilian corpses, huddled on the quays of Dublin. The soldiers had fired hastily and without orders; but if ever a slipshod killing deserved to be called a 'massacre', the killing in Bachelor's Walk deserves that name. For comparisons between Larne and Howth are odious and revealing. At Larne, 30,000 Orange rifles were landed while the police and the coastguards and the soldiers slept: at Howth, the landing of 1,500 Nationalist rifles could only be expiated in blood. And the Army, which refused to march against Ulster, had shown no unwillingness to meet the Nationalist Volunteers. Under these circumstances, it matters very little whether three thousand civilians were slaughtered, or three hundred, or thirty, or three: there are stains in Bachelor's Walk which nothing will ever quite wash away.

The news spread through Ireland with extraordinary rapidity; by Monday, 27th July, the Nationalist Army had been increased by almost every unenrolled reservist in the South. The two forces, Nationalist and Orange, swayed perceptibly towards each other, finger on trigger. Mr Redmond, appalled but polite, and parliamentary to the last, demanded the formal adjournment of the House of Commons. On Tuesday, Austria declared war on Serbia. The Foreign Office felt the strings of diplomacy snapping one by one. Mr Churchill prepared to set his Fleet in motion. And Mr Asquith retired, peacefully, amid a litter of Irish maps and statistics, to compose some kind of a speech on his Amending Bill, now obsolete. It was on Thursday, 30th July, while he was engaged in these pursuits, that he received a telephone call from Mr Bonar Law. Would he come to Mr Law's house in Kensington? He would indeed. Mr Law, it appeared, had suddenly been struck by the fateful condition of Europe, and it now occurred to him – about a month too late – that only a united England could exercise a soothing influence upon the fury of Austria and the ambition of Germany. Sir Edward Carson had agreed reluctantly; though in *his* case one is tempted to inquire whether the wrath of Southern Ireland was not more persuasive than the fate of Europe. But the point was that not only Mr Law, from motives of patriotism, but Sir Edward, from motives of convenience, was now prepared to postpone the Amending Bill indefinitely. Mr Redmond was thereupon approached, and he, too, agreed. On 30th July, so far as its leading figures were concerned, the Irish Civil War had yielded to a greater.

Within the next three days the people of England realized that they were to be sucked into the whirlpool of European affairs. The week-end was the meeting of the past and the future. Crowds of Bank Holiday-makers, mingling their gaiety with an almost roseate premonition of horror to come, lingered around the post offices, the telegraph offices, the railway stations. On Sunday, 2nd July, the Cabinet's pacifists began to incline towards war, and the Opposition leaders, hastening into London from their country house parties, wrote a joint letter to the Prime Minister, offering him their support in any move he might feel called upon to make.

So ended the Tory Rebellion.

Could its effect upon Ireland be prevented with the same ease? Could Mr Redmond *still* flatter himself that he exercised an almost planetary influence upon the tides of Irish opinion, that from his lunar sphere in Westminster he could tug them any way he pleased? Sir Edward, possibly, could be sure of Ulster's support in a mere postponement of Home Rule; but the mind of Ulster, compared with that of Southern Ireland, was as easy to read as a child's spelling book.

Sir Edward Grey appeared to be in doubt. On Monday, 3rd August, while explaining to the Commons how it had come about that England's honour was secretly and irrevocably involved, he remarked: 'One thing I would say: the one bright spot in the very dreadful situation is Ireland.' He then returned to his painful task of revealing, for the first time, that private agreement which had left France's northern coasts at the mercy of the German Fleet. Whether Belgium were invaded or not, it became very clear that England would find it a matter of some difficulty to keep out of war: and in the midst of these melancholy prospects the 'bright spot' of Ireland shone with all the penetrating intensity of a complete illusion.

III

John Redmond was no feminist. He even disapproved of women's meddling in politics, though politics had been their playground since the beginning of Western history. Under the circumstances, it is not surprising that he cared little for Margot Asquith, whose interest in politics was, to say the least of it, an extremely personal one. But Mrs Asquith, whatever her faults, has never been accused of backwardness, and on Saturday she had written a little note to Mr Redmond in which she suggested (1) that in a 'great speech' he should offer all his soldiers to the Government, or (2) that he should write and offer them to the King. And Mr Redmond, strange to say, answered that he was 'very grateful' for the letter. 'I hope,' wrote Mr Redmond, 'that I *may* be able to follow your advice.'

Caught up, perhaps, in the dizzying flights of English patriotism, or animated once again, and once again to his cost, by his sense of duty and decency – he did follow, in some measure, Mrs Asquith's advice. That afternoon of the 3rd, as Sir Edward Grey solemnly conjured out of nowhere his 'bright spot' of Ireland, Mr Redmond turned anxiously to an old colleague of his called John Haydon. 'I am thinking of saying something,' he whispered. 'Do you think I ought to?' 'That depends on what you are going to say.' 'I am going to tell them that they can take all their troops out of Ireland, and we will defend the country ourselves.' 'In that case you should certainly speak,' said Mr Haydon.

Grey was on his feet for nearly an hour more; Bonar Law said a few words: and then, in a tense silence, Redmond arose to speak. 'There are in Ireland,' he said, 'two large bodies of Volunteers. One of them sprang into existence in the South. I say to the Government that they may tomorrow withdraw every one of their troops from Ireland. I say that the coasts of Ireland will be defended from foreign invasion by her sons, and for this purpose armed Nationalist Catholics in the South will be only too glad to join arms with the armed Protestant Ulstermen in the North. . . . We offer to the Government of the day that they make take their troops away, and that, if it is allowed us, in comradeship with our brethren in the North, we will ourselves defend the coasts of our country.'

He sat down. The applause, intermittent at first, had grown deafening. Along the packed Tory benches, papers were being waved, and men who had been his bitterest enemies stood up to cheer him. Ireland's leader, the successor of Parnell, had just rendered an enormous service to the British Empire and ruined his own career. For within the next two months the bright spot of Ireland grew dim, and dimmer, and was at last invisible: and the lightnings which succeeded it illuminated the utter disgrace of John Redmond. But the end of John Redmond has fortunately passed beyond the limits of this story. He listened, impassively and without pleasure, to the cheers of the Commons; and afterwards, when an acquaintance – it was Mr P. J. Hooper of the *Freeman's Journal* – congratulated him on providing all of that day's news for the Irish papers, the answer was a significant one. 'How do you think they will take it?' said Mr Redmond.

IV

On the evening of 4th August, Sir Edward Grey 'watching from the windows of the Foreign Office the lights springing out in the dusk, said to a friend, "The lamps are going out all over Europe; we shall not see them lit again in our lifetime." Whatever happened, the world would never be the same again.' (Buchan, p. 98.) It was already no longer the same. A week ago, England had been, or rather had appeared to be, a distracted country, condemned to a feeble and fatal neutrality; now she was a single nation. An almost incredible vigour animated and united every one of her warring particles. Not the least curious was the change which had overtaken Mr Asquith. He was no longer the leader of a pacific Liberal Government and he never would be again; but he was for a little while to be the country's leader. His weariness and fatalism had disappeared, and 'his manner had all that quiet and reliable force which had once appealed to Queen Victoria and consoled the last days of Campbell-Bannerman.

But as the scene changes, and all the conflicts of the past four years flow together into a new energy, one situation stands out. It is very small, very old-fashioned, and it is rightly invested with a little mystery. Was it on 3rd August or 4th August that Mr Bonar Law paid a private visit to Mr Asquith? The situation is one which you examine with much the same interest which you might give to a cobwebbed bottle of debilitated old brandy: the date on it is unimportant, but it would be amusing to know. The imagination, being free to choose, naturally selects 4th August, with the war but a few hours away.

Mr Asquith has simply recorded that Mr Law came to see him, and that he listened to what his former opponent had to say with a scarcely concealed surprise. So the Unionists had not forgotten, even now, their suspicions and their hatreds! He heard Mr Law through with his usual courtesy. Yes, he answered, he had given his promise and he would keep it: Home Rule was indefinitely suspended. That was all. Mr Bonar Law retired. The door of Number 10, Downing Street closed behind him.

His insignificant black Tory figure was swallowed up in the sunlight of Whitehall.

The Lofty Shade

And England over
Advanced the lofty shade.

The lofty shade advances,
I fetch my flute and play:
Come, lads, and learn the dances,
And praise the tune today.
Tomorrow, more's the pity,
Away we both must hie,
To air the ditty,
And to earth I.

A. E. HOUSMAN

I

On 20th September, 1912, a group of men sat at luncheon in Edward Marsh's rooms in London. Their names were Wilfrid Gibson, John Drinkwater, Harold Monro, Arundel del Re, and Rupert Brooke. They were discussing the plans for the first volume of *Georgian Poetry*.

Georgian Poetry 1911–1912, was published in December and made something of a sensation. It was bound in that particular kind of board which falls apart very easily, and most of the poems in it were equally perishable. If you read it now, you are surprised by the thought that in its time it caused a great deal of excitement; that the reading public, enchanted by this group of young or nearly young men who wrote verses of a musical and romantic nature, began to talk of 'The New Elizabethans'. The expression seems a curious one today. One line of Donne is worth the whole collection put together. And yet, as you turn its pages, you are touched by a lingering magic, and you can, with no very great effort of the imagination, transport yourself back through the years and become one of its first readers. Is it, after all, so very difficult to put oneself in the place of people who saw their arrested, their static notions of respectability disintegrate before their eyes; and who scarcely understood what they saw? When codes, when religions, when ideas cease to move forward it is always in some shining illusion that an alarmed humanity attempts to take refuge. History is a constant witness to this – history which, as its final comment on the death of Liberal England, produced, not merely *Georgian Poetry*, but *Georgian Poetry*'s physical embodiment. For the poems are intelligible; they communicate, with a childlike air of mysterious excitement, the most vague and general of emotions – and to a public which had stopped reading poetry, and which needed to read poetry, that meant a great deal. And then they contain the work of Rupert Brooke.

In *Georgian Poetry 1911–1912* the work of Rupert Brooke provoked particular comment. This was inevitable. All his life he stood out from his surroundings. At that luncheon party at Edward Marsh's, *his* would be the person upon which, could we have watched through the window or the keyhole, we should have bestowed the most of our attention. The other faces would have been interesting, no doubt, but somehow or other they, along with the furniture, would have formed

heard in the poems of Rupert Brooke. And yet, in the opinion of his friends and of a small but increasing public, he was the poet of young England: after his death a larger public reached the same conclusion, and with more enthusiasm. He was then, of course, the poet of a vanished England. But in either case he was considered the representative of all that was best in his times, to have embodied in a curious way the spirit of a lost generation. This may have been true. But it does not mean that he was, even in that vanished England and among that slaughtered generation, a modern poet. Art anticipates. Certain types of human being simply do not exist until a novelist has created them, nature labours to mould herself after the work of a great painter, and truly 'contemporary' poetry is engaged with the shape of things to come. Brooke's poetry was sufficiently eager to appear new, but its best effects had already been anticipated and surpassed; it was born old-fashioned. Hopkins (whom unfortunately he had no chance to read) was far more modern than he, so was Housman, and the prosodic enterprise of Robert Bridges has revealed certain lyric qualities which we are only beginning to appreciate today. These men would have seemed to the readers of *Georgian Poetry* the voices of the past: and yet, sad to say, it is *Georgian Poetry* which has slipped soundlessly into the past, while the voices of Hopkins and Housman and Bridges remain.

But to the examiner of pre-war England, its youngest poetry is full of meaning. How faithfully that poetry sought the refuge of the past and found – in the sunlit ruins of the Romantic Revival – a place where the encroaching sounds and fears of the twentieth century were quite un-heard and unfelt. There was no Poets' Rebellion. Until the very out-break of war, the poets stayed unresponsive to the changing times; stubborn, sweet, unreal, they were the last victims and the last heroes of Liberal England. And in the midst of them, a little in front of them, as one who takes his place before an effective background, there stands the engaging figure of Rupert Brooke.

II

The son of a Rugby master, and grandson of a Canon of Bath, Rupert Brooke was born in 1887 and educated at Rugby and Cambridge, appropriately the University of poets. Of his last term at Rugby he wrote: 'As I looked back upon five years I seemed to see almost every hour golden and radiant, and always increasing in beauty as I grew more conscious.' It was true that he thereupon became aware of 'transience, and parting, and a great many other things', and that he subsequently expressed this awareness both in prose and in verse; but somehow or other it was never very convincing. *Golden and radiant and always increasing in beauty* – this was to be the theme of Brooke's life. It was also, in a time of profound revolution in thought and behaviour, the main theme of *Georgian Poetry*, with a gentle counterpoint of formal sorrow and happy despair.

At Cambridge Brooke assumed, imperceptibly, unaffectedly, a leading place – he was sincere, friendly, shy but not modest, astonishing to look at. Nor is it surprising that at Cambridge, 'whose cloisters have ever been consecrated to poetry', he should have become a poetical socialist, that he should have fallen under the spell of the Sidney Webbs. Undoubtedly the shape of their arguments – the strong prose, the vigorous thought, the feeling that infuses the whole of lives given up to the betterment of mankind – blinded him to the meagre conclusions which might be found at the end of them. As Edward Marsh says, who wrote a Memoir of him, 'Rupert wore his socialism with a difference.' He did, indeed. Class-consciousness he found 'not inspiring'; what he tried to hammer into the heads of his fellow socialists was a faith in the goodness of man. But sometimes even he was forced to doubt. Sometimes it seemed that goodness alone would not bring about the necessary millennium; and then he began to wonder, with infinite reluctance, whether 'the best hope isn't in an upheaval of some kind', though speculations like these always gave him pain. Such was the socialism of Rupert Brooke, and it would be unkind to expect more of a young man who once said to a fellow member of the radical *Carbonari* – 'There are only three things in the world. One is to read poetry, another is to write poetry, and the best of all is to live poetry.'

Yet he was not one of those *dilettante* socialists who, arguing for effect and amusement, and because it was the fashion, were drifting already through the drawing-rooms of Mayfair. He pitied the poor man with all the sincerity which springs from an enthusiastic heart and a comfortable income. He genuinely longed for the reform of abuses and the destruction of privilege. If only everyone – rich and poor, worker and capitalist – would just be good! Meanwhile one could live the life of poetry.

It might seem, even when we separate from these sentiments those which rightly belong to the stage-play of youth, that here was a young man who was unconsciously something of a *poseur*. But this was not the case. The memories of all who knew him are filled with affection, love, reverence; and the young poet who emerges from them is not merely a charming but a candid figure. And yet – there is no doubt about it – he was always in flight from reality, not fearfully, but rather as one who exercises for the sake of his figure. He fled from it into the practice of verse and the examination of Elizabethan drama; into Ibsen, and the English countryside, and the Common Room of King's; into America, Honolulu, Samoa, Fiji, and Tahiti. Reality was faint but dauntless. It pursued him into uniform and brought him within sound of the German guns at Antwerp; and when he died at last of blood-poisoning in the Homeric island of Scyros, it might have permitted itself a smile of satisfaction. But even then, one cannot help feeling, it arrived too late: he had escaped into Death, with his illusions and his beauty untarnished, just one jump ahead.

This unreality pervades the pre-war volumes of *Georgian Poetry*, to which Brooke was the most typical and eventually the most admired contributor. As one reads through those volumes again, it is a vision of England which seems to haunt them and to give their long exhausted ecstasies that lingering magic. But what an England! – the rural England of Shakespeare and Milton and Wordsworth and Hopkins, gone very soft at the heart. It is an England surprised at those exceptionally becoming moments when 'stars into the twilight steer, Or thrushes build among the may, Or wonder moves between the hills' – *that* kind of an England; an England where passion perspires roses, and the abandoned heart slowly freezes into the sweet complacency of an ice cream; where it is almost always either spring or autumn, or exactly midsummer; where 'I go round corners on the roads' – so Brooke wrote one March – 'shivering and nearly crying with suspense'; where sorrow dies with sunset and even despair is crowned with new-mown hay. That such a vision could spring from a deep love of the country, a real national pride, is altogether beyond doubt; nor is it by any means, or at its most crepuscular, a fading vision. Writers like H. V. Morton still pursue it with diligence and profit, and there is hardly a man who knows that countryside but has experienced it. The strange thing is that it should have been concentrated, unsupported by theories or philosophies, among a group of highly intelligent young men, and – stranger still – that it should have been crowned with the glittering laurels of critical applause.

Could it be that the Georgian poets were truly representative, in some way, of pre-war England? And if this is the case, what did they represent? Did they, as they flattered themselves, awaken a new spirit – at once subtle and fresh – in the heart of English poetry, or were their poems the effect and not the cause of a less particular, a more public emotion? The more one ponders these questions, the more it seems as if they were in whole what the youth of England was in part; that their romantic un-realities came chiefly up from the immature soul of a doomed generation. Immaturity is infectious. In the memoirs of the time the young people – from such glimpses of them as we are vouchsafed – seem at once to fear and to long for reality, and to increase by some inner confusion that outer violence which has been the subject of this book. When War came they welcomed it with a cry of eagerness, as if they had been rescued from the lavender-scented, the nightmare-haunted embrace of a large feather bed.

To this state of mind the pages of *Georgian Poetry* bear evidence. There are people who say, and they may be right, that poetry is not evidence of anything; but where, then, *are* you to look? The novels of Saki seem to promise, on first sight, a careful picture of the youth of the times: but the novels of Saki actually present us with (1) a portrait of Saki – witty, cruel, childish, with a gift for admiring all the wrong things, and (2) a singular anticipation of the young men of 1925. You may search the contemporary writings of Shaw, Wells, Conrad, Gals-worthy, Maugham, and search in vain, for a detailed picture of the pre-war young men. Important writing, strange to say, rarely gives the exact flavour of its period; if it is successful it presents you with the soul of man, undated. Very minor literature, on the other hand, is the Baedeker of the soul, and will guide you through the curious relics, the tumbledown buildings, the flimsy palaces, the false pagodas, the distorted and fantastical and faery vistas which have cluttered the im-agination of mankind at this or that brief period of its history. If the soft and ripe countryside of *Georgian Poetry* is insufficient for 1910–14, one might turn to Compton Mackenzie's *Sinister Street*, a novel which the public devoured with shuddering relish just before the war. There is a great deal of good writing in this book, the characters have life, and the first volume, especially, is haunted with a sense of present changes and calamities to come. And yet – it is really very strange – whenever a scene of great importance is to be played, or a situation of extra subtlety to be explored, it has to take place before the glimmer of ecclesiastical candles, or in summer orchards soaked in moonlight and dew. The youthful characters, in spite of their eagerness, their outward look, are dragged back and smothered in this unreal scenery, and the story, pulled simultaneously backwards and forwards, collapses. *Sinister Street* is second-rate. But it is also highly significant. It has embodied in a very readable form the confusions of a generation. It was from these confusions that *Georgian Poetry* provided a refuge, both for those who read it and for those who wrote it.

Apart for their craving for the unreal, their romance, their ability to communicate with apparent distinction the most undistinguished of emotions, these pre-war poets seem also to have been blessed – or was it cursed? – with an unusual innocence. (The critic might venture to suggest that this was not so much innocence as childishness; that the Romantic Revival, now senile to a degree, was on its death-bed and babbling o' green fields. But let that pass.) Theirs was a level innocence, easily irritated into ecstasy and easily abashed into despair, and nowhere is it more noticeable than in the work of Rupert Brooke. His poem called *Lust* is particularly striking; it begins 'How should I know?' And there are some lines from *The Great Lover* which deserve quotation:

> *These I have loved:*
> *White plates and cups clean-gleaming,*
> *Ringed with blue lines; and feathery, faery dust;*
> *Wet roofs, beneath the lamp-light; the strong crust*
> *Of friendly bread; and many-tasting food;*
> *Rainbows; and the blue bitter smoke of wood.*
>
> . . . . .
>
> *Then, the cool kindliness of sheets, that soon*
> *Smooth away trouble; and the rough male kiss*
> *Of blankets; grainy wood; live hair that is*
> *Shining and free; blue-massing clouds; the keen*
> *Unpassioned beauty of a great machine;*
> *The benison of hot water; furs to touch,*
> *The good smell of old clothes and other such—*
> *The comfortable smell of friendly fingers*
> *Hair's fragrance, and the musty reek that lingers*
> *About dead leaves and last year's ferns. . . .*

These are pleasing lines – rather more than pleasing, in a quiet way. Only one is shocked to realize that both poet and public thought them not inconsistent with their title, and that the sentiment at the heart of them was much admired. Yet anything could happen in those days. Harold Monro, as gifted a poet as any and more gifted than most, was able to write some verses in which he berated man for not being more grateful to his furniture and kitchen utensils, those faithful companions which follow life 'not far behind' and nobody thought this at all odd. Was it the poet who was to blame? or was it that haunted and bewildered and inexplicable and rather sorry phenomenon – the soul of Liberal England?

The Georgian poets were certainly persuasive. How eager they were, how tremulous, and melancholy, and musical! And who deserved these epithets more than Rupert Brooke? Taste should have made him ridiculous by now; history should have made him tragic: and yet he has escaped both ridicule and tragedy. If he had been born thirty years earlier or later. . . . But one can only see him, poised, in an attitude of highly attractive unawareness, on the crossroads of history.

> *A young Apollo, golden-haired,*
> *Stands dreaming on the verge of strife,*
> *Magnificently unprepared*
> *For the long littleness of life.*

This epigram was written about Brooke while still an undergraduate, by Frances Cornford. That it should have been highly thought of at the time need occasion us no surprise when we consider that another poem of hers, beginning

> *O fat white woman, whom nobody loves,*
> *Why do you walk through the fields in gloves,*
> *Missing so much and so much . . .*

was regarded almost with veneration. She was very Georgian. But the epigram, none the less, is an appropriate one, it suits very well with the portraits of Brooke. If a man's destiny is written on his face, then Brooke, you might think, was destined to become a legend. He was beautiful; he composed verses: the combination is irresistible. And yet there is something – some shadow flitting from mouth to eyes, elusive and disturbing – which makes you pause and think again. Is it mockery which you discern there? Or inspiration? Or challenge? Or is it perhaps – uneasiness? 'Magnificently unprepared' has a fatal ring. Was he destined to become a legend; or was he doomed, after all, to finish up as nothing more than an epigram?

III

On 22nd May, 1913, he set forth on a year of travel. He was to go to America first, and come home by way of the Pacific Ocean. The record of his wanderings will be found, in a series of letters and verses, in Edward Marsh's admirable *Memoir* which prefaces *The Collected Poems of Rupert Brooke*. The verses are fragmentary, and the letters chiefly distinguished for that intimate charm, that gift for offering himself unreservedly to his friends, which their author possessed above almost all the men of his time. They also have the quality of an exclamation mark. American hospitality he loved – 'Oh, dear, the tears quite well up into my eyes when I think of a group of young Harvard people I tumbled into – at Harvard.' At Lake George he lay naked on the red-gold beach 'and ate cold caribou-heart, and made tea, and had, oh! blueberry pie'. Hawaii was disappointing, but Samoa – 'There it is; there it wonderfully is; heaven on earth, the ideal life, little work, dancing, and singing and eating; naked people of incredible loveliness.... Can't you imagine what a fragmentary heart I'm bearing away to Fiji and Tahiti? And, oh, dear! I'm afraid they'll be just as bad.' They were. At Fiji he was able to say, 'I prefer watching the *Siva-Siva* to observing Nijinsky'; and as for Tahiti, he discovered there everything his heart could desire except a lost Gauguin. 'It is all – all Papeete – like a Renaissance Italy, with the venom taken out.' 'This afternoon I go fishing with a native girl on a green and purple reef.' These are Pacific commonplaces, no doubt, but they are also a refuge from reality – a refuge even more accommodating than the practice of romantic verse. In the consequent *Tiare Tahiti* people have been known to discover, not merely the immortal youth which belongs to true poetry, but also the tragedy of genius nipped in the bud. And yet such poetry becomes inseparable from his physical memory, it was his background too. He was beautiful, he was 26, he would be dead in little more than a year. Was this so very tragic? There is immortal youth and – youth that is not quite so immortal, the youth of Peter Pan. What would have happened to Brooke's eager spirit when wrinkles devoured the flesh? Would it have been agile enough to escape even *that* reality?

That year of changing scenes and peoples – the naïve Americans, the cannibals in Fiji, the laughing loving children of Polynesia – becomes, in retrospect, no more than a various frieze behind the enchanting person of Rupert Brooke. And when he returned to England, 'the friend' wrote Walter de la Mare,

'who placidly appeared from the ends of the earth seemed as little changed as one who gayly and laughingly goes to bed and gayly and laughingly comes down next morning after a perfectly refreshing sleep.'

Mr de la Mare appears to have been surprised. Surely those spellbound islands should have left some mark upon his versatile and impressionable young friend! Had he not written to say that life was changed for him? And except for a bleaching of the golden hair, there was no mark at all. But should there have been? Never-Never-Land has no geography. Scarcely had Brooke left the 'gentleness and beauty and kindliness' of Polynesia than he was beginning to think of Plymouth – 'Oh, blessed name, oh, loveliness! Plymouth – was there ever so sweet and droll a sound? Drake's Plymouth, English Western Plymouth, city where men speak softly . . . and there is love and beauty and old houses. . . .'

He landed at Plymouth on 6th June. The year was 1914.

IV

The first news of war alarmed him: 'the world seems so dark – and I'm vaguely frightened'. In that growing darkness there lurked Reality, licking its lips, preparing for the final leap. But quite suddenly very different sentiments appeared. He was given a commission in the Royal Naval Division, and now 'the central purpose of my life, the thing God wants of me, is to get good at beating Germans. But that isn't what it *was*. What it was, I never knew. . . . I'm the happiest person in the world.' The songs, the talks, the Elizabethan dramatists, the English spring, and Socialism, and Tahiti – they were nothing. He put them out of his mind. Here was the truth at last – this crouching final illusion, the magical German dragon, crowned and deadly, and breathing fantastical fire.

And so came the last, the most surprising event: for War – that loudest and least amenable of backgrounds – meekly retiring, subdued itself to the personality of Rupert Brooke. Beyond Antwerp, within the reach of shells and death, he slept in a château garden, 'and round corners one saw, faintly, occasional Cupids and Venuses – a scattered company of rather bad statues – gleaming quietly. The sailors dug their latrines in the various rose gardens. . . .' Above the trench in which at last he found himself, and which the Germans refrained from attacking 'seriously', there passed 'once or twice a lovely glittering aeroplane'. And so home to England – a 'remarkable' England. In February 1915, he left with his Division for the Dardanelles.

Just one month before another Georgian poet, scarcely less characteristic, had died in the winter bleakness of a Swiss health resort. James Elroy Flecker could squeeze colour out of words as one squeezes paint out of a tube, and some of his poems – *The Four Gates of Damascus* for instance – are the literary equivalent of a Bakst *décor*. He too fled from reality, the reality of tuberculosis, into the lighter side of oriental religion. But though the best of his oriental work, it is true, remains so Anglo-Saxon at heart that it has something of the effect of an amateur charade, only a very narrow mind would deny that he was a poet. He spent much of his life in the Near East, and one could wish that it had ended there, if only because such a *mise-en-scène* would have been more appropriate. But it was not to be. As he lay in Switzerland, very near his death, he thought of war as he had once known it, at Beyrout. 'Unforgettable the thunder of the guns shaking the golden blue of sky and sea while not a breath stirred the palm-trees, not a cloud moved on the swan-like snows of Lebanon.' He opened his eyes, and the kindly vision fled. Before him were the cold mountains, and beyond them the zones of a colourless war, cutting him off even from his friends. Reality had caught up with Flecker.

But not with Brooke. 'I had not imagined,' he wrote to Miss Asquith, just before he set out for the Dardanelles campaign, 'that Fate could be so benign. . . . But I'm filled with confident and glorious hopes. Do you think *perhaps* the fort on the Asiatic corner will want quelling, and we'll land and come at it from behind, and they'll make a sortie and meet us on the plains of Troy? . . . Will Hero's Tower crumble under the 15-inch guns? Will the sea be polyphloisbic and wine-dark and unvintageable? Shall I loot mosaics from St Sophia, and Turkish Delight, and carpets? . . . I've never been quite so happy in my life, I think. Not quite so pervasively happy. . . .'

The German dragon had almost disappeared, and the old paths stretched before him, more shining than ever and – more empty. His troopship sailed past 'the good smell of land – and of Spain, too!'; past the mountains of Africa where the sea was a jewel, 'and sunset and dawn divine blazes of colour'; past Lemnos 'like an Italian town in silverpoint'; through the phosphorescent Aegean. And then – just as they were preparing to make their landing in a warm and green dawn, on a murderous Gallipoli beach, beneath the Turkish guns – as they watched the shore 'crammed with Fate and ominously silent' – someone said, 'We're going home.' It was nearly true. They retired to Egypt.

The path fades in a shining mist. 'I know what a campaign is,' he wrote: 'It is a continual crossing from one place to another, and back, over dreamlike seas.' On 17th April, they returned to the island of Scyros, from which Achilles went forth against Troy, and where Theseus is buried. In Scyros, Brooke caught blood-poisoning, and died, and was buried there: in Scyros 'like one great rock-garden of white, and pinkish-white marble, with small red poppies and every sort of wild-flower; in the gorges ilex, dwarf holly, and occasional groups of olives; and everywhere the smell of thyme (or is it sage? or wild mint?)' (Brigadier-General Arthur Asquith to his sister.) The background was faithful to the last. He was buried on St George's day, by moonlight: and above his head, on the white wooden cross, an interpreter had written in Greek – 'Here lies the servant of God, sub-lieutenant in the English Navy, who died for the deliverance of Constantinople from the Turks.' 'That infinitely lovable soul,' a friend wrote to his mother, 'that stainless heart...' One would not change any of these words; they were true. As for the legend which seems so profoundly buried in them today – will it perhaps shine again? Will the life of Brooke arouse the curiosity and cupidity of some biographer a hundred or so years from now?

However this may be, with his death one sees the extinction of Liberal England. Standing beside that moonlit grave, one looks back. All the violence of the pre-war world has vanished, and in its place there glow, year into backward year, the diminishing vistas of that other England, the England where the Grantchester church clock stood at ten to three, where there was Beauty and Certainty and Quiet, and where nothing was real. Today we know it for what it was; but there are moments, very human moments, when we could almost find it in our hearts to envy those who saw it, and who never lived to see the new world.

Bibliography

Addison, the Right Honourable Christopher, *Politics from Within.*
Allyn, Emily, *Lords versus Commons.*
Askwith, Lord, *Industrial Problems and Disputes.*
Asquith, H. H. (*see Oxford and Asquith, the Earl of*).
Asquith, Cyril (*with J. A. Spender*), *The Life of Herbert Henry Asquith.*
Asquith, Margot (*see Oxford and Asquith, the Countess of*).
Beer, Max, *A History of British Socialism.*
Bennett, Arnold, *The Journal of Arnold Bennett.*
Birkenhead, the 2nd Earl of, *Frederick Edwin Smith, 1st Earl of Birkenhead.*
Blunt, Wilfred Scawen, *My Diaries.*
Brooke, Rupert, *The Collected Poems of Rupert Brooke.*
Buchan, John, *The People's King.*
Callwell, Major-General Sir C. E., *Field-Marshal Sir Henry Wilson, His
  Life and Diaries.*
Churchill, the Right Honourable Winston Spencer, *The World Crisis.*
Cohen, Percy, *The British System of Social Insurance.*
Cole, G. D. H., *The British Labour Movement; The World of Labour;*
  (*with R. Page Arnot*) *Trade Unionism on the Railways.*
Crewe, the Marquess of, *Lord Rosebery.*
Elliot, Walter, *Toryism and the Twentieth Century.*
Figgis, Darrell, *Recollections of the Irish War.*
Fitzroy, Sir Almeric, *Memoirs.*
Fyfe, Henry Hamilton, *The British Liberal Party.*
Gardiner, A. G., *Pillars of Society.*
Gilson, Mary Barnett, *Unemployment Insurance in Great Britain.*
Guedalla, Philip, *Slings and Arrows.*
Gwynn, Denis, *The Life of John Redmond; Traitor or Patriot: the Life of
  Roger Casement.*
Gwynn, Stephen, *John Redmond's Last Years.*
d'Haussonville, Comte, *Ombres Françaises et Visions Anglaises.*
Hamilton, Mary Agnes, *Mary Macarthur.*
Healy, T. M., *Letters and Leaders of My Day.*
Henderson, Fred, *The Labour Unrest.*
Hirst, F. W., *The Six Panics.*
Hobson, Bulmer, *A Short History of the Irish Volunteers.*
Horgan, J. J., *The Complete Grammar of Anarchy.*
Jevons, H. Stanley, *The British Coal Trade.*
Kenney, Annie, *Memories of a Militant.*

355

Kenney, Rowland, *Men and Rails.*
Legge, Edward, *George V and the Royal Family.*
Lloyd George, the Right Honourable David, *War Memoirs.*
Lytton, Lady Constance, *Prisons and Prisoners.*
McCarthy, Lillah, *Myself and My Friends.*
MacDonald, J. Ramsay, *The Social Unrest.*
McKenna, Stephen, *While I Remember.*
McNeill, Ronald, *Ulster's Stand for Union.*
Macready, General the Right Honourable Sir Nevil, *Annals of an Active Life.*
Mallet, Sir Charles, *Mr Lloyd George.*
Mann, Tom, *Tom Mann's Memoirs.*
Martin, Hugh, *Battle.*
Maurois, André, *The Edwardian Era.*
Meech, Thomas Cox, *This Generation.*
Metcalfe, A. E., *Woman's Effort.*
Montgomery, B. G. de, *British and Continental Labour Policy.*
Nevinson, H. W., *More Changes, More Chances.*
Newton, Lord, *Lord Lansdowne.*
Nicolson, Harold, *Portrait of a Diplomatist.*
O'Brien, Conor, *From Three Yachts.*
O'Brien, William, *The Irish Revolution.*
O'Cathasaigh, Sean, *The Story of the Irish Citizen Army.*
Oxford and Asquith, the Earl of, *Fifty Years of British Parliament; Memories and Reflections.*
Oxford and Asquith, the Countess of, *More Memories.*
Pankhurst, Emmeline, *My Own Story.*
Pankhurst, Sylvia, *The Suffragette Movement.*
Peel, George, *The Reign of Sir Edward Carson.*
Perris, George Herbert, *The Industrial History of Modern England.*
Pigou, A. C., *Essays in Applied Economics.*
Pless, Princess Daisy of, *Better Left Unsaid.*
Raymond, E. T., *Mr Lloyd George.*
Rhondda, the Viscountess, *This Was My World.*
Ronaldshay, the Earl of, *The Life of Lord Curzon.*
Rothenstein, Sir William, *Men and Memories.*
Smillie, Robert, *My Life for Labour.*
Somervell, D. C., *The Reign of George V.*
Spender, J. A. (*with Cyril Asquith*), *The Life of Herbert Henry Asquith.*
Spender, Harold, *David Lloyd George.*
Strachey, John, *The Coming Struggle for Power.*
Tillett, Ben, *History of the London Transport Workers' Strike.*
Tracey, Herbert, *The Book of the Labour Party.*
Ullswater, Viscount, *A Speaker's Commentaries.*

Webb, Beatrice and Sydney, *The History of Trade Unionism.*
Willoughby de Broke, Lord, *The Passing Years.*
Wilson-Fox, Alice, *The Earl of Halsbury.*
Wingfield-Stratford, Esmé, *The Victorian Aftermath.*
Wright, Arnold, *Disturbed Dublin.*
Punch, 1910–14.
The Tatler, 1910–14.
The Times, 1910–14.
Returns and Reports of the Board of Trade and the Home Office. Private Information.

Index